THE THOUGHT OF
PAUL TILLICH

THE THOUGHT OF
PAUL TILLICH

James Luther Adams, Wilhelm Pauck,
Roger Lincoln Shinn, Editors,
with the assistance of
Thomas J. S. Mikelson

An American Academy of Arts and Sciences Book

Harper & Row, Publishers, San Francisco

Cambridge, Hagerstown, New York, Philadelphia,
London, Mexico City, São Paulo, Sydney

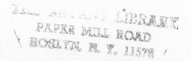

FIRST EDITION

Designed by Donald Hatch

Library of Congress Cataloging in Publication Data
Main entry under title:

The Thought of Paul Tillich.

"Printed for the American Academy of Arts and
Sciences."
    1. Tillich, Paul, 1886–1966—Addresses, essays,
lectures. I. Adams, James Luther.   II. Pauck, Wilhelm.   III. Shinn, Roger Lincoln.   IV. American Academy of Arts and Sciences.
BX4827.T53T519 1984   230'.092'4   84—48255
ISBN 0-06-060072-1

85 86 87 88 89 HC 10 9 8 7 6 5 4 3 2 1

Photo: James K. Mellow.

Contents

Preface

The story of the origin of this book is the key to its intention and its content. It began with a request from Victor A. Weisskopf, who was president of the American Academy of Arts and Sciences from 1976 to 1979. He is not only one of the world's famous physicists, he is also, in the words of Harvard University's citation for an honorary degree in 1983, "the conscience of the American physics community." Weisskopf said to James Luther Adams, "While I am president of the Academy I would like for you to do something to make the significance of Paul Tillich's work widely recognized among the Academy's membership of scholars in all disciplines."

As a result, the Academy requested and received a grant from the National Endowment for the Humanities to launch a project on the meaning of Tillich, who died in 1965, for the historical era following his career. The Academy invited a group of Tillich scholars to a meeting in 1979, in New Harmony, Indiana, a historic American utopian community and the site of the Paul Tillich Park, where Tillich's ashes are interred. The conference discussed the concept of a book to be edited by James Luther Adams and Wilhelm Pauck, who cochaired the meeting.

Following the conference, the coeditors invited a group of writers to contribute chapters for the book. Regrettably Wilhelm Pauck died during the work on the book, but his public address at the New Harmony meeting comprises chapter 2 of this book. After Pauck's death Roger L. Shinn joined the editorial team.

The present volume is not intended to be another of the many books that, in all their variety, analyze and interpret the thought of Paul Tillich. Its aim is to ask the meaning of his style of thought and imagination for a wide range of contemporary human issues, some of which had not appeared in anything like their present form during his lifetime. To do this the authors have, of course, looked at Tillich's own work, in varying ways and in varying degrees. But always the purpose has been to see how that work is still influencing or might be brought to influence contemporary human interests and problems.

Given the extraordinary breadth of Tillich's interests and writings, the book has a wide scope. It was Tillich's habit to look at life in its variety—at the political, economic, technological, psychological, artistic, religious scenes—and to move from concrete concerns to a theological center, then back out into the particulars of life. To set some limits to so wide an arena, the editors decided early to select only writers who live in the U.S. The two who live in England, Albert Friedlander and John Powell Clayton, have had extensive American experience. No introverted nationalism is implied in that decision; it is simply the modest effort to do one part of an inquiry that is going on simultaneously in other parts of the world.

Although the writers come from varied disciplines, their writings frequently converge on some familiar themes: ultimate concern, autonomy, New Being, heteronomy, Protestant principle, theonomy, *Kairos,* the demonic, ontological and technical reason, the appreciation and criticism of religion, utopian aspiration, and criticism of utopias. The editors have not tried to eliminate these overlappings, since they involve almost no repetition. On the contrary, people are often surprised at the discovery of new vistas on familiar themes. The attempt either to enter into or to challenge Tillich's work usually leads to surprises.

The editors gratefully acknowledge the assistance of the National Endowment for the Humanities; John Voss, executive officer, and Corinne Schelling, associate executive officer, of the American Academy of Arts and Sciences; Harriet Ritvo of the American Academy; Karen Smith for secretarial assistance; Jane Blaffer Owen, founder of the Tillich Park and hostess at the meeting in New Harmony; Marion Pauck, coauthor of the recent biography of Tillich, who helped at many stages of the development of this book; Victor Nuovo and Robert Scharlemann who translated Tillich's "Letter to Emanuel Hirsch," which appears in this volume for the first time in English; Maria Grossman, librarian of the Andover-Harvard Theological Library and the Tillich Archives, and Alan Seaburg, curator of manuscripts at Andover-Harvard Library; Harvard Divinity School and Union Theological Seminary, for their encouragement to the editors; James K. Mellow for use of his photo of the sculpture of Tillich by James Rosati at the Tillich Park in New Harmony; and the editors at Harper & Row, John Loudon and Matthew Chanoff. We are especially grateful to the American Academy of Arts and Sciences for making available the assistance of Thomas J. S. Mikelson as assistant editor. It is surely significant, in the storms of our times, that the American Academy of Arts and Sciences, no stranger to the boundaries of its changing times, has sponsored this scholarly dialogue concerning the ongoing relevance of the work of Paul Tillich, an eminent interpreter and disturber of the twentieth century.

James Luther Adams and Roger L. Shinn, editors.

Van Gogh's *Starry Night* has the character of going below the surface. It is a description of the creative powers of nature. It goes into the depths of reality where the forms are dynamically created, . . . those depths in which the tension of the forces creates nature.

 —PAUL TILLICH, "Existentialist Aspects of Modern
      Art," in *Christianity and the Existentialists*

van Gogh, Vincent.
The Starry Night (1889).
Oil on canvas, 29 × 36¼
(73.3 × 92.1 cm).
Collection, The Museum of
Modern Art, New York.
Acquired through the Lillie P.
Bliss Bequest.

1. Introduction: The Storms of Our Times and *Starry Night*

JAMES LUTHER ADAMS

The title of this essay is at odds with the frontispiece, van Gogh's *Starry Night*. The hound and the horn seem to be running in opposite directions. It is this contrast, however, that marks the profile of Paul Tillich's chosen vocation as a philosophical and apologetic theologian.[1] In one aspect of this vocation he has been unrelenting in the recognition and delineation of the disruptions, the storms, of our times. In this sense, he is an existentialist theologian providing a mirror of this "stormy" situation, at the same time issuing a protest in the name of authentic human being. The dark storms, however, are not to be endured without light in the night. Here we see the contrasting feature of his vocation in his attempt to find a new and effective word of religion redemptive in its power. In his view one cannot comprehend religion if one does not recognize its inner tensions and even its ambiguity.

TILLICH'S YES AND NO TO RELIGION

Insofar as religion is a "superfluous consecration" of the forces that have given rise to disruptions, "the first word to be spoken by religion must be a word spoken against religion." But this word must be also a transforming word that transcends, or rather goes deeper than, the surface realities. Characteristically, Tillich finds transforming elements represented in the arts, and especially in the visual arts, where often he perceives a "powerful word." He views van Gogh's vividly colorful painting as an attempt to "look into the depths of reality, below any surface and any beautification." This painting, says Tillich, reveals a "disruption of the creative powers of nature." It plumbs to below the surfaces where the forms are dynamically created.[2]

During his lifetime, Tillich witnessed world wars, acute economic depressions, political reversals, revolutions, and incredible holocausts. He served as a chaplain in the German army of World War I, ministered there to countless of the injured, and officiated at the burial of hundreds of the dead. It is not widely known that Tillich, under that stress and largely as a result of it, suffered a temporary breakdown and had to be withdrawn from the front. Following the war, he experienced the rise of nazism and fascism and became an exile to the United States. This constant witnessing of blood-soaked carnage apparently gave him a sense of the ineradicable anxiety and dread of death in the human situation, perhaps influencing him in the direction of the existentialists. Accordingly, he adopted psychological categories as fundamental not only for understanding human existence but also for reality as a whole. I was told by a student that in a lecture on twentieth-century thought, Donald Fleming of the Harvard faculty characterized Tillich's writings as unique, for the average theologian, Protestant or Catholic, tends to brush aside despair and the darker side of human experience.

In Germany, as elsewhere, the religious crisis with its despair brought about a "return to religion," in Tillich's view an ominous return to sham spirituality. Writing in 1922 at the time of an inflation that nearly wiped out the middle class in Germany, Tillich, discussing the religious crisis, made the following trenchant comment:

It would be an annihilating judgment about our time, more annihilating than ours is about the "Wilhelmine Epoch," if a future historian would write about it: "At that time people turned again to religion; . . . in spite of the increase in non-spiritual forces through the economic situation, it was a religious epoch." Such a judgment could be annihilating, for it could be saying, "That time lacked God; in His place, however, it had religion. After having tried technology and world politics, after having tried idolizing the nation, or the class, and having failed in these attempts, it tried religion."

Such attempts, he goes on to say, have failed in all romanticism from the time of Julian, the apostate Roman emperor, up to the present. They always imply a way of "tempting God if the attempt is made for the sake of something other than for God's sake; and it is necessarily a failure. . . . In times of a growing affirmation of religion, even more than in times of indifference and hostility, we need to be reminded that God is a consuming fire."[3]

This warning against the turn to religion as a means toward something else gives point to a story at one time current on the Harvard campus. In appreciation of Tillich's presence there someone is reported to have said that now at Harvard it is possible to use the word *God* and yet remain intellectually respectable. On hearing this, Tillich is said to have raised his hands in indignant dismay. Obviously, this "God" was not a consuming fire.

Tillich's warning against turning to religion for the sake of culture was grounded in his rejection of the notion, a rejection that Tillich found in both Luther and Calvin, that religion (or God) is something detachable, something alongside the culture or the world. This spatializing serves to produce and protect idolatry and complacency, that is, to protect the culture from radical criticism, from the consuming fire of prophetic judgment, and also to "cabin" the creative, renewing power of the really real. This amounts, then, to the virtual worship of particular spaces that Calvin and others have called polytheism. Some of these particular spaces, set apart and worshipped, can include religion or the god of the dictionary, "a supreme Being."

Tillich's formulation is ontological when he says that in principle everything participates in Being, though ambiguously. At the center, or rather in the ground or depth of everything, whether material or spiritual, whether individual or corporate, whether secular or sacred, is Being. God is Being-itself, but not a spatialized supreme "highest Being" above other beings. When religion is authentic, it is openness to and directedness toward "unconditional reality," and proclaims its power and promise, at the same time bringing both the sacred and the secular under judgment. For Tillich, van Gogh's *Starry Night* unveils something below the surface—potent, renewing power, unmanipulable, and unconditional. The "storms of our times" are not to be endured without a supportive and creative element. He refers to this "coincidence of opposites" as a "belief-ful realism," "realism and faith."

APOSTLE TO THE GENTILES

For Tillich there is in God both ground and abyss (Tillich is indebted to Böhme for the meaning of abyss). The demonic, when it appears, is inflated and distorted by the unpredictable, uncontrollable abyss. This appears in primitive art as the exaggeration of eyes or nose or mouth or genitals. In God, just as in human existence, there is this tension between being and nonbeing. God is always struggling against nonbeing. Apparently Paul Tillich had all of these things in mind when he spoke of the depth of reality. The demonic, then, also issues from the depths, and is to be overcome only by a grace that is more powerful. Tillich liked Nietzsche's statement that "will is the power of being in Being."

In adopting this "depth" language, Tillich reveals a certain uneasiness with the vocabulary of height. The word *height* too often suggests flying away from "the really real." In this reference point of depth, Tillich sees all existence and ultimate meaning as unconditional reality, as "grounded in the depths of being itself." In short, Tillich calls us back to ontology, an inquiry concerning the universal structures of being and the meaning of the inescapable reality of that which is beyond all things.

The word *unconditional,* used so often by Tillich, has been a conundrum for many. Karl Barth, in one of his more scornful moments, called it a "frozen monstrosity." Actually, in the history of philosophy it can be traced back even beyond Plato. The term, Tillich says, is a negative symbol for the divine. So far from denoting a frozen phantom, it points to a dynamic, primordial, holy reality, "infinitely apprehensible, and yet ultimately incomprehensible." The adjectival form, *the unconditional,* is preferable to the substantive form, *the unconditioned;* the latter term implies reification, that it is a thing alongside other things. I once asked Tillich if for the sake of bewildered readers he would give a brief definition of "the unconditional." This little-noted definition appears at the beginning of his essay entitled "Kairos" in *The Prostestant Era:*

The term "unconditional" which is often used in this book points to that element in every religious experience which makes it religious. In every symbol of the divine an unconditional claim is expressed, most powerfully in the command: "Thou shalt love the Lord thy God with *all* thy heart and with all thy soul, and with all thy mind." No partial, restricted, conditioned love of God is admitted. The term "unconditioned," or the adjective made into the substantive, "the unconditional," is an abstraction from such sayings which abound in the Bible and in great religious literature. The unconditional is a quality, not a being. It characterizes that which is our ultimate and, consequently, unconditional concern, whether we call it "God" or "Being as such" or the "Good as such" or the "True as such," or whether we give it any other name. It could be a complete mistake to understand the unconditional as a being the existence of which can be discussed. He who speaks of the "existence of the unconditional" has thoroughly misunderstood the meaning of the term. Unconditional is a quality which we experience in encountering reality, for instance, in the unconditional character of the voice of the conscience, the logical as well as the moral. In this sense, as a quality and not as a being, the term is used in all the following articles.[4]

Whatever one may think of the choice of the term *the unconditional,* we must recognize that one of the most creative things Tillich has done is to contrive a series of terms that aim to communicate with fresh power truths whose clarity and relevance were weakened because of careless interpretation and application. Such terms as *theonomy, Kairos, demonic, boundary, the Protestant principle,* and *ultimate concern* have become associated with Tillich's thought. His new terms nearly always were embedded in the tradition, uncovered, newly defined, and applied variously in such attractive ways that many of them have been adopted and adapted by other thinkers, often with little concern for placing them in the context of Tillich's entire outlook.

So much has he attempted in this fashion to approach the modern person alienated from the language of the churches that he has been called an "apostle to the Gentiles." For his part, Tillich early in his career came to view much preaching in Germany as a form of laziness. The conservative preacher seems to think that he has fulfilled his vocation if he mainly repeats the word of Scripture. He contents himself by saying that he has preached the Word, that God must give the increase. If a wicked and adulterous generation has turned a deaf ear, the guilt lies there. It is noteworthy that Tillich reproached the Barmen Synod of the Confessing Churches (which in 1934 heroically issued its famous declaration against the Nazis) with having used merely traditional language incapable of speaking effectively to those who in the name of intellectual integrity were already alienated. The Confessing Churches relentlessly purged from their language everything associated with the neo-Protestantism (and liberalism) of the years 1730 to 1930. Tillich spoke of their effort here as "extravagant," though he acknowledged the need for some "self-purification" in face of the past. He early became aware that this group could not unite anti-Nazi Christians against the regime. For one thing, its fixated language excluded the liberals.[5]

In Tillich's view, "the Word of God is any reality by means of which the eternal breaks with unconditioned power into our contemporaneity." It is not a question any longer of a direct proclamation of the religious truths as they are given in the Bible and tradition, for "all of these things are torn down into the general chaos of doubt and questioning." Hence the need for new terms.

Wilhelm and Marion Pauck, in the first volume of their biography of Tillich, writing of opposition at Harvard to Tillich's ideas and vocabulary, report that "one philosopher went so far as to call Tillich's thought 'unintelligible nonsense.' " Nevertheless, the response of students to his magnetic power was enormous. In commenting on the Tillichian vocabulary, the Paucks say somewhat wryly that "he himself had not created many of the terms he used, but had borrowed them from other thinkers and by subtle transformation made them his own."[6] It is not sufficient to say this, because these terms used by Tillich were delicately interconnected with respect to his total outlook. To understand one term is to understand all of them. Every term supposes the background of his ontology, epistemology, philosophy of history, and doctrine of God.

Wilhelm Pauck demonstrates this convincingly with reference to the term *unconditional.* The term was one used by Tillich's teacher, Martin Kähler, at Halle, in ways and in contexts that suggest that Tillich may have adopted the term from him. Pauck writes:

For example, in discussing "the living God" in contrast to "the absolute" of Schelling's idealism, Kähler writes: "If one conceives the universal as the precondition *(Voraussetzung)* of everything determined, it appears as the unconditioned which conditions everything else. This translation of the presupposition of thought into the ground of being *(Daseinsgrund)* implies the identification of the indetermined and the indeterminable unconditioned or, in other words, the simple, with "the supreme being." Thus everything determined is regarded (or signified) as something less, as something that in the last resort is not or ought not to be, while that which transcends everything real is considered as that which truly has being *(das wahrhaft Seiende).*

Then, in conclusion, Pauck goes on to say:

> This terminology was certainly not the special property of Kähler, but one will not go wrong in thinking that the very fact that he used it must have been of importance to Tillich, who employed it throughout his life. In this connection, it should be noted that Kähler warned again and again that one should not think of God as a being among beings, as if he were an object, and that particularly one should not speak of him as "the supreme being," a phrase which Kähler called meaningless *(Inhaltsleer).*[7]

The Harvard dissenters were by no means the first in America to mark the difficulty of Tillich's concepts. *The Protestant Era* (1948) was rejected for publication by a major American house. After this publisher had held the manuscript for two years I urged that a decision be made. It turned out to be a rejection. Later on I learned that a "reader" for the publisher, a prominent theologian, in advising against publication, said the book contained a lot of "German gobbledygook" that would find few buyers. Pauck and I then took the manuscript to the University of Chicago Press. Fred Wieck immediately made a contract not only for it but also for the entire *Systematic Theology.* Tillich wished the contract to call for six volumes, but the press restricted the contract to three. After the first volume of this work appeared, Professor Arnold Bergsträsser, a learned, exiled German scholar, a political scientist, and an admirer of Tillich's writings, found so much historical, philosophical, and theological lore as well as vocabulary presupposed that he suggested that we prepare an annotated companion volume for each of the three volumes. He was aware of the fact that for decades Tillich had been giving lecture courses and seminars on Western thought from the pre-Socratics to the present. He wished especially for us to trace the historical lineage of Tillich's conceptual thesaurus.

Tillich himself was aware of the difficulty of his theological language and could rise to humor about it. Once he said to me, after I had complimented him on the style of a new publication, "Jim, from having to learn English, I learned that one need not be obscure to be profound." He recognized, however, that the offering of a new language must needs give offense. Another time, when we were preparing essays in *The Protestant Era* for publication, I could not fully understand the intended meaning of several paragraphs in his text. When I consulted him about the problem, he looked at the passages for some time and then said, "I haven't the slightest idea what I intended there. Leave them out."

WILL: THE NERVE OF TILLICH'S THOUGHT

Attempts have been made repeatedly to identify the nerve of Tillich's whole outlook. Some such attempt is highly pertinent, so that one may avoid rendering primary that which is derivative or secondary in his thought. That nerve may be seen most clearly if it is sought by placing his outlook and lifestyle in the context of the whole religious philosophical development of the West. Tillich's philosophical education was achieving its maturity and solidity at a time when a topic being discussed most vigorously was the identification of meanings and tensions in the history of Western philosophical and religious thought. Windelband, for example, had considered these questions toward the end of determining how one should write the history of philosophy. Dilthey identified three basic themes found in Western thought: naturalism, the idealism of freedom, and objective idealism. Troeltsch, Tillich's major contemporary and mentor, had devoted a lifetime to the search for "the fundamental idea" of Christian and Western culture, trying to understand the basic changes, the periods or phases of development. In one of his essays he spells out the Western tradition and the contemporary period by defining the essence of "the modern," and Tillich, in his youth, published a substantial essay on the same topic.[8] Recently, Trutz Rendtdorf, a major German Troeltsch scholar, in a public lecture at the University of Chicago (April, 1984), attempted to understand and interpret the fundamental differences between contemporary theological positions in terms of how each position has interpreted and reacted to the meaning of modernity.

Tillich, in the midst of the intellectual ferment of his time, with a classical and comprehensive education behind him, recognized that the problems of thought in his time needed to be set in the whole intellectual history of Western culture, ancient, medieval, and modern. As one way of responding to this, he perceived a persistent tension within every generation between those who believed that the will is primary in the nature of reality and those who believed that the intellect is primary. The former could trace their heritage, Tillich believed, from Augustine. "Augustine is the philosopher of will," Tillich writes, "and especially of the will which is love. . . . Love is original being; the power of love is the substance in everything that is." In the Middle Ages, Augustine's ideas were represented by the Franciscans (especially Bonaventura), Duns Scotus, and Ockham and, later, by Luther and Böhme, and then by Schelling at the beginning of the nineteenth century. Those who saw the intellect as primary could claim as their ancestors Aristotle, Thomas Aquinas, the Dominicans, the British Empiricists and, more recently, the positivists and analysts in philosophy. Tillich writes, "These two lines of thought have made the Western philosophical movements full of life and tension." Against this sweeping backdrop of Western thought, Tillich provides a more detailed analysis of the same tension between will and intellect as primary during the nineteenth century. The later Schelling (the philosopher of will, as contrasted with the earlier Schelling, the philosopher of nature) was influenced powerfully by Jakob Böhme, whose writings were called to Schelling's attention by the Roman Catholic theologian, Franz von Baader. For Schelling, Tillich writes, "Will is original being. It is being itself. We can describe being most adequately in terms of will. Being is not a thing; it is not a person; it is will."[9]

Schelling was a major influence on Tillich as also on C. S. Peirce, who once said, when asked to describe his philosophical position, "You may call me a Schellingian."[10] It was Schelling's emphasis on will as the essence of being that drew Schopenhauer's interest, though Schopenhauer, later an important influence on Thomas Mann as well as on Tillich,[11] turned this emphasis in a new direction. For him, will in human life is perpetually restless, always ultimately unsatisfied in its own longing, and finally desirous of its own cessation in a state of resignation. Here, says Tillich, Schopenhauer achieved, quite independently, the vision of Buddhism (overcoming of self in a formless self) and Hinduism (return to the Brahman principles, the eternal ones), and also set the philosophical stage for the later thinking of Freud (death drive) and Nietzsche, who rejected Schopenhauer's "resignation" and affirmed instead the "will to power."[12]

This line of intellectual influence from Schelling to Schopenhauer to Nietzsche, Tillich argues, must be understood as the source of concern for the primacy of the will in the later thinking of Bergson, Heidegger, Sartre, and Whitehead (the century's great metaphysician, according to Tillich).

In this tradition, called voluntarism, Tillich placed himself. For him, this was the basic nerve of Western mentality, the object of perennial attention in its philosophy and theology. The term *voluntarism* recurs in Tillich's writings, sometimes only in passing. Tillich's voluntarism must be understood not only as an intellectual matter but also as an element of his inner experience, his trauma in the midst of World War I, and his new realism, which became a "belief-ful realism." As has been generally recognized, and as was recognized by Tillich himself, his whole philosophical and theological outlook is fundamentally autobiographical.

The term *voluntarism* is only a century old, having been defined by Ferdinand Tönnies as a philosophy in which the element of the will is primary. For Tönnies, the term *will* encompasses the affections as in Augustine. Tillich was familiar with Tönnies's use of the concepts *Gemeinschaft* and *Gesellschaft*, "community" and "society," and used this distinction from Tönnies in his own thought.[13] It seems evident, therefore, that he also knew of Tönnies's views on voluntarism. One of the most elaborate expositions of the idea of voluntarism after Tönnies was by Friedrich Paulsen, who borrowed the term from Tönnies and popularized it in his *Introduction to Philosophy*, which was read widely and which Tillich certainly knew. Paulsen used this conception to present a "voluntaristic psychology." For the English translation of Paulsen's book, William James provided a lengthy introduction asserting that he would like to promote a wide reading of it. "I should be glad if these introductory words of mine would procure for the *Introduction to Philosophy* a readier reception by American and English students," he wrote.[14]

Whitehead has asserted that the first task of the metaphysician is to choose the root metaphor for interpreting reality. He saw the history of modern thought in terms of root metaphors, as the attempt to interpret reality first in Galilean-Newtonian mathematical terms, and later in Darwinian, evolutionary terms. In his own interpretation, Whitehead chose psychological concepts, viewing all of reality in terms of perception (prehension) and memory. His philosophy, as a result, has sometimes been called "pan-psychism." In short, Whitehead may be compared to Tillich in that both of them chose psychological terms for the interpretation of reality—ontological, societal, and psychological—though of course the meanings they attached to these terms differ. In this sense, Tillich also can be called a "pan-psychist."

Tillich goes beyond Paulsen's voluntaristic psychology to a voluntaristic ontology. In doing this, as we have said, he recognizes that the approach is found in classical form in the writings of Augustine. Although Augustine lived in a time of skepticism, says Tillich, "he overcame this skepticism with the experience that in the depths of the soul—of one's own soul—the truth is dwelling, that it is to be found in one's own soul."[15] It must be remembered too that both the Old and the New Testaments are oriented to the will and the love of God. In Rom. 7:22-24, Saint Paul finds within himself two wills struggling with one another: "For I delight in the law of God, in my inmost self, but I see in my members another law at war with the law of my mind and making me captive to the law of sin which dwells in my members. Wretched man that I am! Who will deliver me from this body of death?"

The Augustinian approach rejects the attempt of human beings to penetrate the outer world; that world can be understood only by turning inward with the assumption that in one's own existence one will find the clue to all of existence, indeed to existence itself. Here is an interpretation of existence in terms of inner experience, long before contemporary depth psychology and modern existentialism. It must be kept in mind that for Augustine, evil does not result from the fact that humans are flesh but from perverted will —humans give to the creature what belongs alone to the Creator, and this is idolatry.

Of special significance for later philosophy was Luther's awareness of the dark underground of demonic forces in himself and in society, leading him to the "hell of despair," and to call out for the transforming power of faith. This conflict of wills Jakob Böhme reads back into the mysterious dynamic in God, which he calls *Urgrund.* The cleavage between the wills is rooted in God himself. Through the human abuse of freedom the will of affirmation becomes disjoined from the integrating will in God, and demonic self-affirmation becomes self-inflation. The self-affirmation, however, cannot sustain itself; it requires partial participation in the divine will. In this restricted sense, God may say to rebellious Lucifer, "When me you fly, I am the wings."

Although Tillich interprets the history of thought as a dynamic tension between those who believe will is primary and those who believe intellect is primary, and sides with the former, he nonetheless assigns to reason a variety of functions. He speaks of ecstatic reason, the depth of reason, antonomous reason, technical reason, and technological reason. For him, intellect is not measurable, detached intelligence but the whole range of cognition in its broadest sense of participation in being. It means, following the Latin (inter/legere), to "read between" or participate in. It means becoming aware of the structure (Logos) of everything that is. The world as will is "instinct, drive, trend, dynamics," a "dynamic element of all reality." Intellect participates in that reality and seeks to discern its structure. Tillich was fond of Nietzsche's aphorism that "Spirit [intellect] cuts down through life," discerning the authentic and the inauthentic in the midst of sheer vitality. The intellect also discerns the tensions and contradictions in reality as well as the harmonies in its structure. Thus Tillich sees "the reality" as primary, the intellect (the participation and awareness) as secondary.

In selecting the psychological metaphors will and intellect to interpret ontology, other metaphors that are societal, political, domestic, and organic are also interpreted within a psychological context, metaphors such as the kingship of God; the Kingdom of God; the fatherhood of God; God as a bridegroom as in Hosea; the church as the body of Christ; Covenant; society as an organism (the dominant metaphor of the Middle Ages); and the concept of the demonic, one of Tillich's most widely adopted concepts today.

Tillich's method and concept of correlation is to be understood as a dynamic interrelating of the powers, dynamic powers in reality and history, ever finding new expression. In Troeltschian fashion, he strives again and again for tentative synthesis, in contrast to a Hegelian logistic approach. So when Tillich, as apologetic theologian, insists that one must listen to "the times" he is saying that one must listen to the unique manifestations of the ontological will, in a truly kairotic fashion. The word used by Schelling to designate the depth of reality disclosing itself was *das Unvordenk-liche*, that which precedes and transcends thinking, a word adopted from popular usage meaning "from time immemorial" or "time out of mind." Tillich's view is close to Schelling's when he writes that we have only a dim view of the depth of reality because it precedes and transcends thought so that intellect, in and of itself, even in its broadest sense, cannot encompass and comprehend it.

Tillich envisions our living within being, within this as dynamic will. That will is recreative but subject to demonic perversion due to the abuse of human freedom (Augustine again). We must listen to how that will manifests itself creatively and ambiguously in each new time. That manifestation is *Kairos,* being revealing itself in new crisis and new opportunity. One must listen to that, perceive what the *Kairos* is, and respond to it, lest one fail to be timely. Even then, one's response involves risk; the response may be the wrong one or the time may not be right. This risk is never absent.

For Tillich, the central *Kairos* of history is the New Being, Jesus as the Christ, but there are, he believes, also other "times," *Kairoi,* in which time is being uniquely fulfilled. (See Langdon Gilkey's discussion of New Being in chapter 17 of this book.) The word *Kairos* is drawn by Tillich from Eph. 1:9–10: "For he has made known to us in all wisdom and insight the mystery of his will, according to his purpose which he set forth in Christ as a plan for *the fullness of time,* to unite all things in him, things in heaven and things on earth."

Three nineteenth-century thinkers in the voluntarist tradition created concepts that revolutionized the climate of thought for the twentieth century. Marx (ideology), Freud (psychoanalysis and rationalization) and Nietzsche (resentment) all undercut the bourgeois conventions, laying open the realities of class structure and the depths of human inner experience. Tillich saw himself and his generation as the heirs of that revolution, and he knew that his work must somehow speak to the challenges it presented. Tillich wrote, "I belonged to the first generation; I tried to show what it means for Protestant theology that not the surface consciousness but the underground of human existence is decisive in human experience and relations. The concept of ideology revealed the interest of the ruling classes in preserving their power by producing a transcendent system to divert the masses from their immediate situation of disinheritance."[16] Here is a clear bit of evidence of Tillich's concern to address the implications of voluntarism in both their social and their psychological aspects.

In Tillich's early European career, his emphasis was primarily (not exclusively) on the sociological implications of his theology; in his later American career his efforts were aimed more (but not entirely) at treating depth-psychological implications of the voluntarist principle. His shift of emphasis may be interpreted as a change of focus within his continuing commitment to a voluntarist position. The shift occurred, it seems safe to say, because of Tillich's concern that his work respond to the questions of the changing times that were rising in ever new forms. Before World War II, Tillich saw in the *Kairos* the churning energies of social class newly exposed by the application of insights of Marx as they shaped the human experience in both creative and demonic ways. After World War II, after the holocaust, after the bomb, Tillich perceived that the most haunting human questions had to do with the vacancy or "void" within the human, spiritual experience. He saw numbness, the loss of hope, the depth of anxiety and despair as psychological realities given birth by the disruptions of the twentieth century. For him, then, the deepest question of the postwar *Kairos* was the question of the inner "courage to be in spite of" the threatening landscape and the ominousness of the future. In the dark night of the mid-twentieth century, in the face of meaninglessness, Tillich discerned, however, in addition to threats, a creative promise symbolized powerfully, for example, by van Gogh's *Starry Night.*

TILLICH THE APOLOGIST

If we turn now again to Tillich's conception of the apologetic theologian, a false reading must be rejected. The apologist may be a defender of the faith in a sense, but the faith is not available in a neat package except with authoritarian sanctions. Nor is faith to be defended against outsiders. The apologist is engaged in an internal dialogue, a dialogue between himself as Christian theologian and himself as non-Christian. The apologist's inner dialogue is personal and at the same time more than personal inasmuch as each inner voice corresponds to many voices outside the self.

Apology, therefore, possesses public relevance when the struggle is first personally authentic.

Early in his career, Tillich identified himself as an apologetic theologian, defining the role as "the art of answering questions." As a young pastor in Berlin, he became aware not only of the nagging doubts of many parishioners but also of the virtual indifference of those no longer troubled by doubts—they simply had rejected Christianity and every other religion. He was convinced that others of conservative mentality identified the faith with the status quo in politics and economics, "a superfluous consecration."

At the age of twenty-six, Tillich, with a young colleague, Richard Wegener, initiated for the laity a series of apologetic sessions to be repeated in several sections of Berlin; *Vernunft-Abende* they called them. In preparation for this enterprise, Tillich wrote a lengthy, compact document defining the methods and goals of Christian apologetics. He surveyed various conceptions of apologetics from early Christianity to the present day, giving attention, for example, to the ferreting out of the heretic for excommunication and persecution. This thirty-page document (1913), a remarkably mature statement for one his age, is still extant, and its ideas were echoed in later writings down to his third volume of the *Systematic Theology* (1963).

Besides this document we have in the archives manuscripts of five of the lectures presented by Tillich in sessions of those evenings on apologetics. Years later, moreover, Tillich prepared a tentative preface ("A Personal Introduction") for his *Systematic Theology*. For reasons I do not know, he did not use this preface, and it has remained unpublished. Soon, however, the Tillich seminar at Trinity College, Oxford, in consultation with the Paul Tillich Societies in Germany, France, and the United States, plans to publish the document. It is concerned entirely with a consideration of his systematic theology as apologetic theology, and also systematic theology as the grounding for apologetics. In 1913 he had spoken of theoretical apologetics as a philosophical inquiry and of practical apologetics as a theological discipline.

In this "Personal Introduction" Tillich begins by saying that for twenty years it had been his "passionate desire" to develop and write a systematic theology, but that the project was delayed.

Among the reasons for the delay he speaks of the external situation, the series of wars, revolutions, and emigrations. He does not mention the fact that by reason of his own emigration he was obliged to learn to lecture and write in the language of his adopted country. Instead, he asserts that for the enterprise of preparing a systematic theology a person can never know enough to venture beyond the publication of essays, particularly because of his own "personal and spiritual inadequacy." The attempt at the enterprise indeed is "almost blasphemous," calling for judgment and forgiveness.

On the other hand, the situation presented a favorable element. The same historical events that made normal academic existence nearly impossible "provided experiences and ideas that no amount of learning could ever have given." This variety of experience caused him to live, as he often said, on the boundary, between contrasting positions.

On both sides many other voices participated. The dialogue, however, was conducted dialectically in the teeth of tense experience, not "from book to book." Of this process he says that "through dialectical affirmations and negations truth is discovered." As we have seen, Tillich saw differences of insight as the result of tensions and ambiguities within the dynamic "will" of being itself. The dialectical process, however, is not a resort to relativism. Data do not speak until they are spoken to, and then one listens, finds common ground, and learns to ask the right questions. The new questions arise from the individuality of each historical "situation." Through the questions one discerns the *Kairos*. This is Tillich's method of correlation, a way of uniting "message" and situation." The process of discovery is learning to listen for truth wherever it appears as a manifestation of grace. The theologian carries within him, as a member of a faith community, the criterion of the New Being. This criterion constitutes a recurrent theme of the present volume.

When considering Tillich as an apologist, one must not forget that he was a Lutheran Christian. That he was not a narrow Lutheran is evident from the strong interest of Catholic theologians in his work (initiated by the Catholic theologian and friend of Tillich, the Jesuit Gustave Weigel and carried on by a host of Catholic theologians in various countries) and the deep appreciation that

Jews have expressed for Tillich's courageous commitments to Jews in Nazi Germany as well as for his sensitive treatment of "the Jewish question." Jews were in the Berlin Kairos Circle of which Tillich was a prominent member.[17] Late in his life, Tillich's personal theological horizons expanded even further through his contacts with Eastern cultures. Nevertheless, at the center of his apologetic interest has been an attempt to give meaningful expression to the Pauline-Lutheran doctrine of justification by faith through grace. His approach to the doctrine was influenced by his teacher, Martin Kähler, who taught him that doubt is an aspect of faith and therefore is also "justified." Doubt presupposes meaning and therefore is part of the work of God, thus having theological significance. The apologetic theologian must listen to the voices of doubt within and without. If doubt is suppressed or ignored, the dialectic of faith collapses and the church becomes stagnant.

In Tillich's view, typical neoorthodoxy refuses to listen and is, therefore, nondialectical. It is all too prone merely to "proclaim" the Word, even to the extent of pushing philosophy aside, and of derogating the findings of modern historical criticism as theologically trivial. What comes from on high is decisive. But it is not enough, Tillich believes, to be grasped by the vertical. It must be explicated and applied on the horizontal as well. To be sure, for Tillich the Bible is the primary witness.

In the unpublished preface to *Systematic Theology,* Tillich states clearly that his theology is biblical in character even though he uses few biblical quotations. Biblical and systematic theology must supplement one another. A systematic theologian must refer to and depend on the work of biblical theologians. Biblical criticism (which Tillich calls one of the greatest stories in intellectual history, equal to the growth of science) is necessary and does not diminish the "divine nature" of the Bible, but makes it more manifest.

Many of Tillich's essays exemplify the dialectical method of his listening. As we have observed, in face of the widespread view that religion long ago lost its charisma as matter for art, Tillich has discerned hidden religious import there, spelling out a whole set of ideological as well as social-ethical and mystical categories for the identification of the false and the true. He has examined the many dimensions of *Existenz*-philosophy in similar dialectical fashion. Nowhere else is there such an elaborate comparison and contrast as Tillich's between Marxism and Christianity. He traces these themes from Creation and Fall to the eschaton. Tillich takes delight always in the nuanced multiplication of distinctions and classifications, Yes and No. Even as late as 1948 he published an article entitled "How Much Truth Is in Karl Marx?"[18]

Tillich's relation to Marxist ideas and movements reveals an interesting ambiguity. As a young theologian in Germany, Tillich had been willing to suffer the rebuke of Brandenburg Consistory (of which his pastor-father was a member) after he spoke at a meeting of a Marxist organization. Later in his career in the United States, when we were preparing essays for publication in *The Protestant Era,* after he had approved all essays for inclusion and after I had translated all of them, he changed his mind about including an essay on the class struggle and religious socialism, saying to me, "I can't possibly include this, it would destroy me in this country." Also, Tillich and I were for a time on the board of editors of *The Protestant,* a magazine in which he published many articles. Tillich left the board because he came to believe the journal editor was a sedulous "fellow traveler" with the American Communist party. It must be kept in mind that at the time Tillich was making these decisions about his relation to Marxism in this country, the prevailing national atmosphere here successfully kept American universities from hiring Marxist faculty personnel. In any event, in Tillich's various essays on Marx, as well as in the Supplement at the end of this volume, one sees how Tillich the theologian dialectically asks questions as well as answers them. In this way he displays what is meant by understanding human being ontologically as the being that raises questions about the meaning of its being.

In a book such as this one, a word must be said concerning the development of feminist theologies in relation to the influence of Tillich. Since Tillich's death, feminist theologians increasingly have exposed the limitations of male-dominated religion and theology. The theological work of Mary Daly, one of today's most outspoken antimale feminist theologians, has been influenced by the thought of Tillich, as the methodology of her work shows. *Beyond God the Father* is one way of speaking about God above the God of theism.[19]

Beyond God the Father specifically employs (or goes beyond or against) practically every element or category in the Tillichian theology from beginning to end. Apparently, however, Daly does not take into account Tillich's discussion of possible lines for development of the desexing of theology set forth in the final pages of *Systematic Theology,* part 4. Tillich then would find Daly's desexing of theology as wholly appropriate but would agree possibly with other critics of Daly who believe that she, in seeking to right old wrongs, has succumbed to a naiveté about women and a lack of interest in the truths that arise from the male experience.

THE STRUCTURE OF THIS BOOK

Now to turn to the contents and structure of the present volume. Tillich, it will be recalled, held that the apologetic theologian must practice his vocation in all realms of experience. The chapters that follow aim to present Tillich's thought in a wide spectrum of current culture, also looking to the future. It should be noted, however, that important spheres of the dialogue do not receive systematic attention—such as the philosophy of history, the system of the sciences, the theory of symbols, the doctrine of the church, and technology, all of which were important concerns of Tillich and are treated extensively elsewhere.

The first chapter and the chapter by Wilhelm Pauck present an introduction to Tillich's thought and life by two scholars who not only knew Tillich personally over many decades but also worked with him closely in various endeavors. Pauck reviews Tillich's life and the development of his thought, showing continuities and discontinuities. He emphasizes the autobiographical nature of Tillich's theological work, but points out also his grasp of human history as a context of his thought. Tillich desired deeply to interpret the Christian message for persons living in the twentieth century, a century that had lost its theonomous character.

Next, three authors look at Tillich's larger world view, especially his political theory and practice. Roger Shinn, in chapter 3, views Tillich as the "interpreter and disturber of contemporary civilization," looking at Tillich's understanding of the world, especially his response to the Nazi situation and the inner cries that produced it. Shinn examines Tillich's most central concepts—revolutionary reason, theonomy, the demonic, the Protestant principle, and

Kairos. He then looks at the deepening traumas of civilization since Tillich's time, and closes with a discussion of Tillich and some of his critics, notably Bonhoeffer.

In chapter 4, Walter Weisskopf focusses on the three large themes contained in Tillich's book of 1933, *The Socialist Decision:* the romantic, the bourgeois, and the socialist principles. He discusses Tillich's view of the crisis in Western culture as a loss of "reason grounded in depth dimension" and the emergence of "technical reason" in the bourgeois era. Weisskopf then discusses twentieth-century socialism and capitalism and closes with reflections on contemporary Western culture in light of Tillich's analysis, especially of his concern for the religious dimension—the absolute and unconditional.

Dennis McCann, in chapter 5, looks at eschatological questions raised by Tillich's theology. He compares the creative tension of Marxism and prophetism and looks at Tillich's solutions in comparison with the work of J. L. Segundo and Reinhold Niebuhr, finally looking at the present impasse in theology and the relevance of Tillich's thought for possible future advances.

The two following essays deal with Tillich's long-time concern with the issues of depth psychology that were emerging in his times and the relationship of those issues to the tasks of theology. In chapter 6, William Rogers maintains that Tillich was actively concerned about issues in psychology and psychotherapy early in his career and always kept close and fruitful ties with thinkers in that field, ties that had significant influence in both directions. Those relationships with persons in psychology were especially important in the years after Tillich emigrated to the United States. Rogers then suggests several of Tillich's concepts that offer a fruitful connection between psychology and theology. Through his work, says Rogers, Tillich influenced the whole field of pastoral psychology in this country.

Ann Ulanov, in chapter 7, compares several concepts in Tillich's thought with concepts in depth psychology, noting the fruitful interchange. She examines especially Tillich's concepts of the power of the demonic, the fall from harmony into estrangement, and the juxtaposition of lasting archetypes with changing symbols. Ulanov concludes with a discussion of Tillich's concepts of anxiety as "terror of being," "meaninglessness," and "guilt and condemnation."

The arts, especially painting and literature, were for Tillich among the surest indicators of the condition of the times; thus he both sought out artists and took seriously their work as much as any theologian in this century. In chapter 8, Nathan Scott views Tillich as a theologian of culture who found, even in the secular, something ultimate. For him, autonomous culture, having begun with the Renaissance and Reformation, opened the way to exploitive capitalism, which was reaching its end in the twentieth century. In this situation, Tillich was engaged with writers in the vanguard of modernism and believed that their literature corroborated his estimate of contemporary culture. He died before the growth of postmodernism in literature, but Scott surmises what Tillich's response to it might be were he alive today.

Robert Scharlemann, in chapter 9, discusses Tillich's view of the relationship between art and reality. Tillich's religious thought, says Scharlemann, moves from expressionism to a new realism. For him, religious art is art that expresses the depth of culture where meaning and spiritual substance are found. To understand art, one must distinguish between what it depicts and what it expresses. The meaning of art is in what it expresses, no matter what it depicts. Depth content, for Tillich, shows in and through the physical character and objective structure of things. The depth content of postexpressionist art, believes Scharlemann, is in "technological subjectivity," and he illustrates his point by examining the musical *Jesus Christ, Superstar.*

Three authors now discuss Tillich in relation to non-Christians and those in new American religious movements of the past fifteen years. In chapter 10, Rabbi Albert Friedlander expresses appreciation of Tillich from a Jewish perspective. Though Christ is at the center for Tillich, Friedlander believes that when Tillich defines religion unpolemically, Jews and Christians can meet. Tillich was courageous in his thought and in his lived relationships with Jewish people, especially in Nazi Germany, but he also was sometimes wrong about Judaism, says Friedlander. Overall, Tillich's moral vision, his choice of the God of time against the gods of space, endears him to many Jewish people.

In chapter 11, Joseph Kitagawa discusses Tillich's evolving understanding of the relation between Christianity and other major religions. Near the end of his life, Tillich provided some helpful ground rules for encounter among religions. In his earlier writings, he saw the solution to human existence as the New Being in Jesus, whereas in later years, after a trip to Japan and conversations with scholars in world religions, he gained an increased respect for the religiousness in the depth of all religions.

Jack Boozer, in chapter 12, reviews the work of several thinkers who have analyzed recent American religious movements and asks how Tillich might view those movements. The new religions are successful because they fill a void that traditional churches fail to do. Boozer believes that Tillich would support new religious movements when they challenge the secular, destructive culture, but that he would criticize them when they become neurotic and demonic.

At this point, the emphasis shifts more directly to philosophy and theology. As several writers in this volume suggest, Tillich works from the stuff of experience (political-social-economic) toward theology in his method of correlation. But this is not just a one-way movement from reality to theology. From theology, Tillich then moves toward the culture again in order to provide interpretations of it.

In chapter 13, John Smith, a philosopher, sees Tillich as an interpreter of religion in a post-Enlightenment world. In part, Tillich resists this world, its neglect of the ecstatic, its impoverishment of a reason that it reduces to technical reason. But in part Tillich accepts and welcomes this world. He accepts its freedoms, its scientific knowledge, its rejection of heteronomy. His concept of religion as ultimate concern enables him to be a critic of much conventional religion, an advocate of faith. It enables him to relate religion and science, avoiding the two common temptations: to dictate religious beliefs to the sciences, and to retreat in the face of science to a merely inward religion. In the face of the positivistic tendencies of our time, he reaffirms the importance of both the sacred and the demonic.

David Tracy, in chapter 14, believes that while there is no ongoing school of Tillichians, Tillich touched all present-day theologians by teaching them how to ask religious-theological questions. Especially in his method of correlation Tillich demonstrated how theology must always address a new situation and reinterpret the resources of the tradition for a new time. Tracy argues that issues of global suffering and oppression are more urgent than the Enlightenment issues of reason and revelation on which Tillich's theology focussed. In our situation of "radical pluralism," even among theologians, the important thing, however, is not to repeat Tillich but to "employ his mode of inquiry." In that way, Tillich still teaches us.

Three theologians now turn here to deal with more specific theological questions. In chapter 15, John Powell Clayton sees Tillich as a thinker constantly in process, constantly revising earlier ideas. His system could not be a success finally because of his own conviction that every system is transitory and "none can be final." In the total achievement of his written work, however, there are magnificent fragments. The enduring value of Tillich's theology is not a system but his way of doing theology *kata Kairon*, discerning the "signs of the times."

Thomas O'Meara, in chapter 16, deals with Tillich on Catholic substance. It is a sign of the ecumenical spirit of our times, and the ecumenical importance of Tillich, that David Tracy, a Roman Catholic theologian, wrote the comprehensive chapter "Tillich and Contemporary Theology" quite without any accent on specific Catholic-Protestant issues. O'Meara concentrates on Tillich's formulation of Catholic substance and Protestant principle, showing why Tillich, although in some ways sharply Protestant, has an attraction for and an interest in Catholic theology. Three elements in Tillich's thought, believes O'Meara, have attracted Catholic thinkers: first, Tillich's concern for and respect for ontology; second, Tillich's belief that there is something holy in every era of culture; and third, Tillich's mystical search for an immediate experience of the presence of the Spirit in culture.

Chapter 17, by Langdon Gilkey, is the most "doctrinal" chapter of this book. Gilkey's discussion centers on Tillich's doctrine of the New Being, with particular reference to his beliefs about Christ. Gilkey makes the case that, far from starting with ontology in general and then struggling to fit Christology into it, Tillich has a central concern for the doctrine of the New Being, from which he moves "backward" into ontology and outward into a wide range of concerns. New Being is the paradigm for all other religious symbols, the religious ethical model for all finite entities, and the picture of a creative community or creative individual. Gilkey then lays out the consequences and issues that follow from Tillich's central concept. The key issue is that "the religious," not "the philosophical or scientific," is the pathway to the universal. A true symbol points beyond itself; and so also must Christianity.

In Chapter 18, Gilkey assesses the overall role of the theologian in the light of Tillich's achievement. Because God is identical with being, because religion and culture are interrelated as are theology and philosophy, philosophical and theological questions and answers lie on both sides of theological dialectic. The theologian as a public figure must stand in culture and know its questions, must stand in the church and interpret its message. The work of theology should illumine culture, interpret the message of the religious community, interpret human finitude, and interpret (politically) the drive toward justice. Overall, theology should offer hope, the *Kairos*.

The final essay in this volume is a translation of an open letter from Tillich to Emanuel Hirsch, a document little known among us in this country, one of the great polemical and apologetic utterances of the century. It is the most comprehensive statement of Tillich's critique of nazism, at the same time a demolishing attack on one of his closest friends, the learned Emanuel Hirsch who became the outstanding Nazi (German Christian) theologian.[20] In 1927, however, Tillich had published a review of Hirsch's work, *The Philosophy of Idealism and Christianity* (1926), speaking of it as "perhaps the most mature work on the subject in the last twenty years."

We should observe that Tillich's letter was published in 1934, a year after the Nazi seizure of power, also shortly after Tillich's arrival as an exile in New York to become a professor at Union Theological Seminary. In preparing the letter for possible publication in Germany, Tillich probably feared that the Nazi censor would prohibit its publication. Presumably for this reason the letter scarcely mentions national socialism by name.

Since some of the readers of the present volume may not be familiar with Hirsch's writings, and since some knowledge of them is presupposed in the letter, it is fitting here to give a brief, if oversimplified, account of Hirsch's outlook.

For Tillich the propitious place in the search for truth is the dialogue with representatives of varying, and even opposing, resources in the current historical situation. Accordingly, he speaks of his "living on the boundary." For Tillich, the term boundary is also the point at which one recognizes the limits of human being and human capacities in face of the divine majesty. For Hirsch (who uses the Greek term *Horos* to mean boundary), "the sacred boundary" is the God-given order of Creation, the order of grace, in the German race and in a divinely given "blood covenant." Here he points to what he called the "hidden sovereignty of the *Volk.*"

Tillich, for his part as a theologian of culture, crosses the boundaries, indeed lives on both sides, of certain selected and contrasting perspectives of social existence and of social movements. For Hirsch, however, the boundary of race must not be crossed, for the consequence would be a disastrous dissolution of law and order. One's total orientation must be to the German race. Love of neighbor, admonished in the gospel, must be the love of the German race. It is demonic to ignore this authority by promoting internationalism, ecumenism, pacifism, or democracy, which only amounts to chaotic and endless chatter that lacks binding obligations. This faith is rooted in a "myth of origin," in blood and soil.[21] In Tillich's view, this faith possesses no eschatology because it worships an absolutized, finite entity sealed from criticism and open to nothing essentially new. This produces a self-enclosed, completely perverted, and demonized sense of *Kairos.* Here Tillich agrees with Barth in criticizing Hirsch's identification of the eschaton with a specific, finite time. Indeed, Tillich praised Barth for helping to save all contemporary theology from "forgetting the deity of God."[22] Tillich disagrees with Barth, however, in that for Barth the eschatological has a supernatural character, removed from history. For Tillich, the eschatological is ambiguous, both historical and beyond history.

In the German faith Tillich sees the elimination of the prophetic element in Judaism and Christianity in favor of a rigid and primitive sacramental, spatialized grace available only at the hands of the God of the Germans. Without the authority of the "sacred boundary" *(Horos),* Hirsch asked, how may the character and conscience of the nation, and especially of the youth, be shaped? In all of this, Tillich finds Hirsch appropriating and perverting concepts that Hirsch found in the religious socialism of the Kairos Circle. In short, Hirsch transformed this religious socialism into national socialism, a fearful and destructive idol, or Moloch.[23]

NOTES

1. The concept of the "apologetic theologian" is discussed later in this chapter.
2. See Paul Tillich, "Existentialist Aspects of Modern Art," in *Christianity and the Existentialists*, ed. Carl Michalson (New York: Charles Scribner's Sons, 1956), 128–47. In this essay Tillich examines various dimensions of existentialist paintings of the twentieth century and selects Picasso's *Guernica* as a mirror of the disruptions of our times and a protest against the insanity of a war-torn world. This chapter is one of Tillich's most concise statements of the relationship between religion and art and one of the best that any twentieth-century theologian has written on this matter. See also Wilhelm and Marion Pauck, *Paul Tillich: His Life and Thought* (New York: Harper & Row, 1976), vol. 1, *Life*, 75–79, where the Paucks discuss Tillich's relation to the expressionist painters, especially Cézanne.
3. Paul Tillich, "Religiöse Krisis," *Vivos Voco* 2 (1922): 616–21.
4. Paul Tillich, *The Protestant Era*, trans. James Luther Adams (Chicago: University of Chicago Press, 1948), 32.
5. In connection with the events of those same years, it is important to remember that Tillich thought that Karl Barth had betrayed Religious Socialism by remaining quiet on the issue of anti-Semitism while Tillich and others had published public theses on the matter as early as 1932.
6. Wilhelm and Marion Pauck, *Tillich: His Life and Thought*, vol. 1, *Life*, 171.
7. Wilhelm Pauck, *From Luther to Tillich: The Reformers and Their Heirs* (San Francisco: Harper & Row, 1984). Cited with permission from Harper & Row and Marion Pauck.
8. Paul Tillich, "Das Christentum and Die Moderne," *Schule und Wissenschaft* II (1928): 121–31, 170–77.
9. The issues of will and intellect are discussed at length in Paul Tillich, *Perspectives on 19th and 20th Century Protestant Theology*, ed. Carl Braaten (New York: Harper & Row, 1967), 191ff. The passages quoted here are from pp. 192 and 193.
10. The German philosopher Schelling, a major mentor of Tillich, proposed a typology of spaces that briefly goes as follows: (1) Orientation to particular, limited spaces (such as a grove, the sea, a territory, a race, a nation), a fixated tradition exempt from criticism—polytheism. (2) Orientation to a changing hierarchy of gods—monarchical polytheism. (3) Radical dualism, bifurcation of good and evil, an unstable schizophrenia—Zoroastrianism. (4) Devotion to one God the Creator of all spaces, yet holding all spaces under a universal judgment—exclusive monotheism. These differentiations prevail across the apparent boundaries of culture and religion. Tillich occasionally refers to this typology. Like Schelling, Tillich conceives of history as a struggle between time and space, but Tillich goes beyond Schelling, claiming that time can be the corrector of space. The spatialization of time is idolatry, what Tillich called a "demonic sacramentalism." One entire volume of Tillich's collected writings is entitled *Der Widerstreit von Raum und Zeit*, (vol. 6, *Gesammelte Werke* [Stuttgart: Evangelisches Verlagswerk, 1963].) Tillich distinguishes between the sacramental and the prophetic. Sacramentalism is oriented toward the present while the prophetic is eschatologically oriented. Either can become demonic: Demonic sacramentalism elevates what is finite without criticism while demonic propheticism is false prophecy. Tillich saw in nazism and capitalism tendencies toward demonic sacramentalism, the elevation of the finite beyond criticism.

Even religion can become demonic in this sense of "demonic sacramentalism."
11. There is an interesting connection between Tillich and Thomas Mann as well. Mann, in preparing the manuscript of *Doctor Faustus*, corresponded with Tillich, asking him to describe the climate of theological issues in early twentieth-century Germany. Tillich wrote lengthy answers, many of which were used by Mann in the novel. See Gunilla Bergsten, *Thomas Mann's "Doctor Faustus"* (Chicago: University of Chicago Press, 1963), especially 34–45.

12. It distressed Tillich that Nietzsche was so frequently misunderstood and misrepresented. Tillich, therefore, attempted several times, as did others such as Heidegger, Jaspers, and Fromm, to correct the erroneous, prevailing interpretations of Nietzsche's concept of will to power, showing it to be much more profound than the vulgar concept that many scholars had associated with the rise of nazism. For Nietzsche, Tillich insists, "power is the self-affirmation of being. Will to power means power to affirm one's power of living, the will to affirm one's own individual existence." See Tillich, *Perspectives on Nineteenth and Twentieth Century Protestant Theology*, 198–207; and idem, *The Courage to Be* (New Haven: Yale University Press, 1952), 24–31. Tillich has pointed out that Nietzsche proclaimed the death of God but reclaimed God as "creative life." He challenged whatever opposed life, and what challenged life the most then (and still does) is the "objectivating" nature of bourgeois thinking and acting wherein means replace ends and people become objects of analysis and control. See also idem, "Nietzsche and the Bourgeois Spirit," *Journal of the History of Ideas* 4, no. 3 (June 1945): 307–9. These concerns of Nietzsche's were also concerns of Tillich's, as Walter Weisskopf shows in this volume.

13. Paul Tillich, *The Socialist Decision*, trans. Franklin Sherman (New York: Harper & Row, 1977), 75.

14. William James, "Introduction," in Friedrich Paulsen, *Introduction to Philosophy* (New York: Henry Holt and Co., 1926), vii.

15. Paul Tillich, unpublished, undated lecture, on cassettes 1211–12, Tillich Archive, Andover Harvard Library.

16. Tillich, *Perspectives on Nineteenth and Twentieth Century Protestant Theology*, 199.

17. The Kairos Circle is a name used to refer to the group of Religious Socialists centered in Berlin after World War I, a group of which Tillich was a prominent member.

18. Paul Tillich, "How Much Truth is in Karl Marx?" *The Christian Century* 65, no. 36 (1948): 906–8.

19. See Mary Daly, *Beyond God the Father* (Boston: Beacon, 1973). Mary Ann Stenger has written a remarkable article on the influence of Tillich on Daly. See Mary Ann Stenger, "A Critical Analysis of the Influence of Paul Tillich on Mary Daly's Feminist Theology," *Encounter* 43 (Winter 1982): 219–38. See also Rosemary Ruether's review of Mary Daly's latest book, *Pure Lust: Elemental Feminist Theology*, where Ruether shows that Daly still acknowledges "glimmers of truth" in some male culture, naming Paul Tillich as one of those males in whom there is a "glimmer of truth." *Unitarian Universalist World* 15, no. 6 (15 June 1984): 14. See also Joan Arnold Romero, "The Protestant Principle: A Woman's Eye View of Barth and Tillich," in *Religion and Sexism: Images of Women in the Jewish and Christian Tradition*, ed. Rosemary Radford Ruether (New York: Simon and Schuster, 1974), 336. See also Paul D. Hanson, "Masculine Metaphors for God and Sex Discrimination in the Old Testament," *The Ecumenical Review* 27 (1975): 316–24. Hanson discusses feminism as a prophetic element in present-day history, as a manifestation of what Tillich would call the *Kairos*.

20. For an extensive discussion of the Tillich-Hirsch exchange, see Walter F. Bense, "Tillich's Kairos and Hitler's Seizure of Power: The Tillich-Hirsch Exchange of 1934–5," in *Tillich Studies: 1975*, ed. John J. Carey (Tallahassee, Florida: The Second American Consultation on Paul Tillich Studies, 1975), 39.

21. The concept of the "myth of origin" was used before Tillich by the Roman Catholic political scientist Carl Schmitt, who later became a Nazi. It is possible that Tillich adapted the concept from Schmitt.

22. Paul Tillich, "What Is Wrong with the 'Dialectic' Theology?" *The Journal of Religion* 15, no. 2 (1935): 145.

23. When I first arrived in Germany in 1936, I met anti-Nazi Christians who not only knew Tillich's letter but were deeply grateful for it. In the same visit, I called on Professor Hirsch at the University of Göttingen, and from his lips heard the "gospel" of German Christianity. In the course of the conversation he drew an analogy between the order of subordination in races and the differences of vocation between a scholar and the maid who had just served us tea. Speaking of Judaism, he said that his conscience had often pained him when he was obliged to read a Scripture lesson in church from the Old Testament.

2. To Be or Not to Be: Tillich on the Meaning of Life

WILHELM PAUCK

To be or not to be: That is the question.
—SHAKESPEARE, *Hamlet*

I identified myself (almost dangerously) with figures like Hamlet. My instinctive sympathy today for what is called existentialism goes back in part to an existential understanding of this great work of literature.
—PAUL TILLICH, *On the Boundary*

Paul Tillich's career was extraordinary. When he retired from Union Theological Seminary at the age of sixty-nine, after he had taught there with remarkable success for twenty-two years, he went to Harvard University as a University Professor and served there with the highest distinction. After six years, he had to retire again in compliance with the rules of his appointment. His influence upon the public was then very great both in this country and in Europe. It made no sense for him to become an emeritus. Therefore, he accepted a distinguished theological professorship at the University of Chicago. He planned to leave this post at the end of the academic year 1965–66, shortly before his eightieth birthday —again not to retire but to assume the Alvin Johnson chair of philosophy at the New School of Social Research in New York. His death on October 22, 1965, put an end to these plans.

Shortly before he left Union Theological Seminary in 1955, Tillich had been the Gifford lecturer at the University of Saint Andrews in Scotland, and during the succeeding years, while he held posts at Harvard and Chicago, he taught for single academic terms at the universities of Hamburg and Zurich. During these years he reached large audiences. Hundreds of students filled his classes; hundreds and sometimes thousands, young and old, came to hear his lectures and sermons. He spoke frequently on radio or television broadcasts. His books were widely read; the more popular ones, for example, *The Courage to Be* and *The Dynamics of Faith*, reached a circulation of more than 100,000 copies each. His *Collected Works (Gesammelte Werke)* comprise fourteen volumes in addition to the three volumes of the *Systematic Theology*, his magnum opus, and three volumes of sermons.

At the end of his life, Paul Tillich thus enjoyed great acclaim and exercised wide influence. To those of us who followed his career from its beginnings and who knew him intimately, this caused no surprise, for we were aware that he was a man of unusual personal power and that his impact upon other persons had been profound in all stages of his life. It was remarkable that his outreach became deeper and deeper even during the last phases of his career. It was after the publication in 1948 of *The Protestant Era* that he first became well known to the general public. He was then in his early sixties.

In 1949, while Tillich was a visiting professor for a semester at the University of Marburg, he traveled throughout postwar Germany. Those of us who saw him in action there can testify to the fact that he was given a wide and enthusiastic hearing. His many friends and the public at large had not forgotten him. They remembered that from the time he had begun his work as an academic teacher in Berlin (1919) until the Hitler government had deprived him of his professorship at the University of Frankfurt (1933), he had become increasingly powerful in religion and public affairs. Indeed, his dismissal had cut short a successful career.

Had he returned to Germany and accepted the calls to academic positions that were extended to him after Hitler's downfall, he would have established himself as an incisive force in the remaking of German intellectual life. As it turned out, he did become very influential in his homeland again, but only gradually. The president of the German Federal Republic decorated him with the medals of the Order of Merit. The city of Hamburg honored him by awarding him the Goethe Prize. Later he received the Peace Prize of the German Booksellers, a distinction that earlier had been extended to such leaders of the mind as Albert Schweitzer, Martin Buber, and Thomas Mann.

Tillich chose to stay in America, where he had built a second career. In a way he continued under new circumstances and new auspices the work he was accustomed to do. For the courses he taught in New York dealt with the same materials he had developed in Germany, and the ideas he expressed in his writings were the same he had outlined and formulated earlier. But he had to learn English as an entirely new language in order to win recognition in America. When he arrived in the United States in November 1933, he was forty-seven years of age, and he did not find it easy to adapt himself to new conditions. With the help of friends among his students, he learned the English language (although he never mastered its pronunciation) and he rethought and reformulated his ideas. Indeed, he believed that in the course of this process his thinking became clearer and more readily understandable. He also accommodated himself with characteristic conscientiousness to the American way of life.

Yet as one who had been forced into exile, he initially considered himself a refugee. When he assumed new professional and social responsibilities, he retained the ways and customs in which he had been reared. Yet he believed that as an American he was permitted to remain the person he was: a German intellectual who by education and profession had become identified with the legacy of his nation. At the same time, he felt that as an American he had become liberated from the provincialism of his inherited ways. Although he remained attached to his upbringing and heritage, he set himself free from them.

THE SECRET OF TILLICH'S POWER

At this point we touch upon the secret of Tillich's inner power, and we can begin to understand why his career unfolded as it did and why it reached such a great climax. He was a deeply loyal man who remained faithful to himself throughout his life. At an early age he felt himself called to the work of a theologian and philosopher, even though as a boy he had dreamed of becoming an architect. He was a humanist in the fullest sense of the word. He knew that human life is fulfilled only when autonomy, that is, the self-determination of individuals, is exercised in the context of a cultural heritage so that they relate to it in a critical and constructive way, namely by assessing it for themselves and then transforming it according to the demands of their destiny.

Tillich was filled with a highly personal sense of the character of civilization. He remembered clearly the lessons he had learned from his teachers and the circumstances in which he had learned them. He was acutely mindful of the insights his friends gave to him. He recalled exactly what impression the reading of books or visits to museums had made upon his mind, and he never forgot productive conversations and discussions. He was an autobiographical thinker. His books are full of references to persons whom he called his teachers.

He felt deeply indebted to his father, a minister and high official of the Evangelical Church of Prussia. He never quite outlived the burden of authoritarianism he had encountered in his parent, but he also remained deeply grateful for the introduction to philosophy he had received through conversations with him during the years of his adolescence. In Tillich's mind, the image of his father was connected with recollections of the places where he had grown up. Until his fourteenth year, he had lived in small medieval, walled-in towns in Brandenburg in the middle of Prussia. He was impressed by their historicalness. Their Gothic churches and their old houses gave him a feeling of continuity with past ages—a feeling that he retained throughout his life. Though later he became a passionate spokesman for the "present," he always retained an attachment to old traditions, customs, and usages.

I suppose that it is characteristic of intellectuals everywhere that they remain mindful of those who first stimulated them to undertake ventures of the mind, but I suspect that it is distinctive of German scholars that they like to consider themselves members of a tradition or "school" established by a prominent academic teacher. Paul Tillich was no exception, even though, strictly speaking, he never belonged to a theological or philosophical school, for he was a highly individualistic person, a creative thinker who felt himself guided by a great variety of intuitions and insights. Yet he often expressed deep gratitude for what he owed to Martin Kähler, a professor of systematic theology, whose lectures and seminars he attended at the University of Halle. What attracted him to this man was that, apart from his being a powerful and impressive academic personage, he combined a sympathetic understanding of the faith of the Protestant reformers, especially Luther, with an openness for the humanism of the German literary and philosophical classics, especially Goethe.

Tillich owed to Kähler a constructive understanding of the doctrine of justification by faith and found himself stimulated by him to apply its meaning also to the realm of intellectual thought. A man, he concluded, may have the promise of being justified, of becoming acceptable in God's sight, despite his being not only a sinner but also a doubter. From this Tillich derived the insight, first, that there is not only a religious and moral self-righteousness but also an intellectual one and, second, that as there is in the Christian Gospel the promise of freedom from pharisaism, so there is in it also the promise of becoming liberated from dogmatism. Tillich himself never assumed the bearing of a dogmatist and insofar as he was conscious of this, he knew himself indebted to Kähler.

He learned other lessons from Kähler that came to constitute important parts of his system of thought. For example, he was impressed by Kähler's advocating a theology of mediation not only between liberalism and orthodoxy, but also between philosophy and theology, between human culture and religion, between the secular and the sacred, between existential questions and theological answers. Kähler also suggested to Tillich the basic tenets of his Christology, namely that the Christian faith is not centered in the Jesus of history but in Jesus as he is proclaimed and believed to be the Christ, that is, the Messiah and Redeemer. Tillich remained conscious of this debt throughout his career.

While in Halle, he also came under the influence of a younger teacher, Fritz Medicus by name, a docent of philosophy who later assumed the philosophical chair at the Zurich Institute of Technology but never achieved a wide influence. He specialized in the philosophy of the German idealists. He soon recognized Tillich's philosophical gifts and developed them. It was he who suggested that Tillich concentrate his intellectual labors on the works of the later Schelling. Thus, he was responsible for Tillich's immersing himself in Schelling's "Philosophy of Mythology and Revelation" from which he derived the stimulus for the conception of many themes of his own theology, for example, the *Kairos* and the demonic. Tillich remained consciously grateful to Medicus throughout the days of his life, and Medicus (who was but a few years older than Tillich) derived deep satisfaction in his old age from the fact that one whose promise he had recognized and furthered had come to attain fame in the realm of thought.

Now it was very characteristic of Tillich that, though never unmindful of what he owed to these and other teachers, he felt that he had learned more from friends his own age and from fellow students. He was a member of a famous corporation of students, the Christian student fellowship "Wingolf." In Halle he was the first officer of its chapter at the university. He presided over many heated discussions about the principles that were to guide the students in their common life. He remembered these times as the most stimulating period of his entire career. In a letter of May 23, 1943 written to Thomas Mann, at Mann's request he reviewed his student years:

> The summer semester of 1907 when I presided over the student corporation "Wingolf," then numbering about seventy men, appears to me until today as the greatest period of my life. What I have become as a theologian, a philosopher, a man, I owe partly to my professors but mostly to this fraternity. The theological and philosophical debates we had then till late after midnight and the personal conversations in which we were engaged before dawn, have remained decisive for my entire life.[1]

All who have known Paul Tillich will recognize the truth and relevance of this statement. He loved to be with and among people and to discuss with them almost any question that happened to be brought up. Throughout his life, from the days of his youth until the years of his old age, he learned more from conversations, discussions, and debates than from books, and everyone who talked with him openly and thoughtfully in order to come to a better understanding of some problem or issue became his "teacher." His writings contain numerous reports of personal discoveries and encounters on special occasions filled with searchings for truth and right decisions. Tillich clearly belongs to the rank of those thinkers who are existentially involved in their thought so that when they are affected in their thinking by others they are touched in their personal being; and when they transmit their ideas to their friends or pupils, they give something of themselves.

This is why Tillich so often tended to become engaged in autobiographical reflection; he published several such interpretations of his work, and his writings are filled with reminiscences of persons and events. What he wrote about himself has become deeply imprinted upon the minds of many of his readers; for example, his concept "on the boundary," which is also the title of the essay by which he introduced himself to the American public in his book, *The Interpretation of History*. [2]

For the same reason, his classroom teaching and his public speaking and preaching had a pronounced personal character. He always spoke in a quiet, even voice, and the ideas that he expounded were often highly abstract and quite complex. But he gave the impression that he was speaking from his innermost self to the personal concerns of his listeners.

He was a charismatic person and the *fluidum* that went forth from him cast many under a spell. Without being self-conscious about it and without making himself important, he was aware of his charisma; and this awareness gave a special color to his sense of vocation. He could not possibly have remained insensitive to his power, for his listeners and readers opened themselves to him in most remarkable ways and sought to get in touch with him through personal encounter or correspondence so as to remain assured of the proximity of his spirit.

THE SENSE OF HISTORY

This charisma of Tillich's was, as I have suggested, expressed through a strong sense of history: first, because the stages of his development were always present to him in his thinking; second, because his thought was permeated with the history of mankind, particularly with cultural history and most particularly with the history of Christian theological and philosophical thought. These two sides of his historical outlook were of course closely connected with one another, for it was in the course of his personal development that he came to know the general history to which he so often referred in his work.

The number of historical allusions that he makes in his books is astonishing. Most of these references show the degree to which he was shaped and determined in his thinking by the philosophical and theological tradition from the early Greek philosophers to the present day.

The thinkers with whom he felt a kinship were always present in his thought: the pre-Socratics, and especially Parmenides with his question, "Why is there not nothing?"; Plato and Plotinus and their teaching on essences; the Stoics and their doctrine of the Logos; Augustine with his teaching on grace and his complex doctrine of God as infinite truth that can be experienced immediately in the depths of the soul, and as infinite will that nobody can ever fully comprehend; Eckhart with his principle that God is being (*Deus est esse*) and Cusanus with his conception of the coincidence of opposites; and then, particularly Luther with his interpretation of the Christian message in terms of justification by faith and with his teaching on the God of judgment and mercy, wrath and love; Böhme with his brooding on God the ground and abyss of being; and then the great German thinkers Kant, Hegel, and most especially Schelling, whose theosophical gnosis Tillich had thought through so deeply in his student days that its suggestiveness remained permanently imbedded in his mind; and finally, the liberal theologians from Schleiermacher to Troeltsch, who had renounced the supernaturalistic authorities of the past in order to attempt a historical interpretation of the Christian religion. In his teaching and writing as well as in private meditations and conversations, Tillich again and again coursed through this history, endeavoring to bring it to bear on the modern cultural and spiritual crisis that he saw through the eyes of such diagnosticians as Kierkegaard, Dostoevsky, Nietzsche, Marx, and Freud.

What was characteristic about the way in which Tillich was at home in this tradition of thought was that he knew the distinctive contribution of the individual thinkers from a thorough reading of their main works, and that he kept this knowledge fresh in his mind, not by rereading the sources but by making them the basis of his own creative thought.

This, his own creative thought, was deeply determined by what he felt to be the urgency of understanding the mind of his own era. He published several comprehensive interpretations of his own times, beginning with the widely read book *The Religious Situation*, [3] first issued in 1926. Indeed, throughout his career, he was engaged in diagnosing the major trends in the common life. Some of his books and articles may be regarded as the reports of one who had an unusual skill in illuminating the culture of his own period with the sharp light of his own critical and constructive insight.

Tillich was always conscious of the fact that he himself had lived through several distinct phases of Western civilization. He felt that in his own youth, from 1886 until 1914, he had become steeped in the spirit of the nineteenth century, with its confidence in the human ability to master nature and all difficulties of life. During World War I, for the duration of which he was stationed as an army chaplain on the German front in France, he experienced the breakup of the self-assurance of this proud civilization. He later often remembered that, during a frightful night on the battlefield of Verdun, he had seen as in a vision the end of his era: the era of feudalistic and militaristic monarchies, the era of Protestant bourgeois civilization. Yet he did not adopt the pessimistic outlook of Oswald Spengler who, in his book *The Decline of the West,* predicted the downfall of Western civilization.

Tillich joined the many young and very young men of post–World War I Germany who bent their efforts toward a rebuilding of European culture and who, with hopeful enthusiasm, set themselves the task of formulating new cultural programs. While he laid the foundations for his own career as a university teacher, he joined a circle of the Religious Socialists in Berlin and soon became their most incisive thinker and leading spokesman. The Religious Socialists hoped to obtain from the educated middle classes a positive understanding of the socialist critique of society and from the leaders of the socialist-democratic parties recognition of the need for a religion of culture. The influence of the Religious Socialists was never broad, but they had many loyal followers among the intellectuals in whom they awakened a culturally responsible and constructive interest in politics. Nazis and Communists then struggled for domination of the German scene, and prospects for the realization of a Religious Socialist program grew dimmer and dimmer. When Hitler came to power, those plans and hopes collapsed.

At that time, Tillich held the influential chair of philosophy at the University of Frankfurt. When the Nazis came to power, he was summarily dismissed. He was fortunate enough, through the efforts of Reinhold Niebuhr, to be invited to the United States. He then hoped that his cultural political program would be carried out on a broader basis under American leadership. He joined the

Fellowship of Socialist Christians and in general supported the platform of the New Deal.

During the Second World War, he was preoccupied with the clarification of war aims. He hoped that once victory over Hitler was achieved, a socially and economically constructive peace settlement would be made within the limits of a united Europe supported by an international union of the nations of the world. When it became clear that these aims could not be attained, due to the outbreak of the "East-West conflict," Tillich resignedly proclaimed the doctrine of the "sacred void," which meant that men should be prepared to bear the insecurity of a possibly long, uncertain period of transition and to wait responsibly for the right moment in which to commence the execution of a realistic program of world reconstruction avoiding all utopianism.

In this third phase of the historical period in which he was living, Tillich felt that he should help his contemporaries to understand the existential problems and difficulties that tend to emerge in a time of cultural transition. Believing that when traditional values lose their appeal or become shattered, many people are overcome by a sense of emptiness, which then causes them to fall victim to the anxiety of meaninglessness, he concentrated his attention upon the analysis of the human situation and the universal need for healing.

Tillich did this in his lectures published as *The Courage to Be* and in his sermons, particularly those published under the title *The Shaking of the Foundations,*[4] but also in the whole context of his labors in theology.

SYSTEMATIC THEOLOGY: THE HUMAN SITUATION AND THE CHRISTIAN MESSAGE

In 1925 Tillich had first projected his own "system" of theology, and he had taught academic classes on it since then. But only as his career neared its end did he proceed to prepare this work for publication, always concerned that it should be relevant to the human situation in a historical era of uncertainty and waiting.

Thus his thought came to be principally directed to the task of developing a systematic theology in which eternal truth as manifested in the figure of Christ is mediated to the changing experiences of individuals and groups, to their varying questions and their categories of perceiving reality. In the effort to fulfill this task, he became preoccupied with two great themes: On the one hand, he tried to understand the human situation as deeply and as fully as possible, paying attention not only to special problems in the life of the churches or in economics and politics but also to the structures of human anxiety, conflict, and guilt. On the other hand, he endeavored to interpret the Christian message in such a way that people of today would be able to understand it as a living gospel that would speak directly to them. He was persuaded that the traditional symbols and forms used in theology and worship, indeed in Christian life generally, were no longer understood properly and, moreover, that for many they had become meaningless. Therefore, he attempted to speak in terms that would be readily comprehended by contemporary people. The Christian symbols and forms of expression should be so reinterpreted that they would again become powerful.

He made a supreme effort to carry out this task. And he was widely understood. Occasionally, he was called an "apostle to the intellectuals, speaking in their language."[5] What is correct about this description of Tillich is that he felt himself to be sent as an interpreter of the Christian religion to intellectuals who had become disaffected from the church and thrown into the spiritual emptiness that in modern life has so often been the result of secularization. It is *not* correct to say, however, that he spoke their language. He understood their condition and felt empathy with them in their anxiety, but he spoke to them in his own language.

For example, in defining religion (which he did not regard as a special province of the human mind, but rather as "the substance, the ground, and the depth of man's spiritual life")[6] he employed the term *ultimate concern.* "Religion," or "faith," he said, "is the state of being grasped by the power of being-itself,"[7] "by an unconditional concern" or by "that which concerns one unconditionally."

This is a unique definition. It is Tillich's own. Several layers of meaning are combined in it. The term *unconditional* is characteristic of the German idealists and their preoccupation with the absolute. The phrase "that which concerns one unconditionally" and, indeed, the whole definition of faith, seem to be a restatement of

Luther's famous interpretation of the First Commandment in the *Large Catechism:*

To have a god is nothing else than to trust and believe him with one's whole heart. As I have often said, the trust and the faith of the heart alone make both God and an idol. If your faith and trust are right, then your God is the true God. On the other hand, if your trust is false and wrong, then you do not have the true God. For these two belong together, faith and God. That to which your heart clings and entrusts itself is, I say, really your God.[8]

In his basic understanding of the Christian faith, Tillich was a Lutheran. He had been brought up in the Lutheran tradition both in his training at home and in his early schooling. As he often testified, this upbringing had formed his mind: It shaped his outlook on life. It is very possible, therefore, that when he formulated his rather abstract definition of religious faith, he had in mind Luther's much warmer and highly suggestive statement. Moreover, the sentence "Faith is the state of being grasped by that which concerns one unconditionally" is a translation from the German *Der Glaube ist das Ergriffensein von dem was einen unbedingt angeht. Ergriffensein* is a much more telling term than *being grasped.* One who is deeply moved or has been laid hold of by something holy is *ergriffen.* A religious service in which the holy becomes present is *ergreifend.* The word *angeht* is only inadequately translated by *concern.* Something or someone "coming upon one" is meant by this *concern.* This word too has religious undertones that are absent from its English rendering.

Another interesting and telling term that Tillich employed in order to build a bridge to a positive understanding of the Christian message for those who have become theologically alienated from the church is *the New Being.* Indefatigably, he explained that the New Being is what is revealed in Jesus as the Christ. When he conceived this rather abstract term *the New Being,* was he thinking of Paul's saying in 2 Cor. 5:17, "If any man is in Christ, he is a new creature: the old things are passed away; behold, they are become new"? It is highly possible that Tillich was thinking of this, because the context of this famous, moving declaration of the apostle refers to Christ as we now know him (namely, no longer after the flesh) and to the reconciliation of the world that God brought through him. In Tillich's understanding, the New Being includes reconciliation as it is actualized in justification by faith and by the forgiveness of sins. It includes also a participation in the "eternal" and the "Kingdom of God" established in history and related to the cultural life as it centers around the "healing reality" that is manifested in the cross of Christ.[9]

It is not my intention to deal with Tillich's theology in detail. I am merely pointing to a difficulty that he produced for himself and his readers when he attempted to avoid the use of conventional theological terms and introduced concepts of his own instead. He was quite conscious of what he was doing. In a seminar he held shortly before his death at the University of California in Santa Barbara, he made this statement:

> I presuppose in my theological thinking the entire history of Christian thought . . . and I consider the attitude of those people who are in doubt or estrangement or opposition to everything ecclesiastical and religious, including Christianity. . . . My work is with those who ask questions, and for them I am here. For the others who do not I have the great problem of tact. Of course, I cannot avoid speaking to them because of a fear of becoming a stumbling block for primitive believers. When I am preaching a sermon—and then I am quite aware of what I'm doing—I speak to people who are unshaken in their beliefs and in their acceptance of symbols, in a language which will not undermine their belief. And to those who are actually in a situation of doubt and are even being torn to pieces by it, I hope to speak in such a way that the reasons for their doubts . . . are taken away. On this basis I speak also to a third group, one which has gone through these two stages and is now able again to hear the full power of the message, freed from old difficulties. . . . [T]hey are able to understand me, even when I use the old symbols, because they know that I do not mean them in a literal sense.[10]

Indeed it was his conviction that the "old symbols," namely doctrines, creedal and liturgical formulas, must be "deliteralized." He did not think that they should be demythologized, but he believed that instead of being interpreted literally they should be taken spiritually. This spiritual meaning he tried to express in terms that he had derived (mostly, so it seems, by a creative intuition or by an intuitive synthesis of ideas) either from historical tradition or from contemporary experience.

Thus he spoke of faith as ultimate concern; of God as being itself (not as *a* being among others, not even the supreme being, and certainly not as an object among objects); of sin as estrangement and of grace as acceptance; of the Holy Spirit as spiritual presence, etc. In explaining the meaning of these terms, he endeavored on the one hand to be as true and profound a diagnostician of the human situation as possible and, on the other hand, to be a clear and truly radical spokesman of the ultimate. He saw all human life as finite freedom beset by false and demonic absolutizations of relative entities and values. For him life was filled with anxiety resulting from the threat of nonbeing that inheres in finiteness, an anxiety that appears in three forms; that of fate and death, that of emptiness and meaninglessness, and that of guilt and condemnation. He saw the divine as Being itself, manifesting itself as the power of being and meaning, that is, disclosing the numinous wonder that there is *being* and *not nothing,* that there is meaning as truth, beauty, goodness and not meaninglessness; that all beings and meanings are dependent, in terms of origin and destiny, upon being itself, the power of being, and their creative ground.

Tillich gave body to these fundamental ideas by letting his thought range over past ages and the present, over problems of thought as well as over the relevance of religion for the whole of civilized life. Throughout his career, he was not only a theologian and a philosopher of religion but also a theologian of culture. One may perhaps say that he displayed a special genius for the work of a "theologian of culture," for an analysis of the mutual immanence of religion and culture, for he had no hesitation, as a theologian, to concern himself with problems of the arts and literature, of politics and economics, of medicine and psychotherapy. His ideal was a "theonomous culture," a civilized life derived from autonomous human decisions in which everything is related to the "ultimate" in the sense that in all cultural activities "the holy," or "the power of being," becomes transparent.

It was his deep fear that modern civilization, having largely ceased to be theonomous and therefore threatened with emptiness, would fall under demonic control. Indeed, he felt that this had already happened, for a time at least, during the Nazi and Bolshevist dictatorships and in similar movements and tendencies throughout Western civilization.

He felt, therefore, that, at present, theology of culture is above all a theology at the end of culture, not in general terms but in terms of a concrete analysis of the inner void of most of our cultural expressions. "Little is left in our present civilization," he said, "which does not indicate to a sensitive mind the presence of this vacuum, this lack of ultimacy and substantial power in language and education, in politics and philosophy, in the development of personalities, and in the life of communities."[11]

Paul Tillich found many close listeners whom he stirred and roused so that they came to see the present situation as he did. He became the admired and beloved teacher of several student generations. Many of them still feel the impetus they received from him and are mindful of the light he caused them to see. But there are hardly any Tillichians. For Paul Tillich formed no school, and he was not really interested in doing so. Time will show how and in what form his work will live on.

NOTES

1. See Gunilla Bergsten, *Thomas Mann's Doctor Faustus* (Chicago: University of Chicago Press, 1969), 34–38. The author prints in parallel columns paragraphs of Tillich's letter and corresponding passages from Mann's novel.
2. Paul Tillich, *The Interpretation of History*, trans. N. A. Rasetski and E. L. Talmey (New York: Charles Scribner's Sons, 1936).
3. Paul Tillich, *The Religious Situation*, trans. H. Richard Niebuhr (New York: Meridian Books, 1956). First German edition, 1926.
4. Paul Tillich, *The Shaking of the Foundations* (New York: Charles Scribner's Sons, 1948). Cf. idem, *The New Being* (New York: Charles Scribner's Sons, 1955); and idem, *The Eternal Now* (New York: Charles Scribner's Sons, 1963).
5. D. Mackenzie Brown, *Tillich in Dialogue* (New York: Harper & Row, 1965), 188.
6. Paul Tillich, *Theology of Culture*, ed. Robert C. Kimball (New York: Oxford University Press, 1959), 8.
7. Tillich, *The Courage to Be*, 172.
8. Martin Luther, *The Large Catechism*, Commentary on First Commandment.
9. Tillich, *Theology of Culture*, 209.
10. As quoted in Brown, *Tillich in Dialogue*, 191.
11. Cf. Tillich, *The Protestant Era*, trans. James Luther Adams (Chicago: University of Chicago Press, 1948), 60.

3. Tillich as Interpreter and Disturber of Contemporary Civilization

ROGER L. SHINN

Paul Tillich never forgot Marx's eleventh thesis on Feuerbach: "The philosophers have *interpreted* the world in various ways; the point, however, is to *change* it." Tillich himself wanted to do both. He sought relentlessly to probe the structures and dynamics of contemporary civilization, to question its purposes, to redirect it. This chapter investigates his way of addressing this civilization and the relevance of his methods in our present time.

WHAT IS "CONTEMPORARY CIVILIZATION?"

The first step is to ask what sense it makes to talk about "contemporary civilization." Is there any such reality? There are huge, diverse societies—American, Soviet, Chinese, Indian, South African. There is resurgent Islam, kicking back against much of modernism. There is Latin America, moving out of feudal into various revolutionary patterns. There is central Africa, where recently tribal societies are becoming nation-states with burgeoning airports and industries. There is Europe—Eastern and Western. The United Nations is a name and an organization, not a description of our world.

Yet this diverse world shares a lot. It all falls under the scrutiny of those humanly launched satellites called spies-in-the-sky. It is all threatened—and most people know that it is threatened—by nuclear destruction. Most of the world experiences the "revolution of rising expectations," and most people know that those expectations are in jeopardy.

This entire world has felt the impact of historic events that began in Western Europe, spread to North America, then moved in varying degrees around the globe, partly by conquest and partly by imitation and adaptation. These events had double roots—social and intellectual—that were deeply intertwined.

The social root was the political and industrial revolutions that led to the institutions of parliamentary democracy and of modern economies. The same revolutions led to capitalist and Marxist ideologies, to new productivity, new life-styles.

The intellectual root was the Enlightenment (and behind it, the scientific discoveries that fed into the Enlightenment). A new kind of rationality entered social life—a rationality hostile to inherited superstitions (although it invented a few new superstitions), critical of tradition, and ambitious for understanding and control.

From these double roots sprang an enhancement of human powers, a consciousness that people can take charge of areas of life once assigned to the gods of fate and chance. These new powers have transformed the shape of societies and modified the ecology of the planet.

In some ways this contemporary form of civilization is genuinely *new*. Oswald Spengler and Arnold Toynbee, of course, found analogies in the "late" periods of other civilizations. Tillich could refer to the ancient "Greek Enlightenment"—one reason why he found the Hellenistic age more fascinating than the classical Hellenic period. But never before did Earth carry 4.5 billion people. Never before was there almost instant global communication. Never before did demonstrating crowds in, say, Tehran, send shivers through corporation offices and foreign ministries around the world. Never before did such cultural symbols as blue jeans, rock music, Coca-Cola, and McDonald's hamburgers move so swiftly from continent to continent. And never before was the military threat to the *whole* world.

All this is "contemporary civilization." To it Paul Tillich responded, in his characteristically dialectical manner, with both a Yes of affirmation and a No of criticism. His affirmation led him to a radical reconceptualizing of inherited ideas and ways of meeting human problems. He appropriated the findings of modern science, the ideas of Marx and Freud, the technologies and political institutions of the present day. But his criticism led him to a reassertion of religion and metaphysics in the face of their positivistic critics, to a reappreciation of ancient myth and story, to efforts to move this society in ways unfamiliar either to traditional or to contemporary habits.

TILLICH'S WAY OF UNDERSTANDING THE WORLD

Tillich combined many methods of understanding the world. No one of them was unique, yet he wove them into a gestalt that was unique in itself and that subtly modified every element that entered into the whole. The starting point was the ceaseless effort to relate the interior experience of individuals to the social-political-economic structures of world history. Tillich constantly struggled to penetrate the microworld and the macroworld.

In exploring inner experience, Tillich drew upon his biblical heritage, his love of the mystics, Kierkegaard's existentialism, and psychoanalysis. In his social awareness he sought to fathom his shattering experiences as a chaplain in World War I, his wakening to the class structure of German society and the disintegrating German political situation, and his discovery of the Marxism that spoke to the postwar situation.

This interpenetration of the inward and the outward concerns characterized the Kairos Circle that organized around Tillich in the first postwar years in Berlin. It flowered in Frankfurt.[1] The "Frankfurt School," drawn from both the University and the Institute of Social Research, was to become famous for its work in drawing together insights from frequently antagonistic Marxists and Freudians. To a Marxist, Freudianism, especially in the version of *Civilization and its Discontents,* may look like a reactionary attempt to "adjust" individuals, with all their seething instinctive vitalities, to the inevitably repressive demands of society. To a Freudian, Marxism may look like an attempt to prescribe socially revolutionary answers to human problems by ignoring the deep, often unconscious conflicts within every individual.

But Tillich with the Frankfurt School asked for "an alliance of Marxism and psychoanalysis." He criticized both when they were taken as dogmatic systems. But he appreciated both as methods for "unmasking hidden levels of reality," for "shattering ideologies and revealing the realities of human existence."[2] That is, both recognized that much human "rationality" is actually the deceptive covering of hidden dynamic forces in the social situation and the psyche.

Tillich then added to this synthesis two other elements, uncongenial to many of his colleagues, but utterly essential to his venture: ontology and biblical prophetic religion. Without ontology, he believed, insight could not penetrate beyond the ephemeral. *"The roots of political thinking,"* he wrote, *"must be sought in human being itself."*[3] To understand our civilization, with its possibilities and frustrations, requires that we ask what it is to be human. And even that is not enough: for humanity is not separable from nature and all being. To ask what it is to be human, we must ask what it is to be. This question drove Tillich to explore both the myths of origins and the more rational enterprise of ontology—the structure of being—as it develops from the pre-Socratic to contemporary philosophers. To a positivistically inclined generation, Tillich might appear disconcerting, as his mind moved from political economic crises to religious myths or to Parmenides and Schelling. Today, after the turmoil of the 1960s and 1970s, that seems not quite so strange.

Yet, Tillich recognized, this ontological concern is incomplete. It goes with a sacramental, mystical appreciation of all life and being. But in looking to the origins of human existence in the structures of being, it misses the breaking in of new possibilities. It seeks the "whence" of human existence, not the "whither." Prophetic religion—and the later European Enlightenment, a somewhat rebellious descendant of biblical faith—points to new possibilities. Human existence—yes, even politics—looks toward "something that does not exist but should exist," for "something unconditionally new that transcends what is new and what is old within the sphere of mere development," for a "new heaven and a new earth," for a reality "that cannot be grasped ontologically."[4]

The relation between the given nature of reality and new possibilities, between ontology and prophetic religion, concerned Tillich through all his career. He raised the problem in his early writings. He returned to it years later in *Biblical Religion and the Search for Ultimate Reality* and in his massive *Systematic Theology*. Tillich's readers still argue as to how he related the two or gave priority to one or the other. Here it is enough to say that it is not easy to hold together his two themes. But they form a powerful combination for the effort to understand and live in contemporary civilization.

To the four themes—psychoanalysis and existentialism, Marxism, ontology, and prophetic religion—must be added one more: the history of culture. From it Tillich learned to appreciate both the human situation and the varieties of human situations. He could write that "the tragic self-destruction of our present world is the result not simply of the particular contradictions bred by that world but also of the contradictions which characterize human life always."[5] To ignore the "particular contradictions" would be to lose the concreteness that he valued; but to ignore "human life always" would be to rush into frantic solutions for passing problems.

The history of culture enabled Tillich to draw upon myth, poetry, drama, philosophy, science, technology, politics, and the visual arts. He had a masterful professional knowledge of the history of philosophy and theology; in other areas his amateur insights often impressed professional specialists. Not many theological writers illustrate their books with pictures or detailed comments on paintings and sculptures. Tillich's method assumes that, to enter deeply into the experience of a culture at any point is to penetrate toward a center that enhances the understanding of all aspects of that culture.

Tillich's approach is akin to that of cultural anthropologists who take as relevant evidence all the institutions, myths, habits, ideas, art forms, and techniques of a society. But Tillich was interested not simply in phenomenological descriptions of societies. His work was oriented toward the ultimate—toward what is good and true. And it was oriented toward action—toward efforts to change the world.

It was a combination of empirical, intuitive, and analytic methods. Tillich's skills were not primarily in empirical research—certainly not in the style of computerized printouts. But he was attentive to historical events—from the menace of Hilter to the tremors of American society. The intuitive element was a tuning of his inner vibrations to the vibrations of the world. "Truth," he wrote, "is bound to the situation of the knower: to the situation of the individual for Kierkegaard, and to that of society for Marx."[6]

Nevertheless, he subjected his observations and intuitions to a critical analysis, both historical and rational, sometimes architectonic in scope.

By bringing together self-exploration (including psychoanalysis), Marxism, ontology, biblical religion, and the history of culture, Tillich forged a method for meeting contemporary civilization. Even those who question his synthesis are likely to appreciate the insights that flowed from it.

SOME CONCEPTUAL TOOLS

In both affirming and challenging contemporary civilization, Tillich developed several conceptual tools that may help a later generation as it relates to a modified historical situation. Four of those concepts—the number is largely a matter of convenience—require mention here: revolutionary reason, theonomy, the demonic, and *Kairos*.

REVOLUTIONARY REASON

The modern era, as Tillich saw it, was borne out of a triumph of a revolutionary reason that wrought scientific, political, economic, and cultural revolutions. It assaulted entrenched authorities of church, empire, superstitious ignorance, custom, inner feeling. Its technology was "a revelation of the power of spirit over matter," an emancipation of many people "from a stupid, beastlike existence."[7] It believed itself to be "the power of truth and justice embodied in man as man."[8] Its enemy was heteronomy—any authority imposed upon human beings from external sources, whether religious, political, or anything else. It confronted heteronomy with autonomy—the authority of the free, rational self.

Tillich rejoiced in that revolutionary reason. His whole life was a protest against heteronomous authority. Speaking of his early family life, he wrote of the "break-through to autonomy which has made me immune against any system of thought or life which demands the surrender of this autonomy."[9] As a young minister he asserted himself against church authorities who questioned his independent thinking. With great personal courage he protested Nazi political authority. When Karl Barth chided him for fighting the obsolete battle against Dostoevsky's Grand Inquisitor, Tillich reaffirmed his challenge to external authority in the form of Barthian biblicism and supranaturalism.[10]

But revolutionary reason, when it lost its humanistic grounding, became "technical reason"—a reason no longer incorporating purpose and value, but a reason of means and ends, a tool of technical progress. "Technical intelligence replaced humanistic reason," and "the technical depersonalization of man spread . . . all over the world."[11] Positivistic reason denied meaning to the most deeply human questions. Technical reason was equally available to industrialized nations winning colonial empires, to bourgeoisie subduing proletariats, to Fascist and Soviet totalitarianism.

What had gone wrong? Reason had become uprooted from its context in human existence and ontological reality. It had been bent to the pursuit of arbitrary objectives rather than truth. It came to revel in a "self-sufficient finitude"[12] that ignored the mystery, the glory, and the terròr of human experience.

To impose authoritative redirection upon technical reason would mean a futile heteronomy. The only creative possibility was theonomy.

THEONOMY

Instead of arbitrary heteronomy or uprooted autonomy, Tillich advocated "a self-transcending autonomy, or theonomy," "an autonomy informed by a religious substance."[13] But how does theonomy differ from religious constraint on autonomous reason —a familiar form of heteronomy? Does not the very term theonomy mean that God *(theos)* replaces the human self *(autos)* as authority? Is this not an effort to revoke the victories of revolutionary reason?

Tillich did not slight such questions. "Theonomy does not mean the acceptance of a divine law imposed on reason by a highest authority; it means autonomous reason united with its own depth. In a theonomous situation reason actualizes itself in obedience to its structural laws and in the power of its own inexhaustible ground."[14] Without theonomy, all ethical responsibility is arbitrary—the subjection to personal caprice or external authority. The disarray of the modern world—both the macroworld of national and international politics and the microworld of alienated individuals—shows the problem. A meaningful response to the world must be related to the "whence" and the "whither" of human life, and these must be related to the grounding of all life in the power of being itself.

Tillich recognized that in the world as we know it there is no perfect concord between autonomy and theonomy, no accomplished "self-transcending autonomy." There is "no complete theonomy under the conditions of existence."[15] In that sense he described himself as living "on the boundary between autonomy and heteronomy."[16] But the point was not to maintain a precarious balance on the razor edge or to keep a foot in each camp. It was to reach toward, or respond to, the possibility of that self-transcending autonomy that is theonomy.

There is no reason to think that people who talk comfortably about God are closer to theonomy than those who never speak of God or who deny God's reality. Tillich's thinking was far too unconventional for any such construction. His examples of theonomy are as likely to be atheists as conventional believers. It is only beyond the creeds of both religion and atheism that theonomy has meaning.

THE DEMONIC AND THE PROTESTANT PRINCIPLE

There is no pure theonomy in human existence because of the continuous eruption of "the demonic." Tillich wrote of the demonic at least as early as 1923.[17] In his later *Systematic Theology* he was able to say with quiet pleasure, "The symbol of the demonic does not need justification as it did thirty years ago when it was reintroduced into theological language."[18]

The demonic is not fanciful, although it has been depicted fancifully in art and myth. It is not simply evil. It is "the unity of form-creating and form-destroying strength"; it is "the form-destroying eruption of the creative basis of things."[19]

The demonic enters into even the most creative historical movements. People involved in heroic struggles against oppression characteristically claim too much for themselves and their cause. "And the claim of something finite to infinity or to divine greatness is the characteristic of the demonic." Fear of the demonic is no reason to avoid action, sometimes revolutionary action. Sin is more often "uncreative weakness" than demonry.[20] But those who would act responsibly in history had better be aware of the demonic.

The protest against the demonic is "the Protestant principle." This principle is "the divine and human protest against any absolute claim made for a relative reality."[21] Although it is illustrated in the Protestant Reformation, it is no sectarian term. Indeed, to claim it for Protestant churches is demonic. Tillich found it in the Hebrew prophets, in atheists resisting the heteronomous authority of churches, in modern art. It was in this sense that Tillich called Picasso's *Guernica* the best example of contemporary "Protestant" religious painting.[22]

The Protestant principle is not a sufficient substance of religious faith, which includes affirmation in message and sacrament. (See chapter 16 in this book, "Tillich and the Catholic Substance.") "But," Tillich believed, "the prophetic protest is necessary for every church and for every secular movement if it is to avoid disintegration."[23]

KAIROS

Tillich faced the familiar problem: how to work for creative social change while countering the demonic tendency that distorts creativity. Revolutionaries usually project utopias. And Tillich had learned from his Lutheran heritage "a repudiation of every kind of social Utopia."[24] The Protestant principle protests against the utopian absolutizing of social programs, and historical wisdom shows the disillusion that follows utopian expectations. Tillich sought a "belief-ful" or "believing realism" in "contrast to unbelieving realism and to belief-ful or Utopian idealism."[25]

The answer came in the theme of *Kairos.* In the New Testament *Kairos* is "the fullness of time," the time of the coming of Christ, the time of the breaking in of God's kingdom. For Tillich this meaning remained decisive, but he looked also for the *Kairos* in every period of history. In Berlin, following World War I, he became the leader of the small Kairos Circle. It is characteristic of Tillich that the group, despite its theological interest, was religiously diverse. One member jokingly described it as made up of "three Jews and three pagans."[26]

Tillich himself said that "the utopian problem was the central issue" for the group. The idea of *Kairos* meant "that the struggle for a new social order cannot lead to the kind of fulfillment expressed by the idea of the Kingdom of God, but that at a particular time particular tasks are demanded, as one particular aspect of the Kingdom of God becomes a demand and an expectation for us. The Kingdom of God will always remain transcendent, but it appears as a judgment on a given form of society and as a norm for a coming one."[27]

The social goal of the Kairos Circle was "religious socialism," an answer to the demonic nature of capitalism in the aftermath of the First World War. Some years later (1933), in Frankfurt, Tillich published the book that remained perhaps his proudest achievement to the end of his life, *The Socialist Decision.* It is a work of anger, imagination, and intellect.

By the standards of most socialist and political literature, it is a curious book. Little in it is programmatic. There is no suggested legislation, no discussion of details of economic organization (although Tillich worked out his ideas in consultation with such able economists as Adolf Lowe and Eduard Heimann). It does not tell how to organize a society, nationalize industries, handle currency, or distribute the results of production. Tillich later said of religious socialism: "It is more than a new economic system. It is a comprehensive understanding of existence, the form of the theonomy demanded and expected by our present Kairos."[28] This obviously is not the stuff of conventional political oratory or party organization.

Yet Tillich's socialism is not merely abstract. Its sharp bite is evident in two ways. First, deriding "moralistic" and "intellectual socialism," he took seriously the class struggle and sided with the proletariat.[29] Second, the Nazis quickly recognized its power and threat. They suppressed the book. And, when Tillich criticized the Brownshirts for roughing up students, authorities dismissed him from the faculty at Frankfurt. A little later, as Adolf Lowe reports it, an official of the Nazi Ministry of Education offered Tillich a chair in theology at the University of Berlin, if he would repudiate *The Socialist Decision.* Tillich laughed in his face.[30]

THE DEEPENING TRAUMA OF CIVILIZATION SINCE TILLICH

The years since Tillich's death in 1965 have often vindicated his insights. Many of his fresh and jolting criticisms of contemporary civilization have become common coinage. But readers still marvel at the comprehensive contours of his thought, at his ability to move every perception to a penetrating grasp of the dynamics of culture and all being.

The post-Tillichian years have brought an intensification of the problems of "technical reason." Some of its triumphs and perils —for instance, in nuclear physics and molecular biology—have mounted ever higher. When the World Council of Churches convened a Conference on Faith, Science, and the Future at the Massachusetts Institute of Technology in the summer of 1979, scientists outdid theologians in pointing to the threats of regnant technical reason.[31] To talk of the trauma of civilization is not to exaggerate.

The most obvious single example is modern weaponry. In an important article of 1964 Jerome Wiesner and Herbert York, famous specialists in the development of weapons, wrote: "Both sides in the arms race are thus confronted by the dilemma of steadily increasing military power and steadily decreasing national security. It is our considered professional judgment that this dilemma has no technical solution." Their hope requires attention to "moral questions and human values—political, social, economic and psychological questions."[32]

A second example is the increasing turbulence following the dispersion of technical reason around the world. The peculiar problems of Western Europe and North America, most manifest in nazism but evident elsewhere also, came (in Tillich's terms) from the divorce of technical reason from revolutionary, humanistic reason. In many nations now the situation is that traditional societies acquire technical reason directly without the intervening development of humanistic reason. This is not to say that the upheavals, for example, in the Middle East, are worse than in Europe; nothing has been worse than nazism. It is rather to point to the universal but variegated trauma of technical reason severed from humanistic concerns and—if Tillich was right—from ontological roots.

A third example is the worldwide economic perplexity. In 1971 British economist E. F. Schumacher observed that the economy of the Western world has run "at full speed, in fact at continuous acceleration" for twenty-five years. One result, he continued, was that "there are more miserable people in the world today than there were twenty-five years ago: more in absolute numbers and a higher proportion."[33] The details may be debatable. What is certain is the dis-ease of a world plagued by inflation, unemployment, shortages of energy and critical resources, and monstrously unequal distribution of goods. Yet all of this has come with—perhaps from—victories of technical reason.

A fourth example, related to the third, is the new consciousness of ecological problems. It would be wrong to say that Tillich foresaw these in any detail. In fact, he took for granted the conventional socialist wisdom of his time and referred to "the earth's virtually unlimited productive possibilities."[34] What he did see was the error of separating human life from its relations with the whole of nature. In an era when most Protestant theology sharply distinguished between nature and history, Tillich insisted on an experiential and ontological unity of the two.

These examples are evidences of the widespread sense that the world has become unmanageable, not because of *Tyche* or *Fortuna* (as in ancient times), but because "they"—the world's politicians, industrialists, generals, revolutionaries—aren't up to managing the forces they try to manipulate. In part the problem is sheer complexity; in part it is that a technical reason has detached itself from humanistic reason and human concern.

A recent custom has developed of referring to a large class of "no technical solution" problems.[35] A civilization, habituated to look for a "technical fix" for its difficulties, finds that it is "in a fix" because technical reason is inadequate. Almost everywhere people recognize the necessity to relate technique to values and commitments. But if these values and commitments are to be more than arbitrary or heteronomous assertions, they must have some grounding in the nature of humanity and of being. And that leads to Tillich's theonomy.

TILLICH AND HIS CRITICS

I shall here deal with two controversies about Tillich and ask how they qualify his criticism of contemporary civilization. The first concerns theological criticisms of religion. The second concerns the relation of intuition to empirical-rational methods.

THE CRITICISM OF RELIGION

It is possible to interpret modern history not as a destructive rebellion against theonomy but as a triumph of human powers over oppressive religion. The most striking theological example, in a specific criticism of Tillich, came from Dietrich Bonhoeffer, the valiant Christian foe of nazism who was hanged in 1945 for his part in the attempt to assassinate Hitler.

In prison Bonhoeffer wrote: "We are proceeding towards a time of no religion at all: men as they are now simply cannot be religious any more." Rather than regret a decline in human sensitivity, Bonhoeffer celebrated the achievement. Tillich, by contrast, constantly tried to show the religious quality of all culture. His famous saying, variously phrased from time to time, is this: "As religion is the substance of culture, so culture is the form of religion."[36]

Tillich could criticize religion as pointedly as Bonhoeffer. He knew its demonic and idolatrous forms, its hypocrisies and its self-indulgences. As early as 1922 he wrote an essay titled "The Conquest of the Concept of Religion in the Philosophy of Religion."[37] Twenty years later he wrote: "The first word . . . to be spoken by religion to the people of our time must be a word spoken against religion,"[38] a word spoken by the Hebrew prophets long ago. He shared with Bonhoeffer a passion toward the "profane," a "passion for the secular."[39] Before Bonhoeffer, he insisted that faith requires political expression.

Yet he affirmed religion. "Religion is the state of being grasped by an ultimate concern, a concern which qualifies all other concerns as preliminary and which itself contains an answer to the question of the meaning of our life." It is not obsolete. "Religion, like God, is omnipresent; its presence, like that of God, can be forgotten, neglected, denied. But it is always effective, giving inexhaustible depth to life and inexhaustible meaning to every cultural creation."[40]

Part of the argument is simply a matter of definition. Tillich rejected much of what Bonhoeffer rejected in religion; Bonhoeffer affirmed part of what Tillich affirmed. But there is still a difference. Bonhoeffer wrote: "Tillich set out to interpret the evolution of the world itself—against its will—in a religious sense, to give it its whole shape through religion. That was very courageous of him, but the world unseated him and went on by itself; he too sought to understand the world better than it understood itself, but it felt entirely *mis*understood, and rejected the implication. (Of course the world does need to be understood better than it understands itself, but not 'religiously,' as the religious socialists desired.")[41]

Bonhoeffer seemed to have Tillich in mind also when he rejected the association of religion with "metaphysics" and "inwardness,"[42] the fascination with the "borders of human existence," and "the existentialist philosophers and the psychotherapists, who demonstrate to secure, contented mankind that it is really unhappy and desperate."[43] Bonhoeffer was saying that a modern world, now come "of age," no longer experienced the old religious feelings. If he was right, Tillich should have trusted his own exultation in revolutionary reason and autonomy, rather than countering it with talk of anxiety and the need for theonomy. The argument is the more persuasive because Bonhoeffer certainly knew the evils in the world of Hitler.

There is a real issue here. Suppose somebody, reading Tillich or Kierkegaard before him, replies, "I honestly don't feel all that anxiety. Maybe, if I try hard enough, I can. But most of the time I know my problems and I try to manage them. Of course, I win some and I lose some. But that doesn't mean that I'm constantly living over a threatening abyss." Is that response the confidence of a healthy, secularized self, or is it the shallowness of a self that lacks the courage to look into its own existence? Could it be, as the Paucks have suggested, that Tillich sometimes projected his own inner turmoil onto an outer world that did not feel it?[44]

Rather than answer, I prefer to let the question stand. In doing so, I would mention that Tillich, as truly as Bonhoeffer, recognized the prevalence of widespread secular contentment ("self-sufficient finitude," as he called it), but he saw demonic and idolatrous tendencies lurking in it. I would point out also that Bonhoeffer sometimes (for example, in his poem "Who Am I?") cultivated the very themes that he seemed to reject in Tillich. I would add that the question concerns not only individuals but a culture that must either genuinely fear nuclear destruction and feel the guilt of injustice, or somehow manage to block fear and guilt out of its consciousness. And I would give attention finally to the lush growth in the 1970s of "religion," often in mystical and exotic forms, a growth that both Tillich and Bonhoeffer would criticize even as they sought to understand it. (See chapter 12 in this book, "Tillich and the New Religious Movements.")

THE INTUITIVE, THE EMPIRICAL, AND THE ANALYTIC

I have mentioned earlier the importance of intuitive insights in Tillich's understanding of contemporary civilization. His intuitions were not impulsive or capricious. He subjected them to empirical checks and to searching historical and rational analysis. But he trusted the artist more than the sociometric reporter to disclose what was really going on. Although he frequently warned against the errors of romanticism, he sometime acknowledged a romantic element in himself. Some of his intuitions about the world seem, in retrospect, to be remarkably discerning. Others are questionable. Should an understanding of contemporary civilization pay more attention to the empirical methods of the social sciences?

The doctrine of *Kairos* is a case in point. It sets a basis for action in the world. Recognizing the demonic and the Protestant principle, Tillich warned against utopian expectations, while looking for creative possibilities in each unique historical situation. Thus Christians, for example, make decisions for the Kingdom of God within their history, even though they will not achieve that Kingdom. Thus Tillich's decision for religious socialism was, at one stage of his career, a decision for the Kingdom of God, even though its aims remained subject to the judgment of God.[45]

This way of thinking can be a strong resource for historical action. It can stir and generate fervor for reform without expecting too much and therefore falling into disillusion after a few losses —or disenchanting victories. Those who had learned from Tillich escaped excesses of the revolts of the '60s, precisely because they saw the demonic joined with the creative element in those revolts; they also escaped the "new narcissism" of the '70s, because they recognized injustices and ethical responsibilities in this changed situation.

But the question concerns the way of recognizing the *Kairos* of a particular historical situation. It came to a focus in Tillich's response to the historical situation following World War II. Instead of the ecstatic fervor of his earlier religious socialism, he felt "the void."

He spoke of the void in the first winter following World War II (1945–46) at a New York meeting of the Fellowship of Socialist Christians. This group, organized by Reinhold Niebuhr in the 1930s, had come to include Tillich and others of the German Religious Socialists, now living in America. So Tillich was among friends, familiar with his doctrine of *Kairos*. He stunned them when he spoke of the void. There were reports in the following weeks that he had lost his only copy of the speech, but at about that time he gave an address in Chicago, where he said, "While after the first World War the mood of a new beginning prevailed, after the second World War a mood of the end prevails." He went on to talk of "the inner void of most of our cultural expressions," of a "vacuum," that might, if appropriated with insight, become a "sacred void."[46] He reaffirmed the doctrine of theonomy, but detached it from political expectations.

My own memory of the New York occasion is still vivid because, as Tillich came under questioning, he called on me, as a student recently returned from European battlefields, for my off-the-cuff opinion. (That way of treating a student as an equal in discussion was one of his endearing qualities.) Taken by surprise, I mumbled an answer, then went home to think. Even as his admiring student, I later ventured to put the question "May it not be that as he probably overestimated the potentialities of that period [following World War I], he may be underestimating the present?"[47]

John Stumme, despite his deep appreciation of Tillich, makes this severe judgment: "The ontological, priestly strain of his thinking overshadowed the eschatological, prophetic thrust of his religious socialism. . . . The angst and meaninglessness of segments of the overclass became his point of departure instead of the oppression of the underclass." Tillich, of course, could reply that alienated underclasses in a dehumanizing society also experience meaninglessness. Ronald Stone has shown that Tillich did not renounce political interests; in the liberal left he remained more active "than the typical professor."[48] When James Luther Adams challenged him on his shift of emphasis, he pointed to his Rauschenbusch lectures, in which he reaffirmed old interests.[49] Yet one wonders whether, if he had written *The Courage to Be* (1952) in an earlier decade, he might not have called it *The Courage to Become*.

Obviously Tillich had a right to decide that his personal abilities were not well adapted to political activity in a country so different from his native land; or to decide that his vocation, as he grew older, was to finish his *Systematic Theology*. His error, if it was an error, was to expand his personal experience into a judgment on an era. In the "Author's Introduction" to *The Protestant Era* he said: "It was the 'ecstatic' experience of the belief in a kairos which, after the first World War, created, or at least initiated, most of the ideas presented in this book. There is no such ecstatic experience after the second World War, but a general feeling that more darkness than light is lying ahead of us. An element of cynical realism is prevailing today, as an element of utopian hope was prevailing at that earlier time. The Protestant principle judges both of them."[50]

That last sentence is an example of Tillich's ability for self-criticism. The preceding sentences are examples of his intuitions at work. They did not tell him that the years ahead would bring experiences of *Kairos* for the black civil rights movement, for the women's movement, for people in nations throwing off colonial domination, for Latin Americans seeking economic and political freedom. To the extent that such movements moved from euphoria to sober realism, they vindicated Tillich's Protestant principle. But he might have gained more from reliance upon the empirical social sciences to check his intuitive sensitivities. Empirical attention might have shown him greater obstacles than he saw for religious socialism after World War I, greater opportunities for action than he saw after World War II.

It is ungrateful to ask for more from a thinker who made an awesomely comprehensive criticism of contemporary civilization in our recent past. It is enough to say that a more empirical analysis also has something to say. It will say it more discerningly if it is sensitive to the imaginative power of Paul Tillich.

NOTES

1. In the Kairos Circle Tillich exchanged ideas with Karl Mannheim, Max Horkheimer, Theodore Adorno, Leo Lowenthal, Friedrich Pollock, Herbert Marcuse, and Erich Fromm. He also continued his long-standing conversations with economists Adolf Lowe and Eduard Heimann.
2. Paul Tillich, *The Socialist Decision*, trans. Franklin Sherman (New York: Harper & Row, 1977), 134 (first German edition, 1933); idem, *On the Boundary: An*

Autobiographical Sketch (New York: Charles Scribner's Sons, 1966), 88, 89 (first edition, 1936).

3. Tillich, *The Socialist Decision*, 2.

4. Ibid., 4, 20.

5. Paul Tillich, "The World Situation," in *The Christian Answer*, ed. Henry P. Van Dusen (New York: Charles Scribner's Sons, 1945), 44.

6. Tillich, *On the Boundary*, 85.

7. Paul Tillich, *The Religious Situation*, trans. H. Richard Niebuhr (New York: Meridian Books, 1956), 49. First German edition, 1926; first English edition, 1932.

8. Tillich, "The World Situation," 2.

9. Paul Tillich, "Autobiographical Reflections of Paul Tillich," in *The Theology of Paul Tillich*, ed. Charles W. Kegley and Robert W. Bretall (New York: Macmillan, 1952), 8.

10. Tillich, *On the Boundary*, 41.

11. Tillich, "The World Situation," 11.

12. The phrase *self-sufficient finitude* is a virtual refrain in *The Religious Situation*.

13. Paul Tillich, *The Protestant Era*, trans. James Luther Adams (Chicago: University of Chicago Press, 1948), xvi; idem, *On the Boundary*, 38.

14. Paul Tillich, *Systematic Theology*, vol. 1 (Chicago: University of Chicago Press, 1951), 85.

15. Ibid.

16. Tillich, *On the Boundary*, 45.

17. See James Luther Adams, *Paul Tillich's Philosophy of Culture, Science, and Religion* (New York: Harper & Row, 1965), 229. Tillich's essay "The Demonic" appears in English translation in Paul Tillich, *The Interpretation of History*, trans. N. A. Rasetzki and Elsa L. Talmey (New York: Charles Scribner's Sons, 1936).

18. Tillich, *Systematic Theology* 3 (1963), 102.

19. Tillich, *The Interpretation of History*, 81, 85.

20. Tillich, *Systematic Theology* 3:102; idem, *The Interpretation of History*, 93.

21. Tillich, *The Protestant Era*, 163.

22. Paul Tillich, "Existentialist Aspects of Modern Art," in *Christianity and the Existentialists*, ed. Carl Michalson (New York: Charles Scribner's Sons, 1956), 138.

23. Tillich, *The Protestant Era*, 230.

24. Tillich, *On the Boundary*, 75.

25. Tillich, *The Religious Situation*, 176–77.

26. John Stumme, *Socialism in Theological Perspective: A Study of Paul Tillich, 1918–1933* (Missoula, Mont.: Scholars Press, 1978), 34, quoting Karl Mennicke.

27. Tillich, *On the Boundary*, 78–79. Cf. idem, "Kairos and Logos," in *The Interpretation of History*. Cf. idem, "Kairos," in *The Protestant Era*. Cf. idem, *The Religious Situation*, 176–77.

28. Tillich, *On the Boundary*, 81.

29. On "intellectual" and "moralistic" socialism, see Tillich, *The Socialist Decision*, 64, 107. Tillich realized that he himself did not belong to the proletariat. His affinities were with intellectuals and with the artistic community that he called "Bohemia." But he pointed to Marx and Lenin as examples of bourgeoisie who "gave to the proletariat its self-consciousness." *The Socialist Decision*, 8.

30. Stumme, *Socialism in Theological Perspective*, 49.

31. See *Faith and Science in an Unjust World: Report of the World Council of Churches'*

Conference on Faith, Science and the Future, vol. 1, *Plenary Presentations,* ed. Roger L. Shinn (Philadelphia: Fortress Press, 1980).

32. Jerome Wiesner and Herbert York, "National Security and the Nuclear-Test Ban," *Scientific American* 211, no. 4 (October 1964): 27–35.

33. E. F. Schumacher, "Small Is Beautiful: Toward a Theology of 'Enough'," *The Christian Century* 88 (1971): 900.

34. Tillich, *The Socialist Decision,* 159.

35. The phrase *no technical solution* comes from Garrett Hardin in his famous essay "The Tragedy of the Commons," first published in *Science* 162 (13 December 1969): 1243–48; and reprinted in many places. Its use here is not meant to imply general agreement between Hardin and Tillich; the differences are many.

36. Dietrich Bonhoeffer, *Letters and Papers from Prison,* ed. Eberhard Bethge, trans. Reginald Fuller (1953; reprint, New York: Macmillan, 1962), 162, entry for 30 April 1944; Tillich, *On the Boundary,* 69–70.

37. Paul Tillich, "The Conquest of the Concept of Religion in the Philosophy of Religion," trans. Kenneth Schedler with the assistance of Charles W. Fox, in Paul Tillich, *What Is Religion?,* trans. James Luther Adams (New York: Harper & Row, Torchbook, 1973).

38. Tillich, *The Protestant Era,* 185.

39. Tillich, *On the Boundary,* 71, 73.

40. Paul Tillich, *Christianity and the Encounter of the World Religions* (New York: Columbia University Press, 1963), 4; idem, *The Protestant Era,* xv–xvi.

41. Bonhoeffer, *Letters and Papers from Prison,* 197–98, entry for 8 June 1944.

42. Ibid., 164, entry for 30 April 1944.

43. Ibid., 165, entry for 30 April 1944; and 196, entry for 8 June 1944.

44. Wilhelm and Marion Pauck, *Paul Tillich: His Life and Thought* (New York: Harper & Row, 1976), vol. 1, *Life,* 316, n. 22.

45. Tillich, *On the Boundary,* 78–81. It is worth noting that contemporary Latin American liberation theologians follow a similar pattern when they acknowledge the transcendent nature of God's Kingdom, yet pursue a particular utopia as their "historical project" in a given situation. They are more ready to use utopian language than Tillich, perhaps because they do not fully share his concept of the demonic.

46. Tillich, *The Protestant Era,* 60. Tillich repeated the theme in his article "Beyond Religious Socialism," *The Christian Century* 66 (15 June 1949): 732–33. Incidentally, he objected to the title assigned that article by the editors. See "Autobiographical Reflections of Paul Tillich," in *The Theology of Paul Tillich,* 12–13.

47. Roger L. Shinn, *Christianity and the Problem of History* (New York: Charles Scribner's Sons, 1953), 218, n. 6.

48. Stumme, *Socialism in Theological Perspective,* 253; Ronald H. Stone, *Paul Tillich's Radical Social Thought* (Atlanta: John Knox Press, 1980), 153.

49. See the discussion between James Luther Adams and Paul Tillich, in "Interrogation of Paul Tillich," *Philosophical Interrogations,* ed. Sydney and Beatrice Rome (New York: Holt, Rinehart and Winston, 1964), 404–6. The first of the Rauschenbusch lectures, "Between Utopianism and Escape from History," was published in the *Colgate Rochester Divinity School Bulletin* 31, n. 2 (1959): 32–40.

50. Tillich, *The Protestant Era,* xxix.

4. Tillich and the Crisis of the West

WALTER A. WEISSKOPF

It is a difficult task to ascertain the impact of a great mind on its time. Such influence is not always directly discernible; it does not consist merely in the explicit use of a thinker's ideas in the writings of others. Ideas, like seeds dispersed by the wind, may inseminate others without their being aware of it. Many ideas on the Western crisis may have been influenced by Tillich.

This is why I will try to show what this impact could and should have been. Tillich reformulated classical theology and philosophy, the thought of Hegel, Marx, and Freud, and existentialism into a system that had a direct influence on American theology and an indirect influence on wider Western thought.

This chapter centers around and begins with Tillich's *The Socialist Decision.* [1] In this work Tillich was influenced by the German political situation in the early 1930s. However, his argument reaches into deeper dimensions. He developed a tripartite and dialectical scheme; its substructure is historical, but it is rooted in ontological and psychological dimensions. [2]

The tripartite scheme of *The Socialist Decision* involves three principles: the romantic, the bourgeois, and the socialist principles. In line with Tillich's holistic approach these terms have ontological, psychological, and historical meanings. The scaffold is the historical political structure in the Germany of the 1920s and 1930s; the romantic principle represents the German conservative movements, the German National parties allied with big business, and the National Socialist movements with support among the *"Lumpen"*-proletariat and the unemployed middle class youth; the bourgeois principle stands for the supporters of a liberal capitalist free-market economy and for a democratic society; and the socialist principle for Marxist socialism in the Weimar Republic, the Social Democrats, and the labor unions.

POWERS OF ORIGIN

This political and historical scaffold reaches deep down into the roots of human existence. Tillich traces the romantic principle back to the "mythical powers of origin." This term refers to the original bonds that tie human beings together in the early phases of history as well as in early infancy. Essential for this state is the unity of man, world, nature, and God. Tillich mentions the ties to father and mother, blood relations, the roots in the soil, the dependency on the circle of vegetative existence in interchange between man and earth and supranatural powers. The romantic principle originated in a culture in which consciousness, reason, purposive action, and conscious goals are not yet predominant. The world is viewed in terms of an eternal circular movement, Nietzsche's idea of eternal return. This culture tries to answer the question of the "whence"; the "whither" is not envisaged.

In his *Systematic Theology* Tillich describes this state as "dreaming innocence": a state of nonactualized potentialities, transposed by myth and dogma into the historical past; but this state of dreaming innocence appears also in the development of the individual before the growth of consciousness.[3] Erich Neumann also uses a mythical symbol for this stage, the "uroboros," the serpent that bites its own tail, expressing the primeval unity of man and world.[4] Tillich, talking about myths and powers of origin, sees in this state a universal source of conservative political movements. This shifts the discussion of politics to a deeper dimension. Political conservatism assumes a different character if seen not merely as a class conflict but as a deeply rooted trait of mankind.

"The state of dreaming innocence drives beyond itself."[5] This metaphysical presupposition is of utmost importance in Tillich's philosophy of history; it assumes a force that drives existing forms toward the new, toward transcendence.

In his distinction between dynamics and form—an ontological dichotomy characteristic of all being—Tillich describes the dynamic as something that "underlies most mythologies and is indicated in the chaos, the *tohu-va-bohu,* the night, the emptiness, which precedes creation." Again, he says, "The dynamic character of being implies the tendency of everything to transcend itself and to create new forms."[6] The *dynamic* is another term for a part of what in *The Socialist Decision* Tillich calls the powers of origin; but it includes the drive toward the new as part of these powers.

In Western history Tillich sees two breaks with the powers of origin: Jewish prophetism and the Enlightenment. He talks (as later in the *Systematic Theology*) about "the creative powers of origin that press beyond the original point of origin."[7] In Judaism this drive contains the experience of the "ought to" *(Sollen)*. The moral demand is projected into time; history is seen as driving toward the realization of an ethical imperative. The powers of origin become the *beginning* of history, pointing toward an *end* of history. The basic idea of religious socialism, that history is governed by an ethical imperative leading toward a fulfillment, has its origin in Jewish prophecy.

THE BOURGEOIS PRINCIPLE

In Tillich's dialectical interpretation, the "thesis" is represented by civilizations rooted in the powers of origin. The "antithesis" develops because of the tendency, innate in the powers of origin, to transcend themselves (as in Jewish prophecy and in the Enlightenment). In Western history this led to the emergence of the bourgeois principle.[8] This term includes all facets of Western society as it developed during the last two hundred years: capitalism, individualism, democracy, with natural science, technology, and economy as the dominant spheres of life. The term *bourgeois* accepts the Marxian view of the bourgeoisie as the ruling class; but Tillich's term *the bourgeois principle* includes all of the elements of modern society: utilitarianism, positivism, liberalism, autonomous this-worldliness, rational purposive thought, and action. The acceptance of things as they are is replaced by the striving for material progress. The bourgeoisie attempt to tame the external world by subjecting it to their purposes through scientific knowledge and technology; the unconditional becomes conditioned. Bourgeois individualism cuts the social bonds in the individual psyche and in social groups. Therefore, the actually existing bonds of the social order require explanation and justification. This has been accomplished by the belief in the harmony, nay identity, of individual and social interests. According to Tillich, liberalism believes in the natural harmony, the invisible hand; democracy in an *"artificial harmony,"* in the possibility of subjugating nature, people, society, and history to reason through persuasion, education, and political action. The belief in harmony is supported by a belief in progress accomplished by human action. The viability of capitalist society depends on the belief in harmony.

The decline of the bourgeois principle and the Western crisis are caused, in part, by the impossibility of maintaining this belief in the economic field. Free-enterprise liberalism became untenable with the organizational revolution, the growth of big business, the countervailing power of unionism, and the growth of governmental intervention and control; with the breakdown of international free trade and of the international gold standard, followed by the shift to manipulated currencies and regulated international trade; and finally with the Great Depression of the 1930s. It undermined the belief in the automatic self-regenerating powers and in the harmonious beneficence of the free market. Some of this had not yet happened when Tillich wrote *The Socialist Decision.* However, what has happened since has shown clearly that the bourgeois economy and society are in reality not a harmonious network of autonomous individuals but are dominated by organized interest groups, by political action, and by irrational forces.

An important cause of the decline of the bourgeois principle and of the Western crisis was and is the emergence of autonomous consciousness and the demotion of reason from ontological to technical reason. Autonomous consciousness "suppresses the depth dimension of being."[9] The finite becomes the exclusive object of knowledge; action is directed, not toward the new as such, but toward material "progress." The unknown and the incalculable are pushed aside in favor of certainty and calculability. Vitalistic power is diminished by rational efficiency. Revelation is replaced by education. Nothing is insoluble; there is nothing that cannot be manipulated.[10] When autonomy becomes established dogma, it creates an emptiness that is then filled again by "romantic" movements.[11]

In the *Systematic Theology* the idea of autonomous consciousness is enlarged and clarified by the dichotomy of ontological and technical reason. Ontological reason "is the structure of the mind which enables the mind to grasp and to transform reality. It is effective in the cognitive, aesthetic, practical, and technical functions of the human mind." In the concept of technical reason, "reason is reduced to the capacity for 'reasoning.' *Only the cognitive side* of the classical concept of reason remains, and within the cognitive realm only those cognitive acts which deal with the discovery of means for ends." The main difference between ontological and technical reason is that the first encompasses all of human activity, not only the cognitive aspects. "Even emotional life is not irrational in itself."[12] Eros, intellectual love, and *appetitus* drive the mind toward the true and the good. Ontological reason is not confined to certain spheres of human existence; all of them, including the passions, emotions, and feelings have a rational structure.

In the realm of technical reason the ends are accepted as given "from somewhere else." The consequence is that ends are provided by nonrational forces. Critical reason has ceased to exercise any controlling forces over norms and ends. Here again we find one of the main sources of the Western crisis: the demotion and reduction of reason to reasoning or technical reason.[13] The latter is the basic pillar on which our present civilization rests. By this demotion of reason, important dimensions of human existence—such as the spiritual dimension; the realm of meaning; the normative dimension; the realm of values; the transcendental dimension; the realm of the unknown; the depth dimension of being, worship, mystery, faith in things unseen; the affective dimension of fantasy, imagination and intuition; the communal dimension of close relations to the "thou"; and the realm of love—were excluded from the rational cognitive sphere.[14] Means-ends rationality aiming at purposive efficiency has pushed the search for meaning, the grasping of essences, intuition, mystery, and the entire realm of ideas and ideals into the sphere of the irrational. The limits of the irrational were thus vastly extended. This removed the intellectual, psychological, and spiritual possibility of reasoning about ends and taming the "passions" through reason. Thus, irrational forces and movements were unchained in two world wars; in national socialism; in Stalinism; and in the growth of force, violence, terror, and crime in the West. An antinomy developed in bourgeois civilization between reason reduced to technical reasoning, and the depth dimensions of human existence.

THE BOURGEOIS PRINCIPLE AND THE POWERS OF ORIGIN

In *The Socialist Decision* Tillich discusses this situation in terms of the interdependence of autonomy and myth of origin. He sees here a parallelism between a political and a spiritual situation. The bourgeoisie and the principle of autonomous reason are dependent on the powers of origin for establishing a viable society. Bourgeois civilization and its autonomy of technical reason are seen as a mere antithesis, as the manifestation of a critical principle, a corrective, not a system that can stand on its own; the complete realization of the bourgeois goals of unrestricted freedom and uninhibited technical reason would destroy society. The situation in the 1980s, with its threatening destruction of mankind and of its natural environment by forces unleashed by science, economy, and technology, seems to bear out this view.

J. A. Schumpeter has advanced the idea that the bourgeoisie requires protective political strata to maintain social order.[15] Hence the bourgeoisie made alliance with prebourgeois classes in England and Germany. Schumpeter also believed that the critical intellect and its bearer, the intelligentsia, undermine the basic bourgeois values such as private property and the family. In *The Socialist Decision* Tillich concludes likewise that the bourgeoisie has to ally itself with those political movements that are rooted in the powers of origin, with "romantic" conservative groups and parties. This is what happened in Western countries, but especially in Germany in the period between the two world wars. The bourgeois capitalist states, even when ruled by social democratic and labor parties, became nationalist. In nationalism the bourgeoisie found social bonds of cohesion, which were related to the powers of origin which were lacking in its own principle. In the United States of the post–World War II period, however, nationalism has been weakened by economic, ethnic, social, religious, occupational, and regional groupings that broke through the overall cohesion of the nation in favor of smaller units.

The essence of Tillich's existential and historical scheme is a dichotomic and dialectic structure consisting of the antinomy between and interdependence of the powers of origin and the bourgeois principle. The bourgeois principle is the antithesis to the romantic conservative principle rooted in the powers of origin. However, true to his dialectic view, Tillich detects in bourgeois society itself an antinomy between the two principles; the bourgeoisie has to ally itself with the conservative forces, mainly by embracing nationalism.

MARXIST PROLETARIAN SOCIALISM

Tillich sees in socialism an antithesis to the bourgeois principle;[16] but it too is rent by a dichotomy. On the one hand, it radicalizes bourgeois immanentist and materialistic ideals. On the other hand, socialism rejects the bourgeois belief in natural harmony of interests and the belief that harmony could be established by political action under capitalism. Socialism saw disharmony and disequilibrium in bourgeois society caused by class struggle, and it projected the achievement of harmony into the "classless" society of the future. For the present, the disharmony of bourgeois society requires the use of political power in the class struggle, in central planning, and in the dictatorship of the proletariat.

In Tillich's view socialism is not merely a movement of the proletariat representing one particular interest group among others. Socialism sees the proletariat as the historical instrument that will bring about the classless society. Thus it has also a universal aspect. It aims at a new form of human existence, a new life-style, and a new form of society, all symbolized in the term *classless society*. The proletariat is thus viewed as the carrier of a universal movement. The socialist principle also has ontological roots. Socialism expresses a force in human existence, a primordial drive spurred by the "demand" for transcendence, by the expectation of the new.[17] It represents another breakthrough like prophetism and humanism.

In *The Socialist Decision* Tillich does not define what he means by socialism; he seems to accept the traditional Marxist definition. However, in earlier writings he mentions as goals of socialism rational structuring of the economy; freeing life of contingencies; justice in the economy; elimination of conflicts between classes, nations, and religious denominations. Justice is for him an essential characteristic of socialism: "One can debate how justice in the economy and polity can be carried out; but there can be no doubt that justice has to be willed." From his socialist viewpoint he rejects vigorously the idea that the distinction between rich and poor is a divine necessity; that misery, war, and racial hatred must always exist; that one has to make the economy into a battlefield of everybody against everybody else; and that the state is merely an organization of power. Those who propagate these ideas do not know anything about socialism. For Tillich socialism aims at the realization of the Christian ideal: changing the world according to the idea of justice and Christian love.[18]

However, according to Tillich, the socialist principle is also a product and continuation of the bourgeois principle. Socialism aims not only at revolution but at the realization of the bourgeois promises of harmony, progress, and human autonomy. It also accepts the economic and technological goals of bourgeois capitalism. Even the means to accomplish these goals—bureaucratization, technology, and economic growth—have become very similar in socialism, communism, and capitalism. Thus socialism is confronted with the same problems as bourgeois society: the necessity to vitalize the creative aspects of the powers of origin, and to synthesize them with autonomous immanentist reason. The failure to do so, and the fact that socialism succumbed to the same one-dimensionality as bourgeois capitalism, was one of the factors that caused the failure of Marxian proletarian socialism.

If we try to apply some of Tillich's ideas about socialism to the present American scene, we have to separate his universally applicable concepts from what is time- and culture-bound in his socialist writings. His ideal of religious, but nevertheless Marxist, proletarian socialism never took hold in the United States. However, the antinomies and contradictions he uncovered in bourgeois society and in the socialist principle and their ontological and existential roots are still at work in the West. Tillich interprets the course of history in terms of antithetical, dialectical forces. Bourgeois society and socialism are antithetical in relation to each other, but they are also split in themselves by dialectical contradictions. When we now look at American developments, we find again dialectical contradictions, but in different forms.

SOCIALISM AND MANAGERIAL CAPITALISM

Marxist proletarian socialism was not victorious in the West. Although in large parts of the world its ideology and terminology have been adopted as the official creed, the social and economic reality is very different from anything Tillich envisaged in his preemigration writings. However, one of the socialist goals (control and planning by collective organizations and governments) has made great inroads, even in the Western, nonsocialist countries; they have become mixed economies where large organizations of business, labor, and government struggle for power and a larger share in the social product. In the Eastern world and all over the globe, totalitarian and authoritarian systems, also of a mixed character, have emerged.

In the West, outside the United States, socialism led to the formation of labor- and social-democratic parties and to political unionism. In the United States, unions as an economic interest group have become part and parcel of a capitalist system; their collectivistic character fits well into a socioeconomic system of large organizations. This capitalism could rightly be called a collective managerial society;[19] in all sectors (business, labor, government, political parties, etc.) large organizations are manipulated by managers who administer the money and the assets of others but do not own them. The "owners" (stockholders, union members, voters, taxpayers) have, in fact, lost control, although they are still legally the "sovereigns." Bureaucratization of economic, political, and social life is the pervasive characteristic of this system; it matches the bureaucratization in the totalitarian countries.[20] However, modern, especially American, managerial, large-scale capitalism created the affluent society and raised large groups of the proletariat to the life-style of the bourgeoisie, consequently called middle class. This is a far cry from the expectations and predictions of Marxian proletarian socialism (which in 1933 Tillich expressed in *The Socialist Decision* and in his German writings about religious socialism) with its hopes for a classless society.

Nevertheless, much of what Tillich says in *The Socialist Decision* about the inner conflicts of socialism can be viewed as the inner conflicts not merely of socialism, but of Western society in general. However, the basic Western conflict between the powers of origin and technical reason assumed a different form in the United States. Here there are no conservative political parties such as the Tories, the British Conservatives, the German National and Center parties who represent the powers of origin. Here there is no feudal aristocratic conservative tradition and class. *Here the bourgeois principle and capitalist value-attitudes,* with the belief in harmony and progress, *represent the conservative, traditional orientation;* and the opposition against this conservatism by various progressivist movements rests on the same bourgeois beliefs in eventual harmony and progress. On the American scene the political conflict is between two wings of the Western creed: the conservative, pro–free-enterprise orientation versus democratic, progressive, governmental liberalism of the New Deal type.

Nevertheless, the powers of origin have also been at work on the American scene. They found their expression in a series of "revolutionary," rebellious, sometimes destructive, movements. What came to be called "the counterculture," or "adversary culture" played a prominent part in these trends.[21] They are recent eruptions of the suppressed powers of origin and a rebellion against an essential aspect of the bourgeois principle, namely impulse control, against what Max Weber called "worldly asceticism" and "the Protestant ethic." The "spirit of capitalism" (or the bourgeois principle) consisted originally of a combination of "rational" efficiency and strong external and internal discipline. However, this discipline disintegrated gradually after the material and spiritual destructions of the First World War.

Tillich saw this disintegration as an eruption of the demonic, especially in the form of the Nazi movement, a rebellion against the bourgeois principle. He also saw a demonic element in the modern economy because of its destruction of the human substance through unemployment, exploitation, and poverty.[22] Tillich saw *social* demonics in the breaking of the human person by an overwhelming social organization: "The demonic of the state, the church, the economy is visible where the bonds of society are misused and lead to society's self-destruction."[23] He also saw the demonic, even the satanic, in the ethical relativism of bourgeois society, which empties reality of its meaning. (The demonic arises from the tension between the destruction and creation in human existence and history; the satanic is destruction without creation).[24]

"Our time and all social strata are facing the abyss of meaninglessness."[25] The essence of Tillich's analysis is that the suppression of the powers of origin in bourgeois, capitalist society must lead to the eruption, and thus to the destruction, of the Western way of life. The same powers of origin are at work in such revolutionary, destructive movements as militant nationalism, jingoism, racism, sexism, extremist ethnicism, and in the counterculture and adversary culture. There is a rebellion against the meaninglessness and value-emptiness that result from bourgeois utilitarian means-ends rationality. The rebellion is also directed against the discipline that capitalist technical rationality requires. This rebellion aims at the liberation of deep-seated "irrational" drives, irrational only because of their contrast to the bourgeois life-style. These trends have, however, permeated beyond fringe groups and have affected the entire temper of life in the West.

"RATIONAL WORK" AND "IRRATIONAL LEISURE"

The economic root (by no means the only root) of this rebellion is the affluent society. Our economic attitudes suffer from inner contradictions. In our work life we are supposed to proceed methodically, systematically, "rationally," and practice discipline and self-control. Our leisure life is dominated by what I have called "subjectivistic consumerism."[26] We are supposed to act out our drives, instincts, and desires without inhibitions. What libertarians call "freedom to choose" has become a call to limitless orgies of consumption. We are continuously exhorted—with the help of the mass media—to engage in frantic buying, apparently for the sake of more variegated experiences, feelings, emotions, thrills, "kicks," sensations. This attitude is not confined to hippies, flower children, drug users, and the like, but permeates our entire style of consumption. We are continuously challenged to go on a binge of consumption. This orientation has become necessary in our economic system which, for the sake of continuous, unlimited economic growth, requires unlimited expansion of spending and consumption of the most irrational kind.

Tillich's antinomy of the powers of origin and autonomous

consciousness is reflected in this split of disciplined rationality in work and uninhibited consumerism in leisure; it is one source of the Western crisis. This antinomy is related to what is so frequently deplored: the disintegration of traditional bourgeois and civic values and virtues, the lack of moral restraints, and the corruption of manners. The walls of morality and of control of the passions are crumbling in the (to us) most important sphere of life—in consumption—and the effects are spreading into all other spheres. The decline in excellence, education, intelligence, literacy, and also economic productivity is related to unchained subjectivistic consumerism. The ideal of "doing a job well" is disintegrating together with the Protestant ethic and disciplined bourgeois rationality. Orgiastic consumption has become a general way of life.

One aspect of the Western crisis is seen as the "permissive society." This term refers to the loosening of moral restraints in all spheres of life: in the family, personal relations, and sex; in consumption habits and dress; in the growing laxity of performance and achievement, keeping obligations, punctuality, precision, honesty; in laxity in the fulfillment of contracts and obligations; in the permissive treatment of crime, especially white-collar crime; in the growing acceptance of corruption in business and government. In Tillich's terms, autonomous consciousness and purely technical expediency combined with impulse control have repressed the "powers of origin." They have broken out of the dungeon of their repression and have overwhelmed reason, rationality, and moral restraint. The permissive society, unchaining the passions of sensuous satisfaction in mass consumption, is the modern counterpart to Tillich's antithetical forces opposing the bourgeois capitalistic mode of life and thought. These trends can be understood as a transformation and/or disintegration of bourgeois values—in other words, as the crisis of the West.

THE DOMINANT THEMES

We have tried to show how some of Tillich's ideas have opened new vistas on the crisis of the West. His ideas about socialism are actually dealing with this crisis. It is appropriate to summarize them at this point.

1. Tillich has shifted the discussion from the economic and political level to the ontological and existential dimension.

2. He presented a dialectical scheme for historical development, influenced by, but not identical with, either Hegelian or Marxian dialectics, because it applies to the existential and ontological as well as to the historical sphere. His tripartite scheme—the romantic, bourgeois, and socialist principles—refer to historical phenomena of the political structure of Germany in the 1920s and early 1930s; however, they are also rooted in the structure of human existence.

3. The *romantic principle* is related to the myths and powers of origin. In this symbol "lower" and "higher" dimensions are combined. The powers of origin include the demonic and the satanic. In contemporary parlance, they include what Freud called the id, this "melting-pot of seething excitations," this "subterranean dynamic" of "primitive and irrational" impulses, as Thomas Mann described it.[27]

   However, the powers of origin also include the forces that are tying human beings together through blood relationships such as the family, the clan, the tribe; and the bonds that tie people to the soil, to an area, a space, and each other. Tillich talks about the powers of origin because they point to the primeval, preindividuation stage of humankind; to the state of human beings before consciousness and individuation. However, these powers of origin also contain the sacred, the holy, the mystery, the participation in the divine dimension that has been universally expressed in myths, rites, cults, and religious beliefs and institutions.

4. The *bourgeois principle* also represents the extension of a sociohistorical phenomenon into the existential sphere. It stands for basic human characteristics such as individuation, consciousness, reason, and autonomy. Bourgeois culture stresses consciousness against being, self against the world, individualization against participation, form against dynamics, and freedom against destiny, thus splitting apart the dialectical unity of human existence and history.[28]

5. The key to the understanding of the Western crisis is to be found in these antinomies. The forces and bonds of origin keep society together; consciousness and individuation break

through and transcend the state of original unity and dreaming innocence, and drive toward the new. The crisis of Western society, like every historical crisis, consists then of inner conflicts, contradictions, antinomies. The bourgeois crisis is caused by the neglect of one branch of the antinomy, of the powers of origin, in favor of exclusive reliance on individuation, autonomy, and reason. Similarly, the demotion of reason from encompassing, ontological to instrumental, technical reason is an aspect of this crisis.

6. *The socialist principle* is, according to Tillich, beset by antinomies similar to those of the bourgeois principle. On the one hand, the socialism Tillich has in mind in *The Socialist Decision* is imbued with the same spirit of autonomous consciousness, rationality, empirical knowledge, and with the belief in the possibility of manipulating society and history. However, in its eschatological faith in a harmonious "classless" future, it performs a leap into a transcendent dimension, although in the form of an "immanent" end of history.[29] The belief in such a transformation from class rule into classlessness amounts to a belief in a miracle, incompatible with the stance of "scientific" socialism. This antinomy contributed to the failure of Marxian proletarian socialism; but this contradiction goes beyond socialist doctrine. It is a symptom of the deep ailment of Western culture: Technical reason clashes with the hope for a future, based on eschatological immanentist expectations.[30]

7. Tillich's socialist writings stem from the time before his emigration to the United States and therefore do not cover events after 1933. He did not, in his later writings, offer an explanation of why the hopes of religious and Marxist socialism were not fulfilled. However, as far as his thought moved along ontological and existential lines, it is *mutatis mutandis* applicable to the present American scene. In the United States the absence of a specifically socialist movement did not prevent the deterioration of individualistic entrepreneurial capitalism into collective managerialism. However, because in the United States there was no feudal romantic tradition connected with the powers of origin, the bourgeois principle itself became the traditional conservative force. Oppositional

powers of origin were at work in nineteenth-century transcendentalism and in populist political movements. They broke into the open again in the counterculture and adversary culture in the post–World War II period in the form of "irrational" movements ranging from militant nationalism, racism, sexism, ethnicism to counterculture, deculturation, permissiveness, licentiousness, violence, terrorism, and crime. A disintegration of "rational" discipline and impulse control, still retained in the sphere of work, took place in the sphere of leisure and was supported by the economic desire for unlimited economic growth and for unrestricted spending.

THE RELIGIOUS DIMENSION: THE UNCONDITIONED AND THE ABSOLUTE

Tillich, from his earliest German writings to his *Systematic Theology*, regards the course of history as a superstructure of ontological and existential dimensions. Every historical crisis is a special manifestation of the structure of human existence and of the antinomies of being. There are no "solutions" for "crises" rooted in the ontological and existential structure; they cannot be solved as malaria can be wiped out by DDT. These dichotomies cannot be eliminated as long as people and world are what they are now, and as long as the "end of history" has not arrived. Any hope for such an end on an immanent level is futile. History consists of swings of the pendulum from thesis to antithesis, from the repressing to the liberated repressed forces. The crisis of the West is the decline of the West and the emergence of a new configuration, a new system of values and institutions which, like previous systems, will contain conflicting elements.

The "solution" of the crisis lies in the direction in which history may develop and in the resurrection of certain dimensions repressed in Western culture. Such a "solution" was indicated by Tillich already in 1919: "If socialism . . . wants to create a new intellectual and social life, it must penetrate from autonomy to 'theonomy,' that is to a grasping of the unconditioned in all phenomena."[37] This applies not only to socialism but to all attempts of finding a way out of the Western crisis. During the last four hundred years Westerners have suffered from a historical repression of the unconditioned and the absolute. Modernity has found no place for it in either thought or action. However, although humans are conditioned beings, they partake, through the mind and soul, in the unconditioned and in the absolute or, in other words, in the dimension of the divine.

In his posthumously published *My Search for Absolutes,* Tillich circumscribes the absolute as "the categories and polarities that make understanding of reality possible; . . . the unconditional character of the moral imperative, regardless of its contents, and the principle of justice—acknowledgment of every person as a person. Finally, there [is] *agape,* love, which contains and transcends justice and unites the absolute and the relative by adapting itself to every concrete situation." The absolutes point to the most basic absolute of all, being itself, "the ground of truth and of the good. . . . The experience of the Absolute-itself is experience of the holy, the sacred."[32]

On the American scene today a revival of religion is taking place in a great variety of forms and on different levels. They range from the renewed stress on sectarian fundamentalism, revivalist preachings, and widespread interest in and practice of meditation, to the many cults and sects—some with demonic and satanic undertones —that attract youth away from the spiritual emptiness of bourgeois life. There is also a new interest of sociologists and philosophers in religion.[33] There is talk about the return of the sacred.[34] This longing for the sacred, the holy, the *tremendum* and *fascinosum* is the "solution" of the Western crisis. It is, of course, no solution in fact. It indicates, however, the direction in which the dialectical pendulum of history swings: from people who consider themselves autonomous masters of themselves, the world, and society, to the revival of the belief in a divine dimension comprising the unknown that limits all human powers. If this is the wave of the future, Tillich certainly has shown us this way in prophetic vision.

NOTES

1. I have used the German edition of Tillich's *Die Sozialistische Entscheidung,* vol. 2, *Gesammelte Werke* (Stuttgart: Evangelisches Verlagswerk, 1962), 219 ff., and the English edition, *The Socialist Decision,* trans. Franklin Sherman (New York: Harper & Row, 1977). Hereafter these volumes are referred to simply by their

respective German and English titles. When I have paraphrased Tillich's thought, I have used either my own or Professor Sherman's translation.

2. A remark about Tillich's dimensional scheme is in order. In his *Systematic Theology* (Chicago: The University of Chicago Press, vol. 1, 1951; vol. 2, 1957; vol. 3, 1963) he distinguishes five dimensions: reason, being, existence, life, and history. Everything human participates in all dimensions. By *being* Tillich means being as such, including everything that "is" in distinction from "nothingness." *Existence* is used in distinction from *essence;* existence stands here for the phenomena of this world. In *Die Sozialistische Entscheidung* Tillich uses the term *being* synonymously with *existence.* I shall, however, in discussing *Die Sozialistische Entscheidung,* use the term *ontology* to refer to being and to existence, because at this stage Tillich had not yet made his later clear-cut distinction between being and existence.

3. Tillich, *Systematic Theology* 2:31ff.

4. Erich Neumann, *Origin and History of Consciousness,* 2 vols. (Princeton, N.J.: Princeton University Press, 1954). First German edition, 1949.

5. Tillich, *Systematic Theology* 2:34 (italics added).

6. Ibid., 1:79, 81.

7. Tillich, *Die Sozialistische Entscheidung,* 239.

8. Ibid., 264ff.

9. Ibid., 244.

10. Ibid., 245.

11. Ibid., 265.

12. Tillich, *Systematic Theology* 1:72, 73 (italics added), 72.

13. See Walter A. Weisskopf, *Alienation and Economics* (New York: Dutton & Co., 1971), 37ff.

14. Ibid., 190.

15. J. A. Schumpeter, *Capitalism, Socialism, and Democracy* (New York: Harper & Brothers, 1950), 139ff.

16. Tillich, *Die Sozialistische Entscheidung,* 274.

17. Ibid., 279.

18. Tillich, *Christentum und Sozialismus,* vol. 2, *Gesammelte Werke,* 29–33. (Hereafter *Gesammelte Werke* is referred to as *GW.*)

19. See James Burnham, *The Managerial Revolution* (Bloomington: University of Indiana Press, 1960).

20. The collective organizational and managerial element in Western economies could be regarded as a partial "victory" of socialism. However, in the United States it was brought about by entirely different socioeconomic forces. Large-scale corporate capitalism developed for reasons of capital accumulation and technology. Managerialism developed as an instrument of corporate organization and bureaucratization. This is why its similarity to socialism is rarely stressed. Burnham, in *The Managerial Revolution;* and Adolf A. Berle and Gardner C. Means, in *The Modern Corporation and Private Property* (New York: Macmillan, 1932; revised ed., New York: Harcourt, Brace and World, 1967) saw this relation clearly; but ideological reasons prevented either Marxists or free-enterprise economists from admitting the "socialist" aspect of the bureaucratized, managerial corporate economy.

21. Theodore Roszak, *The Making of a Counterculture* (Garden City, N.Y.: Doubleday, Anchor Books, 1969). Also Daniel Bell, "The Cultural Contradiction of Capitalism," in *Capitalism Today,* ed. Daniel Bell and Irving Kristol (New York: New American Library, Mentor Books, 1970).

22. Tillich, "Das Dämonische," in GW 6 (1963), 42–71.
23. Ibid., 52.
24. Ibid., 45–46.
25. Ibid., 69.
26. Weisskopf, *Alienation and Economics*, 105.
27. Thomas Mann, "Freud and the Future," in idem, *Essays of Three Decades* (New York: Alfred A. Knopf, 1947), 416–17.
28. Tillich, *Systematic Theology* 1:71ff, 163ff.
29. Tillich, *Die Sozialistische Entscheidung*, 281.
30. Crudely speaking, immanentism is the belief in the Kingdom of God on earth, such as the belief in the thousand-year Reich, or the classless society. Tillich calls it "essentialism" (*Systematic Theology* 2:23). Eric Voegelin in *The New Science of Politics* (Chicago: University of Chicago Press, 1952), 107ff., talks about the fallacy of the "immanentization of the Christian eschaton." Tillich discusses the relation between immanent and transcendent elements in Protestantism and religious socialism in *The Protestant Era* (Chicago: University of Chicago Press, 1948), chaps. 11 and 17.
31. Tillich, *Christentum und Sozialismus*, vol. 2, GW, 25.
32. Paul Tillich, *My Search for Absolutes* (New York: Simon and Schuster, 1967), 124–25.
33. See Jacob Needleman and George Baker, eds., *Understanding the New Religions* (New York: Seabury Press, 1978).
34. Daniel Bell, in *The Bulletin of the American Academy of Arts and Sciences* 31 (1978): 29ff.

5. Tillich's Religious Socialism: "Creative Synthesis" or Personal Statement?

DENNIS P. M^cCANN

When Paul Tillich was still a struggling young *privatdocent* at Marburg, he was asked to prepare an essay for *Kantstudien* assessing the continued relevance of Ernst Troeltsch's philosophy for theology. Ever alert to new opportunities, he used the essay to present Troeltsch's "philosophical problematic" as "the negative presupposition" for any future constructive projects in theology, especially his own. In all three of the areas in which Troeltsch had made a contribution—philosophy of religion, philosophy of history, and social philosophy—Tillich saw the problematic of "the absolute and the relative,"[1] and in all three areas he noted Troeltsch's failure to actually achieve his goal of a "creative synthesis" between them.

Troeltsch's philosophy of religion, he claimed, applies the acids of historical criticism to the false absolutes of dogmatic theology. But it tries in vain to establish the substantively "religious a priori" needed to construct an alternative. Similarly, after having relativized all historical absolutes, Troeltsch's philosophy of history seeks "the unconditional meaning of history." But the "Europeanism" that he hoped would embody the highest cultural values of the Western Christian and humanistic traditions is itself only "a chance by-product of the stream of contingencies." Not surprisingly, Troeltsch's social philosophy betrays the same difficulty. His emphasis on "natural law" leads him to advocate the principle of formal democracy, but both "his ideal of humanity and his fear of utopian absolutes" keep him from making a wholehearted commitment to "socialist democracy."[2]

In each area Troeltsch defines the problem but not the solution;

and in each area Tillich presupposes this definition, while envision-
ing a different solution. Instead of seeking "the true religion in the
depths of all religion," he hopes to find it "beyond all religion."
Instead of basing his "creative synthesis" on the chance configura-
tions of modern Europe, he calls for grounding the meaning of
history "in the Unconditional itself." Instead of restricting his
commitment to socialism "within the limits of humanity, systems,
and forms," he awaits "the breakthrough of the Unconditional,"
which will mark the birth of "new community."[3] Each of Tillich's
new solutions, however, requires a "qualitative" transformation of
both thought and action, in short, a response to "the Unconditional" adequately understood only in terms of "grace."

Throughout the vast theological literature that he went on to
produce, nowhere do these elements converge so brilliantly and
so poignantly as in *The Socialist Decision.* Written in haste during the
fateful summer and fall of 1932, it testifies to Tillich's hope that
the collapse of the Weimar Republic would mean the prelude to
this promised transformation. It bears witness, in other words, to
Tillich's faith in "the breakthrough of the Unconditional," not just
as an abstract truth about religion "beyond religion," but as a
concrete *Kairos* for resolving the crisis of Western culture. The
continued relevance of Tillich's philosophy for theology, therefore, may well depend on what we can make of *The Socialist Decision.*
In addressing this issue, I will focus more on the theoretical framework implicit in it and less on its practical implications (which
Walter A. Weisskopf treats in chapter 4 of this volume). I will
compare its fundamental understanding of myth and praxis, faith
and ideology, with positions represented by Reinhold Niebuhr's
Christian realism and Juan Luis Segundo's liberation theology.
Since these positions dramatize the current impasse in practical
theology, I hope to use them to ask whether Tillich's "creative
synthesis" actually succeeded where Troeltsch's had failed, and in
what way it might help to further the development of practical
theology today.

THE CREATIVE TENSION OF MARXISM AND
PROPHETISM

From this distance it may be difficult to appreciate just how bold
The Socialist Decision really was. As Tillich declared rather ponder-

ously in the book's foreword, "the socialist decision is a decision *of* socialism and a decision *for* socialism." Yet even with this fanfare we may still be unprepared for what follows. For in defiance of conventional political wisdom, Tillich sought to prevent the triumph of nazism by bringing about an alliance between the proletarian socialist movement and its enemies among "the revolutionary groups within political romanticism."[4] Since both groups depended on "the powers of origin," the socialist principle might accommodate the hopes and fears of both in a compromise based on more than political expediency and intellectual confusion. But as it turned out, *The Socialist Decision* came too late. Having bullied their way into the coalition government of January, 1933, the Nazis soon confiscated Tillich's book as it sat waiting in the warehouse. Be that as it may, our concern is not whether Tillich's proposal would have worked had it seen the light of day, but whether it still holds promise as a framework for analyzing contemporary society and politics. Whatever the superficial similarities and differences between Germany in the early 1930s and America in the 1980s, this issue can be resolved only by taking a fresh look at Tillich's theory of politics and myth. How are these elements distinguished and related? How do they converge in Tillich's concept of historic "principles"? What strategies of analysis do they open up? Are these strategies still relevant today?

The most important thing about Tillich's theory is that it strives to be at once both ontological and historical. "The roots of political thought," he says, "must be sought in human being itself."[5] Anyone familiar with even the outlines of Tillich's thought will hardly be surprised by this assertion. But placed in the context of the ideological battles of that time, it represents a bold attempt to reconcile the seemingly irreconcilable perspectives of historical materialism and philosophical idealism. Tillich's strategy follows from his understanding of "human being." Since for him it includes the totality of nature and history, of religious symbol and social structure, in which and from which human consciousness develops, he can thus affirm the "thrownness" of existence along with Heidegger as well as the dynamism of historical change along with Marx. Nevertheless, given his sense of the direction in which the socialist principle must unfold, his analysis emphasizes the ontological dimension of this totality. He therefore concentrates on the myths and symbols that give rise to political thought.

Among these, Tillich places "the myth of origin" at the center. For it is the "whence" *(Woher)* of existence—the cycle of birth and death, the ties to mother and father, soil and blood, religious cult and social group; in other words, the reality into which each of us is "thrown"—that is disclosed in the myth of origin. Within this myth the "whence" is recognized and sanctified, and human beings are thereby bound to it as to a way of life. In this way the myth of origin provides "the root of all conservative and romantic thought in politics."[6]

Were this all there is to the myth of origin, it would hardly raise questions. Politics would consist simply in perpetuating the primordial patterns of existence. But the origin is also "creative" and therefore "ambiguous." Even though it remains fundamentally cyclical, the origin also "brings us forth as something new and singular" and as such affords us the possibility of experiencing what Tillich calls "the demand." When this happens, we are "no longer simply bound to the origin." The "whence" becomes problematic, and thus compels us to address the question of "whither" *(Wozu)*. For in Tillich's view, the "whither"—the possibility of achieving "something unconditionally new" in history—demands a "break" with the myth of origin, which lies at "the root of liberal, democratic, and socialist thought in politics."[7] Although Tillich does not lend further precision to these concepts, at least his purpose in using them is clear. Humanity's quest for justice must be grounded in "the true power of being," which is "the origin in truth." Since the "whither" that breaks the myth is just as much a disclosure of the origin as is the "whence" itself, both must be accounted for in genuine political thinking.

Within the baselines laid out by these ontological definitions, Tillich proceeds to a historical analysis of society and politics. The link between history and ontology is forged in his concept of principle. As Tillich defines it, "A principle is the real power that supports a historical phenomenon, giving it the possibility to actualize itself anew and yet in continuity with the past."[8] His notion of principle, in short, follows from his understanding of human being. Since human being is always concrete, a principle always refers to the dynamism of particular social groups and the individuals who are "thrown" together in them. The unfolding of the socialist principle thus calls for tracking the interplay of "whence" and "whither" in the historic situation of "proletarian being."

Such an analysis will seek to show three things: First, while political romanticism is oriented to the powers of origin, it is incapable of serving as a creative historic principle. Reacting against the definitive break with the myth of origin accomplished by Judeo-Christian prophetism and the Enlightenment, romanticism seeks to restore the "whence" by suppressing the "whither." But since the "whither" is also a part of the origin in truth, romanticism can never be more than a protest.

Second, while the bourgeois principle did successfully break with the myth of origin in the name of Enlightenment "autonomy," it has now been radicalized to the point where its conception of the "whither" is no longer plausible. In short once the Enlightenment's faith in "natural harmony" was shaken by the paradoxical consequences of economic liberalism, the bourgeois principle was faced with a dilemma: either reject the unconditional demand of the "whither" and retreat toward the "whence" represented by political romanticism, or accept the unconditional demand in its latest manifestation as the socialist principle. Whichever choice is made, it results in the eventual disappearance of the bourgeois principle.

Third, what then of the socialist principle? Since it has emerged as the consciousness of proletarian being in the class struggle, all three elements, "the power of origin, the shattering of the belief in harmony, and an emphasis on the demand" manifest themselves in it. Thus its struggle against the bourgeois principle embodies a properly dialectical conception of both the "whence" and the "whither." But the socialist principle can do this only to the extent that its break with the myth of origin carries on the prophetic tradition of Judaism and Christianity. In other words, "socialism is prophetism on the soil of an autonomous, self-sufficient world."[9]

This analysis, of course, provides the theoretical justification for "the socialist decision." On the one hand, political romanticism expresses a legitimate protest against the total eclipse of the powers of origin envisioned by the bourgeois principle. On the other hand, the powers of origin are also operative in the struggle of the proletariat. If the socialist principle can recover its own relationship to the origin as this has been broken and yet preserved in prophetism, and if at least the revolutionary elements in political romanticism can be convinced that their own demand is authentically realized in the socialist principle, then a basis exists for a political coalition between them. Otherwise, the bourgeoisie will barter away its autonomy in exchange for security, the proletariat will remain politically impotent, and fascism will triumph by default. The socialist decision, in other words, is a choice between socialism and barbarism.

However politically astute or naive Tillich's call for a coalition, its theoretical integrity depends on maintaining a creative tension between prophetism and Marxism. Although Marxism is defined as the "socialist self-consciousness" of the proletarian movement, it clearly does not exhaust the socialist principle. Since Marxism radicalizes the bourgeois principle of rational criticism, it can only remain immanent within history and therefore subject to distortion. By contrast, the principle of prophetic criticism in some sense transcends the historical process: "The expectation of a 'new heaven and a new earth' signifies the expectation of a reality that is not subject to the structure of being, that cannot be grasped ontologically."[10] Prophetic criticism, in other words, bears an unconditional demand that relativizes all immanent expectations. It is able to do this because its transcendent perspective resists objectification and therefore remains paradoxically rooted in both the "whence" and the "whither."

This claim undoubtedly requires some explanation. Prophetic criticism enhances rational criticism by reorienting it toward both the origin and the demand, while rational criticism enhances prophetic criticism by serving as a check upon its tendency to interpret in purely formal terms what is unconditional in both. Ever so easily prophetic criticism may degenerate into either an otherworldly spirituality or an abstract moralizing. By the same token, rational criticism easily may degenerate into a "dogmatic Marxism" that sponsors similar errors.[11] In either case, when this happens the unconditional demand remains "impotent against the actual forces of society."[12] Since the socialist principle cannot unfold without overcoming dogmatic Marxism, Tillich proceeds to a more detailed analysis of its problems.

In light of the rediscovery of "the young Marx" and the failure of the German Communist party, Tillich accuses dogmatic Marxism of betraying the proletarian situation by objectifying Marx's dialectical understanding of history. This process of objectification has produced two major distortions both in theory and in praxis: First, Marx's "historical materialism"—in other words, the claim that "the 'matter' of history" is "socially productive humanity, . . . not an overarching 'reason' "—is reduced to "a materialistic doctrine of human nature" in which the cultural "superstructure" and the economic "substructure" are related as effect to cause. Consistent with this dogma, ideology and false consciousness are no longer understood dialectically in relationship to a "true consciousness" of the actual structures of society. Instead, they are seen as deviations from an abstract norm of materialist orthodoxy. Such theoretical reductionism is not without practical consequences. Since dogmatic Marxism dismisses "all prebourgeois elements in bourgeois society as expressions of false consciousness," it is unable to understand the proletarian movement's own relationship to the powers of origin. It thus needlessly drives these elements into the camp of political romanticism. Second, Marx's "historical dialectic"—in other words, "the peculiar notion that history moves forward toward its goal, as it were, *behind the backs of the bearers of historical action*"—is also reduced to a "law of cause and effect." As a result the "historical dialectic" no longer provides orientation to the interplay of freedom and necessity in historical praxis; instead, it becomes a principle of pseudoscientific "calculability." Once dogmatic Marxism embraces reductionism, the proletarian situation inevitably splits into two opposing factions: one intellectualist, the other, voluntarist. In the former a speculative concern for predicting revolutions becomes a substitute for historical praxis; in the latter, passionate but arbitrary action becomes a substitute for critical insight into the dynamics of historical change. These distortions suggest that "socialism has permanent cause to suspect itself of being an ideology."[13]

Given the direction of Tillich's criticism, the point then is to link the failure of dogmatic Marxism to a basic problem common to all forms of political thought: the problem of objectification (*Verdinglichung*). Objectification, for Tillich, is a thought process that inevitably produces "ideology" or "dogma." No longer definable simply as "the ideas of the ruling class," ideology becomes a generalizable condition, "a false consciousness, [representing] nothing other than the willful self-affirmation of old social structures that are being threatened and destroyed by new ones."[14] Such willfulness is manifest conceptually in the formation of static ideas whose structure resists truly dialectical thinking. If ideas are flexible enough to be transformed even as the new social structures are transforming the old, they remain properly dialectical and in no sense ideological. All the same, since the process of objectification is so pervasive as to be found not only in bourgeois but also in socialist thought, the problem is how it may be overcome. Is there any perspective that ultimately resists objectification?

Tillich's response to this question is predictably dialectical. On the one hand, only the critical awareness stemming from the proletarian situation resists objectification: "What in any other place happens only through reflection, and therefore by chance, happens here of necessity and without rational argumentation. What in any other place is possible only for individuals—to see through the social ideologies—happens here among the masses without any effort, through their sheer existence. The natural, instinctive reactions themselves drive towards justice."[15] On the other hand, only the transcendent perspective of prophetism ensures that this critical awareness reflects the unconditional demand without distortion. In short, Tillich's response is that only a religious socialism providing a "creative synthesis" of both perspectives suffices to overcome the problem of objectification. Before venturing an appraisal of Tillich's creative synthesis, we should clarify the problem of objectification still further by comparing his sense of it with the theological discussions of faith and ideology offered by Niebuhr and Segundo.

A COMPARISON OF TILLICH WITH NIEBUHR AND SEGUNDO

While it is clear that Tillich was a formative influence on Niebuhr's growing awareness of the significance of myth in religious and political thought,[16] it is also clear that Niebuhr's mature work on the question of ideology diverged from Tillich's approach in important ways. In *The Nature and Destiny of Man,* for example, Niebuhr defines "ideology" as essentially a religious problem, similar to the problem of "idolatry" addressed by the prophets of Israel. Consistent with the categories of his theological anthropology, Niebuhr describes it as a form of the "sin" of "intellectual pride."[17] Ideology is not just a consequence of the finite character of all knowledge; it is also a refusal to admit the limits imposed by finitude. Such "pretense" is just one more manifestation of the "original sin" of humanity's rebellion against God. An essentially religious problem, however, can only admit an essentially religious solution. Niebuhr therefore insists that the "ideological taint" in all human thinking and acting can be removed—if at all—only "in moments of prayerful transcendence."[18] Only such moments can shatter "the false sense of self-sufficiency and universality of spirit," because only these allow "grace" to enter and purify the human heart.

Niebuhr's view might easily be dismissed as pious platitude, were it not for the way in which he establishes its relevance to social conflict. By juxtaposing his "Christian interpretation" of ideology to those offered by Marx and Mannheim, he argues that such moments are indispensable if the problem is ever to be adequately resolved. While he credits Marxism with "the discovery of the ideological taint in all culture," he also criticizes it for "mistakenly confining this taint to economic life."[19] His point is similar to Tillich's: Marxist "economism" restricts our awareness of the depth of the problem of ideology, and consequently blinds Marxists to the ideological taint in their own perspective. But he moves beyond Tillich in the implication he draws from this point. Since therefore even proletarian thought is tainted, Niebuhr does not see it playing any special role in overcoming the problem of ideology. In drawing this conclusion, he is in partial agreement with Mannheim against Marx. For although Mannheim's "sociology of knowledge" distinguishes "ideologies" from "utopias" according to their function relative to the social status quo, it does not follow Marxism in criticizing ideologies from the utopian perspective of the proletariat. Instead, Mannheim argues that both perspectives may be transcended in the thinking of a third group, namely, "free-floating intellectuals."[20] Since the perspective of this group is determined by an interest in neither preserving nor destroying the status quo, it is ideally situated to adjudicate social conflict in the name of a transcendent reality.

Although Niebuhr credits Mannheim with showing the full

scope of the problem of ideology, he rejects his solution of it. In his view, it is simply ludicrous to think that the perspective of free-floating intellectuals is any less tainted than those of groups more directly involved in social conflict. The problem with Mannheim's analysis is that—like Marx's—it lacks an awareness of the depth of the problem. If the ideological taint is ultimately a matter of sinful pretense, then surely neither intellectual sophistication nor political enthusiasm is an adequate response to it.

Niebuhr's criticisms of Marx and Mannheim, of course, place his own proposal under a formidable burden of proof. What is to guarantee that his "moments of prayerful transcendence" remain exempt from ideological taint and yet still relevant as a perspective for ideological criticism? Niebuhr's answer to this question illustrates the basic strategy of his Christian realism. On the one hand, even if these moments are given a Christian interpretation as they are in *The Nature and Destiny of Man*, there is no guarantee that the theological perspective so constructed can claim to be untainted. Truth, no less than grace, may be held "in principle but not in fact."[21] In short, Niebuhr does not claim an exemption for his own theology. On the other hand, precisely because the function of such moments is primarily existential rather than cognitive, they remain paradoxically relevant as an ultimate foundation for ideological criticism. By touching the "heights and the depths" of the individual, "prayerful transcendence" places personal existence under the scrutiny of prophetic criticism. Since such criticism remains essentially religious, its political relevance is necessarily limited by the degree to which individual politicians and social activists allow themselves to be judged by it.[22] In short, Niebuhr's Christian realism insists on a religious solution to the problem even at the risk of compromising its relevance to social conflict.

By contrast, Juan Luis Segundo's liberation theology risks compromising the religious nature of the solution even while heightening its political relevance. At the heart of his book *The Liberation of Theology* is a bold rethinking of the relationship between "ideologies and faith."[23] Like Niebuhr and Tillich, Segundo takes up this issue as part of an attempt to stake out a position responsive to the challenge of Marxism. In contrast to those who would "de-ideologize" faith by equating the Christian gospel with "a specific political option,"—say, a Marxist understanding of revolutionary praxis

—Segundo argues that "faith" and "ideologies" must be both distinguished and related in a "deutero-learning process." His point, following Mannheim, is that no perspective—least of all either Marxism or Christianity—can raise an absolute claim to truth; that all perspectives are ideological in one way or another; and that the important task is to adopt the ideology most appropriate to the current historical circumstances.[24] Given these assumptions, what is the relationship between faith and ideologies?

Working from a model derived from developmental psychology, Segundo argues, on the one hand, that faith and ideologies are "inextricably intermingled" insofar as "a person lives it (the undifferentiated totality of faith and ideology) *subjectively* as an absolute value"; on the other hand, that they are distinct inasmuch as faith claims to "possess an *objectively* absolute value," while ideology is "grounded in arguments whose value is relative."[25] Once a "crisis" develops, the totality begins to fragment, and either irrational resistance or a mature capacity for ideological change may ensue. Segundo's hope, of course, is to form an "elite of mature Christians," a community of those who, having passed through the crisis, are now able to risk creating new ideologies in order to develop the possibilities implicit in faith.

Not surprisingly, this general conception of ideologies and faith determines his view of Christian theology and its role in the struggle for liberation. What is surprising, however, is the way in which Segundo applies this concept to the traditional norm of theology, namely "biblical revelation." Since "God's revelation never comes to us in pure form, . . . it is always fleshed out in historical ideologies." The religious ideologies of the Bible, in other words, function as a "provisional but necessary . . . bridge between our conception of God and the real-life problems of history." Thus, for example, Israel's policy of exterminating its enemies at the time of the Conquest of Canaan must be regarded as "the ideology that faith adopted" then. Similarly, Jesus' preaching of "freely proffered love and nonresistance to evil" is "another ideology, not . . . the content of faith itself." What, then, is the meaning of Christian faith? According to Segundo, this question may be answered by shifting attention to "the pedagogical intent of the whole scriptural process." Once this is done, it becomes clear that faith itself is "the spirit of *freedom for history, of taste for the future, of openness for the provisional and relative,"* in short a *"freedom for ideologies."* That this understanding of faith is implicit in biblical revelation is evident from Jesus' promise to send the Holy Spirit, which gives ultimate sanction to the "deutero-learning process" going on in the succession of ideologies.[26] What remains normative for Christian theology thus is not the ideological content of Jesus' teaching but the "process of learning how to learn" that he discovered and committed to us as the gift of faith.

While this distinction obviously "gives liberation theology great freedom to move, in principle, through the Scriptures and to work with the faith,"[27] it also places Segundo under a burden of proof of his own. He must show that this theory represents a theologically adequate account of Christian faith. Although he does try to identify his view with Saint Paul's understanding of faith and freedom, the link is so formal as to be less than convincing.[28] Given Segundo's definitions, there is no reason in principle not to speak of the teachings of Jesus as "ideology." But he fails to recognize the way in which even the ideology of Jesus remains normative for substantive Christian faith. By equating Christian faith with a commitment to a strictly formal deutero-learning process, Segundo goes beyond relativizing its content to risking its elimination altogether. Since only "the ideology that faith adopts" is substantive, its content can only emerge from the historical circumstances in which the deutero-learning process goes on. If that is the case, Christian faith may gain new political relevance, but only at the price of its critical role vis-à-vis ideologies.

The practical consequences of the differences between Niebuhr and Segundo may be seen in their diverging interpretations of Christian eschatology. For Niebuhr the Kingdom of God remains a symbol of the paradoxical reality of the grace and truth of Jesus Christ. It serves as a reminder that in history sin is overcome in principle, but not in fact. In other words, it discloses the paradoxical limit of what can and cannot be hoped for in those "moments of prayerful transcendence." As a guide to political thought and action, the Kingdom of God thus communicates a "religious reservation" against the pretensions of social movements of whatever political stripe. It is, in short, the most profound symbol of prophetic criticism as Niebuhr understands it. From Segundo's perspective, however, this religious reservation represents not an ultimate principle of criticism, but one more outmoded Christian ideology. Since it tends "to throw a dash of cold water" on the political enthusiasm necessary for "real-life revolution," it in turn must be relativized by the deutero-learning process. Instead of reading the Kingdom of God as "something metahistorical and a disgusted turning away from real-life history,"[29] Segundo's elite of mature Christians should see it as symbolizing the urgent need to create or adopt new ideologies truly suited to the requirements of real-life revolution. In other words, although Niebuhr and Segundo agree on the practical consequences of this eschatological reservation, the latter denounces these as evidence of outmoded ideology while the former identifies them with the substance of Christian faith.

Such is the impasse between Niebuhr's Christian realism and Segundo's liberation theology. Were their differing approaches merely idiosyncratic, they would be of little interest here. But, in my opinion, this is not the case. Niebuhr's theological interpretation of ideology, or something very like it, stands behind those who fear the "politicization" of Christian faith. Segundo's discovery of a scripturally based deutero-learning process, or something very like it, stands behind those who seek to overcome the "excessive spiritualization" of this same faith. The question thus becomes how Tillich's theory might help resolve the conflict over the nature of practical theology that this impasse represents.

ANALYZING THE IMPASSE

In the role of sympathetic critic, it seems, Tillich would have accused both Niebuhr and Segundo of objectifying prophetic criticism in ways that distort its basic meaning for the social struggle. Niebuhr's emphasis on "moments of prayerful transcendence" unwittingly reduces prophetic criticism to an abstract form of religious transcendence whose impact is limited to the hearts and minds of individuals. As can be inferred from Tillich's important early essay "Protestantism as a Critical and Creative Principle," Niebuhr's religious solution to the problem of ideology is a variation on the "hypostatization of the transcendence of grace"[30] by which Protestantism tradition has failed to measure up to "the unconditional demand" of prophetic criticism. Segundo's identification of the deutero-learning process with "the pedagogical intent" of biblical revelation also objectifies "the unconditional demand," but unlike Niebuhr's it reduces prophetic criticism to an abstract form of political immanence whose impact is no different from that of rational criticism. Segundo's deutero-learning process, in other words, conforms to the pattern which—according to Tillich—results in "the dissolution of the church into the structures of society and the dissolution of religious knowledge into secular knowledge."[31] In short, his objectification of "the transcendence of grace" results not in its hypostatization but in its elimination as a principle of criticism. By failing to address the problem of objectification, so Tillich would argue, the perspectives of both Niebuhr and Segundo unwittingly prove the truth of their mutual accusations. Since only a religious socialism that is truly a "creative synthesis" can resolve this problem, it remains the most promising basis for a practical theology successfully avoiding both politicization and excessive spiritualization.

So far, then, Tillich's framework of analysis allows us to see the impasse between Christian realism and liberation theology as a struggle over the meaning of prophetic criticism. While this certainly confirms the relevance of Tillich's analysis, it hardly establishes the validity of his alternative. To warrant this claim, any "creative synthesis" based on his alternative will have to meet certain criteria:

1. *If it is to be true to the legacy of prophetism, a creative synthesis must truly mediate the form of grace.* While Tillich often expresses this point metaphorically—"The form of grace may be veiled," for example, "but still it must shine through"[32]—it can only mean that a creative synthesis must represent "the unconditional demand" in a manner that is both substantive and nonobjectifiable. Since "the Unconditional" itself is apprehended as a substantive yet nonobjectified reality, its meaning therefore can only be conveyed in a theological language that remains true to this reality; in other words, in a language that strives to be consistently dialectical.

2. *For a creative synthesis to remain truly dialectical, it must be rooted in the proletarian situation.* "Grace is really grace only if it is present." But as Tillich also insists, since "in every living form

[there is] a hidden form of grace that is identical with its power to be,"[33] grace cannot be identified with the church but must be discovered hidden within the culture in which the church itself is "thrown." Since a prophetic understanding of the *Kairos* reveals the hidden form of grace in culture, a creative synthesis therefore must respond to the *Kairos*. But as Tillich everywhere proclaimed in the years prior to his exile, the *Kairos* for his generation is disclosed in the proletarian situation. A creative synthesis therefore will be truly dialectical only to the extent that it remains rooted in it.

3. *A creative synthesis therefore will carry on the agenda of Tillich's religious socialism only to the extent that it succeeds in establishing a dialectical relationship between prophetic criticism and ideologies rooted in the proletarian situation.* Since the *Kairos* discloses the hidden form of grace in the proletarian situation, theological thinking can only be dialectical to the extent that it reflects this reality. How might this be done? The answer may be found in Tillich's analysis of "objectification." Since both prophetic criticism and ideologies, when detached from the proletarian situation, tend to become objectified in forms that stand in antithesis to one another, the truth of both can be saved only by constructing a dialectic between them to serve as the methodological principle for practical theology. Prophetic criticism must therefore function as a limit-language[34] defining the boundaries of ideologies based on rational criticism. As a limit-language, prophetic criticism thus is dialectically related to ideologies to the extent that its own content remains strictly paradoxical.

This is, I trust, a faithful picture of what Tillich was up to in his critique of objectification. Dogmatic Marxism, for example, ceased to reflect the dynamism of "the proletarian situation" when it gave up the flexibility of dialectical thinking for the rigidity of pseudo-scientific dogma. While this pattern of objectification can be broken only by allowing consciousness to remain open to that situation, such openness can be achieved only by recovering an awareness of "the unconditional demand." The point, of course, is that this kind of analysis is applicable not just to dogmatic Marxism, but to any ideology, or for that matter, to any form of rational criticism whatsoever. In short, the critique of objectification succeeds only by reawakening a sense of the limits of rational thought, and in Tillich's view this sense of limit is communicated only by a limit-language that in itself strives to reflect the Unconditional by remaining both substantive and strictly nonobjectifiable.

While no human language can perfectly fulfill this requirement, in Tillich's opinion a creative synthesis based on prophetic criticism comes close. By confronting ideologies with a deliberately paradoxical discourse concerning the concrete mystery of the "whence" that is also the "whither," prophetic criticism functions as such a limit-language. By allowing the awareness of this limit-reality to confront and be confronted by ideologies, prophetic criticism reveals the dynamism of the proletarian situation and thus helps further the unfolding of the socialist principle. Any creative synthesis seeking to avoid both the politicization and the excessive spiritualization of prophetic Christianity, therefore, must construct a limit-language whose function is dialectical even as its referent remains paradoxical. Tillich's religious socialism and the systematic theology that eventually grew out of it were, I believe, an attempt to construct just such a language.

THE TASK AHEAD

I wish I could conclude this essay by stating my firm conviction that Tillich's strategy succeeded in his day and indeed still has promise in our own; but I find myself stymied in several ways. Let me close, then, by stating my reservations and showing what they may mean. They are of two kinds, but interrelated.

The first set of difficulties is *existential*. The problem here is what, after all, is the basis for the decision that Tillich demands we make? From whatever angle I approach it, the answer always depends on Tillich's sense of the *Kairos*. In light of the *Kairos* religious socialism discovers the form of grace in the proletarian situation. But what is the *Kairos* but Tillich's own deeply personal discernment of history's meaning? Moreover, can Tillich's personal authority provide a sufficient warrant for making "the socialist decision"? The difficulty for me becomes even more pressing when I consider the subsequent fluctuation in Tillich's sense of the *Kairos*. Since his theology reflects "a deepening 'sacred void' of waiting" in the years after World War II,[35] apparently I am asked to accept this passing of the *Kairos* once again on the strength of Tillich's personal authority. What I find distressing about his pronouncements on the *Kairos* over the years is their oracular quality. I am stymied, in short, not because I assume that existential decisions should be so tightly argued as to be virtually risk-free; but because Tillich's use of the *Kairos* principle remains just too intuitive to provide much help in checking the reasonableness of "the unconditional demand" mediated through it.[36]

The second set of difficulties, while *theoretical*, directly follows from the first. Even though Tillich's use of the *Kairos* principle is consistent with his concept of a religious limit-language whose paradoxes dialectically overcome the patterns of objectification, the theoretical problem is whether and to what extent even a religious limit-language actually succeeds in doing this. Given the limits of any human language, it would seem that the requirement of being both substantive and nonobjectified actually presents us with a dilemma. If theology is to be substantive, it inevitably produces "dogma" and therefore is subject to all the problems of objectification. If it is to remain nonobjectified, it is difficult to see how it can communicate anything substantive. My guess is that Tillich was well aware of this dilemma, and tried to show how it might be overcome in a consistently paradoxical theology. He sought, in short, to safeguard the transcendence of the Unconditional even while affirming its historic immanence in religious symbols and social movements.[37]

Nevertheless, what remains unsaid in Tillich's theology may provide the real clue for understanding his response to this dilemma. For Tillich's theology is based ultimately on a personal religious vision of great power and originality. This vision, however, both is and is not Christian in a traditional sense. But neither is it nor is it not Marxist in a traditional sense. It is, as he often hinted, more closely related to the subterranean tradition of the "coincidence of opposites." Ultimately, Tillich's vision stands in the line of Jakob Böhme and Nicholas of Cusa, but unlike their vision, his emerged as a religious horizon for the counterculture of German expressionism. This, at any rate, is the context in which his religious limit-language must be understood. While it may account for the authority and power of Tillich's creative synthesis in his own time, it also suggests that its usefulness may be limited in our own.[38]

So I must conclude by being as tentative about Tillich as Tillich was about Troeltsch. What we have seen is that Tillich's theology was all that he promised it would be. It did emerge from a religious vision "beyond religion," and thus did ground the meaning of history in a way that was strikingly responsive to "the breakthrough of the Unconditional" in the proletarian situation. In short, Tillich's religious socialism was in fact the creative synthesis that he himself had prophesied. But this creative synthesis remains existentially rooted in Tillich's personal religious vision and theoretically grounded in his distinctive theory of religious language. Because these depend so deeply on what remains unsaid in the mystery of Tillich's own being and its relationship to the esoteric culture which nurtured it, they are not so easily detached and deployed as a model for practical theology. Ironically, then, Tillich's creative synthesis remains as much a personal statement as does Troeltsch's. Its relevance to the 1980s may be limited by our willingness and ability to enter into his personal religious vision and make it our own.

NOTES

1. Paul Tillich, "Ernst Troeltsch: Versuch einer geistesgeschichtlichen Würdigung," *Kantstudien* 29 (1924): 351–58.
2. Ibid., 357, 355.
3. Ibid., 355.
4. Paul Tillich, *The Socialist Decision,* trans. Franklin Sherman (New York: Harper & Row, 1977), xxxi, 129.
5. Ibid., 2.
6. Ibid., 4.
7. Ibid., 5.
8. Ibid., 10.
9. Ibid., 100, 101.
10. Ibid., 20.
11. Prophetic and rational criticism are similar insofar as the attempt to read Marxism as a speculative philosophy of history is a secular form of "otherworldly spirituality," and the attempt to turn it into a set of slogans to justify the spirit of militant activism is a secular form of "abstract moralizing."
12. Tillich, *The Socialist Decision,* 107.
13. Ibid., 124–25, 115, 119, 118.
14. Ibid., 117.
15. Ibid., 123.
16. Niebuhr's debt to Tillich is explicitly acknowledged in the preface to his book,

An Interpretation of Christian Ethics (New York: Harper & Brothers, 1935). It is significant that in this book Niebuhr gives clearest and most systematic expression to the "mythical method of interpretation" that was to provide the foundation for his Christian realism.

17. For a reconstruction of Niebuhr's theological anthropology, see Dennis P. McCann, *Christian Realism and Liberation Theology: Practical Theologies in Creative Conflict* (Maryknoll, N.Y.: Orbis Books, 1981), especially chap. 3.

18. Reinhold Niebuhr, *The Nature and Destiny of Man*, vol. 2 (New York: Charles Scribner's Sons, 1943), 217. Niebuhr contrasts his formulation with the one presented by Tillich in *The Interpretation of History*, trans. N. A. Rasetzki and Elsa L. Talmey (New York: Charles Scribner's Sons, 1936). According to Niebuhr, Tillich's understanding of "the relation of knowledge to the Unconditioned" holds out the possibility of a "formal transcendence over the ambiguity of all historical truth." Niebuhr's appeal to "moments of prayerful transcendence" claims to go deeper than Tillich's "philosophical formulation of this reality" by illuminating the roots of the problem of ideology as sinful "pretense." Given Tillich's religious understanding of "the Unconditioned," it seems that Niebuhr's interpretation unfairly minimizes the significance of Tillich's position. His, too, points toward a religious solution to the problem of ideology, but his discussion of this solution concentrates on the formal conditions of its possible relevance to epistemology. See Tillich's essay "Kairos and Logos," in *The Interpretation of History*.

19. Reinhold Niebuhr, *The Nature and Destiny of Man*, vol. 1 (1941), 197.

20. Karl Mannheim, *Ideology and Utopia*, trans. Louis Wirth and Edward Shils (New York: Harcourt, Brace and World, 1936), 156–64.

21. Niebuhr, *The Nature and Destiny of Man*, vol. 2 (1943), 214–20.

22. In showing the limitations of Niebuhr's position, I do not mean to dismiss it. As I have argued in chapter 4 of *Christian Realism and Liberation Theology*, Niebuhr's "Christian interpretation" of ideology provides one element in a "dispositional ethic for politicians." While it is of limited use in adjudicating the theoretical claims of conflicting ideologies, it may still be indispensable for addressing the existential difficulties of politicians and social activists locked in such conflicts.

23. Juan Luis Segundo, *The Liberation of Theology*, trans. John Drury (Maryknoll, N.Y.: Orbis Books, 1976), 97–124.

24. Ibid., 100.

25. Ibid., 107.

26. Ibid., 116, 110, 121.

27. Ibid., 117.

28. Ibid., 121–22. Given his theory of the deutero-learning process, the burden of proof for Segundo involves developing a plausible interpretation of the substantive content of Christian faith. In doing this, he is forced to make wildly improbable claims: For example, the declarations of the Council of Chalcedon concerning the hypostatic union of the human and divine natures in Christ are "essentially methodological symbols" of the relationship of faith and ideologies in this process. Ibid., 108–9. If Segundo means what he says, he may have to enlighten us further on how his views may be reconciled, among other things, with traditional Catholic Christology.

29. Ibid., 145, 147.

30. Paul Tillich, *Political Expectation*, trans. and ed. James Luther Adams (New York: Harper & Row, 1971), 18.

31. Ibid., 36.

32. Ibid., 35.

33. Ibid., 30, 28.

34. I am using the term *limit-language* in the sense given it in David Tracy's seminal work *Blessed Rage for Order* (New York: Seabury Press, 1975), 91–118. There Tracy, following Clifford Geertz, speculates that in general religion is expressive of certain "limits-to" our ordinary experience (for example, finitude, contingency, or radical transience) and disclosive of certain fundamental structures of our existence beyond (or alternatively, grounding to) that ordinary experience (for example, our fundamental trust in the worthwhileness of existence, our basic belief in order and value). Ibid., 93. Religious limit-language discloses these limits-to by pointing to limit-situations that raise limit-questions. Theologies seek to address these limit-questions by formulating theoretical limit concepts. In Tillich's hands, prophetic criticism is a limit-language insofar as it discloses the limits-to all objectification in theory and in praxis. Tillich's theological claim—which, of course, can be disputed—is that prophetic criticism is uniquely capable of disclosing these limits-to theory and praxis.

35. Paul Tillich, "Beyond Religious Socialism," *The Christian Century* 66 (1949): 732–33.

36. In criticizing the *Kairos* principle, I am not ignoring the massive work of theological and cultural analysis that Tillich produced in support of his decision. Tillich's brilliant early work *The Religious Situation* (1932) is typical of such analyses; and, of course, *The Socialist Decision* itself is inspired by his sense of the *Kairos*. My point is not that these analyses are inconsequential but that—as far as I can tell—they always already presuppose the truth of Tillich's perception of the *Kairos*. In other words, he not so much infers the presence of the *Kairos* from these analyses as he presupposes the presence of the *Kairos* as a principle for interpreting them. As a result, although he does provide a general theology of history in which *Kairoi* are to be expected, he does not provide an argument for regarding any particular situation as a *Kairos* apart from his own "prophetic" sense of the present moment. In my opinion, while Tillich's view of the *Kairos* is consistent with his concern to avoid objectification in both theology and critical social theory, its apparently decisionistic implications strike me as problematic both for theory and for praxis.

37. The dilemma that I have tried to outline corroborates many of the points made in Malcolm Diamond's sympathetic yet critical analysis of Tillich's theology, *Contemporary Philosophy and Religious Thought: An Introduction to the Philosophy of Religion* (New York: McGraw Hill, 1974), 301–89. What I describe here as the problem of "objectification" requiring a paradoxical religious limit-language for its solution corresponds to Diamond's insistence that Tillich sought to transcend "the subject-object distinction" by developing a religious use of "ecstatic reason" that itself remains open to "existential verification." While my analysis has been focused almost exclusively on Tillich's early political writings and Diamond's analysis on his later systematic theology, it is clear—to me, at least—that Diamond's reservations about Tillich's inability to show how religious symbols can legitimately convey anything meaningful about "being-itself" parallels my own reservations about the *Kairos* principle and its relationship to the Unconditional. In both cases the problem is whether Tillich's proposal succeeds in overcoming objectification, and if so, at what price to his constructive theological intention as a whole. Where Diamond and I

differ is in our speculations concerning how that price is to be paid. Diamond sees Tillich achieving consistency by falling into an "existential humanism" that is atheistic in its theoretical structure. I see Tillich achieving consistency by requiring initiation into the esoteric mystical tradition of the "coincidence of opposites." In my view, Tillich was unable to see the allegedly atheistic structure of his own thought, not because he was seduced by the "bombastic" quality of his own language, but because his language did actually mediate what was for him and for many of his disciples a genuinely religious experience. If I am right, then the terrible price exacted by Tillich's solution is the necessarily ineffable character of the insights of that mystical tradition: If the solution to the problem of objectification in both religious and political ideologies requires a mystical apprehension of "the coincidence of opposites," then the prospects for theology as public discourse are bleak indeed. Be that as it may, the point is that my disenchantment with the oracular quality of the *Kairos* principle follows directly from this interpretation of Tillich's response to the dilemma posed by a "prophetic criticism" of objectification.

38. My skepticism in no way is intended as a dismissal of the culture of German expressionism. It does, however, reflect a sense of the enormous difficulty in moving from an expressionistic style in thought and action to the kind of public discourse needed in a rational adjudication of questions of theory and praxis. My sense of the problem is informed by studies analyzing the strengths and limitations of the Frankfurt School's critical social theory. Jürgen Habermas has attempted to develop critical theory as a form of public discourse, but he has been able to do so only by breaking with the style of thinking and acting characteristic of the founders of the Frankfurt School, Max Horkheimer and Theodor W. Adorno. Something similar to Habermas's attempt would have to be made with Tillich's religious socialism before it could overcome the difficulties I have tried to outline here. For background on Habermas and the Frankfurt School, see Martin Jay, *The Dialectical Imagination: A History of the Frankfurt School and the Institute of Social Research, 1923–1950* (Boston: Little, Brown and Co., 1973); and Thomas McCarthy, *The Critical Theory of Jürgen Habermas* (Cambridge, Mass.: MIT Press, 1978).

6. Tillich and Depth Psychology

WILLIAM R. ROGERS

Perhaps the two most critical questions in depth psychology are "How can we appropriately understand the complex and often inaccessible dynamic interactions that occur beneath the conscious surface in psychological life, affecting behavior, memory, belief, symbolization, and interpersonal entanglements?" and "How can we utilize the interpersonal dynamics of therapeutic relationships to enable a new, more aware, and 'freer' (less distorted and defensively bound) mode of human existence?"

Attempts to elaborate answers to such questions through methods of analysis and intervention, especially in the clinical work of Freud and Jung early in this century, gave rise to intriguing, profound, and useful psychodynamic theory. That theory—with its view of fundamental opposition in the "depth" structure of motivation and its articulation of defense mechanisms like repression, projection, illusion, displacement, and transference—illuminated an infrastructure to explain the unwitting alterations of the contents of consciousness, the manifest imagery of dreams, the form of social rituals, the structures of perception, and even the character of religious belief. As such it had enormous impact on Christian theology, and not least on the thinking of Paul Tillich.

But while many religious thinkers were suspicious and apprehensive about the psychological assertions emerging from depth psychology, Tillich, almost from the very beginning, welcomed them. Others had felt offended at the psychoanalytic claims that religious belief and practice might be no more than the internally constructed and self-protecting product of wishes, obsessions, projections, and illusions, unconsciously framed as a defense against the inevitable losses, ambiguities, and insecurities of life— especially life experienced as lonely and helpless. When this critique of religion was reduced to matters of transference and unresolved oedipal strivings, the matter seemed even more offensive.

Yet Tillich was quick to realize that the discoveries concerning the workings of the unconscious could aid, not simply threaten, the theological analysis of the ambiguities of existence. Psychoanalysis, both as method and as emerging theory, could help uncover the forms of self-deception, the unacknowledged ruthlessness of tyrannical social programs concealed by pseudoreligious justifications, and the apparently ironic intermingling of faith and doubt even in authentic religious experience. Indeed dynamic psychologies joined hands with theology, and for that matter with Marxism, in unmasking hidden levels of reality. Tillich makes this point clearly in *On The Boundary,* and he acknowledges our resistance against such painful revelations of hidden complexities of reality. Yet, "without this painful process the ultimate meaning of the Christian gospel cannot be perceived. The theologian, therefore, should use these means for exposing the true condition of man as often as he can rather than propagating an idealism that smooths over the ambiguities of existence."[1]

THEOLOGICAL STRUCTURE AND OPENNESS TO PSYCHOLOGY

The theological structure that provided his early methodological openness to psychological thought was set at Halle (1905–07). Tillich comments: "One thing we learned above all was that Protestant theology is by no means obsolete, but that it can, without losing its Christian foundation, incorporate strictly scientific methods, a critical philosophy, a realistic understanding of men and society, and powerful ethical principles and motives."[2] Not only did his studies reflect a significant dialogue among humanistic and social scientific disciplines, but also his circle of friends included many in the arts, in philosophy, and in psychology.

When he began to teach in 1919 at the University of Berlin as a *privatdocent,* he reports, "I lectured on subjects which included the relation of religion to politics, art, philosophy, depth psychology, and sociology."[3] And he began to develop a "theology of culture" that tried to interweave the theological notions with psychological and sociological analyses. Tillich describes himself as being caught up in the social upheavals of the 1920s in which he was particularly interested in learning more about what the psychological forces were that motivated people. This was a period when the collapse of the social structure led to strong experiences of disillusionment; when relationships with respect to authority, education, families, sex, and friendship were in creative chaos. But the chaos could easily take on demonic form. For hungry and lost people are not very discriminating about the sources of their food; and totalitarian capitulation was precisely the spectre that Tillich feared. In this context, "psychoanalytic ideas spread and produced a consciousness of realities which had been carefully repressed in previous generations. The participation in these movements created manifold problems, conflicts, fears, expectations, ecstasies, and despairs, practically as well as theoretically."[4] It was a time of upheaval, a time of malaise, a time of emptiness, a time of longing, a time haunted by the sense of not being able to see yet what would emerge, a time of hollowness. The '20s were also times of personal struggle: Tillich's sister died, he divorced his first wife, and he married Hannah Werner in 1924. Into all this came the urgent need to integrate political, ethical, and psychological analyses with his theological perspective.

When Tillich was forced to leave Germany and invited to begin a new life in New York City in 1933, his associations with psychological colleagues increased. He came to state very boldly the necessity for interaction with depth psychology:

For external and practical reasons it became impossible to maintain the relationship to artists, poets, and writers which I enjoyed in postwar Germany. But I have been in permanent contact with the depth-psychology movement and with many of its representatives, especially in the last ten years. The problem of the relation between the theological and the psychotherapeutic understanding of men has come more and more into the foreground of my interest, partly through a university seminar on religion and health at Columbia University, partly through the great practical and theoretical interest that depth psychology has aroused in Union Seminary, and partly through personal friendship with older and younger analysts and counselors. I do not think that it is possible today to elaborate a Christian doctrine of man, and especially a Christian doctrine of the Christian man, without using the immense material brought forth by depth psychology.[5]

Now, who were these older and younger psychologists and psychotherapists? Even before coming to America, Tillich had been influenced by his childhood friend Eckart von Sydow, who introduced him to the writings of Freud in 1912.[6] Tillich had read Rilke partly because of what he saw as a "profound psychoanalytic realism." He had also been intrigued by the psychoanalysts Kurt Volstein and Heinrich Goesch. Goesch had been a house guest and later gave Tillich a partial analysis. Tillich also experienced a brief and incomplete series of analytic sessions with Christian Hermann during the time that Hermann was lodging in Tillich's Berlin apartment.[7]

In New York, Tillich formed what was called the "New York Psychology Group," meeting for the first time just two days before Pearl Harbor, December 5, 1941 and running until 1945. This group was made up of Ruth Benedict, Erich Fromm, Rollo May, David Roberts (teaching religion and psychiatry at Union Seminary in New York), Seward Hiltner, Francis Whits (a Jungian analyst), John Everett (a theological student), and Goddard Booth (working in psychosomatic medicine), as well as Hannah Tillich. Also into that group came temporarily people like Henry Bane (psychoanalyst), Elined Kotschnig and Violet de Laszio (Jungians), and Ernest Schachtel (doing his early work with Rorschach testing). They organized a series of seminars on the psychology of faith in 1942, the psychology of love in 1942–43, the psychology of conscience in 1943–44, and the psychology of help in 1944–45.[8]

Several themes seem to have particularly fascinated Tillich in these discussions. One was the respect for detail and immediacy in the understanding of experiences of transition and transformation in therapy, detail that seemed to deepen traditional categories of salvation and redemption. The movement from despair and meaninglessness was well documented by his clinical colleagues— though not sufficiently so, in Tillich's judgment, for they failed to take into account the full context of ontological anxiety and hope. Another theme of importance included the erotic, a reality that Tillich saw in earlier religious sensibilities, but which had been "lost, relegated to a forgotten truth," in Christian theology. Both its demonic and creative possibilities were important to Tillich, and came to be elaborated further on the basis of psychoanalytic insights.[9] Tillich also explored the functions of guilt and the confessional, making important critiques of both the intellectual and routinized religious practices, and the temporal and ontologial limitations of psychoanalytic "confessions." The latter might alleviate internal and psychodynamic conflict, minimizing the power of the superego, but fail to deal with the sense of lostness or isolation of the self from that which transcends temporal existence.

Above all, Tillich was appreciative of the way the depth psychologists attempted consistently to probe beneath the surface of reality, even though this might be a painful pilgrimage. The process of moving through suffering, ambiguity, darkness, and denial was essential, Tillich realized, to both effective psychotherapy and the journey of faith. The experience of negation and the confrontation with the void seemed essential to a reintegration with the "spiritual presence." Only on the far side of such experiences, he sensed, could one genuinely know the "power of being, taking nonbeing into itself without being overwhelmed by it." This reality was attested to historically as central to Christianity, but reexperienced with integrity in what he came to call "radical faith"— faith not yet packed with explicit belief content, but consisting of profound trust, acknowledgment, and gratitude for having been brought through the "dark night of the soul."[10]

It was precisely these broader reaches of "ultimate concern" that Tillich felt were not taken seriously enough by his psychological colleagues. True, they helped unmask the ambiguities of existence; but they gave little help in understanding the essential fullness of creative intention in human possibility or the ultimate ground of transforming power by which even therapeutic change occurred. And it was to such theological and ontological questions that Tillich gave increasing attention.

Having identified some of the sources of influence from depth psychology on Tillich's thought, it now becomes our more important task to trace some of the lines of impact that Tillich himself had, and could have, on contemporary psychological developments. In fact it could be argued that of all the areas of cultural influence stemming from Tillich's work, the area of psychology and psychotherapeutic practice has been the one most seriously and profoundly affected.

This could be demonstrated in two ways: one, through the range of major psychological thinkers, movements, institutes, and publications that reflect serious engagement with his thought; and the other, through an enumeration of some of the salient ideas themselves that hold significance for the psychological disciplines.

THE SCOPE OF TILLICH'S INFLUENCE ON PSYCHOLOGY

It is not an exaggeration to assert that Tillich has influenced major psychological theorists in Europe and America across nearly the entire spectrum of "schools of thought." Particularly among the depth psychologists—psychoanalysts, neo-Freudians, (Jungian) analytic psychologists, and object-relations psychologists—has his work been important. But it also resonates through substantial groups of humanistic, existential, phenomenological, and what might be called interdisciplinary or "boundary" psychologists.

Within psychoanalysis, Tillich's work has been especially influential on people like Rollo May, Karen Horney, Erich Fromm, Erik Erikson, Robert Lifton, and Hannah Arendt. His insistence on plumbing the most profound spiritual depths of malaise, on looking searchingly into the experiences of despair and anomie that often pervade the most complex intrapsychic dynamics, pushed these psychoanalysts to see their clients in a new perspective. His careful distinction between neurotic anxiety and ontic anxiety pressed their understanding of psychopathology beyond an analysis of topographic tensions in the id-ego-superego structure, or "alarm bell" mechanisms, or even the unsuccessful self-deceits of idealized and protective self-images. It moved toward a view of the fundamental and universal threat of nonbeing itself—an anxiety not only irremovable but also potentially constructive, insofar as it may raise the most ultimate questions of meaning. Rollo May explores such issues most specifically in *The Meaning of Anxiety,* as well as in his later work on *Existence.* [11]

In *Existence,* May also demonstrates the influence of Tillich's thought on guilt, for it became increasingly inadequate to locate guilt as simply a product of infantile introjections of social constraints via the mechanisms of the superego. Just as the analysts came to see the ramifications of "ontic" anxiety, so they came to see the depth of "ontic" guilt—a discomforting awareness of the violation of potentialities for being, both in the self and in one's relations to others and to nature. Manipulation, projection, defensive ego structures, and even depressive reactions could be seen as veiled, and for the most part unconstructive, efforts to deal with a primary sense of broken fidelity to the ultimate ground and potentiality of being.

Tillich also questioned the primarily individualistic orientations of the analysts, challenging them to take up the profound social questions implied in his root ontological principle of the "self-world correlation." The self can never be understood in itself, but only in dynamic interaction with a "world"—especially a world of significant others. Perhaps Erich Fromm can be seen as working most explicitly with this theme, both in his direct study of *Psychoanalysis and Religion* and in his explicit social analysis, *The Sane Society.* [12]

More recently this subject-object dimension of psychological development, held as Tillich would have insisted within a deeper context of relationship, has been expanded by the "object-relations theorists" Harry Guntrip, D. W. Winnicott, W. R. D. Fairbairn, John Bowlby, and Ana-Maria Rizzuto. The fact that both Guntrip and Rizzuto come at this theory not only with attention to clinical issues but also with explicit training and concern for theological questions deepens their analysis of attachment, separation, and internal representations of God as these develop amid the context of early human relationships.

Tillich was, of course, especially concerned about broader cultural issues, especially the breakdown of a cultural context that might support symbolically as well as institutionally the affirmation of a meaningful center of existence. The tragedies of post–World War I Germany had shown all too vividly the precarious temptations of both anarchy and totalitarianism that exist when a coherent cultural and religious system has been shattered. Tillich used as a psychological metaphor that hunger which lures anxious men and women to lunge uncritically at any morsels of coherent hope, even when the forms in which they appear may be as tyrannical and dehumanizing as Nazi power and the myth of Aryan supremacy.

This perspective, especially coupled with a psychoanalytic view of the drive toward ego identity, the defensive concealment of aggressive impulses, and the tendency toward displacement and transference in affective relationships (particularly toward authority figures), can be seen as influencing conjointly some aspects of so-called "Critical Theory" in the "Frankfurt School." Certainly Tillich's theory of culture seems to be reflected in the Frankfurt method of examining the "secret" (ultimate concerns) lying beneath the specific forms, policies, and images of a given society, rather than superficially amassing a cluster of fragmented "facts" in attempting to portray what either society or individuals were about.[13]

Tillich's influence on Erik Erikson also involved social as well as individual theological sensitivities. The importance of dealing with questions of ultimate concern emerged as a very explicit aspect of Erikson's culminating "life stage" of "ego-integrity vs. despair." Without coming to terms with ultimate questions, Erikson pointed out, we are in danger of a psychological collapse before the final acknowledgment of death. We are in danger, as well, of failing in the task of each generation to provide guidelines of meaning and security to the next: "For if there is any responsibility in the human cycle of life it must be that one generation gives to the next that strength by which it can come to face ultimate concerns in its own way—unmarred by debilitating poverty or by neurotic concerns caused by emotional exploitation."[14]

Clearly Erikson's interest in virtues like basic trust, identity, love, and care, as well as his conception of "homo religiosus," was deeply influenced by Tillich. The overcoming of estrangement or the "power to unite what has been separated" pervades Erikson's sensibilities. And as Robert Coles points out, Erikson, like Tillich, stood self-consciously "on the boundary," transcending an age, a nation, and a discipline with gracious and profound vision: "Both men made a home out of boundaries, and in the course of doing so, edged rather close to a new one, the kind that separates intelligent scholars from particularly inspired intellectual and spiritual leaders—in Gabriel Marcel's words 'vivifying minds.' "[15]

In a similar vein, the psychiatric work of Robert Lifton also reflects the influence of Tillich, as well as of Erikson. Lifton's concern with unraveling the dynamic complex of suffering in "survivors"; his sensitivity to the interpretation of global ethical issues; his concern with matters of personal bafflement, numbing, and growth; and most especially his attention to the powerful symbolic components of the culture and of the construction of the "self"— all reveal elements of an ontological and therapeutic perspective that carries the mark of Tillich.[16]

Beyond these psychoanalytic developments, Tillich's thought has also been deeply intertwined with that of the Jungian analytic therapists. Ann Ulanov, in chapter 7 of this volume, details components of that relationship, but any review of Tillich and depth psychology would be remiss not to allude to such an important connection. It is remarkable to trace not only the specific parallel elements of thought between Jung and Tillich—for instance the archetypal character of symbolic forms, the basic categories of the individual and the collective, the functions of the demonic shadow, and the trust in ecstatic experiences of the power of being—but also to recognize the fundamental similarities of their *structure* of thought. Both have a profound confidence in the refinement of a dialectical method that looks at elements in opposition and moves subtly back and forth in approaching a higher truth. For Tillich this is termed the "method of correlation"; for Jung it is the principle of "enantiodromia." In both it is a weaving of the subject and object, the existential and essential, the question and answer, the mundane and the sacred, the particular and the eternal. For both, the ontological character of all reality, especially the reality of brokenness and suffering in human experience, is never to be denied. And for both there is an ultimate trust in a transcending unity.

While Tillich seems to have drawn upon Jung in some areas, particularly the ideas of symbolic form, his own ontological work had a clear influence in return on Jung's followers. See for instance James Hillman on the structure of Being and the nature of the soul, or June Singer on the character and context of the soul.[17]

There are other people working on the boundary of psychology and theology who have given explicit attention to their rootage in Tillich on the one hand and Freud and Jung on the other: Peter Homans, Ira Progoff, Ernest Becker.[18]

Within the more existentialist, phenomenological, and humanistic traditions in psychology, Tillich's influence has been felt by European figures such as Ludwig Binswanger, Medard Boss, and Victor Frankl; and by American writers such as Adrian Van Kaam and Carl Rogers.[19]

The "boundary" writers to whom I refer include a significant group of persons who have worked self-consciously on the boundary between psychology and theology, influenced not only by the content but also by the correlational method of Tillich.

Preeminent in this group are the late Seward Hiltner and Paul Pruyser. Responding especially to issues of psychoanalysis, these men have vigorously explored the ramifications of a "dynamic" psychology, with convincing insights into the clinical process itself as well as into the theoretical dialogue between disciplines. Hiltner's work in particular, growing out of experiences with Tillich's New York Psychology Group and practical engagement as Director of the Council for Clinical Training, came to fruition in his clear leadership of the American pastoral psychology movement—a leadership that showed unmistakable marks of Tillich's exploration of the ambiguities of faith, the suspicion of easy explanations of redemptive transformation, and the affirmation of a legitimate theological method arising from the "questions" implicit in existental and therapeutic contexts. A careful examination of the *structure* of major works by Hiltner *(Preface to Pastoral Theology* and *Theological Dynamics)*[20] also shows the subtle influence of Tillich's insistence on fundamental categories that are capable of sustaining *systematic* formulation of theory in relation to the history and structure of knowledge, as well as in relation to the dynamic subtleties of lived experience. The same impressive structural and epistemological capabilities are evident in Paul Pruyser's *A Dynamic Psychology of Religion.*[21]

The work of such psychologist-theologians has also spawned an important second and third generation of influence from Tillich. This is especially evident in the work of Peter Homans, Donald Browning, Leroy Aden, and myself; as well as more recently in the thought and clinical experience of people like Donald Capps, Judith Van Herik, Roger Johnson, Walter Lowe, Lucy Bregman, and David Barnard.

In addition to his influence on individual psychologists, Tillich also had an impact on the functioning of several important institutions and journals dedicated to psychological theory and practice. Among these were the William Alanson White Institute in New York and the Menninger Foundation in Topeka, Kansas. His intellectual influence is seen in the journals of *Psychiatry, Orthopsychiatry, Pastoral Psychology,* the *Journal of Pastoral Care,* and the *Bulletin of the Menninger Clinic.*

TILLICH AND A CONSTRUCTIVE THEORY OF PSYCHOTHERAPY

Beyond citations of specific psychological thinkers and institutions whom Tillich has influenced, we need to move to a constructive indication of the emerging psychological theory that may be further broadened in the light of his thought. What follows is a series of suggestive directions that such expanded work might take. Depth psychology has grown from, and given form to, the psychotherapeutic experience. Most of these comments will bear on that experience.

CENTEREDNESS VERSUS ANNIHILATING OPENNESS

Essential to the traditional task of therapy has been a process of liberating individuals from psychodynamic (and social) constraints that have "bound" their energy, constricted perception, and unconsciously dominated behavior. Psychotherapy has typically involved the unpacking of a complex and often hidden cargo of repressed memories and attachments—a bringing to consciousness of denied and sometimes baffling intrapsychic realities that had effectively "closed" the person off from meaningful relationships and creative living. Such closure has often been seen as connected to provincial ideas, beliefs, and rituals. At times it has been viewed as simply a succumbing to the tyrannies of unexamined, and often traumatic, events and relationships, repeated unsuccessfully because of their inaccessibility to awareness. In any event, the therapeutic effort was designed to "open" the individual both to the reality of the self and to the complexity of the world.

As such, the therapeutic endeavor has been not unlike the challenges of a religious awakening or, indeed, the goals of a liberal education. In each there has been concern to overcome narrow bias and blindness, and to enhance possibilities of new vision, variety, and possibility.

But while such an aim has been laudable for many in the past, we seem to be in a period now when the vast majority of people, in the Western world at least, are not so much "bound" by narrow beliefs and attachments, but rather lost within an overwhelming vagueness and lack of commitment to any ideal or relationship.

The modern problem, as Tillich so well described it, may have far more to do with the threat of annihilating openness than with the constraints of a narrow closedness. We appear to be open to all manner of belief systems, all manner of child-rearing practices (including frequent abandonment), all manner of sexual expression, all manner of consumer appeals, all manner of political thought, all manner of expression in the arts. Toleration is carried to a relativistic and listless fault. There are no cultural heroes.

There is distrust of "the system." There are no compelling goals. As Philip Rieff puts it: "We can live freely at last, enjoying all our senses—except the sense of the past—as unremembering, honest, and friendly barbarians will, in a technological Eden."[22]

A psychotherapy that sees its major goal as "opening" persons to experience may falter seriously in attempting to help in such a predicament. Instead, it might even tragically exacerbate the very problems of anxiety and helplessness in the face of annhilating openness.

What is needed is a psychotherapeutic understanding and mode of relationship that gives as much attention to the formation of meaning and "centeredness" as to analyzing the fragmentation and tyrannies of the past. What is needed is a sense of that spiritual center that can hold personal reality in focus and can inspire a sense of purposive dedication. True, we do need to respond to the pain and bewilderment of people whose lives seem utterly ungrounded, floating, dislocated. And we need to do so empathetically. But Tillich helps us see how the therapist must also be ready to stand beside clients (and friends) in awe of the power of reintegration, which brings with it a sense of direction and destiny. And ironically such emergent centeredness is often experienced as the enabling of a more profound freedom.[23]

SEPARATION VERSUS REUNIFICATION

A major strand of this thought in Tillich has to do with his characterization of the fundamental life processes. These processes, he argued, are always marked by movement from centeredness, through self-alteration, and toward return.[24] The notion of centeredness entails a dynamic movement between integration and disintegration—a dynamic that is elaborated by aspects of depth psychology that speak of chaotic and disruptive unconscious forces violating and confounding the psychic economy, as well as of forces moving toward ego identity. The idea of a synthesizing movement toward identity (centeredness) finds particular expression in Allport's concepts of integration and "propriate striving."[25]

But the connection of "self-alteration" and the psychotherapeutic process has not been thoughtfully developed, and it could well be. For in the therapeutic relationship itself there is a "going out" from the self in which the client relinquishes the safety (and rigidity) of previous forms of self-concealment and enters imaginatively into an altered perspective on reality and personal history. Furthermore, the dangers of resistance, over-identification, or an "unresolved transference" that could inhibit the therapeutic effectiveness of the relationship could also be understood more deeply in the light of Tillich's perspective on the self as alienated from itself—or as merged with a "world" in such a way as to be incapable of "returning" through a new (redeeming) process of self-transformation.

This aspect of return, furthermore, has more layers of significance than merely the "working through of the transference" and a thrust toward a more viable self-identity. Looked at from Tillich's perspective, this dimension of therapy could be seen by the psychologist as a more essential reestablishment of one's total ontological connectedness. That is, the ends of therapy go beyond analytical and self-conscious existence, beyond *"leben und arbeiten,"* even beyond a stable formation of ego identity, to a recovery of a sense of participation in essential unity. Tillich would call this a "reunion with the ultimate."

Just as Tillich's own categories of "life process" take their character from his perception of a movement beyond the ambiguities of existence made possible by an essential "groundedness" in the structure of Being, so that realization may have both interpretive and practical force in the work of the psychotherapist. Indeed, without that sort of essential confidence it is hard to see how a therapist could long endure in the courage to face the apparently overwhelming forms of despair, separation, and incompleteness that so often are presented in therapy. The "power of Being" is truly revealed in those forms of transformation by which reunification is enabled both in personal life and in the ultimate context.

AUTHENTICITY VERSUS CERTAINTY

One of the most critical debates in contemporary psychology is between those whose primary interest is in precision and certainty in the formulation of psychological knowledge versus those who strive for modes of understanding that have fullness and authenticity in relation to the lived struggles and meanings of human experience. On the one side there is concern for scientific rigor, exactness of measurement, elegance of research design, control of subjects, quantifiable data, and replicable procedures. On the other side there is concern for naturalistic settings, holistic data, ecological validity, open discovery, and human communicability. Stated in terms of traditional positions in scientific inquiry, this tension between the demands for certainty and the desire for authenticity can be identified as the debate between claims for internal validity versus the need for external validity.

Psychology had a difficult battle in the twentieth century, attempting to take a legitimate place alongside the "hard" sciences. In part that was a battle to overcome the general and hypothetical character of some of the clinically based theories that had grown especially out of depth psychology. It is little wonder that beleaguered researchers in the emerging experimental areas of psychology tried to define their terms with greater exactness, to isolate dependent variables, and to study behavior under controlled conditions.

But the desire for certainty, even as it has begun to influence clinical research, may have gone too far. The problem is well stated by Bronfenbrenner:

Especially in recent decades, research in human development has pursued a divided course, with each direction tangential to genuine scientific progress. . . . The emphasis on rigor has led to experiments that are elegantly designed but often limited in scope. This limitation derives from the fact that many of these experiments involve situations that are unfamiliar, artificial, and short-lived, and that call for unusual behaviors that are difficult to generalize to other settings.[26]

Strong voices in psychology have spoken out against the narrowness of research based on tachistoscopic flashes, nonsense syllables, eye blinks, arbitrary word sequences, and marginal temperature variations.[27] A particularly thoughtful essay on this tension has been written by John Gibbs.[28]

While some connections have been drawn between this debate and the work of Kant—particularly his theories of the interaction between conception and perception—it seems intriguing and highly suggestive to imagine ways in which Tillich's thought could illumine this issue in psychology. For instance, Tillich's careful methodological distinctions between the functions of technical reason and the character of ontological reason would be clarifying. (See chapter 4 of this volume, "Tillich and the Crisis of the West.") Certainly both have an important bearing on truth, but the technical and manipulative function of reasoning necessary for certainty in science *must* be seen within broader ontological structures of reality—structures that include authentic human experience. Tillich was just as impatient with obscure pedantry in theology as he was with sterile "facts" in the social sciences. Both demand to be understood in their human importance as well as in their historical context.

It is valuable to explore in this connection the ontological significance of the psychotherapeutic project itself as similarly moving beyond "technical" functions of clinical scoring devices, procedural strategies, or behavioral conditioning techniques. To be sure, some behavior changes can be made with relative "certainty," just as some experimental correlations can be made with certainty. And some therapists can even hypothesize apt cognitive interpretations that may be "correct" but completely unliberating to the patient. But until the therapist is able to face the profound mystery and particularity of another's life in a way that respects personal language and idiosyncratic variations of perception, there will be little hope of authentic understanding. And until there is a sustaining appreciation for more ultimate significance, there will be little authentic change.

Therapy, like psychological research, must finally see itself in the context of that ontological unity to which Tillich so frequently and cogently pointed. The estrangement and brokenness of human experience, like the fragmentation and divisiveness of knowledge in psychology (or any discipline), must be taken seriously. But in a sense it can only be taken with full seriousness when it does not have to be taken with ultimate finality; within a context of faith in something beyond that brokenness, we can risk full exposure to the reality of the struggle, the suffering, the incompleteness. Such a risk, as Tillich so well said (and lived), may be possible only through radical confidence in that reconciling, reuniting power of Being, which comes on the far side of profound (personal or social) experiences of dislocation through which we have been sustained and transformed.

Such experiences are potentially present at the heart of the

therapeutic encounters of the depth psychologist. To be a participant in them is to be powerfully moved. To see them in the light
of a fundamental spiritual process of centeredness, self-alteration,
and return is to celebrate their essentially awesome and uniting
generativity. To be attentive to the magnitude of new possibility
emerging from such transformations is to be less patient with the
quantifiable and "certain" conclusions obtainable on matters of
relatively much less consequence. And to be renewed in this gracious process is to be humbled and inspired to gratitude. May the
future of depth psychology itself be so transformed!

NOTES

1. Paul Tillich, *On the Boundary: An Autobiographical Sketch* (New York: Charles Scribner's Sons, 1966), 88. First edition, 1936.
2. C. W. Kegley and R. W. Bretall, eds., *The Theology of Paul Tillich* (New York: Macmillan, 1961; rev. ed., New York: Pilgrim Press, 1982), 10.
3. Ibid., 13.
4. Ibid., 13–14.
5. Ibid., 18–19.
6. Wilhelm and Marion Pauck. *Paul Tillich: His Life and Thought* (New York: Harper & Row, 1976), vol. 1, *Life,* 8.
7. Ibid., 81.
8. The most careful research on the New York Psychology Group is being done by Allison Stokes, Ph.D. candidate in American studies, Yale University, on the basis of transcriptions and notes taken in the group by Seward Hiltner.
9. Cf. especially Paul Tillich, *The Religious Situation* (Cleveland: World Publishing Co., 1967). First German edition, 1926.
10. Paul Tillich, *The Courage to Be* (New Haven: Yale University Press, 1952), chaps. 5, 6.
11. Rollo May, *The Meaning of Anxiety* (New York: Ronald Press, 1950); idem, *Existence* (New York: Basic Books, 1958); Ernest Becker has more recently taken up this line of discussion, with specific reference to his indebtedness to Tillich, in *The Denial of Death* (New York: Free Press, 1973).
12. Erich Fromm, *Psychoanalysis and Religion* (New Haven: Yale University Press, 1950); idem, *The Sane Society* (New York: Holt, Rinehart and Winston, 1955).
13. For an analysis of the social and psychological forces at work in the Frankfurt School as well as a review of Tillich's friendship with Max Horkheimer, Theodor Adorno, Leo Loenthal, Erich Fromm, etc., see Martin Jay, *The Dialectical Imagination* (Boston: Little, Brown and Co., 1973); or some of the primary work by Theodor Adorno, for example, "Sociology and Psychology," *New Left Review,* nos. 46 and 47 (1967–68).
14. Erik Erikson, *Insight and Responsibility* (New York: W. W. Norton and Co., 1964), 133.
15. Robert Coles, *Erik H. Erikson: The Growth of His Work* (Boston: Little, Brown and Co., 1970), 409. For further discussion of the influence of Tillich on Erikson, see the work of Ernest Wallwork, "Erik H. Erikson: Psychosocial Resources for

Faith," in *Critical Issues in Modern Religion*, ed. Roger Johnson and E. Wallwork (Englewood Cliffs, N.J.: Prentice Hall, 1973), 322–61.

16. See especially R. J. Lifton, *Death in Life* (New York: Simon and Schuster, 1967); and idem, *The Life of the Self* (New York: Simon and Schuster, 1976).

17. James Hillman, *Re-Visioning Psychology* (New York: Harper & Row, 1975); June Singer, *Boundaries of the Soul* (New York: Doubleday, Anchor Books, 1953).

18. See, for instance, Peter Homans, *Jung in Context* (Chicago: University of Chicago Press, 1979); or Ernest Becker, *The Denial of Death* (New York: Free Press, 1973).

19. Of special interest to some researchers would be the tape-recorded dialogues between Tillich and Rogers and between Buber and Rogers maintained for a time by the Counseling and Psychotherapy Research Center of the University of Chicago.

20. Seward Hiltner, *Preface to Pastoral Theology* (New York: Abingdon, 1958); and idem, *Theological Dynamics* (Washville: Abingdon, 1972).

21. Paul Pruyser, *A Dynamic Psychology of Religion* (New York: Harper & Row, 1968).

22. Philip Rieff, *The Triumph of the Therapeutic* (New York: Harper & Row, 1964), 4.

23. The allusions here are to Tillich's work on freedom and destiny in his *Systematic Theology*, vol. 1 (Chicago: University of Chicago Press, 1951) and in his *Courage to Be* (New Haven: Yale University Press, 1952).

24. See Paul Tillich, *Systematic Theology*, vol. 3 (1963), part 4.

25. Cf. Gordon Allport, *Becoming* (New Haven: Yale University Press, 1955), 47–51.

26. Urie Bronfenbrenner, "Toward an Experimental Ecology of Human Development," *American Psychologist* 32 (1977): 513.

27. See, for instance J. J. Jenkins, "Remember that old theory of Memory? Well, forget it!" *American Psychologist* 29 (1974): 785–95; and U. Neisser, *Cognition and Reality* (San Francisco: W. H. Freeman and Co., 1976).

28. John C. Gibbs, "The Meaning of Ecologically Oriented Inquiry in Contemporary Psychology," *American Psychologist* 34 (1979): 127–40.

7. The Anxiety of Being

ANN BELFORD ULANOV

> Man's life is abundant life, infinitely complex, inexhaustible in its possibilities, even in the vitally poorest human beings.
> —PAUL TILLICH, "Heal the Sick; Cast Out the Demons," in
> *The Eternal Now*

> We hear the voice of that depth; but our ears are closed. We feel that something radical, total, and unconditioned is demanded of us; but we rebel against it, try to escape its urgency, and will not accept its promise.
> —PAUL TILLICH, "You Are Accepted," in *The Shaking of the Foundations*

In his willingness to combat the anxiety of nonbeing, Paul Tillich received and welcomed anything that promised to enlarge his—and others'—courage to be. As a scholar he was passionately caught up in the spiritual conditions of his times, trying to create a structure of understanding that would support a life of meaning.

Unlike most theologians, Tillich was deeply receptive to depth psychology. Its insights engaged his heart as well as his mind, his visceral reactions as well as his speculative thought, his own strong anxieties as well as his calm theological mind. He knew doubts, compulsions, splits within himself, all of which aroused suffering and uncertainty in him as well as fascination, a fascination summed up best, perhaps, in his absorbing interest in the demonic, upon which he shed so much light in his epochal essay of 1926, "The Demonic: A Contribution to the Interpretation of History."[1] He even suffered anxiety about the future of his systematic theology, as many of his friends attest in their memories of his worried questions about whether his ideas would last beyond the grave.

Yet Tillich knew a serene largeness of being, too, a largeness so evident in the quality of his humanity, his love of life, his high good humor, above all his impatience with narrowness and moralism. His being was ambiguous, ambivalent, flawed, spacious, full of images and insights. He was a man to whom the history of thought was the life of the imagination. He cared about Being and about particular human beings. He always saw the specific person there before him and addressed his remarks to the other person's deepest self. I remember when I first met him as a student at Radcliffe, how generously and with what seriousness he listened to me, as he did to almost all young persons. He was much more than the recent gossip about his problems with women suggests. He saw women as individual persons, complete in their own right, and he called them forward from the distant background position into which they were so often thrust, to affirm their own being. Tillich's perceptiveness of other persons' deep longings is what so touched his audiences, I believe.[2] And that perception lives on still in the printed words of his sermons.[3] Students and seekers of all types and occupations flocked to his lectures, for they heard in him a friendly call that recognized where they were, and with it a stern call that summoned them to come more fully into their own being. They heard themselves addressed by a man with all the perceptiveness and compassion of one who knew in himself what he called "the anxiety of nonbeing."

Tillich knew something more as well. He knew what I would call, in an extension of his concept, the anxiety of being. I am talking about the anxiety so many of us feel about the being that is there before us, within us, around us, the being that is available to us with its abundance of possibilities, its many complex facets, there to be lived, and, even more anxiety-producing, for us to live and to realize. This anxiety, aroused by the astounding fact of being, came very early to Tillich. He said that at the age of eight he was amazed that there could be something rather than nothing.[4]

In 1936 Tillich wrote about the principal metaphor that summed up his being: He lived on a series of boundary lines among many opposites—Europe and America, Philosophy and Theology, Faith and Doubt, Church and Culture.[5] He found his standpoint there, in that in-between place of inclusion and exclusion, a place he defined as both-and, though his harshest critics were to accuse him of being neither-nor. This boundary place expressed his anxiety of being. It signalled his reaching out to include all manner and forms of disciplines from which to build his theological system, and his worry about the effectiveness of including so much.

A theology that embraced all of human life—that was the task Tillich set himself, and it was often a nasty one. His concept of the "God beyond God," for example, brought down upon him severe rebukes for what seemed to persons of faith a windy abstractionism, and for what seemed to persons of precise and logical thought a cloud of vagueness. Yet for Tillich, his notion proposed an important meeting place for all the many persons who live on opposite sides of the boundary lines, those for example of confessional faith on one hand and those drawn by strong but undefined yearnings toward the divine on the other. Tillich took his stand there, on the perpetual border between strong opposing factions, trying to include the perspectives and experiences of each, despite the double exposure to criticism this occasioned. I believe he stood there between disciplines because on the other side of his own boundary line of nonbeing, with its special difficulties, rested being with its irresistible anxieties. And where he stood, we may stand again to see and understand the richness of opposing ideas brought to confrontation and rapprochement.

CORRESPONDENCES BETWEEN THEOLOGY AND DEPTH PSYCHOLOGY

In this way, we may point to the many lines of correspondence between Tillich's systematic theology and depth psychology—lines that he used like grappling hooks hurled across the point of intersection of the two disciplines, and that we can continue to use in the same dramatic way. For example, his deep appreciation of the power of the demonic forces that can capture a person is very much like a basic concept of object relations theory. That theory focuses on the psyche's mechanism of splitting away from consciousness impulses that the ego cannot tolerate. If the splitting is too extreme, these impulses will assume a demonic autonomous life that can usurp the ego's control and fragment what Tillich called the "center" of the person. Without that center, a person's humanity will be lost.[6]

A correspondence of matching importance can be found between Tillich's stern insistence on the unavoidable, tragic, but still free, fall of humanity from harmony into estrangement, and Freud's and Melanie Klein's understanding of the death instinct as a force that threatens to destroy human beings from within them. Unlike many of Freud's own followers, Tillich accepted the death instinct as a tough fact about life, as mysterious in its source as life itself.[7] Together, the life and death forces produced for him the inescapable ambiguities of life, a truth expressed by Klein in her epochal formulation of the "depressive position."[8] In early infancy, she saw, a child achieves the capacity to accept ambivalence, to recognize that all goodness is mixed with badness and that motives and emotions are not pure. Tillich agreed with his friend Karen Horney's insistence that the ambivalences in culture, with their far-ranging mixtures of good and bad, also must be seen as crucial determinants of mental health and illness. The theologian's vivid descriptions of our existential predicament—an estranged and disordered freedom—and our flight from it into the restrictions of neurosis or the excesses of psychosis, echo the psychoanalyst's graphic portrayals of mental disturbance.

Tillich found in Jung's distinction between lasting archetypes and changing symbols a solution to an ancient Catholic-Protestant conflict. For Catholic theology, the revealed symbols of faith are known, fixed, and unchangeable. For Protestants, religious symbols emerge spontaneously from the experiences of individuals and groups. Each side of this religious boundary offers something valuable but also poses a serious danger. On the Catholic side, there is a continuity to religious symbols but the constant threat of a lifeless rigidity in fixed doctrines that no longer catch persons with a transformative power. On the Protestant side, there is life to symbols but the danger of their coming and going without clear continuity or objective permanence. Tillich saw a solution to these problems in Jung's distinction between the fixed archetypal potentialities that are all around us and the infinitely variable symbols in which the potentialities present themselves. The archetypal possibilities are differently realized as they fit different individual and social needs. Thus permanence and change work together in religious symbols and can be made to come together in religious life generally.[9]

Tillich's perception of the truth latent in Freud's criticism of religious faith as nothing but the projection of childish wishes for a protecting and authoritative father leads directly to a very large question for Tillich: What is the "screen" upon which the projection is cast? The answer came for Tillich out of the resources of his theological system: "The screen is our ultimate concern. . . . [T]here is something that precedes the act of projection. . . . It means that if we use the father image in order to symbolize our ultimate concern, then the ultimate concern is not the father image. Rather the ultimate concern is the screen into which the father image is put."[10] Thus Tillich left open a way for many persons unable to enter the Church through confessions of faith. He offered them the possibility of finding their own symbols for life's meaning, a meaning he saw as enclosed within the universal human longing for connection to the divine.

Here Tillich knew a special affinity with the existentialist analysts. They shared a common root in Heidegger's examination of the capacity of *Dasein* to shape being. They shared a common emphasis on the power of symbols to illuminate the character of human existence in its relation to being itself. A less obvious, but vivid connecting point between the analysts and the theologian was Tillich's insistence on the central human resource of what he called "the courage to be" and the notion of the will that the existentialists shared with Otto Rank.

Tillich's formulation of the Yes in God that overcomes the No in God, of the Being that embraces its own nonbeing, and of the nonbeing that "drives being out of its seclusion [and] forces it to affirm itself dynamically,"[11] reaches back to the philosophy of Schelling. It also reaches forward to include Jung's later notions about God's "unconscious side," put forth so controversially in his book, *Answer to Job*. Tillich's emphasis on the anxiety-creating and anxiety-allaying functions of words connects with the work of Jacques Lacan. Lacan sees the human capacity for language as a creative bridge across the gap left in every child by the alienating discovery that it is not part of the large being of its mother, nor even a part of an imagined being that it somehow shares with the mother, but is only a solitary *"moi,"* separated and alone. Such a function of words, as creating links between self and other and between self and reality, bridges another gap, as Tillich sees it, that between our essential human nature and our existential estrangement. Words cross the gap, yet at the same time resound with our trembling awareness of the gap's existence.[12] But Tillich goes further: He sees the being of words as rooted in the originating Word of God, "the Word cutting into all words."[13]

Tillich pressed the practitioners of depth psychology to expose to consciousness their own ontological roots, to discover by what buried notions of being their particular systems of psychological theory were fed.[14] He rightly claimed that his own investigations into what it means to be a part of those "structures which are presupposed in any encounter with reality"[15] were directly relevant to the working analyst who each day must deal with the healing of the shattered being of specific persons.

It is precisely here, with these important questions of what it means to be, of how particular persons come into being, and from what sources of being healing can come, that Tillich's work remains useful to the practitioners and theorists of depth psychology. The initial link between Tillich and depth psychology is in this area of nonbeing and anxiety, which announces a threat to every person's life in three kinds of attack (as Tillich describes them): of fate and death, of meaninglessness and emptiness, and of guilt and condemnation. The connection between the disciplines is deepened for us when, as depth psychologists or theologians, we contemplate the anxiety on the opposite side of the boundary line, the anxiety of being. We look now, not at how our being is menaced, but at how it has become being in the first place, and what conditions foster the capacity to be.

In depth psychology a shift of emphasis has occurred in recent years, one that mirrors the crossing of the boundary line from the anxiety of nonbeing to the anxiety of being. As depth psychologists have moved into ever earlier years of human life in their etiologies of psychic disorder, their attention has shifted from latent pathology to the mysterious early beginnings of the human self. Their focus now centers on how a person comes to be at all. Freud began with what he saw as the oedipal conflict of the four- to six-year-old. Klein pushed the theory into the preoedipal years, as early as a child's first year. D. W. Winnicott investigated the very first months of a child's life—and so on. Can we not say that depth psychology projects in this way onto an earlier and earlier chronology the age-old religious quest to relate to the power and presence of being at the source? Depth-psychological theories have become a new vehicle of relationship to the mystery of life. In what have become passionate metapsychological and metaphysical disputes, we can see new religious wars taking shape in analytical societies. This drawing near to the borders of religion from the psychological side, with no matter what rawness of feeling, gives impetus to another movement of thought that Tillich firmly supported and took as a resource for his own system, the discipline of pastoral counseling. There he saw the resources of God's grace and human skills in healing combined, a boundary line successfully negotiated.

Tillich's great interest in the wondrous event of grace begins his crossing from nonbeing to being. Grace, says Tillich, *happens* to us in those moments when reunion spans separation, recognition conquers estrangement, and reconciliation accepts that which is rejected. Grace *is* our capacity to open to the healing power of faith: We are grasped by that which concerns us ultimately. Grace is given us mysteriously, in an encounter of persons; without it, Tillich sees no hope of anyone becoming a person at all.[16] In this construction of grace, Tillich anticipates some of the major developments of depth psychology since his time.

In the explosion of interest in D. W. Winnicott's formulation of transitional space, the very origin of the capacity "to be" is explored in the early infant-mother relationship. Winnicott states the point radically: "There is no such thing as a baby," but only a "nursing couple."[17] In the new Chicago school of Heinz Kohut and his followers, and in the work of Otto Kernberg, the healing of the radical early narcissistic wound to being is examined methodically, as a result of which Kohut, Kernberg, and the others arrive at the point from which Tillich started: "A person becomes a person in the encounter with other persons, and in no other way."[18] Analysts of several schools direct their attention to the intricacies of such an encounter through developing complicated and enlightening theories about the transference-countertransference interaction, that laboratory in the analyst's office where person-to-person encounters are investigated, lived, and reflected upon all at once. Thus the simultaneous presence of many dimensions of being is achieved.

In trying to heal narcissistic injury, what analysts attempt is the establishment of being at the core of personal identity. In working with those called "borderline personalities," in the language of depth psychology, because they slip and slide back and forth across the borders of sanity and psychosis, analysts attempt to cement together a center for being out of many fragments of their patients' personalities. In working with those persons called "neurotic," analysts attempt to strengthen what Tillich would call the forces of being to embrace the forces of nonbeing. The existentialist analysts investigate the dynamics of "ontological insecurity," as R. D. Laing puts it, and the resources of being available to overcome it.

The shift in depth psychology from a focus on pathology to a focus on the origins of our capacity to be corresponds to the shift from the anxiety of nonbeing to the anxiety of being. One form of anxiety leads to the other. What originally appears as a boundary line separating the dimensions of being and nonbeing turns out, on closer inspection, to mark the point of their junction. Tillich declares that the character of the anxiety of nonbeing depends upon the kind of being it tries to negate. He describes three levels of threat to persons that correspond to our bodily, spiritual, and moral existence. Thus for Tillich our anxiety over the quixotic nature of fate and the approaching final verdict of death threatens our "ontic self-affirmation." The task of our courage to be is to affirm existence in the face of this threat. Our anxiety over the immediate meaninglessness or ultimate emptiness of our lives, or of our time, or of history as a whole, threatens our "spiritual affirmation," both in our personal selves and in our cultural life. Our courage once again is demonstrated in our efforts to take these doubts into ourselves, to claim them without suppressing them or overcompensating for them with fanatical assertions of belief, to carry the doubt and live the meaning we know, even if it is not a final, clear, and altogether positive meaning. Our anxiety and guilt at making wrong choices and the threat of ultimate condemnation of our motives or our actions—of the whole sorry mixture of good and bad—threatens our "moral self-affirmation." Courageous self-acceptance, even though we see very good reasons for finding ourselves unacceptable, answers this last threat to our being.

It is faith, as Tillich understands it, that finally conquers all three forms of anxiety of nonbeing. By "faith" he means the state of being grasped and caught up beyond ourselves, by the "God beyond God." This being grasped changes the geography of our being, for faith is "not a state which appears beside other states of mind. . . . It is the situation on the boundary of man's possibilities. It *is* this boundary."[19] The three forms in which anxiety of being appears describe what it is like to live at that boundary, a line we have arrived at when we have discovered the courage to be, and have learned what it means to experience being as including nonbeing.[20]

THE THREE FORMS OF THE ANXIETY OF BEING

ONTIC TERROR

The first form of anxiety of being, which parallels Tillich's understanding of the threat of "fate and death" in the anxiety of nonbeing, confronts us at the ontic level in the form of a terror of being. It is what is there that frightens, not what is not there. Something exists antecedant to nonbeing and that something feels the threat of negation. When we permit ourselves to be conscious of this antecedant being, we feel panic. How shall we hold it all? How can we live with it? How can we embrace its many dimensions? We are anxious about having any being at all. We know what Tillich means when he writes that we close our ears to our own depths. We know what Jung means when he writes, "Everybody would pay anything, his whole fortune, to avoid going into himself."[21]

The work of depth psychologists attests to this primal fear of being as a resistance—as Freud puts it—to the life of unconscious mental processes flowing through us, night and day, from birth to death. How to include this different order of being with its confusion of images, affects, impulses, and drives? Its principles of organization differ frighteningly from the rules of conscious thinking that proceed according to an orderly logic, that provide us with a shared language, a goal-directed behavior, and a series of clear separations, between subject and object, self and other, and gratification and delay. Unconscious processes of thinking proceed according to principles of contiguity and association, of expressive behavior and violent intensity of emotion. Imagery is wildly inflated. In the unconscious, there is no separation of self and other, of subject and object, or of time and space. How, then, can we make room for its driving, pulsating life within the demands of daily reality functions?

The anxious threat of being takes a double form. Seemingly chaotic unconscious emotions and drives swamp our consciousness, and at the same time our conscious existence may so aggrandize *its* being that it leaves no portals open to us to receive and assimilate the forces of being that live in the unconscious. The anxiety of being shows itself as a fearful uncertainty in the face of an overwhelming number of life forms. We are anxious that we will be swept away, lost in currents of undifferentiated emotions, needs, and drives, never to be able again to form ourselves into a discrete entity, to become a person who can hold it all. We are also anxious over its opposite, that we can become a person. This last is what Otto Rank calls the "life-fear," the fear that one can indeed become an individual differentiated from the group, yet still somehow remain related to the group. It is the anxiety that inevitably accompanies the bringing of something new into being. The free-floating, unorganized affect that characterizes the anxious state presses on one's consciousness to find its appropriate channels of expression.

Anxiety of being shows itself again in our anxiousness about the unlived life in ourselves. Because we are afraid, we shut off being. We refuse to admit into awareness all the bits of being available to us—in our emotions, images, ambitions, needs, hurts, longings —and so they remain there in the shadows, undeveloped and unrealized.[22] We will not open our attention to new ideas, to new kinds of music, painting, literature. We will not engage in discussions of threatening political issues. We will not expose ourselves to the strippings of prayer. We shut up tight to guard an ego fortress. And so the unlived life, existing there unconsciously around the fortress, stirs in us, surrounds us, threatens us with the possibility of violent eruption. Unlike those passionate words of Stravinsky in a newspaper interview shortly before he died, "I want to be awake! awake!" our cry to ourselves is "Go to sleep"—and we do. We retire before our time because we fear we cannot make room for all the being in us.

The answer to anxiety of being, at what Tillich calls the ontic level of self-affirmation, is not courage, as it is with nonbeing. It is something that proceeds from that courage—love. Love holds our small being in its own larger reality, making room for us to come to be, not unlike Winnicott's "good-enough" mother who holds a situation together for her child, keeping in readiness new pieces of the world to hand the child when it is open to take them up, to inspect them, to make use of them. Love alone confers the power to be. It is the only way that the anxiety of being can be overcome. Love as a holding, a letting-be, a making-provision for being to come into life, permits the unorganized affect of the anxious state slowly to take shape and emerge in the specific being of an attitude, an emotion, an idea, or an action. Love makes room for us to find our way into being. Tillich's frequent use of the image of an embracing or holding "ground" of being points to the reality of this love, which he sees as imbued with "the feminine element of being." He was one of the first theologians to insist on inclusion of such a feminine element of being in our traditional masculine concepts of God.

ANXIETY OF MEANING

The second form of the anxiety of being parallels Tillich's discussion under the rubric of nonbeing of the anxiety of "meaninglessness and of emptiness," which gnaw at our spiritual affirmation. Here the issue is not the meaning that is absent, but the meaning that is present, there, even in the experience of loss of meaning. We know how deeply we fear facing who we are or what is there around us. We know how quickly we construct false idols to shield us from reality. The destruction of meaning involves the destruction of our idols. It is a frightening process, but one that pries us open, blasts us apart sometimes so that we can find the presence of what there is behind our idols, demanding our unguarded inspection of it.

One of our most successful ways to avoid being is to hide among the pseudoissues of nonbeing. We inflate and generalize what faces us, making grandiose, abstract, and hence unanswerable the most concrete bits of being facing us at any particular moment. For example, we may ask the unanswerable question "What is the meaning of suffering?" and thereby cleverly avoid a much more immediate question, "What am I to make of this suffering afflicting me now? To what use can it be put?" The plight of a person suffering narcissistic disorder gives ample evidence of the nature of this dodge. The aggrandized images of self are so exaggerated that no experience of a real self can come into existence and fill the inner emptiness threatening the person. Everything in oneself and in others falls short and betrays expectations. So a person fills with rage and envy and develops an eloquent *I-told-you-so* rhetoric of justification for endless complaining. The available possibilities —of risking dependence on a lover, a friend, or an analyst, for example; or of permitting grief over not having been valued as a person in one's own right; or of registering a sense of helplessness in not knowing how to do a task one has never been taught to handle—all get swept away in cosmic questions that are really pseudoquestions. "Why is there evil?" we ask. "Why are people so false?" "Why does no one ever understand?"

Paul Pruyser questions Tillich's whole distinction between neurotic and existential anxiety, asserting that the latter always disguises a version of the former. I would not go that far. We do know formless anxieties about the meaning of events and the ultimate meaning of human history, I believe. The way to meet those anxieties about the existence of meaning, however, is to face whatever bits of meaning may have presented themselves to us in our lives. The question then shifts from the abstract "Why did this happen?" to the concrete "What has happened?" We focus on seeing what is there in the small but immediate and concrete chunk of being that is presented to us, in an attitude, a quarrel, a job opportunity, an insult, physical suffering, a dream, a historic event, a cultural moment. The problem is not a lack of meanings, but too many of them. We see multiple meanings, ambivalent meanings, even opposite meanings, especially when we look at large historical currents, political issues, or problems of global dimension. It is the abundance of meanings, small and large, that so confounds us. How do we hold them all in awareness? How do we find a pattern or patterns in them?

Anxiety of being about our spiritual affirmation, lacking or faltering as it may be, shows itself in a threatening multiplicity of possibilities, an abundance that may overwhelm our capacity to make rational order out of them. Our systems of thought turn out to be too small, too tight, and yet we fear the loss of them. We defend ourselves by fanatic insistence upon the small order we see while rejecting the larger order we may be shown. Unlike Paul

Ricoeur's Job, who renounces the narcissism of his finite perspective for the sake of the larger whole Yahweh has revealed to him, we flee into a defense of our small and partial view, making it into an idol that inevitably must collapse and be smashed into pieces.[23] It is too small to hold the being given it. We are forced to let go of it because we cannot consent to let it be and see what is there in us and around us.

Anxiety of being about our spiritual affirmation shows itself too in the threat with which specific bits of being face us now, with their own meaning exposed to us, to be seen by us. Their presence frightens us. We may indeed glimpse something profound and essential in such experiences. We may indeed know the conviction in any particular moment that this is it, that this is life addressing us, that here we are met, confronted, handed something of utmost importance. How can we take it in?

The anxiety of being is the opening to the being given us in such little fragments of experience, a piece of the whole, a small perception of reality. The answer to such anxiety is again, not the power of courage, though it may issue from courage; it is a responsive opening, a motion of love, a love tough enough not to pull all into itself, a love that allows us to be ourselves. Tillich says, "in the recent psychotherapeutic literature the relation between power-drive and love is in the foreground of interest. Love has been more and more acknowledged as the answer to the question implied in anxiety and neurosis."[24] The answering love is a love that opens us to itself and makes us receive it.

REFUSAL TO BE

The last form of the anxiety of being corresponds to Tillich's use of "guilt and condemnation" in his categories of the anxiety of nonbeing, and to the level of moral affirmation. Here the issue is our guilt before the fact of being, our refusal "to be" in our failure to live the unlived life in us, our refusal to receive the being in the fragments of experience that are offered to us. We put our anxiety in place of being. We refuse the incarnation of being in concrete pieces of attitude, action, relationship, projects, and especially the way it turns up in the mistakes we make, when we cling instead to our emptiness and our grandiose questions. Being for us means deep suffering—but not true being. Our guilt is not over wrong choices, or even mixed choices, as Tillich describes the anxiety of nonbeing at this level. Our guilt is over the many choices constantly presented to us with which to face being as it is, true being. Our anxiety is challenged by such a fullness of choice. It is an anxiety so serious that we would rather destroy or deny the choices than risk their realization. Viktor Frankl presses this point vividly, and challenges all our notions of being, when he insists from the authority of his own experience that even in the deprivation and degradation of being in a concentration camp, people were confronted with choices of how to react, with what spiritual attitude to choose to meet suffering and death.[25] Even in such a place, in the most savage conditions, being presents itself for the taking, insisting on our responding, summoning us to do so.

Our anxiety of being over our moral self-affirmation shows itself, then, in our awareness of that summons "to be," that command to be our true self. We know that we must discard our counterfeit self, must let being incarnate itself. We know that we are being drawn into a partnership where being itself is at stake, where our continuation of life is in question. In old-fashioned anthropomorphic language, this is what was meant by doing God's will, or not doing it, and making God suffer as a result. Jung writes of the same phenomenon in his language of the ego and the self. The self, the center of the whole psyche, wants to come into being. It depends on the ego's consciousness to receive it. The ego is the portal to reality and realization for the self. The self is the source and refuge of the ego's efforts.[26]

As the experience deepens, our anxiety of being over the perils of moral self-affirmation shows itself, not as condemnation, as it does in the anxiety of nonbeing, not as suffering the wrath of God in the exclusion from his presence, but as just the opposite. We are made anxious now by the presence of God and the abundance of God's grace. We cannot face a presence that can turn a disastrous blow into a source of renewal, a grace that points to the fact of goodness dwelling there, real, alive, in the midst of terrible evil, a grace that can tenderly expose our much-needed defenses to the stripping action of love. And so we resort to unlived life, and to a flat refusal of the bits of being that have been given us. We sense in those fragments the presence of Being itself. We recognize that we might become all that we could and should be. Like animals on the alert to the presence of an alien, we sense what looks like God's possibility approaching our actuality that is really God's actuality approaching our possibility. We are made anxious by our awareness that if we became all that we could be, the intensity of being would be too much for us. Life is more threatening than death. We really could live fully right up to the end, even in illness, poverty, or degradation. Those blessed handicapped persons who have found a vocation in their very illness or deformity give evidence of such a capacity "to be."[27] So do countless unnamed others, as grand in their ways as the fabled Mother Teresa in hers, all those who become a source of life in the ministry to the sick, the abandoned, and the dying.

We are anxious about such unimaginably large pieces of being coming to us in such little, unmistakably real and attainable bits and pieces, because though very small, these fragments, when really received, will push us right into God. It is too much for us, with all that life rushing to us and through us, to find Being itself present in us.[28] Worse yet, the anxiety of being, met and lived through here in this life, throws us wide open to the threat of a life resurrected from death, a life where we see God face to face, where there is given to us not fragments of being, but a large being identifiable by its "abundant life," "infinite complexity," and "inexhaustible possibilities." At that point, we hear the complete words being addressed to us. We feel totally summoned, unconditionally demanded of, made to respond. We are promised a fullness of being.

This radical anxiety of being can be met only by love. Only love is strong as death, the author of the "Song of Songs" tells us. Tillich's notion of "ultimate concern" must be both enlarged and diminished into something more concrete in order to house this anxiety of being. The relationship at the boundary line must evolve with all the specific marks of each person's and each faith-group's relationship to God, conditioned by the bits of being given and accepted by them in the conflicts and disjunctions of their particular historical time and social structure. This relationship at the boundary will bear the marks of a concrete communication with God, even if it is in silence. It will mark a presence, even if one is only aware of an absence. It is still being that is addressed concretely, being concretely accepted, being lived, being chosen and responded to in this relationship at the boundary. This is love: present, concrete, real enough to sustain us even though it is not exhausted in all its forms in this experience, however large or transforming.

This is what Tillich meant, I believe, in that moving sermon "You Are Accepted." Receive being. It comes to us. It seeks us out. It shows itself to us, even when it must do so in a hidden form. We do not need to *know* as much as we need to *receive* what is given. We do not need to *understand* as much as we need to *live* the relation to being in any way in which it offers itself to us. This is the legacy of Tillich, his way of living being as he knew and felt it address him. This is his grateful way of receiving its fragments and quickly sharing them. For this, we can follow him and be thankful.

NOTES

1. Paul Tillich, "The Demonic: A Contribution to the Interpretation of History," in idem, *The Interpretation of History*, trans. N. A. Rasetski and E. L. Talmey (New York: Charles Scribner's Sons, 1936). Originally published as "Das Dämonische, ein Beitrag zur Sinndeutung der Geschichte," in *Gesammelte Werke*, vol. 6 (Stuttgart: Evangelisches Verlagswerk, 1963).

2. See Paul Tillich, "Heal the Sick; Cast Out the Demons," in *The Eternal Now* (New York: Charles Scribner's Sons, 1963), 58–61, where he asserts that everyone longs for salvation.

3. See Paul Tillich, *The Shaking of the Foundations* (New York: Charles Scribner's Sons, 1948); idem, *The New Being* (New York: Charles Scribner's Sons, 1955); and idem, *The Eternal Now*.

4. Personal conversation with Tillich in Hamburg, Germany, 1958. Cf. Wilhelm and Marion Pauck, *Paul Tillich: His Life and Thought* (New York: Harper & Row, 1976), vol. 1, *Life*, 2.

5. Paul Tillich, "On the Boundary: An Autobiographical Sketch," first published in *The Interpretation of History;* later published as a separate volume, *On the Boundary: An Autobiographical Sketch*, in a translation revised by Tillich (New York: Charles Scribner's Sons, 1966).

6. Paul Tillich, "The Meaning of Health," an address to the New York Society of Clinical Psychiatry, 14 January 1960, in idem, *The Meaning of Health: Essays in Existentialism, Psychoanalysis, and Religion*, ed. Perry LeFevre (Chicago: Exploration Press, 1984), 165–73.

7. See Paul Tillich, "You Are Accepted," in *The Shaking of the Foundations*, 158.

8. See Tillich, "The Meaning of Health," 166–67.

9. See Paul Tillich, "Remarks," in *Carl Gustav Jung, 1875–1961: A Memorial Meeting* (New York: Analytical Psychology Club, 1962), 30; see also Ann B. Ulanov, *The Feminine in Christian Theology and in Jungian Psychology* (Evanston: Northwestern University Press, 1971), chap. 5.

10. Paul Tillich, "Psychoanalysis, Existentialism, and Theology," *Pastoral Psychology* 9, no. 87 (October 1958): 16–17.

11. Paul Tillich, *The Courage to Be* (New Haven: Yale University Press, 1952), 179.

12. See Paul Tillich, "Existentialism, Psychotherapy, and the Nature of Man," in *The Nature of Man in Theological and Psychological Perspectives*, ed. S. Doniger (New York: Harper & Row, 1962), 52; see also idem, "Anxiety Reducing Agencies in Our Culture," in *Anxiety*, ed. P. Hoch and J. Zubin (New York: Grune and Stratton, 1950), 17–26.

13. Paul Tillich, *Love, Power, and Justice* (New York and London: Oxford University Press, 1954), 33.

14. See Tillich, "Psychoanalysis, Existentialism, and the Nature of Man," 47.

15. Tillich, *Love, Power, and Justice*, 19, 23.

16. See Tillich, "You Are Accepted," 155; idem, *The Dynamics of Faith* (New York: Harper & Row, 1957), 111–12; and idem, *The Courage to Be*, 166.

17. D. W. Winnicott, *Through Pediatrics to Psycho-Analysis* (New York: Basic Books, 1975), 99; see also *Between Reality and Fantasy: Transitional Objects and Phenomena*, ed. S. A. Grolnick and L. Barkin in collaboration with W. Muensterberger (New York: Jacob Aronson, 1978).

18. Tillich, "Existentialism, Psychotherapy, and the Nature of Man," 51.

19. Tillich, *The Courage to Be*, 188–89.

20. Ibid., 179.

21. C. G. Jung, *The Visions Seminars*, 2 vols. (Dallas: Spring Publications, 1976), 1:30.

22. I use the phrases *bits of being* and *fragments of being* to refer to the pieces of a whole experience we retain in the form of an image, a feeling, a symbol, a partial insight that can reconstruct the focus of the whole. We may, for example, find an image for a long-range goal in our work that connects us to what we see as the value of the whole of our work even though we have not yet achieved that goal. We may have a feeling about a sexual experience that gives us access to our identity as a whole man or woman, even though we have not yet achieved what Freud would call the complete genital stage of development. We may find a symbol for God that opens to us the meaning of religious faith without our being fully in possession of a whole faith. We may gain partial insight into a long-standing hostility we have felt toward a friend, an insight that conveys to us a sense of resolution for the whole of the problem, even though we have not yet reached such resolution. The value of emphasizing the "fragments" or "bits," as I have put it, is that we are relieved from the pressure of a punitive superego that operates according to an all-or-nothing set of standards. Such a superego says that either we possess the whole of something or we have nothing. Such a superego insists that either we reach a perfect solution to a problem or we accomplish nothing. Because we do not in fact ever achieve perfection under such superego dictates, we feel only that we fail, have nothing to show for our efforts, and as a result fall into hopeless discouragement. To stress the positive value of receiving and using the fragments of the whole that we do possess and can reach changes our discouragement into confidence. We see what we can do, what we can accomplish. This perception encourages in us a fresh, positive general outlook as well as helping us accomplish specific tasks.

23. See Paul Ricoeur, *Freud and Philosophy: An Essay on Interpretation* (New Haven: Yale University Press, 1970), 548–49.

24. Tillich, *Love, Power, and Justice*, 22–23.

25. Victor Frankl, *From Death-Camp to Existentialism: A Psychiatrist's Path to a New Therapy* (Boston: Beacon Press, 1959).

26. See C. G. Jung, *Aion,* vol. 9, no. 2, *The Collected Works,* trans. R. F. C. Hull, (New York: Pantheon, Bollingen Series 20, 1959), 23–36.

27. See Mother Marie des Douleurs, *Joy Out of Sorrow,* Barry Ulanov and F. Tauritz (Westminster, Md.: The Newman Press, 1958).

28. See Ann B. Ulanov, "The Christian Fear of the Psyche," *Union Seminary Quarterly Review* 30, nos. 2–4 (Winter-Summer 1975): 140–52.

8. Tillich's Legacy and the New Scene in Literature

NATHAN A. SCOTT, JR.

Among the major Christian thinkers of this century Paul Tillich is rivaled only by Nicolas Berdyaev and Jacques Maritain in attention bestowed upon literature and the arts. Tillich's elected vocation was (as he phrased it) that of "philosophical theologian," and the three volumes of his *Systematic Theology,* in the extraordinary feat of imagination that they represent, amply attest to his commanding genius for constructive work in this mode. But, even in his most formal and systematic writing, his overriding preoccupation never ceased to be that which formed the theme of his first important public lecture, before the Berlin chapter of the Kant Society in April of 1919, "On the Idea of a Theology of Culture" (*Ueber die Idee einer Theologie der Kultur*). Indeed, no other theologian of the modern period was more entitled than Tillich to make Terence's declaration *humani nihil a me alienum puto.* For throughout his long career, there was never a statement of his, no book or essay or lecture, that was untouched by a great animus toward all simple disjunctions between religion and culture. Religion, as he maintained over and again in his now famous formula, "is the substance of culture, culture is the form of religion."[1] And it was this principle that controlled his entire theological program.

Unlike Kant, who associated religion with reason in its practical mode, or Schleiermacher, who conceived it to belong to the realm of feeling, Tillich wanted always to deny that religion by itself constitutes a special realm of life or involves a special function of the human spirit. On the contrary: it represents, as he insisted, that dimension of depth or of ultimacy that informs all aspects of spiritual life—in the degree to which we are by way of being grasped by an *ultimate concern,* by "something absolutely serious and therefore holy, even if [it is] expressed in secular terms." Indeed, far from being a particular sphere of life and thought alongside other spheres (of morality and politics and art), religion, in Tillich's conception of it, is nothing other than "the state of being grasped by something unconditional, holy, absolute"—and thus it actualizes itself not only in myth and dogma and cultus but in all the forms and protocols of human culture. "No cultural creation," as he felt, "can hide its religious ground," and its religious ground is formed by the "ultimate concern" to which it bears witness; for that, he insisted, is what religion is: "ultimate concern."[2]

Tillich did not, of course, in these definitions want to *identify* religion and culture, but he did want to avoid the error that T. S. Eliot cautioned us against, "of regarding religion and culture as two separate things between which there is a *relation.*"[3] And, with a touch of drollery, Tillich liked to say that, to prove that the world is fallen, one has only to remark the fact of "a religious culture beside a secular culture, a temple beside a town hall, a Lord's Supper beside a daily supper, prayer beside work, meditation beside research, *caritas* beside *eros.*"[4]

AUTONOMY, HETERONOMY, THEONOMY

Now there are two types of polity, in Tillich's view, that tend to disrupt the natural coinherence of religion and culture: His term for the one is "autonomy," and the other he designates as "heteronomy." The human world takes on the style of autonomy when the self *(autos)* is conceived to be the source of the basic law *(nomos)* or of the fundamental order of life. The autonomous culture is one everywhere pervaded by a spirit of "self-sufficient finitude," and its radical secularity forbids the acknowledgment of any transcendent source of meaning. Whereas a heteronomous culture is one in which the fundamental order of the world is conceived to have its source in something other than *(hetero)* the untrammeled creativity of the autonomous individual. "Heteronomy imposes an alien law"[5] on the various forms of man's spiritual life—in the manner, say, of the ecclesiastical tyrannies of the late Middle Ages or of the political tyrannies of modern Fascist and Communist totalitarianism. And both the autonomous and the heteronomous modes are antithetical to that order of things which in Tillich's lexicon is spoken of as "theonomy"—his term for the kind of cultural order that prevails when the *theos,* or the dimension of transcendence, is freely acknowledged and thus wins spontaneous expression in all fields of life and thought. In a theonomous culture there is no arbitrary imposition of heteronomous authority: nor is the reigning principle that of "self-sufficient finitude" since, in such a dispensation, "the ultimate meaning of existence shines through all finite forms of thought and action; the culture is transparent, and its creations are vessels of a spiritual content."[6]

These patterns—which are rarely to be encountered in their pure ideality—do not, in Tillich's view, arise by way of volitional acts of elective preference: On the contrary, they emerge out of the restless thrusts and counterthrusts of social-political and intellectual history, and they are not consequent upon any kind of contrivance or deliberate purposing. Nor do the special commitments and assumptions constituting the autonomous or heteronomous or theonomous orientation wholly belong to that region of thought which defines a people's conscious understanding of itself and its world: They are, rather, beliefs and attitudes that operate largely at the level of what is tacit and taken for granted, and there they form the ground out of which come all the explicit statements that a culture makes through its art and literature and religion and politics. It is this subterraneanly dynamic and inexplicitly formulated structure of assumption and belief that comprises in a given period what Tillich called "the religious situation,"[7] and he conceived the task of a theological analysis of culture to be that of deciphering this unconscious but altogether decisive faith, which is the shaping principle at work in the legislation and metaphysics and art and all the other formulated monuments of a particular time and place. For, as he insisted, "in the depth of . . . [even the most intransigently] autonomous culture an ultimate concern . . . is implied."[8] And, as he believed, to disclose this fact in a closely detailed way, with reference to the cultural reality of our own period, is to offer a kind of *preparatio* for the advent of a new theonomy.

Indeed, the scene presented by his own time convinced Tillich that we are moving toward the end of the whole experiment in autonomy initiated by the *Aufklärung.* The Renaissance, in the powerful revolt it launched against the ecclesiastical heteronomy of the late Middle Ages, marked the first step in the direction of an autonomous culture; but artists and thinkers otherwise so diverse as Titian and Raphael, Dürer and Cranach, Erasmus and Melanchthon, Colet and More, Spenser and Shakespeare are surely to be thought of as commonly reflecting the degree to which the Renaissance was (as Tillich's somewhat stilted English puts it) "still in the spiritual power of an unwasted medieval heritage."[9] Nor can one easily fail to notice, for all its radical innovativeness, how deeply the Protestant Reformation (most especially in its first great strategist, Martin Luther) was steeped in its Catholic inheritance. But the Enlightenment, though drawing a part of its initial inspiration from the Reformation, quickly lost its early religious substance and tended ever more insistently to sponsor an essentially secular witness in behalf of "the scientific world view."

In Tillich's sense of things, the great drift of the age, especially with the advance of the nineteenth century, was toward a new kind of order marked above all else by the hegemony of what he calls "technical reason,"[10] by which he means that predatory spirit that prompts the people of the modern period to approach the things and creatures of this world with the prime intention of simply making them obedient to one or another enterprise of science or engineering. In short, technical reason—which in Tillich's system of thought is the exact equivalent of what Heidegger calls "calculative thinking"[11]—fosters a kind of grasping manipulativeness that wants to turn everything to practical account, to convert everything to use. And this kind of sensibility inevitably forfeits at last any real sense of the sheer ontological weight and depth of the world. The result, says Tillich, is the loss not only of "a common spiritual ground but [also of] a common spiritual purpose."

In the public sphere, the reign of technical reason prepared the way for a ruthlessly exploitative capitalism, and for the accompanying misery of the proletarian multitudes who could find no shelter against the irrationalities of a laissez-faire economy. And in the private sphere, since "the service of the mechanism of mass production" offered no favorable basis for the preservation of traditional communities, the controlling logic of a society under the sway of technical reason tended to separate "individuals from one another in spiritual loneliness and competition."[12] So, as Tillich concluded, "It is not an exaggeration to say that today man experiences his present situation in terms of disruption, conflict, self-destruction, meaninglessness, and despair in all realms of life."[13]

Yet of nothing was he so much convinced as that this "vacuum of disintegration can become a vacuum out of which creation is possible, a 'sacred void,' so to speak, which brings a quality of waiting, of 'not yet,' of a being broken from above, into all our cultural creativity." Indeed, he was persuaded that a theology of culture relevant to the circumstances of our time must be "a theology of the end of culture,"[14] in the sense of its needing to reckon with the primary fact of the age—which he took to be that of an autonomous order at the end of its tether, one stricken by the inclement weathers of its own devising and inchoately waiting for and yearning after some new dispensation. It was such a diagnosis of the basic "religious situation" of the modern period that consistently guided and informed all Tillich's reflections on the cultural scene and, since he conceived literature and the arts to offer a kind of barometer registering the deeper currents of thought and feeling, he constantly reserved a large place for them on the agenda to which he addressed himself as a theologian.

It may, of course, be felt to be somewhat surprising that one as fascinated as Tillich was with such figures as Rilke and Kafka and Eliot and Sartre expressed no inclination to accord literature a status any different from that which Durkheim assigned to religion —namely, that of an "eminent form and . . . concentrated expression of the . . . collective life."[15] But, at least in his published work, there is no evidence of his ever having moved beyond the canons of *Geistesgeschichte* criticism to the point of considering the literary imagination as possibly a mode of *knowing* that may offer the theologian something more than merely a reflection of the "time spirit." Yet, though his general perspectives in this area remained those of the *Geisteswissenchaftler,* at the time of his death in 1965 his engagement with the vanguard in literary life had been unremitting for over fifty years, and he never ceased to feel that the important literature of this century corroborated and ratified his own estimate of where we stand—near the end of the modern age.

ART AND THE EXPERIENCE OF THE VOID

Now it is not at all difficult to understand why Tillich should have thought that "only those cultural creations have greatness in which the experience of the void is expressed."[16] For in the formative years of his career, he was most immediately surrounded on the German scene by poets such as Georg Trakl and Gottfried Benn and Georg Heym, by playwrights such as Frank Wedekind, Georg Kaiser, Ernst Toller, and the young Bert Brecht, and by novelists such as Heinrich Mann and Franz Kafka—all of whom, in varying degrees, were prepared to view European civilization under something like the metaphor of Thomas Mann's *Der Zauberberg*, as a sort of sanatorium filled with tuberculars whose high-colored cheeks and spirited manner at once disclose and conceal the insidious *maladie* by which they are afflicted. And such a view of the European world, as a kind of Heartbreak House, was also being expressed in the 1920s with a fierce irony by painters like George Grosz and Otto Dix and Max Beckmann. This whole movement was for Tillich deeply affecting, and he never lost the impulse to turn first of all to German expressionism when he wanted to cite paradigmatic cases of modernist insurgency in literature and the pictorial arts.

Tillich's cultural interests were by no means, however, limited to German developments, and he, *Weltbürger* that he was, offered a large response to the full range of that canon making up the modern phase of literature. And what is to the point is that this is a literature, in most of its great exemplary models, that asks, as it were, for some such assessment as Tillich proposed and that, indeed, he could himself reasonably regard as confirming his view of the general course taken by cultural life as the modern experiment in autonomy approached its end.

The modern movement in literature not only embraces the classic avatars of the twentieth-century avant-garde—Apollinaire, Proust, Rilke, Joyce, Pound, Yeats, Eliot, Kafka, Malraux, Faulkner—but also reaches back here and there into the nineteenth century, to such figures as Flaubert and Dostoevsky, Rimbaud and Baudelaire and Mallarmé. Given the kind of perspective on this whole tradition that our present vantage point affords, we are not likely to feel that its greatness may be easily gainsaid. And in part its special kind of power derives from the imperial audaciousness with which it has addressed itself to "the immense panorama of . . . anarchy"[17] presented by the modern world. This is an anarchy that has registered itself perhaps most fundamentally in an "enormous dream of . . . the mortality of [the] gods"[18] and in a sense of the consequent disarray of the human city. The iconoclasm of the Enlightenment proved successful to a degree doubtless far beyond its own expectations, for by the beginning of the nineteenth century, a great enervation was beginning to overtake all those pre-Kantian certitudes of the *fides perennis* about the possibility of our moving upward along a sort of analogical ladder from the phenomenal world of nature and history to a noumenal world where the Divine Principle reigns over the whole of the Great Chain of Being. And, finding itself deprived of that metaphysical machinery for the ordering of experience that had been available to the countless generations of the past, the literary imagination began to have a sense of being overborne by what Wordsworth (in "Tintern Abbey") called "the weary weight/Of all this unintelligible world."

Poets and novelists and dramatists are not, of course, metaphysicians, and their task is that not of fashioning metaphysical systems but of making symbolic forms out of imagined characters and actions, out of meters and tropes and narratives. Yet if their patternings of experience are to have order and proportion, they must have at hand some basic perspective or method of construing the world's affairs that permits them to locate significance and to bring things into focus. Which is to say that, though, to be sure, the artist is not a metaphysician, he yet needs a sort of metaphysic, or at least some fundament of value wherewith he can discover what Henry James called "the figure in the carpet." Better it may no doubt be that he should not himself have to invent this primary structure of belief or method of vision, that he should rather simply inherit it from his culture and thus not need to expend on the search for principles of order creative energies that might otherwise be more happily invested in distinctively literary endeavor. But once the whole scientific and critical effort of the Enlightenment began to be felt in full force, it became apparent that the old myths and coordinating analogies that had long sustained Western reflection were, many of them, fast withering away under, as Keats called it (in *Lamia*), "the mere touch of cold philosophy"—or were suddenly becoming (in a phrase from Eliot's "Burnt Norton") like "bits of paper, whirled by the cold wind."

And thus, after Blake, as the modern writer faced into the new climate of a post-Christian age, he discovered, as the late R. P. Blackmur once said, "almost the whole job of culture . . . [to have] been dumped on . . . [his] hands."[19] By which one may take Blackmur to have meant that, amid the wilderness delivered to us by the Enlightenment, the writer—bereft now of all those categorical certainties and integrative myths that had traditionally centralized and ordered the literary imagination—found himself obliged to invent new world hypotheses, new systems of value and belief, if *as an artist* he were "to make a beginning and to make toward an end."[20] The central quest, in short, of modern literature in its classic phase was for a new "vision of the whole,"[21] or for some way whereby it might be found possible once again to dwell in a "whole present."[22]

So it went from the time of Leopardi to that of Rimbaud and Dostoevsky, from the time of Hölderlin to that of Flaubert and Laforgue. And, indeed, the people of our own century who incarnate the very idea of modernity—the Joyce of *Ulysses,* the Eliot of *The Waste Land,* the Rilke of the *Duino Elegies,* the Pound of the *Cantos,* the Virginia Woolf of *To the Lighthouse,* the Kafka of *The Castle,* the Brecht of *St. Joan of the Stockyards*—are all artists whose work is most fundamentally driven by that effort which Eliot early discerned to be the main force behind Joyce's book of 1922: namely, the effort to find "a way of controlling, of ordering, of giving a shape and a significance to the immense panorama of . . . anarchy which is contemporary history."[23] Theirs is a literature everywhere filled with a sense of the immense poverty that has overtaken the modern world as a result of the eclipse of God, of that old sun that once lit up all the seasons and spaces of humankind. True, it is—with such exceptions as the later poetry of Eliot and Auden, and the fiction of Bernanos and Mauriac and Greene, and the drama of Claudel—a predominantly secular literature, and one whose negations are often very radical indeed. Yet, for the kind of sensibility at work in *The Waste Land* or in *The Castle* or in *Nausea* or in *Waiting for Godot,* it would seem that the experience of the death of God is itself, somewhat paradoxically, a religious experience.

Meursault, for example, the little clerk in an Algerian shipping firm who is the protagonist of Camus's *The Stranger,* is convinced that his is a godless universe in which no sure sign of divinity can anywhere be descried. But his way of reckoning with this fact makes it apparent that, for him, it is a *theological* fact, that he conceives the silence or the absence or the death of God to be the most important reality that any man can confront: For him the universe, absurd though it be, is still a religious universe whose final meaning is to be found in God (whether God be absent or dead). And it is such a *coincidentia oppositorum* that is often by way of being brought into play in much of the great literature of the modern period, where the negations of a radically secular spirituality, by reason of their very radicality, evoke perceptions of an antithetical order—so that the opposites coincide at the heart of darkness. Which perhaps in part explains why a Paul Claudel at the beginning of his career could find in the testimony made by Rimbaud's *Une Saison en Enfer* and *Les Illuminations* "la révélation du surnaturel," so much so that he accounted this half-mad apostate his very Father in God. The void, in other words, into which he was plunged was, as Tillich would say, a "sacred void," and thus, as Claudel was eager to declare, the blasphemies and negations of Arthur Rimbaud in a strangely circuitous yet decisive way prepared him for his vocation as a Catholic: "Rimbaud seul a eu une action que j'appellerai séminale et paternelle et qui me fait réellement croire qu'il y a une génération dans l'ordre des esprits comme dans celle des corps."[24]

So, despite its general secularity, the literature forming the central canon of the modern period is often distinguished (as I have elsewhere remarked) by "an austere religious grandeur that is an expression of the stringent honesty and courage with which . . . [it moves] through tracts of the spirit left darkened by the recession of older codes and beliefs." And the claims it makes upon us—which are often exigent in the extreme—are those of "a kind of unconsecrated scripture arising out of the innermost chambers of the heart in a straitened age."[25] It is, in other words, a literature that, in the great vibrancy and poignance it gives to the disquiet of radical agnosticism, proves wonderfully responsive to analysis under the sorts of perspectives that Tillich advanced. For, however much it forsakes the *analogia entis* of the "perennial philosophy," its penchant for the *analogia extremitatis* makes it a body of testimony answerable in various ways to the proposal that "only those cultural creations have greatness in which the experience of the void is expressed."

Tillich was not, of course, an aesthetician or a literary critic or a cultural historian, but a theologian. Yet when due allowance has been made for the speciality of his basic interests, one cannot but be struck by the appositeness of his general analysis of modern culture to the spiritual tonality that predominates in much of the important literature of the modern period. But one is likely also to be equally struck by how inapposite is his vision of things to the main tendencies being represented by the literary imagination of the present time.

THE POSTMODERNIST SITUATION

Over the past twenty years we have grown, increasingly, to feel that in the affairs of literary life we stand now at a great distance from the age of modernism, so great indeed that it has become a matter of convention to regard the contemporary insurgency as reflecting a quite new reality, what specialists in *Tendenz* have, by their various advertisements, taught us to speak of as "postmodernism." The advent of this new dispensation—at some point no doubt in the 1950s—is difficult to locate precisely: nor does this whole enterprise even now have the sort of coherence that lends itself to swift and easy description. Perhaps its beginnings are to be found in the *alittérature* of Samuel Beckett and Nathalie Sarraute and Michel Butor and Alain Robbe-Grillet and various others who suddenly came to the fore with a good deal of aggressiveness at the end of the '50s—or perhaps it was in the strange fables of Jorge Luis Borges and Vladimir Nabokov that these beginnings first appeared. And Alain Robbe-Grillet's *For a New Novel* undoubtedly deserves to be thought of as presenting in something like the terms of theory an important early formulation of the new poetic, though on the American scene it has rough counterparts in such statements as Susan Sontag's *Against Interpretation* and William Gass's *Fiction and the Figures of Life*.[26] But, wherever we are to locate its beginnings or the more decisive expressions of its self-justification, we know ourselves to have been surrounded since the early '60s by a kind of literature that, when considered in relation to the styles and idioms that won prevalence after "the generation of 1914," seems to be rather a new thing.

It may be that what is most notable in verbal art of the present time is its retreat from the sort of imperial imagination that so generally marked the characteristic expressions of modernist sensibility. For the new vanguard has very little patience with the old "cult of the 'human' " and "the old myths of 'depth.' "[27] So it wants to purge its work of the old anecdotalism, of the old eloquence, in order that it may be nothing more than "mere literature." Before we have gone far into Robert Musil's *Der Mann ohne Eigenschaften* (The man without qualities, written between the early '20s and the early '40s), we are told that no "serious attempt [will] be made to . . . enter into competition with reality"—which would seem to be quite the sort of decision that has been reached by those of our contemporaries who most emphatically represent the postmodernist tendency. Not for them any attempt at finding stratagems for "giving a shape and a significance to the immense panorama of . . . anarchy which is contemporary history," since, like Musil and his hero Ulrich, they suppose that "everything has now become non-narrative": so they take it for granted that, given the intractability of those public realities of the age that we call conditions, it is futile to try in any way to alter or subdue or transfigure our broken and bullying world.

True, there are numerous contemporary writers of distinction who keep the kinds of commitments that we associate with classic modernism—Ellison and Bellow and Styron and Updike, for example, on the American scene, or Günter Grass in Germany, or Doris Lessing in England. And, of course, there is the great looming presence of Solzhenitsyn. But it is not to *Invisible Man* and *Mr. Sammler's Planet* and *The Cancer Ward* and *The Tin Drum* that we will turn for evidences of that contempt for storytelling and that passion for *meta*fiction which belong to our present moment. If we think just of our own American situation and just of our novelists, it is rather such figures as John Barth and Thomas Pynchon, Donald Barthelme and William Gass, Ronald Sukenick and Raymond Federman, Robert Coover and Gilbert Sorrentino whom we will have in mind, for it is in their work and that of their confreres that we encounter key examples of the new period-style of postmodernism.

At a certain point in Malcolm Lowry's *Under the Volcano* the Consul, Lowry's alcoholic protagonist, remarks to his friend, M. Laruelle, how wonderfully tequila sharpens and clarifies his thoughts, his perceptions, his general view of the world—which prompts his friend to reply that surely this is not the case with respect to "the things . . . on which the balance of any human situation depends." The Frenchman says ironically, "Your Ben Jonson, for instance, or perhaps it was Christopher Marlowe, your Faust man, saw the Carthaginians fighting on his big toe-nail. That's like the kind of clear seeing you indulge in. Everything seems perfectly clear, because indeed it is perfectly clear, in terms of the toe-nail."

But this, argues William Gass, is precisely what literary fictions come to—"life in terms of the toenail."[30] And so it would be maintained today by many of his contemporaries who are bent on producing a fiction that is absolutely figurative. They take it as axiomatic that there is a great discrepancy between art and the objective world, a discrepancy indeed so immense that literature cannot hope to deal with things "out there" except by way of fantasy and conceit, by way of farce and parodistic joking. So, everywhere, we find that element of waggishness that Ortega long ago suggested we might expect to find in a literature retreating from the fact-world. "The waggery may be more or less refined, it may run the whole gamut from open clownery to a slight ironical twinkle, but it is always there"[31]—in Joseph Heller's *Catch-22*, in Donald Barthelme's *Snow White*, in Thomas Pynchon's *V.*, in Kurt Vonnegut's *Slaughterhouse-Five*, in Ishmael Reed's *Mumbo Jumbo*, in Raymond Federman's *Take It or Leave It*, in Ronald Sukenick's *98.6*, and in many another of the most representative fictions of the present time. And, as Ortega would insist, the penchant for jesting is inevitable in a literature so thoroughly insistent on its own fabulism, on the fictive character of its own constructions; which is to say (in his phrase) that it is "doomed to irony" by its fascination with the world as it appears "in terms of the toenail."

John Hawkes, who in such books as *The Beetle Leg* and *The Lime Twig* and *Second Skin* and *Travesty* has written some of the most brilliant essays in the new mode, says: "I began to write fiction on the assumption that the true enemies of the novel were plot, character, setting, and theme.... "[32] This declaration springs from the very heart of postmodernist doctrine in the poetics of fiction and puts us immediately in mind of the general discredit into which "story" has fallen. For it is now the Catholic faith of the people who carry (as Matthew Arnold called it) "the tone of the centre" that the act of storytelling inevitably presupposes a great illusion, that the world is somehow susceptible of comprehension. And it is no doubt the case that story does tend to suggest that we dwell in a universe that is in some measure finally decipherable.

The storyteller presents us with lovers who become separated or with a child who becomes lost in a forest and, as the British philosopher W. B. Gallie puts it, invites us to ask, "What happened to them next? And, after *that*, what happened? And *then* what happened?" The prime requisite of a story, Gallie says, is "followability,"[33] and to tell a story is to imply that the human world is itself something followable: It is to imply (in a figure of Frank Kermode's) that the human order proceeds in something like the manner of a clock, that the *tick* is followed by a *tock* and that the interval between the two is "charged with significant duration."[34] And, when one thinks of such typical modernist texts as *The Magic Mountain* and *Ulysses* and *The Sound and the Fury* and *Man's Fate,* one feels that what distinguishes them in part is their fierce commitment to the kind of explanation that literary narrative entails. But, for the generation of John Hawkes, there is an utterly absurd discrepancy between all plots and the world "out there": so character, setting, theme, stories—these things are conceived to add up to nothing but a kind of self-nullifying fraudulence, a kind of futile revenge that the storyteller takes against the pervasive contingency of existence.

And, of course, the great conclusion drawn is that, since the language of literary art can make no significant contact with reality and is condemned to an irremediable "blindness," since it is (as Richard Poirier says) merely "a form of energy not accountable to the orderings anyone makes of it,"[35] all it can offer, therefore, is oblique commentary on its own *problématique.* Literary fictions, as we are told by the new vanguard, are and ought to be "self-reflexive," their chief interest lying in the degree of radicality with which they subvert any expectation of their making reference to a reality extrinsic to their own internal grammar of myth and metaphor. It is, in other words, the very "inability [of the novel] to transcend the solipsism of subjectivity and language [that] becomes the novel's chief subject and the principle of its form."[36] Or such at any rate is asserted to be the case by the Catholic faith that today forms the literary conscience of the postmodernist insurgency.

So it is not at all strange that in Barthelme's *Snow White* and Federman's *Double or Nothing* and Barth's *Giles Goat-Boy* and Pynchon's *Gravity's Rainbow* and Sorrentino's *Splendide-Hotel*—to cite merely a few representative cases—we are struck by a strange depthlessness, for given the kind of retreat from the public world of our time that these writers are negotiating, it is inevitable that theirs should be texts that "exhaust their necessity as soon as they have been seen, since to see them is immediately to understand to what destructive purpose they are exhibited."[37] They are very determined, indeed, not to "compete" with the realities that press in upon us, and thus their knotty arabesques are quite thoroughly decontaminated of all the old *profondeurs*. Which makes it inevitable that such a hermeneutic as Paul Tillich's—with its expectation that the artist shall be committed to some *theoria* or vision of "the human condition"—should suffer a considerable frustration when it encounters the literature that comes today from the new avant-garde.

A SURMISE ABOUT TILLICH AND POSTMODERNISM

One of the reasons, of course, why Tillich considered the literary and visual arts to present the theologian with highly significant data was that the artwork, as he felt, is charged with what he called "import." In an early essay of the 1920s, for example, he said:

If we imagine the import (or ultimate meaning) to be the sun, and form the orbit of a planet, then for every form of culture there is proximity to and distance from the sun or the import. . . .

The import is not this or that individual psychological element, nor is it biographical or sociological or national. . . . The essence of the import lies beneath all these subjective factors. It is a certain attitude toward reality. It is an interpretation of ultimate meaning. . . .[38]

Or we may say, using the term he employed more frequently in his later years, that he considered every serious work of art to be one bearing witness to some "ultimate concern," to be one reflecting an effort of the imagination to take hold of its world *in the dimension of ultimacy.* "No artistic expression is possible without the creative rational form, but the form, even in its greatest refinement, is," as he insisted, "empty if it does not express a spiritual substance."[39]

Now the terms *import* and *ultimacy* and *spiritual substance* make reference to what the artist's design discloses regarding that which is conceived to be the essential "ground" of the human enterprise, the fundamental *source* of creativity and vitality and order. And they also make reference to whatever the artwork may disclose regarding "those places in life where we come up against that which is not pliable and disposable"[40] and where we confront some truly radical hazard or threat. The dimension of ultimacy, in other words, may appear, paradoxically, in terms of some vision that the artwork projects either of that which is the positive ground of life (namely, the sacred) or of that which promises in the end to subvert and annihilate the human endeavor (namely, the demonic). And Tillich took it for granted that genuine greatness in the arts, though having also other roots, is necessarily consequent in part upon the artist's having searched experience to the point of having won some really integral vision of the human situation in that range of things over which the term "ultimacy" presides. He quite understood, of course, that one cannot "grasp import disengaged from form": as he says (and the italics are his), *"Substance or import is grasped by means of a form and given expression in a content."*[41] By this he meant that that sense of ultimate value (or disvalue) that knits together a given poetic economy is incarnate within a particular structure of trope and dramatic gesture and may, therefore, be apprehended only in the degree to which we consent not to go round but *through* "the well-wrought urn." But however much the dimension of the work of art denominated "ultimate concern" may require to be encountered in and through *la vie des formes,* it is nevertheless, in Tillich's view, always there— at least in those poems and novels and dramas that carry that special resonance belonging to major literature—and it is this that opens literary art (even in those of its phases that may be insistently secular) to religious analysis.

The whole phenomenon of postmodernism is, to be sure, something with which Tillich never reckoned, and one cannot undertake to surmise just what his response to it would entail, though he would no doubt be more than a little astonished at the resoluteness with which the literary imagination in these past years has deliberately expelled from its world "the dimension of ultimacy." And he might well be inclined today very much to radicalize his proposition of the 1940s about a theology of culture relevant to the contemporary scene needing to be "a theology of the end of culture . . . [committed to] a concrete analysis of the inner void of most of our cultural expressions."[42] For the void that one meets now in the literature of the new mannerism hardly gives off even the slightest intimations of the sacred, not even in the negative way that permitted the testimony of a Rimbaud to prove so fertile in the religious formation of a Paul Claudel: It is, indeed, as Warner Berthoff has recently suggested (in a figure drawn from Robert Musil) "a literature without qualities."[43]

Yet, though one hesitates to speculate in any detailed way about how Tillich would respond to postmodernist styles in literature, of one thing we may be fairly certain—namely, that he would not at all be inclined to face them in a spirit of scoffing censoriousness; far from it. Those who knew him well can easily imagine him reading some of the currently stylish books of our period and then nodding his great leonine head and murmuring ruminatively, *"Ja . . . ja . . ."*—which, as those who were familiar with the Tillichian *Ja* know full well, would mean "Let's wait and see." Indeed, as he said in the great sermon called "Waiting": "Our time is a time of waiting; waiting is its special destiny."[44] And, believing this in a deeply serious way, he constantly represented an unfailing generousness and hospitality in his approach to contemporary ferment in the arts, as in all other fields of cultural life. As his whole doctrine of "the Protestant principle" fully indicates, he was by no means afraid to "test the spirits" (1 John 4:1), but he was fearful of doing so prematurely, lest some possibility be thereby foreclosed, in perhaps even the unlikeliest place, of new discernment and discovery.

True, the void (as Tillich would call it) in our literature just now often seems—given the rigorously careful extrusion of "the old cult of 'the human' " and "the old myths of 'depth' "—to be something quite absolute, something utterly dry and vacant and unpromising. And thus we may feel perhaps, as Warner Berthoff suggests, a kind of convergence between religious paradigm and secular literary enterprise,[45] in the sense of something having been enacted analogous to that process which Saint Paul describes as *kenosis*.[46] But, rough and imperfect though it may be, if Professor Berthoff takes his own analogy seriously, it is a little strange that the element in it that prompts some hopefulness about the future of literature seems not to modify the general moroseness with which he scans the current scene. For when they do make some use of kenotic theory (which has always been riddled with ambiguity), the classic formulations of Christological doctrine declare in effect that the *kenosis* was not, as it were, absolute, that the Son of God in his self-abasement *never ceased to be God,* the second person of the Holy Trinity. And, similarly, Warner Berthoff's analogy should remind us that, however much many of those forming the new avant-garde seem bent on emptying themselves of even the merest commitment to the great traditional aims of mimetic literature, *they do nevertheless remain writers,* and many of them writers of immense gifts.

So maybe, in a spirit of patient anticipation, we should tarry with them a while longer. *Ja.* . . . Let us wait and see. Or so at any rate Tillich, one suspects, would advise. Though, *meanwhile,* he would doubtless be wanting to find ways of encouraging them to perform an act of *anamnesis*—of remembrance of that in which the greatness and the glory of modern literature in its finest moments consist: namely, its determination to *cope* with "the human condition" and to find new stratagems for "giving a shape and a significance to the immense panorama" of confusion and disquiet that continues to surround the days of our years.

NOTES

1. Paul Tillich, *Theology of Culture,* ed. Robert C. Kimball (New York: Oxford University Press, 1959), 42.
2. Paul Tillich, *The Protestant Era,* trans. James Luther Adams (Chicago: University of Chicago Press, 1948), 59, 57.
3. T. S. Eliot, *Notes Towards the Definition of Culture* (New York: Harcourt, Brace and Co., 1949), 31–32.
4. Tillich, *The Protestant Era,* 59.
5. Ibid., 46.

6. Ibid., xvi.
7. See Paul Tillich, *The Religious Situation*, trans. H. Richard Niebuhr (New York: Henry Holt and Co., 1932).
8. Tillich, *The Protestant Era*, 58.
9. Ibid.
10. See Paul Tillich, "The World Situation," in *The Christian Answer*, ed. Henry P. Van Dusen (New York: Charles Scribner's Sons, 1945), 1–44.
11. See Martin Heidegger, *Discourse on Thinking*, trans. John M. Anderson and E. Hans Freund (New York: Harper & Row, 1966), 43–57.
12. Tillich, "The World Situation," 13.
13. Paul Tillich, *Systematic Theology*, vol. 1 (Chicago: University of Chicago Press, 1951), 49.
14. Tillich, *The Protestant Era*, 60.
15. Emile Durkheim, *The Elementary Forms of the Religious Life*, trans. Joseph Ward Swain (London: George Allen and Unwin, 1915), 418–19.
16. Tillich, *The Protestant Era*, 60.
17. T. S. Eliot, "*Ulysses*, Order, and Myth," in *Critiques and Essays on Modern Fiction*, ed. John W. Aldridge (New York: Ronald Press, 1952), 426.
18. Ihab Hassan, "The Dismemberment of Orpheus: Reflections on Modern Culture, Language, and Literature," *The American Scholar* 32, no. 3 (Summer 1963): 463.
19. R. P. Blackmur, *The Lion and the Honeycomb* (New York: Harcourt, Brace and World, Harvest Books, 1955), 206.
20. Roy W. Battenhouse, "The Relation of Theology to Literary Criticism," in *Religion and Modern Literature: Essays in Theory and Criticism*, ed. G. B. Tennyson and Edward Ericson, Jr. (Grand Rapids, Mich.: William E. Eerdmans Co., 1975), 87.
21. See Stephen Spender, *The Struggle of the Modern* (Berkeley-Los Angeles: University of California Press, 1963), 79–97.
22. See John Holloway, *The Colours of Clarity* (London: Routledge and Kegan Paul, 1964), chap. 1.
23. T. S. Eliot, "*Ulysses*, Order, and Myth," 426.
24. "Rimbaud alone had an influence that I shall call seminal and paternal and that makes me really believe that there is a formative power in the order of the mind as in that of the body." (Ed.'s translation.) Claudel to Jacques Rivière, 12 March 1908, *Jacques Rivière-Paul Claudel: Correspondance, 1907–1914* (Paris: Librairie Plon, 1926), 104.
25. Nathan A. Scott, Jr., *Negative Capability: Studies in the New Literature and the Religious Situation* (New Haven: Yale University Press, 1969), 30.
26. Alain Robbe-Grillet, *For a New Novel*, trans. Richard Howard (New York: Grove Press, 1965), originally published as *Pour un nouveau roman* (Paris: Les Editions de Minuit, 1963); Susan Sontag, *Against Interpretation* (New York: Farrar, Straus and Giroux, 1966); William Gass, *Fiction and the Figures of Life* (New York: Vintage Books, 1972).
27. Robbe-Grillet, *For a New Novel*, 29, 23.
28. Gass, *Fiction and the Figures of Life*, 59–60.
29. Jose Ortega y Gasset, *The Dehumanization of Art* (Garden City, N.Y.: Doubleday, Anchor Books, 1956), 43.
30. "John Hawkes: An Interview," *Wisconsin Studies in Contemporary Literature* 6 (Summer 1965): 149.

31. W. B. Gallie, *Philosophy and the Historical Understanding* (New York: Schocken Books, 1964), 45, 22–50.

32. Frank Kermode, *The Sense of an Ending: Studies in the Theory of Fiction* (New York: Oxford University Press, 1967), 45.

33. Richard Poirier, *The Performing Self: Compositions and Decompositions in the Languages of Contemporary Life* (New York: Oxford University Press, 1971), 40.

34. Gerald Graff, *Literature Against Itself: Literary Ideas in Modern Society* (Chicago: University of Chicago Press, 1979), 53.

35. Roland Barthes, *The Pleasure of the Text*, trans. Richard Miller (New York: Hill and Wang, 1975), 17.

36. Paul Tillich, "Religiöser Stil und religiöser Stoff in der bildenden Kunst," in *Das neue Deutschland* 9 (1921): 155.

37. Tillich, *Systematic Theology*, 1:90.

38. Harvey Cox, *The Secular City* (New York: Macmillan, 1965), 262.

39. Paul Tillich, "On the Idea of a Theology of Culture," in *What Is Religion?*, ed. James Luther Adams (New York: Harper & Row, 1969), 165.

40. Tillich, *The Protestant Era*, 60.

41. See Warner Berthoff, *A Literature Without Qualities: American Writing Since 1945* (Berkeley-Los Angeles: University of California Press, 1979).

42. Paul Tillich, "Waiting," in *The Shaking of the Foundations* (New York: Charles Scribner's Sons, 1948), 152.

43. Berthoff, *A Literature Without Qualities*, 24.

44. In the second chapter of the Epistle to the Philippians (vs. 7) Saint Paul speaks of Christ having "emptied himself" (ἑαυτὸν ἐκένωσεν), of his having laid aside his divine attributes for the sake of dwelling for a time on earth and entering into the drama of human history.

9. Tillich and the Religious Interpretation of Art

ROBERT P. SCHARLEMANN

Tillich's idea of a theology of culture, or of an interpretation of the religious dimension in culture, is doubtless one of the most influential aspects of his thought. One can think of a number of reasons why that might be so. But of them perhaps the two most important are, first, that it offers a way to understand theology as something other than the repetition or interpretation of a doctrinal tradition and, second, that it speaks to the situation of many in the modern period who have sought to span the chasm between the religious and the cultural without denying the autonomy of the cultural. On both these counts Tillich, in his person as well as in his thought, provided a pattern that could be followed. In a vivid way, James Luther Adams sees Albrecht Dürer's *Heller Altarpiece,* in which the author had removed the band of clouds that in Raphael's painting of the same subject had separated the terrestrial and the celestial, as a visualization of Tillich's conception.[1]

At the same time, it is also true that few of those whose religious interpretation of culture was inspired by Tillich's suggestion carried it out in the manner that he projected. For to provide a theology of culture by following the process through which unconditional depth content (what religion means by the name *God*) breaks the cultural forms demands a rare kind of receptivity and theological erudition. Hence it seems advisable here first to recall what his conception was and only then to ask what can be seen today as the religious or theological content in works of art.

ART AND REALITY

In retrospective remarks made in 1961,[2] Tillich named three things that led to his interest in drafting a theology of culture. The first was the "moment of inspiration," "almost a revelation," occasioned by seeing the *Madonna with Eight Singing Angels* of Sandro Botticelli in the Kaiser Friedrich Museum in Berlin.[3] Subsequently he was introduced to expressionist painting and, in that connection, wrote a review of two books on religion and art, one by Eckart von Sydow, his friend from early youth, and the other by G. F. Hartlaub; it was published in 1921 under the title "Religiöser Stil und religiöser Stoff in der bildenden Kunst."[4] What had become clear to him was that art is related to the religious through its expressive power and that this power is independent of the subject matter. Finally, on his own, and perhaps as a result of an early desire to become an architect, he familiarized himself with the Bauhaus style of architecture, characterized by its *Sachlichkeit,* its objectivity or practicality. Material objectivity associated with realism and expressionistic power associated with the notion of breakthrough became key elements in his interpretation of art. Indeed, the relation of these two elements forms a central problem for his whole systematic thought; and the move from expressionism to a new realism also describes a progress in his religious thought, from a beginning orientation to the principle of identity (1915) to the notions of breakthrough (1919) and realization (about 1926). "Self-transcending realism" in his philosophy of history, the "new realism" of his sacramental theory, and the attitude of "belief-ful realism" in facing the present are all variations upon this same theme.[5]

Equally important for Tillich's theology of art, which is part of his theology of culture, is a distinction between what a work of art can "represent" or depict and what it can "express." The terminology itself does not play a prominent role; in fact, Tillich can even speak of what "expression" can "represent."[6] But it is obvious that he is acquainted with the distinction itself, and on at least one occasion he calls attention in particular to the phenomenon of "expression."[7] Representation has to do with the appearance of things, and expression has to do with something that makes itself known through the outward appearance without having an appearance of its own. A grimace, for example, can be represented; it is something that appears to our physical senses. But the disapproval that a grimace may express cannot be represented, or depicted; it can only be expressed through the representation of the grimace itself. Representations are what we perceive through one or all of our physical senses; expressions are what we feel or sense as conveyed with and through the representation. In terms of this distinction, one can say that the quality of the "holy," with which a religious or theological interpretation of art is concerned, can never be depicted, but it can be expressed. For this reason it is easy to see why the expressionist element of style took on particular importance in Tillich's reading of works of art, for this style uses artistic techniques in order to have what is represented in the painting serve as the expression of another dimension of reality.

When things express a meaning through their appearance, they are examples of what Tillich in the 1920s called a "sense" *(Sinn)*. "Sense" is something between a thought and a thing—it is, as Tillich also called it, "spiritual substance," a unity of thought and thing. The primary example of such a sense is a word; for under one aspect it is a perceptible thing, a figure that can be heard or seen, and under another aspect it is a thought, distinguished from a mere scratch on the page or an unintelligible sound because it carries and calls forth a thought. Though Tillich appears to have taken this use of the word *Sinn* from Edmund Husserl, it gets developed differently under the impact of Martin Heidegger's *Being and Time* and is then brought into association with Tillich's theory of symbols. What distinguishes a symbol from a mere thing is that a symbol is a thing that also conveys a meaning. A tree may be only that—a tree. Or it may also be a symbol—a tree that not only appears as such but also expresses an import. Customarily we may limit the realm of "sense" to language; for we are all familiar with words as thought-things, and we can readily see how a word is at once a visually or acoustically perceptible material and the conveyor of an intelligible meaning—we cannot listen to the word *tree* without its making us think of a tree; in that regard it is both substantial and spiritual. We are less familiar, however, with the fact that other physical entities, whether artifacts or natural things, have the capacity for conveying a meaning through their physical appearance. They can be symbols.

By what faculty do we become cognizant of what is expressed, in contrast to what is depicted? According to a fairly common usage, we can say that we "feel" or "sense" it. Thus, with reference to his *Improvisation No. 30*, Wassily Kandinsky could say, "The 'content' of the picture is what the spectator *lives* or *feels* while under the effect of the form and color combination."[8] But in this connection Tillich also takes advantage of Heidegger's existentialist analysis and uses the word *concern*. It is through concern that the worldliness of the world is opened to us, and what a work of art expresses is made known through how it elicits concern from us. If the concern is "ultimate," or "unconditional," then what is expressed is a religious sense.

Art is not religion. But the relation between the two in a theology of art is easily confused, and Tillich is easily misunderstood if one does not attend to the difference between two ways of defining such terms as *art*.[9] A "generic," or classifying, kind of definition is reached by identifying the properties that are common to all things in a group and that make them members of that group, and then by relating the specific and individual differences of the objects to that general property. But such definitions are not suited to delimiting the spheres of such objects as art and science, which result from the activity of reason or spirit. For this purpose a "constructive," or constitutive, definition serves better. It identifies and differentiates its objects not according to general and specific properties but according to the mode of self-world relation that is implied. The possible modes in which the self can relate itself to its world are what Tillich called the "necessary functions" of spirit or mind; and the realms of reason or spirit are not generic properties of objects but products of the various necessary functions. Generic definitions are formulated in view of the object and its qualities as they appear; constructive definitions have in view the self's relation to objects and the characteristics of this relation that are implied in and exhibited by products of the relation. For the former kind of definition, one looks at the objects; for the latter, one looks at our looking at the objects.

Juxtaposing a generic and a constructive definition of art may make the difference clearer. A work of art is defined, let us say, as an object that is the product of human effort, which shows skill in its making, and which expresses meaning, beauty, or similar qualities. Against this generic definition, let us set a constructive one:

A work of art is an object that is the product of a theoretic relation between the self and the world whose intention is to express the realness of the real in the object rather than to grasp its form. This latter definition is, as a matter of fact, a close paraphrase of Tillich's definition of art; and it makes clear that we can understand a constructive definition only to the extent that we can see the act, the relation of self to world, of which the object is the product or embodiment.

In many instances, of course, things that fit under the title of *art* according to generic definitions or ordinary usage will also belong there according to constructive definitions. Nevertheless, there are cases in which something might be art by generic definition or common usage but not by a constructive definition. Common usage always provides an initial guide for understanding which things exemplify a certain definition. Hence, if one formulated a constructive definition of art that had no connection with anything that is usually called art, the definition would be defective. Yet, at the same time, common use is not the final criterion, and what is commonly called art (as is kitsch, for example) may not merit that title; and what may not commonly be called art (Joan Miró's surrealist *Acrobats in the Night Garden,* for example, may look indistinguishable from a schoolchild's drawing) does merit the title in a constructive definition.

According to constructive definitions, we can say that a scientific statement is "scientific" because it is the product of a self-world relation in which the self is neutralized, the relation is that of grasping the form of the reality, and the object is one that can appear directly or indirectly to our physical senses. Similarly, a work of art is "artistic," or aesthetic, because it is the product of a self-world relation in which the self is individualized; the relation is that of expressing the quality of realness (what Tillich called *Gehalt*) in the object; and the object to which the work refers, as the source of its "inspiration," is one that is given to "feeling" rather than to the physical senses, appearing "at" or "upon" physically perceptible objects and embodied in them.

Bearing in mind the distinction between representation and expression and the character of constructive definitions, one can give this account of the place of art in Tillich's systematic thought: Art belongs to theoretical, not practical, reason; that is to say, the function it serves is that of receiving reality rather than that of transforming reality. Despite the fact that the making of a work of art might seem to involve a doing, or a transformation of reality —a sculptor does seem to transform a boulder into a statue—the relation of self to world that is implied in the work is still theoretic. Its intention is not to make reality different from what it is but to show a dimension of reality that does not otherwise appear.

In his 1919 essay, "On the Idea of a Theology of Culture,"[10] Tillich adopted a wording from Johann Fichte, whose *Wissenschaftslehre* he had studied, and from Friedrich Schleiermacher in order to describe these relations. What characterizes the theoretic relation, which involves science and art, is that the mind, or spirit, endeavors to take the object into itself; by contrast, what characterizes the practical relation is that the mind endeavors to inject itself into reality, to transform it in the direction of what, in the mind's judgment, it should be. Although Tillich subsequently made little use of this wording, the idea it expresses is one that stayed with him. He thus construed both science (cognition) and art as activities in which the mind conforms itself to the way in which reality is what it is. What is taking place when, in the presence of an object, we say, "This is a tree," is that the mind is forming its own thought so as to conform with the way in which the real object shows itself. In the presence of an appearing tree, we cannot think, "That is a lion," if we intend to "know" reality.

Art, too, implies a relation in which the mind conforms with the real. But unlike cognition, which grasps the form and with it the content *(Inhalt)* of reality, art expresses the import *(Gehalt)*—the quality of realness or the depth content—of reality. A painting of a tree, a poem, and a musical composition are all theoretical expressions of the realness of the real. Both science and art, then, are ways of receiving reality, but the one receives it through grasping its forms and the other through expressing its quality of realness, its depth. Conceivably a single set of words—for example, "I read, much of the night, and go south in the winter," from T. S. Eliot's *Waste Land*[11]—might serve both cognitive and aesthetic purposes, depending on whether they are read as part of a poem, where the versification and structure indicate this intention, or with a view to obtaining biographical information. Science is more important in the rise of a spiritual situation; art, in the interpreting of it.

This systematic placing of the two does not take into account that aesthetic forms themselves differ from cognitive ones, an omission that, curiously, is found in all of Tillich's treatments of the topic. It is a notable omission, for there is obviously a formal difference between the two as well. Mathematical physics differs from music not only because it is formal while music is expressive, but also because cognitive forms are not sensuous forms. The form that we hear in music as an octave can also be put as an arithmetic ratio; but the sensuous form as we hear it is not the same as that ratio. One of the consequences of this difference appears in language. The cognition contained in a statement may be put into other words, in a paraphrase or in another language, and we can recognize that the two wordings say the same thing. The poetic sense of a verse or line cannot be transferred in that fashion. Thus, "This is a tree" and "Das ist ein Baum" do say the same thing, cognitively speaking; but they do not say the same thing aesthetically. They are the same science but not the same art—they "judge" the same way because of the cognitive form, but they "sound" different because of their aesthetic form. This results not from the difference between grasping forms and expressing depth but from a difference in forms themselves.

Tillich's basic interest, however, lay not with a philosophy of art but with a theology of art based on the relation between surface and depth content. This relation provides the principle for a typology of artistic styles. True, Tillich has no single typology; he even disclaimed the possibility of providing a complete set of types, and he used different ones on different occasions.[12] Nevertheless, what runs through all of them, and is especially important for the religious interpretation of art, is a triplex pattern derived from the distinction between theoretic functions when they are directed to surface forms and content and those same functions when directed toward the depth content. In "profane," or secular, styles, exemplified by impressionism and realism, natural appearances, whether subjective or objective, predominate over the expression of depth content; "religious" art, exemplified by romanticism and expressionism, is a style in which the expression of depth content prevails over the representation of natural forms; and in "classical" art, exemplified by classicism and idealism, there is a balance between the expression of depth content and the appearance of natural form.

Besides being drawn from a constitutive definition of art, this typology also shows the rooting of Tillich's reflections on art in the visual arts rather than in music or literature. For the illustrations that he uses of "natural form" are taken from paintings, in which it is easy to ascertain whether or not concrete things like trees and abstract ones like cubes are represented in their natural appearance. It is not quite so clear what would count as a "natural" form in music, though one could imagine that harsh dissonances might be considered a disruption of the natural form, or that the experimental music of, say, Karlheinz Stockhausen, which has fragments of melodies that are interrupted by other sounds or are composed to be played in arbitrary sequences, might equally well be heard as breaking natural forms, that is, the familiar melodies, tempi, and sequences.

At all events, however, what distinguishes a work expressing depth content is that what speaks from it is a power or meaning, a "spiritual substance," coming in and through the visual, acoustic, or otherwise perceptible subject matter, rather than the subject matter itself. Thus, one's attention in van Gogh's *Starry Night* (1889) is directed not so much to the celestial scene itself but to an eeriness that addresses a viewer through it. The disruption of natural appearance does not result from a lack of skill, nor does it strike the beholder as merely odd or idiosyncratic; it expresses something, a depth of being.

What expressive art reveals is a dimension of depth in being, though that depth need not be the "unconditional" or "ultimate" depth.[13] This dimension can be manifested in two contrasting ways—either naturalistically, as the mystery of the givenness of things in their normal appearance, or religiously, as the "divine-demonic ground" of things. When authentically revealed, it is not a subjective meaning imposed upon the work of art or its contents; it is as real as is the surface appearance, coming to the viewer from the work and through the form and content of what is there. Power and meaning, as Tillich put it in his essay "Nature and Sacrament," are not separated from the physical character and objective structure of things; they appear "in and through"—or, in a better wording, "at" and "upon"—those structures.[14] In the twentieth century they can appear, however, only by disrupting and distorting the normal appearances.

In this, the modern world differs from the medieval world,

whose spirit was expressed in the architecture of its cathedrals, particularly the stained-glass windows, which tell one of the most eloquent parables the Western world possesses. Depth, in them, is the daylight; surface, the window figures. Inside a cathedral, one sees the light only as it comes through the stained glass. But the light shining through has the effect of letting the figures in the windows stand out on their own. From this point of view, one is always simultaneously seeing both the window figures and the light by which they are illuminated and made real. Each figure appears simultaneously in its own right—we see the shepherd, the king, the rose, for what they are—and also as pointing to the light, which shines through it. The biblical word for this relation is *glory*. Daylight "glorifies" the window figures, and they "glorify" it. For Western Christendom, these windows were at their time a parable of the glory of God on earth. They are still capable of being recalled, and they are the image in the background when Tillich refers to the "transparency" of the finite to the infinite. But the metaphysics of translucence they imply does not tell of the disruption of worldly content that is a mark of the twentieth-century experience of reality, and they say nothing about the possibility of an artistic expression of religious depth today, that is, in a period after the religious tradition and its symbols have been subjected to the critique that bears the name of Enlightenment.

That possibility is dependent on another consideration, as Tillich, who was always concerned about the present, knew very well. Artists cannot be convincing if their works incorporate less of the apprehension of the real than has already been incorporated in past works. Once the dread of the abyss has appeared to modernity, as it did in the expressionism of the early twentieth century, something about the depth of reality has been seen which cannot subsequently be forgotten without peril of losing one's self as oriented to reality. This is the reason why a theonomy of translucence, which does not express that dimension, cannot seem real today. What is at stake here is fundamentally the question of truth in art; it is the question not of whether one style is more correct than another, or Cézanne's painting truer than Gauguin's, but of whether the meaning seen in a work of art has a connection with reality.

In earlier periods of history, the line between significance and reality was not so clearly drawn, and it may still be possible on occasion to dwell in the significant without being troubled by the real. But it can be done only at a heavy cost. In the end, one cannot be satisfied with an art that is merely meaningful if it does not bear a connection to one's understanding of what reality is. One reason for this is that art does bear on reality; indeed, its intention is to express the realness of the real. If, then, what it presents seems to be unrealistically decorative ("prettifying," or "beautifying," Tillich sometimes called this kind of art),[15] one might take it as a nice occasion to escape from reality, and one might even like it; but one cannot regard it as conveying *to* the viewer the reality of the real. It is to art what science fiction is to science. It may have its value for diversion, but it cannot fulfill the necessary function of the aesthetic faculty.

The way that significance and reality are connected with each other in a work of art is, of course, different from scientific knowledge—as is noted in Archibald MacLeish's oft-mentioned remark that a poem does not "mean," it just "is." "Truth [in art] is that of signifying, not that of historical or scientific validity," Tillich wrote.[16] In cognitive statements, as works of science, the meaning is located in the statements themselves (what we understand them to be saying) and contains a draft of the intended reality, but the reality itself is presented in some other fashion, dependent finally on our physical senses. In works of art, however, both the meaning and the reality are found in the work itself. The artistic sense, which is constituted by the play of colors, sounds, shapes, and rhythms, discloses at the same time the world that the sense intends. It "is" what it intends; what it expresses is found at the same place as what it depicts. This coexistence of meaning and reference in a work is often mistakenly thought to collapse the difference between the two. The contrary is the case. We can distinguish the significance that, for example, a painting of a landscape bears and the reality it expresses. Because we can do so, we can recognize whether it is meaningful but not true, or both meaningful and true. In the latter case it not only has a perceptible significance but also is the corresponding reality. One might use the word *authenticity* to designate the truth of art instead of *correctness,* which applies to the truth of science; but it is truth that is involved in both.

This consideration is especially important for artistic presentations of religious subject matter. Can art today not only signify but present reality, when the reality is that meant by the religious subject matter? Tillich confessed to a divided mind about this question. Some paintings—of which he cited Sutherland's *Crucifixion* as an example—suggested to him that expressionistic art can indeed revive traditional religious symbols. But in the main he thought otherwise. Such expressionistic works as Georges Rouault's *Miserere* did not convince him that the religious subject matter portrayed was made contemporaneous.[17] In this sense even expressionistic religious art may seem untrue.

Nonetheless, the expressionistic style acquired importance for theology of art because it could show how religion, as the direction toward the unconditional, appears as a "breakthrough," existing at those places where the unconditional breaks through as the reality in all entities, the necessity in all values, and the meaning *(Sinn)* in all personal life.[18] This style of painting, with its disfiguring of everyday appearances, portrays its subject matter, or content, as insignificant; nature possesses no luster or sheen; it is robbed of its illusion, its glory. Moreover, what "speaks" from expressionist painting is something that evokes dread, a shudder at the abyss. The painting is "about" this rather than about the objects painted. The dissolution of everyday forms, however, is not intended to sacrifice form to the formless vitality of things; instead, as Tillich insisted against Georg Simmel, it strives for a new form which, paradoxically, is to grasp a depth content that of its nature cannot be grasped.

TECHNOLOGICAL SELF-CONSCIOUSNESS IN POSTEXPRESSIONISM

The intention, then, of a theology of art is, as Tillich put it in 1919, to follow the process by which the depth content breaks into the form, as "the meaning, the spiritual substance, without which the form has no significance" or, stated differently, as the reality experience present in the work. The process in which this spiritual substance emerges is "grasped in the content [of the work] by means of the form *(an dem Inhalt mittelst der Form)*"; for it is a process in which the content disappears in the plenitude of the spiritual substance that "flows into the form." The form becomes increasingly inadequate; the reality breaks through the form that is to contain it, and yet "this bubbling over and shattering is itself still a form."[19] The religious interpreter of art describes this process from the standpoint of the *Gehalt* itself, in other words, with the aim of saying what it is that is breaking through and seeking to be formed.

An example may serve to clarify these terms and their relations. Let us assume that we are dealing with a landscape painting and that it is recognizably a work of art—van Gogh's *Landscape with Olive Trees* (1889). The "form" of the work is that of a landscape; its "content" is made up of the things that appear in the work (mountains, trees, grass); and the depth content, the *Gehalt* or spiritual substance, is the power that speaks to a viewer from the painting, eliciting concern about being or not being at all. This much is obvious enough. But to see the interrelation of the aspects somewhat more analytically than Tillich, we can follow the course of the adjectives that apply to them. Paintings are characterized by such terms as "skillful," "eloquent," "powerful"; landscapes may be "beautiful," "serene," and the like. The depth content that breaks through is "holy," in other words, awakening both dread and hope with respect to the being of anything at all. If, as in van Gogh's *Landscape,* the content becomes accidental and the form is left to float free, then the landscape, by losing its connection to trees, mountains, grass, and other such things that belong to it, becomes open to new content. The form is still there—landscape —but what is seen in the landscape is a power or eloquence. In the everyday world, we cannot have a landscape without the content of a landscape. But what is happening in van Gogh's *Landscape* is that something still recognizable as a landscape is losing its everyday objects. No longer can it be characterized—as might Gaugin's *Tahitian Landscape* (1891) or even van Gogh's earlier *Orchard* (1888)—in terms ordinarily used of landscapes. It requires terms applied to the power of the realness of the real. Van Gogh's is "an eloquent landscape," one that "speaks" to a viewer.

Here we notice what has happened. The term *eloquent,* which is otherwise used to describe the character of the painting, but not of its subject matter, is now used to refer to the subject matter. The artwork has become a landscape. It can literally, though paradoxically, be said to be a "powerful landscape," or "landscaped power"; for this combination of words names a form whose content is no longer its own subject matter, except in an accidental fashion, but the power that speaks through it. Finally, this depth content is "religious" to the extent that what speaks through the painting is not only a cosmic quality (say, the turbulence or even the saving, destructive power of nature, as in Faust's invocation "Nature immense" in Berlioz's *La Damnation de Faust*), but something of ultimate concern, the depth of being and not being at all. Then the painting has "holy" eloquence, which speaks a Yes and No upon its subject. It is an eloquent and holy *landscape,* not just an eloquent painting.

In this terminology, a landscape painting of a "secular" type might be described as a "skillful" painting of a naturally "beautiful" (or ugly) landscape—the ordinary forms and content of the artwork and its subject matter remain intact. This type is, incidentally, driven to absurdity musically in John Cage's *Four Minutes and 33 Seconds*—the work consists of having a pianist sit at the keyboard for the stated length of time and then close the piano. The aesthetic form here has no content that could, by reason of its becoming accidental, express the power of depth. It is like an empty tautology. A "classical" portrait of the landscape mentioned can be described as a "beautiful" painting of a "beautiful" landscape—beauty is the meaning of the work and also of its subject matter.

In expressive, or religious, style the same work can be described as a "powerful" (an eloquent, a "holy") landscape. The Yes that a painting like van Gogh's landscape makes known lies in our still being able to recognize it as a landscape; the No lies in the disruption of the forms of ordinary objects. In this work, though not in later expressionism, the Yes still predominates over the No; there is a creative, saving quality present, which is sealed, as it were, by the cloud at the top in the center of the painting, a cloud whose shape can be seen, without unduly taxing the imagination, as that of a mother and child. The very nebulousness of this figure may foretell times to come; but there is no doubt that it is there, casting its light upon the turbulent Earth below. The work was painted by a man who, hovering between sanity and insanity, committed suicide not long after. Yet what it bespeaks is not insanity or irrationality, but the radiance of a Yes that outlives the destruction of earthly form.

Tillich's theology of culture read the depth content not of isolated works but of whole cultural periods. This is why the style in which the masses were painted served to interpret the history of spirit in his *Masse und Geist*. [20] This is also why expressionistic painting, with its sense of dread, of cosmic guilt, and of redemption in a love-mysticism that eradicates individuality in a one-and-all, was important for a theology of culture in the first half of the twentieth century and why, later, Tillich could see a connection between pop art ("the art of non-art," or "the death of the concept of art") and death-of-God theology.[21] In the last quarter of this century, however, one sees something different from what Tillich could see in expressionism. The pluralism of styles, which defeats any effort to find a dominant style as the unity of the period, and the experimentalism practiced everywhere attest to a new kind of experience, one that has survived expressionistic disruption and moved to an activity based on a recognition of the structure of reflexivity and of a certain "double agency" at the root of self-consciousness; and the place at which the relation of surface and depth is focused is that of self-consciousness and conscience instead of the appearance of nature.

In 1912, to define his expressionism as against the earlier impressionism he had studied, Franz Marc wrote in the periodical *Pan:* "Today we seek behind the veil of appearance the hidden things in nature that seem to us more important than the discoveries of the Impressionists. . . . We see this [inner spiritual] side in the same way that earlier ones suddenly 'saw' violet shadows and the atmosphere surrounding things."[22] Of the present, it could be said that, in contrast to expressionism, the main insight has to do with a "hidden" subject in technological reason. Not the veil of appearance or the flow of abstract form, but technological subjectivity is where the dimension of depth makes its presence known. From this point of view, the plurality of styles and interest is not just a coexistence but a genuine pluralism of style, that is, a reflexivity that amounts to a conscious style of stylings. Through all styles the pervading unity is not another style of the same order but a search for a style by which to use the first-order styles—in other words, a style of styles, or the reflexivity of style.

This thesis about the present—that it is an age of the doubling of consciousness and technique upon itself—cannot be given the necessary substantiation in the compass of one article, nor could it be made entirely convincing simply through an examination of art, no matter how extensive. Let it serve here as no more than a proposal, and let me illustrate what it means by reference to a work, now over a decade old, in which the essential aspects converge. At the intersection of the popular and the cultivated, of youth culture and tradition, of the acoustic and the literary, is a work exhibiting the conscience and self-consciousness of a culture of mass communications (self- and star-promotion), the surface and depth of human doing (a double agency), the metaphysics of technique, a religious subject matter to which the authors appear to have a living relation, and a reflexivity of style. I mean the rock opera *Jesus Christ Superstar*. It was written and composed by Andrew Lloyd Webber and Tim Rice in 1970, though two selections, "Superstar" and "John Nineteen Forty-One," are from a year earlier.

Rock is, in part, a style of its own, characterized by the use of a driving rhythm based on eighth notes of equal duration, a distinctive meter (often 4/4, with accent on the second and fourth beats of the measure, instead of on the first and third), and a freedom for such previously forbidden harmonies as parallel fourths and fifths, to say nothing of dissonances and portamenti. But, in part, rock represents a reflexivity of style also, a style of using styles, melodies, and harmonies, ancient as well as modern and recent. It is, accordingly, a style of music and a style of the styles of music.

Rice and Webber disclaim any confessional interest in Christianity. Yet their opera gives evidence of a living concern with the passion story. It provides not a decorative rendering, a false piety, but an encounter with the meaning of the story. Nothing shows this more than the freedom with which the authors reconstruct the gospel story. Unlike such traditional passions as those of J. S. Bach and Heinrich Schütz or such contemporary ones as Krzysztof Penderecki's, this one makes no effort to be faithful to the exact words of the New Testament. It reinterprets that text in a process that Heideggerians would call a dismantling and reconstructing.

In another respect too, the opera is significant. Tillich remarked that no contemporary metaphysics can be true without incorporating the element of shuddering in the presence of the depth of being; that is why Hegel's metaphysics could not be simply resuscitated. The remark can be corroborated for music by a comparison of Igor Stravinsky's neoclassicism with Mozart's classicism—in Stravinsky the negative has already asserted itself and must be conquered, whereas in Mozart it has not yet asserted itself; Mozart's is a music of the original goodness of creation, whereas Stravinsky's is of the redemption of creation. A similar corroboration lies in Rudolf Otto's analysis of Bach's "Sanctus" in the *B-Minor Mass.* From Bach's "enraptured and triumphant choric hymn," no one would gather "that the Seraphim covered their faces with two of their wings" and that Isaiah, in his vision, had declared, "Woe is me! For I am lost."[23] Not the least of the authenticity of the Rice-Webber opera comes from its incorporating this element, though in a remarkable way, almost benignly, with a sense of the grace beneath it, as a kind of quizzical self-reflection: Mary Magdalene's blues melody, "I Don't Know How to Love Him," concludes with the words: "He scares me so / I want him so / I love him so." Judas repeats it later: "He scares me so." Most dramatically it emerges in Judas's recognition that he has been, unwittingly, a double agent: "My God . . . I've been used / And you knew all the time / God I'll never ever know why you chose me for your crime / . . . You have murdered me!" But this outburst passes, as it is transmuted into the voice of Judas, who wonders at what has happened: "Did you mean to die like that? . . . Don't get me wrong—I only want to know."

This element is all the more significant because of the form of the whole. The drama of the opera has the form of self-assertion, specifically that self-promotion or star-promotion that is characteristic of modern mass communications. It exemplifies what Tillich called "technological reason." The actors are promoters of a superstar, and talk about God is one of the promotional means. Technological reason has no aspect of depth or dread; it is pure calculation of means for ends. Yet here something steals into it, a depth subject, which is understood only in a paradox of human technique. The promotional thinking of the human persons turns out to be the working of a hidden subject "God." Human subjectivity is a double agent, at one and the same time a doer and a representative of another. That is to say, the religious dimension becomes manifest when the autonomy of promotive reason is out-tricked, outcalculated, by a subject acting through it. The paradoxical form (in Judas's "You have murdered me!") makes this trickery different from Hegel's *List,* or cunning, of history. Yet this reason maintains its integrity to the end. It does not shrink back from the threat of an abyss. Despite feeling that "he scares me so," the promoters continue to carry out their plans.

Unlike the case of expressionist painting, which served as Tillich's guide, the natural forms here are not disrupted but preserved and carried to their end—calculation, suspicion, planning, success, failure, accusation, demands, self-serving attitudes, love, egoism, and altruism are preserved in a self-consciousness for which they are equal possibilities. But a gracious duplicity is revealed when the natural and human are shown to be the instruments—free, at that—for a power acting through them. Whatever horror is connected with the negativity that is in the depth of subjectivity is perceived when it has, as it were, already been corrected or graced. Art reveals subjects and objects that are hidden in the persons and things of everyday. Here too what it reveals is not only the Judas, with whom potentially anyone can be identified, and the whip-lashing—the sound of the thirty-nine lashes in the "Trial Before Pilate" is starkly realistic—which is potentially the import of every realism, but also, when the aesthetic transcends itself to express the religious, the unconditional subject named "God" and the unconditional power of being named "grace."

These are indications of how the religious experience expressed in art today seems changed from that of expressionism as Tillich analyzed it. The period of disruptive spirit seems to have ended and given way to a spirit of agency. If art and metaphysics after Kierkegaard, Schelling, and Schopenhauer must include the dread of the abyss, then perhaps after the discovery of computers, they must also include the technological self-consciousness in face of the calculability, or the promotive quality, of the depth. In one point of comparison, however, the religious situation has not changed. The symbol of resurrection has not been recovered. What follows the death of Jesus and concludes this rock opera is a wordless, almost sentimental and nostalgic string music, entitled simply "John Nineteen Forty-One" and containing only a hint of something new and still to come. John 19:41 reads: "Now in the place where he was crucified there is a garden, and in the garden a new tomb where no one had ever been laid."

NOTES

1. James Luther Adams, *Paul Tillich's Philosophy of Culture, Science, and Religion* (New York: Harper & Row, 1965), v.

2. Paul Tillich, "Zur Theologie der bildenden Kunst und der Architektur," in *Gesammelte Werke*, vol. 9 (Stuttgart: Evangelisches Verlagswerk, 1967), 345–55. (Hereafter, *Gesammelt Werke* is referred to as *GW*.)

3. Ibid. Cf. Paul Tillich, *On the Boundary* (New York: Charles Scribner's Sons, 1966), 28; First edition, 1936. Cf. Wilhelm and Marion Pauck, *Paul Tillich: His Life and Thought* (New York: Harper & Row, 1976), vol. 1, *Life*, 76. Cf. Paul Tillich "I'll Always Remember . . . One Moment of Beauty," *Parade*, 25 September 1955, 2.

4. Paul Tillich, "Religiöser Stil und Religiöser Stoff in der Bildenden Kunst," in *GW* 9:312–23. The two books Tillich reviewed were Eckart von Sydow, *Die deutsch expressionistische Kultur und Malerei* (Berlin: Furche Verlag, 1920) and G. F. Hartlaub, *Kunst und Religion, ein Versuch über die Möglichkeit neuer religiöser Kunst* (Leipzig: Kurt Wolff, 1919).

5. See Tillich's 1929 essays, "Realism and Faith" and "Nature and Sacrament," in *The Protestant Era*, trans. James Luther Adams (Chicago: University of Chicago Press, 1948), 66, 101. See also idem, *The Religious Situation*, trans. H. Richard Niebuhr (New York: Meridian Books, 1956), 16; first German edition, 1926; first English edition, 1932. See also his 1930 essay, "Kult und Form," *GW* 9:324–27.

6. Paul Tillich, "Protestantism and Artistic Style," in idem, *Theology of Culture*, ed. Robert C. Kimball (New York: Oxford University Press, 1959), 73.

7. Paul Tillich, "Art and Ultimate Reality," in *Cross Currents* 10 (1959): 1–14.

8. Sheldon Cheney, *A World History of Art* (New York: Viking Press, 1952), 896.

9. See Tillich's 1922 essay, "The Philosophy of Religion," in idem, *What Is Religion?*, ed. James Luther Adams (New York: Harper & Row, 1969), 41, 54.

10. Paul Tillich, "On the Idea of a Theology of Culture," trans. William Baillie Green, in *What Is Religion?*

11. T. S. Eliot, *Waste Land*, 1, 18, in *The Complete Poems and Plays of T. S. Eliot* (London: Faber and Faber, 1969), 61.

12. The simplest typology is that of naturalism, idealism, and expressionism. Another has four types, depending on whether the content and the style are religious or nonreligious. See Paul Tillich, "Existentialist Aspects of Modern Art," in *Christianity and the Existentialists*, ed. Carl Michalson (New York: Charles Scribner's Sons, 1956). A third typology coordinates five elements of style (imitative, subjective, idealist, realist, expressive) with types of religion. See idem, "Protestantism and Artistic Style." A fourth has six types: impressionism and realism, both form-dominated; romanticism and expressionism, both *Gehalt*-dominated; idealism and classicism, both exhibiting a balance of form and *Gehalt*. See idem, "Religiöser Stil und religiöser Stoff in der bildenden Kunst," *GW* 9:312–23. Tillich wrote a number of essays on architecture as well, some of which include practical suggestions for building, and he also discussed some works of literature; but it is clear that his theory of art and its relation to religion is guided by the visual arts.

13. Tillich, "Zur Theologie der bildenden Kunst und der Architektur," *GW* 9:348.

14. Tillich, "Nature and Sacrament," 101.

15. Tillich, "Existentialist Aspects of Modern Art," 146.

16. Tillich, "Religiöser Stil und religiöser Stoff in der bildenden Kunst," 321.

17. Tillich, "Existential Aspects of Modern Art," 143, 144.

18. See Tillich's 1919 essay, "Über die Idee einer Theologie der Kultur," *GW* 9:11–31.

19. Ibid., 38, 39, 48, 37.

20. Paul Tillich, *Masse und Geist,* in *GW* 2(1962):35–90. See the résumé of this work of 1922 in Adams, *Paul Tillich's Philosophy of Culture, Science, and Religion,* 90–93.

21. See Tillich's 1964 essay, "Der schöpferische Durchbruch," *GW* 8 (1970):435.

22. Franz Marc, as quoted by Nick Baldwin, "Seeing Nature's Spiritual Side," on the Franz Marc exposition in Minneapolis, *Des Moines Sunday Register,* 25 May 1980.

23. Rudolf Otto, *The Idea of the Holy,* trans. John W. Harvey (1923; reprint, London: Penguin Books, 1959), 85–6.

10. Tillich and Jewish Thought

ALBERT H. FRIEDLANDER

> The similarity between the thoughts of Tillich and Jewish thought perhaps consists in this: the Jews are also unable to represent or to depict God, that is, the Absolute.
> —MAX HORKHEIMER, *Werk und Wirken Paul Tillichs, Ein Gedenkbuch*

> One may doubt, indeed, that Tillich and the Bible are even talking about the same God. The God who is described by Tillich as "being itself" seems to have very little in common with the God of Abraham, Isaac, and Jacob. . . . Might Tillich not have done better to have gone back to the Mosaic conception of God in the Book of Exodus . . . [of] God . . . not as an It but as a Thou . . . as moral challenge, not as objective existent . . . ?
> —BERNARD MARTIN, *The Existentialist Theology of Paul Tillich*

Jews are aware of Paul Tillich as a controversial Christian theologian. Seen from the vantage point of the outsider, Tillich's Christianity looms over all his works. The more he is attacked by Christian thinkers, the clearer his position as a Christian appears to us. The points that are argued in this very Christian debate deal with the open or closed stance of the Christian toward other religions; they are centered upon a traditional, as against a radical, Christology; they are concerned with matters of Christian dogma. The attempt is often made to pull this walker upon boundary lines into the center of the tradition, to reject the enlargement of the religious area lest it attenuate Christian faith. Even Bonhoeffer was concerned about Tillich's attempt "to interpret the evolution of the world . . . in a religious sense—to give it its whole shape through religion."[1] But it is precisely at this point that Tillich becomes most interesting to Jewish thinkers, to Jewish thought which has always ignored boundaries between the secular and the sacred, which lives in the tension of polarities that find very clear expression in the writings of Tillich.

THE MAN AND HIS TEACHINGS

What Tillich taught is important to Judaism—important enough for us to start our own controversies about him, to challenge and to reject, to approve and to accept what he has to say. However, it is not only the teaching but also the teacher that matters to Judaism. We listen to Tillich the theologian because Tillich the human being *extraordinaire* cast his lot with the Jewish people in dark times. Max Horkheimer, in his recollections about their shared university life, states that well before 1933 Tillich's courageous, moral statements in public utterances stamped him a foe of the Nazis.[2] Tillich was always proud to declare that he was the first non-Jew thrown out of his professorial post, in 1933, as an enemy of the Nazis. His was an existential involvement with the Jewish people: through his friends, through his understanding of the Jewish dimension within the Christian heritage that formed him. The actual lecture in Frankfurt that led to his expulsion was given as part of the anniversary celebrations of the philosophic faculty at that university. The lecture traced the abiding influence upon classic German literature and philosophic thought emanating from Spinoza and continuing through Marx. As the audience left the lecture hall, Tillich heard one of his colleagues exclaim, *"Nun will man uns auch noch zu Juden machen!"* ("Now, they even want to turn us into Jews!") The expulsion order arrived shortly after this event.

A great teacher instructs by his life as much as by his writings. Some time should be spent contemplating this act of courage. However, this aspect of Paul Tillich also exists in written form. In a little-known lecture series of 1953, in Berlin, Tillich formulated this aspect of his teaching with crispness and cogency. Less than a decade after the war, in an atmosphere filled with guilt and defiance, within a language that had not yet unlearned the barbarisms of the previous decade, Tillich gave four lectures titled "The Jewish Question, a Christian and a German Problem."[3]

Tillich did not quote Amos in that first lecture, which dealt with aspects of guilt. But Bible scholars can find similarities: the same cadences, the same controlled anger. Tillich spoke of five types of guilt. First, there was the absolute guilt of the murderers, of certain groups and individuals who could be viewed separately from the other Germans. Second, he spoke of the guilt that no German could evade: the moral responsibility that was not accepted, the voices that remained silent, the individuals who made not one move to save their fellow human beings. Next, he looked at the audience surrounding him and spoke of the guilt of repressed knowledge, of hiding from oneself, of encapsulating past trauma deeply within one's self in the hope that it would never break forth into the new life that did not want to know what happened in the past. This could only lead to the fourth type of guilt: that one would really forget the past! More tragedy resided in that fact than in the earlier patterns of self-deceit. Finally, he warned the Germans not to take these moral questions into the area of bookkeeping, not to calculate carefully that the hurt they had suffered wiped out their own guilt of involvement in concentration camps or wanton murder. It was a hard lecture to give; but Tillich felt that he had to present the unacceptable face of Christianity—in the immediate past as well as in the Church's history and in the Gospels—before the Jewish question would open itself to full Christian awareness. *Present day dialogue between Judaism and Christianity would have been impossible without this type of honest self-examination.*

The second lecture dealt with anti-Semitism itself, but also with the use of stereotypes endemic to all contemporary discourse. Jew and Christian can be instructed by the description of the intolerant person who clings grimly to the abstraction instead of accepting reality: "In the encounter with the actual Jew the stereotype is shattered. It cannot be realized. But the anti-Semite wants it to be true, and therefore views the individual Jew as 'the exception.' Typological thinking is unhistorical. It is not permitted to recognize that personalities and groups are subservient to historical change."[4]

And Tillich guided his audience and our society through a post-holocaust world where outsiders are not permitted actual existence but remain "the stranger," "the Jew"—figures of speech that to this day characterize our relationships to others. Tillich emphasized the point:

The stranger? I would recall the answer which Hamlet gives the soldier who says: "By God, this is surprisingly strange," namely, "Then call it welcome as a stranger."

For the German subconscious, "the Jew" is too close to be welcomed as a stranger, and not close enough to be experienced as part of one's own. . . . The mirror which Judaism presents to the Germans emerges out of a prophetic tradition and has therefore a particular meaning and a particular authority.[5]

But the Jew—and Judaism—was no stranger to Tillich. It may also be said that the teachings found throughout his works are a mirror that he holds in front of a suffering people in order to make them realize that the stereotypes of the outside world are not held universally, that in the eyes of the brother the basic nature of his suffering sibling remains unchanged. Tillich saw a religious dimension to this encounter that had to be grasped before understanding could take place: "Within the history of the Jewish people there exists something singular and unique, which can only be understood in the light of a religious analysis."[6]

The Berlin lecture here becomes an outline of Tillich's basic religious position, so that the audience can understand a structure that includes both Jews and Christians, who are both unconditionally concerned with the holy, which they cannot reject, which cannot be limited in time or in space. As far as Tillich is concerned, this excursion into theology is at the heart of dialogue between the religions. The audience is reminded that

the Holy is never completed. . . . It contains within itself the tension between that which is and that which is to be. . . . It has the character of polarity as priest and prophet. . . . If the priestly pole alone remains, the sacramental becomes magic; if the prophetic pole alone remains, the proclamation becomes the law. . . . The history of the relationship between Judaism and Christianity is determined through this polarity.[7]

This polarity, whether between the church structure and the prophet, or as seen within the realm of Jewish life, leads to an understanding of the categories that dominate both Christianity and Judaism, the categories of time and space. The sacrament is bound to space, and a historical understanding of Judaism sees it in the framework of the polytheism surrounding it, finding its power within space but also its limitation, whereas the prophets of Israel are time bound, reaching out into the future:

Abraham is called forth, out of space, into time. The bonds of space which he had in common with all, dedicated through sacraments, are broken. This does not mean that space as space is denied. After all, he is to go into a land which God will show him. But this space of the future is left undetermined. The future is . . . the decisive mode of time.

Exodus is the going forth out of space, that is, out of Egypt. The line of time is the line of history, is the line of monotheism, and is the line of justice.[8]

It is at this point, recognizing the Jews as the people of time, recognizing the shared goals of the two religious traditions, that Tillich begins to point towards their unity even through their diversities:

The God of the genuine monotheism is . . . the God of history and of time . . . and Judaism endures for all time as a thorn in the flesh of all who deify space, all nationalisms and imperialisms. Within the interconnections of this history belongs Christianity as well . . . in the attack upon the particularistic, nationalistic tendency within Jewish history . . . by a Christian universalism which . . . collected chosen ones out of all . . . the peoples . . . although the belief that the messiah had already appeared could lead to a new bondage within space.[9]

Jewish thought must inspect this aspect of Tillich's teaching with some hesitation. Deeply aware of the polarities within the Jewish tradition, of particularism and universalism in a creative tension present in all times and places of Jewish existence, we cannot apply this formula to a specific historical situation— whether the time of Jesus or the contemporary emergence of the state of Israel—and impress upon this a pattern assigning particularism to one group and universalism to the other. There is a sense in which Tillich always longed for the Jew to be the true prophet in time.

He only reluctantly accepted that those dynamics of history that he acknowledged also transformed the Jews and made them less a "righteous remnant" and more experts in survival. In his Berlin lectures, Tillich spoke with a touch of sadness about "the attempt of Judaism to create its own space for itself, through the Zionist movement . . . the old paradox." Accepting that the run-of-the-mill Jew cannot be criticized for not wanting to be of time, for finding space for himself, "can one then demand that . . . only because he is born as a Jew, he must belong to the righteous remnant? Evidently one cannot do so."[10] But Tillich does express the hope that the space that Israel has found for itself as a land of its own might lead to a new realization of the prophetic spirit in a new incarnation.

The lecture series concluded with specific demands made upon Christianity which, again as mirror images, come to instruct Jewish thought. Historical circumstances had plunged early Christianity into a pattern where the salvation of the individual became central to the New Testament message; but it had grown away from the Hebrew Scriptures where "the fate of the nations is seen in the light of the prophets' message."[11] Christianity has to learn from Judaism. Hence Jewish thought must be brought to terms with the realization that it has to teach—and that it cannot teach without learning from its neighbor.

Finally, Tillich called for Christianity to combat its own anti-Judaism. In the days since Vatican II, much has been done in this area. Tillich also demanded recognition for Judaism as the representative of prophetic criticism directed against Christianity (but surely also against itself). The image presented to both Christianity and to Judaism is of converging lines:

Judaism has something which has already come, that is, the covenant with God made with it in the past . . . Christianity also has something which does not rest in the past but in the future, that is, the symbol of the second coming of Christ. These are converging lines; and nevertheless the fundamental difference endures, that is, the reference to the Christ who has come, within Christianity, and the reference to the messiah who is expected within Judaism. . . .

The only argument which you can have against the Jewish argument is to be witnesses that through the coming of Christ there really has appeared a new reality. . . . It is an answer of being. Perhaps . . . out of Christian Being there will emerge a strength of breaking into pieces the demon of anti-Semitism and which will fashion a new community between Christians and Jews, not only within the German people but among all Peoples.[12]

Again, the lecture says no more than the life, but it says as much as the life.

MUTUAL ACCEPTANCE AND REJECTION

The basic kinship between the thoughts of Paul Tillich and contemporary Jewish thinking rises out of the common Judeo-Christian tradition, out of the Bible and out of shared experiences in the last days of Palestinian Jewry and the first days of the Christian fellowship. It also emerges out of our own situation, out of a prewar Germany and the experiences of the holocaust. At the beginning of the twentieth century, the great German Jewish thinkers—Buber, Cohen, Rosenzweig, and Baeck—had a parallel development to Tillich in terms of their theological formulations. The old nineteenth century optimism and liberalism was shattered by the events of the twentieth century. Tillich's letter to Thomas Mann regarding his own theological education could have been written by liberal Jewish scholars of that time: "I adhered to liberal theology [Ritschl, Harnack, and Troeltsch], for its scholarly superiority was unquestionable . . . but it lacked insight into the 'daemonic' character of human existence."[13]

Let me go back here to a comparison I made between Leo Baeck and Tillich that still seems valid to me. It sees a basically liberal pattern in Jewish and Christian thought, vitiated by the anguish and doubt of a century of brutality, uncertain at times, but possessed of the same vital energy riding out of the tension of polarities. Some years ago, a German study by Heinz Zahrnt characterized the Christian theologians in terms of the prepositions they employ. Karl Barth uses "over"—God is over, above the world; the strength of his discovery of the loving God is here weakened by the distance that removes God from concrete history. Rudolf Bultmann uses the "over against" to let humanity confront God in an existential decision. The Christian *kerygma* is thus a call to present-day life and out of it—but the Gospels lose reality and become a demand rather than a gift. And Tillich uses "in"—God meets humanity in the reality of the world, in all being, in the immediate and unconditional aspects of human being. According to Zahrnt, this, too, has its flaw. God and world come to intermingle to the point where all is God and people can no longer recognize the world, where all is world and people can no longer find God. Actually, that aspect of the analysis is weak in that Jesus remains in the center of Tillich's thought, is the criterion of all revelation, and the *Geistgemeinschaft* within the church does mean that there are Christian sentinels upon the boundary line.

Yet it is clear that the drive toward the universal is strong enough to create areas where Christian and Jewish thought can meet. Where religion is defined unpolemically by Tillich—"the name for the reception of revelation is 'religion' "[14]—there can be discourse between Jewish and Christian thought. It does not mean that there will not be rejection. As Tillich said: "the problem is not the right of rejecting that which rejects us; rather, it is the nature of this rejection."[15] And he refers to the "dialectical union of rejection and acceptance in the relation of the two groups." Authentic religions validate each other, and not only in terms of their shared encounter with the ultimate. The structure of faith and the natural self-affirmation of the believer create the condition for the self-affirmation of the other. The dialectical union of acceptance and rejection, with "all the tensions, uncertainties, and changes which such dialectics implies,"[16] creates an open boundary between Judaism and Christianity where even the necessary rejection of the other brings us closer to it.

Tillich instructed both Judaism and Christianity when he wrote:

The exclusive monotheism of the prophetic religion is not due to the absoluteness of one particular god as against others, but it is the universal validity of justice which produces the exclusive monotheism of the God of justice. This, of course, implies that justice is a principle which transcends every particular religion and makes the exclusiveness of any particular religion conditional.[17]

Support is here given for every doubter and rebel, every Socratic gadfly challenging the religious establishment's position on the meaning of the inherited truth. The way from the finite to the Infinite remains incomplete, and the "tensions and uncertainties" of religious belief are a necessary aspect of the truth of religious experience for the individual and for the group.

In Jewish thought, controversies *l'shem sha-mayim* ("for the sake of heaven") have always been welcomed. The minority opinion is always recorded in the Talmud, and the final word upon the most heated argument is that "these and those are both words of the living God." Despite all the instruction Tillich gives us, it is harder to apply this to the discussion between our religions—perhaps because these are often still patterned after the medieval disputations where the end result was often forced conversions or the burning of books, and where the outcome was predetermined.

Nevertheless, when we look at the dialogues between Franz

Rosenzweig and Eugen Rosenstock-Heussy, between Martin Buber and many Christian colleagues, the shared experiences of the Christian clergy and the rabbis on civil rights marches, and the integrity of Christian scholars exploring Judaism and Jewish scholars examining the Christian tradition—then we understand Tillich's dialectical union of acceptance and rejection. It can and does happen. It is predicated upon natural self-affirmation and self-confidence, an aspect of the life of religion that is totally removed from fanaticism. Fanaticism, viewed by Tillich as an endemic sickness within religion, is an aspect of weakness. And it is a weak Christianity that attacks Judaism. That is why Tillich could write:

After the shock of the encounter with Islam the Church became conscious of Judaism as another religion and anti-Judaism became fanatical. Only after this was it possible for governments to use the Jews as political scapegoats to cover up their own political and economic failures, and only since the end of the nineteenth century did religious anti-Judaism become racial anti-Semitism, which was—and still is—one of the many ingredients in the radicalized nationalistic quasi-religion.[18]

Whether or not we accept this observation as an adequate sketch of the development of modern anti-Semitism, we can and do accept the implied prescription for authentic religious development which must accept the opposing faith within the framework of divine justice.

DISAGREEMENT IN LOVE

Jewish thought disagrees with Tillich in many areas. In citing Rabbi Bernard Martin's doubts about the central point in Tillich's teachings concerning God,[19] we are basically confronting normative Jewish thought on that point. Horkheimer is, of course, eager to claim congruence between Tillich and Judaism, and Ernst Bloch similarly sees himself echoed in Tillich's position toward utopia: "To be human means to possess utopia."[20] But it must be admitted that Tillich's many Jewish friends and students, including this writer, respond to both life and teaching with the attempt to find resonances with both in their own lives and thoughts. It is not an incorrect procedure, as long as Tillich's own warnings are heeded and the opposition is not explained away but recognized and respected. Tillich's Christianity remains Christianity, with Jesus as the manifestation of the New Being and the criterion for revelation, and with his transmoral ethic of agape, which has to be understood ontologically. Bernard Martin sees this clearly, even where he welcomes Tillich's Christology: "Tillich's Christology . . . has not only succeeded in presenting a conception of the Christ that is meaningful and relevant to modern man, but has also a-voided the divinization of Jesus and . . . absurdities . . . characteristic of much traditional Christian thought."[21]

That kind of defense within Jewish thought may well be considered an attack within the Christian domain, but it does at least open the Jewish tradition to the deep understanding that Tillich had for the biblical text and for many aspects of the Jewish tradition. The emphases differ, and we live and die in these emphases. In the face of utmost darkness, Judaism stresses human goodness at a point where Tillich would rather insist upon the courage to accept the evil resident in man.

Again, a personal memory introduces itself here. A few months before Tillich died, I sat with him in his garden in Easthampton. We discussed a textbook I was preparing on the holocaust, and we came to talk about Leo Baeck, a rabbi and teacher of the Jewish community, who continued to instruct and teach his congregation even when rabbi and congregation were imprisoned together in the concentration camp. I have reported that conversation elsewhere;[22] but there remains an ongoing argument about the use of truth in a situation of crisis. Leo Baeck counseled and taught his fellow inmates in the concentration camp. At one point, he was informed that the trains leaving his camp (Theresienstadt) were taking the Jews not to labor camps or to resettlement places, but to places of extermination. He trusted the informant, but an element of uncertainty remained for him. And he knew that giving this information to the inmates of his camp would destroy hope and the will to live. He decided to wait for more confirmation, and did not pass on this information. When I discussed this with Tillich, he said:

I might have disagreed with Baeck, if I had been in his place, in the concentration camp. But I was not there. I might have shared the last iota of information . . . that the railroad tracks . . . led to certain death. The

full existential truth should always be made available. But the concentration camp . . . was outside our knowledge. . . . Nothing could be done
inside that place to change the fate of those imprisoned there. . . . In the
same way, I believe that the incurable patient should *always* be told the
full truth.[23]

As it happens, most contemporary Jewish thinkers would go
along with Tillich at this point. I cannot do so. I will not *always* tell
the full truth. (At this very time, as I am at work on this chapter,
I regularly visit an incurable cancer patient who has not been told
the full truth.) But if there will be disagreements on matters of
judgment, these disagreements are found on all levels within the
Jewish community, where we feel the right to challenge past and
present teachers and their approach to basic problems of Jewish
existence. Disagreeing with Tillich at this point makes him more
of a teacher to us: Disagreement is not necessarily denial.

Tillich has sometimes been wrong about Judaism. As a product
of mainstream Christian thinking at the turn of the century, he
imbibed prejudices and false information about Judaism from his
earliest days—prejudices that he often fought during his American
period. His inherent sense of justice often tempered the picture of
Judaism he received from the Protestant tradition. Yet there are
certain nuances in Tillich's *Religious Situation (Die religiöse Lage der
Gegenwart)* that indicate inadequate judgment of current Jewish
life. Tillich appreciated the similarities between Judaism, Protestantism, and capitalist society: the "close connection between religion and morality, the high evaluation of personality, the devalua-
tion of the sacramental sphere, the secularization of nature, the
exaltation of the law, religiously inspired intraworldly activity."
That judgment, made in the days of the Weimar Republic, was not
invalid. Yet the Judaism of that time was not divorced from traditional Judaism, and one must disagree with Tillich when he writes:
"The situation in orthodox Judaism is different. It is bound to
tradition and contains valuable religious forces. But it carries them
beneath an armor of Jewish ritualism. Therefore it is not of direct
significance for the religious situation of the present. Eastern Judaism particularly is a reservoir . . . which cannot be directly tapped
by the capitalist West."[24]

In our time, liberal Judaism has drawn so much upon that
Eastern reservoir of faith that contemporary Judaism cannot be

understood without it (and the wave of nostalgia for the vanished Eastern Jewish life indicates that the relationship was certainly present at the beginning of the twentieth century as well). Religious ritual has proved less of an armor and more part of the internal structure of survival for Jewish existence today.

In the same way, Tillich's judgments on Zionism have been overtaken by history. No one would challenge the element of truth in his writing: "Opposition to the movement within Judaism itself is based on the danger which would attend the realization of the Zionist ideal. The peril is that the Jews scattered throughout the world would become foreigners everywhere, that a secular Jewish nationalism might develop and that the universal, messianic, world-uniting mission of Judaism would suffer."[25] Tillich accurately described patterns of thought that existed in the Jewish and non-Jewish community of that time. Implicit within them are assumptions about what Jews should be and what Jews should do. Half a century later, Jews assert the Zionist ideal without becoming foreigners where they live; and it can be argued that a universal, even messianic mission of Judaism is strengthened rather than weakened by a state of Israel, where Hebrew learning and scholarship has given new intensity and extra dimensions to the religion as well as to secular Jewish studies. Yet a bit of this earlier thinking remained within Tillich. The Berlin lecture of 1953 still expressed his fears about that "old paradox [of] . . . Zionism . . . the attempt of Judaism to create its own space for itself."

In a way, Tillich's very love and respect for Judaism and the Jewish people made him demand conformity from them: conformity to a great image of the Jews as the priest-people of the God of time, who should remain special, should continue as unique in the world. Rabbis demand this, as well; but out of a framework of Jewish existence where secularity itself can be an expression of the continuing task. In a sense, we see the Jew and then his Judaism; outside observation often begins with the other polarity. In February of 1980, at a Protestant academy in Tutzing near Munich, I engaged in a dialogue with Karl Rahner on the same theme. Here, too, I found the insistence upon seeing the Jew as the Jew should be in terms of the divine word, rather than viewing Jewish life as it actually exists. There is a point where we have to disagree with philo-Semitism as much as with anti-Semitism (well, perhaps not as much!). But, in disagreeing with Tillich, we come to love him as well.

INTERPRETER OF THE SCRIPTURES

It can be argued that Jewish thought should find itself most at home in the historical, aesthetic, and philosophical writings of Tillich, where one does not begin with theological presuppositions; but that argument falters the more one explores Tillich's writings. Despite all the attacks upon Tillich's theology by the more fundamentalist critics, it becomes clear that everything he has ever taught is built upon his faith in God, which does not become attenuated or tentative when applied to the problems of society. At the end of *Love, Power and Justice*, Tillich writes: "The problems of love, power, and justice categorically demand an ontological foundation and a theological view in order to be saved from the vague talk, idealism, and cynicism with which they are usually treated. Man cannot solve any of his great problems if he does not see them in the light of his own being and of being-itself."[26]

All of Tillich's writings are religious texts, and equally accessible to Jews. Their challenge to Jewish thought is explicit or implicit; and we listen carefully to what is said and to what is left unspoken. Nevertheless, Jews will be less concerned with his *Systematic Theology* and more open to the sermons. In the sermons we find more of Tillich the individual and the concerned friend. Tillich's understanding of the biblical text shows him related to the Jews who listened to Jeremiah and to the Psalmist. Tillich's knowledge of contemporary Jewish fate makes him our brother, even where we question the lessons he draws from our experience. Thus, Tillich interprets Matt. 27 through a holocaust incident:

In the Nuremberg War-crime Trials a witness appeared who had lived for a time in a grave in a Jewish graveyard, in Wilna, Poland. It was the only place he—and many others—could live, when in hiding after they had escaped the gas chamber. During this time he wrote poetry, and one of the poems was a description of a birth. In a grave nearby a young woman gave birth to a boy. The eighty-year-old gravedigger, wrapped in a linen shroud, assisted. When the newborn child uttered his first cry, the old man prayed: "Great God, hast Thou finally sent the Messiah to us? For who else than the Messiah Himself can be born in a grave?" But after three days the poet saw the child sucking his mother's tears because she had no milk for him.

Tillich's anguish and grief for the mother and child who must have died and for the Jews and their fate reaches out and touches us. He also sees "tremendous symbolic value" in the story. In it, he sees the manger and the tomb of Jesus, which ended his life *before* the tomb became the place of his final triumph. He attacks the "happy ending" motif within Christian thought, which thus does not see the agony of the death, and he sets Jewish thought against this:

After three days the child was not elevated to glory; he drank his mother's tears, having nothing else to drink. Probably he died and the hope of the old Jew was frustrated once more. . . . No consolation can be derived . . . ; there cannot be a happy ending.[27]

Strangely enough, I would argue that the Jew is more optimistic than the Christian here. In unabated waiting for a future event rather than looking at a fulfilled moment of the past, we continue, on our own, asserting life. Other Jewish thinkers would disagree. But there is a consensus among us that these events cannot be made an allegory, that Auschwitz has no symbolic value. *Auschwitz is not Calvary.* It cannot be equated with Calvary. Moltmann understands this configuration under the words *ecce homo* and *ecce deus.* Jews cannot do so. At most, they see man here.

For Tillich, "the Christ must be buried in order to be the 'Christ,' namely, He Who has conquered death."[28] The caesura in life must be final. A new beginning cannot come until the end has come. For us, the messiah need not come out of the grave. But we listen to Tillich not because the death of a child is a symbol, but because he wept when the child died.

Tillich's biblical expositions are marvelously instructive. Interpreting Psalm 139, "The Escape from God," he describes the tensions of contemporary existence with deep perception:

We are known in a depth of darkness through which we ourselves do not even dare to look. And at the same time, we are seen in a height of a fullness which surpasses our highest vision. . . . It is the tension in which modern man lives. . . . To endure it is more horrible and more difficult than anything else in the world. And, yet, to endure it is the only way by which we can attain to the ultimate meaning, joy, and freedom of our lives.

Each of us is called to endure. . . . It is to that vocation that we are called as men.[29]

Our rabbinic sages live in the knowledge of that tension. They taught that in one pocket we should always carry a slip with the words "I am dust and ashes" and in the other pocket, a slip with the words "For my sake was the world created." In the tension of that polarity, we move along our way.

Many years after Tillich, Dorothee Sölle began teaching at Union Theological Seminary. In her book *Die Hinreise* she also supplies a commentary to Psalm 139: "Psalm 139 is the direct expression regarding the identity of the human being; it is one answer to the question: Who am I? What do I seek here in the world? Whither does my life lead? Whence do I come? What does it mean that I exist?[30]

The answers are curious parallels to Tillich's observations. There is the same battle against the pious believer who would flee into doctrine or ritual in order to escape the tensions in which an aware human being is caught. But, for Tillich, the paradox of shining darkness is given in order to assert the absolute role of God: "To flee into darkness in order to forget God is not to escape Him. For a time we may be able to hurl Him out of our consciousness . . . but . . . there is no escape from God through forgetfulness." And this absolute rule is only overcome, as it were, by the Psalmist asking God to lead him the perfect way:

At this moment he *asks* God to do what . . . he does relentlessly anyway. The psalmist has overcome his wavering between the will to flee God and the will to be equal with God. He has found that the final solution lies in the fact that the Presence of the Witness, the Presence of the center of all life within the center of *his* life, implies both a radical attack on his existence, and the ultimate meaning of his existence.[31]

For Dorothee Sölle, that shining darkness is the positive assertion of the ultimate dimension of human existence, something absolutely positive:

On his inward journey, beyond all of our normal possibilities of experiences [the person praying the psalm] has experienced . . . the eternal affirmation of his self. The totality of the world . . . contains an unending YES to all of life. . . .

Identity can only be granted and experienced here because identity is more than our conscious existence and more than our time-bound life;

because our whole life is founded in the mystery of the Absolute. Who am I? The answer goes: God knows me better than I know myself.[32]

The answers complement each other. This may well rise out of the fact that both Paul Tillich and Dorothee Sölle are boundary walkers, fighters against the traditionalism of the church, drawn toward biblical texts in which the human condition is described out of the context of human existence rather than as the product of institutional thought.

Tillich's sermons speak to us of the God of history who is revealed through Israel's pain as the first and the last, the beginning and the end of history. In its valleys of darkness, Israel accepted that revelation in all its universal significance. Whenever national pride suborned this revelation by limiting it to a national god, a breakdown followed:

For Jahweh as a national god is always condemned by Jahweh the God of history. The mystery of Judaism today lies in that fact. [Isaiah] describes two very great figures: Cyrus, . . . the world figure of his time, called by the prophet the shepherd and the anointed, the man of God's counsel; and the servant of Jahweh who represents the saving power of innocent suffering and death. The glorious founder of the Empire had to be the servant of the servant of Jahweh. He had to liberate the remnants of Israel, out of which the suffering servant arose.

. . . there are two forces in our battered world. One is the force of those who, like the suffering servant of God, exist, unseen, in all countries. . . . And the second force . . . is . . . those who . . . rule Empires, and incorporate all the shame and greatness of Empires. . . . But if we turn to the true servants and to the true God whom they serve, the God of history, we shall know of the future.[33]

Jewish thought had its own history of interpretation of the *eved adonai*, the "suffering servant." But Tillich's moral vision in proclaiming the God of time against the gods of space, the power of the spirit against the might of rulers, and the reality of the divine justice moving through the sphere of history will always be cherished by us. And so will Paul Tillich.

TILLICH AND BUBER

How shall we sum up the relationship between Tillich, Judaism, and the Jews? Texts and the life give only intimations of a warm and complex relationship in which the natural confrontation between Judaism and Christianity also takes place. This tends to be forgotten; but nothing is more important than seeing a totality of Christian thought enabling the theologian to confront contradictory beliefs even while celebrating common goals and a shared humanity. But this was Paulus—that extraordinary human being who was a brother to the persecuted and a lover of the Jewish tradition. Is there no clear way of freezing that relationship between Tillich and the Jews into a finished image? No, because it was too important, it was too central to his life. A picture of a man, particularly an intellectual portrait, must always remain unfinished. Hölderlin once wrote:

Die Linien des Lebens sind verschieden,
Wie Wege sind, und wie der Berge Grenzen.
Was hier wir sind, kann dort ein Gott ergänzen
Mit Harmonien und ewigem Lohn und Frieden. [34]

A cloud moves across the sun, and the mountains take on a different aspect. An incident, a friendship, suddenly illuminates a life for us; but the lines of that life move on toward destiny. And so, in order to understand more of Paul Tillich, I would turn toward his relationship with Martin Buber—but with hesitation, and with some uncertainty.

There are those who would challenge the central position we would assign to Tillich within contemporary Christianity. And there are many who would question the role of Buber as a paradigm of contemporary Judaism. It could be argued that he always had more Christian disciples than Jewish students, that he was a universal genius more than a representative of Judaism. In the end, the argument fades away; Buber will be seen as one of the greatest of Jewish teachers of any generation. But the argument must not be forgotten. It enables us to see the strained relationships between the two teachers and their traditions as they meet in friendly confrontation.

Between 1929 and 1933 Tillich and Buber were colleagues at the University of Frankfurt. They had close contacts, which endured to the end. Tillich's memorial to Buber stresses not only the sense of personal loss, but indicates the importance of Buber to Christianity, his seminal thinking, his influence upon Catholic and Protestant thinkers.[35] Carl Hermann Voss, in an important article published in *Midstream* magazine,[36] also reminds us of an article published by Tillich in the June 1948 issue of *Commentary*.[37] In much of this section, I follow Voss's presentation, and must gratefully acknowledge the sources collected in his essay.

The threefold contribution of Buber acknowledged by Tillich and summarized by Voss consisted of: "an existential interpretation of prophetic religion as a message of social justice to be the criterion for political thinking and acting today; the rediscovery of mysticism as an element within prophetic religion; an understanding of the relation between prophetic religion and culture."[38] It is, of course, evident that these teachings came from many sources of that time; but the fact remains that Buber became a decisive teacher for Christians—and for Tillich. Their shared concern with Religious Socialism brought them close to each other, as two incidents show clearly. Tillich's account of the first lets us see the depths of the encounter:

We found each other in the so-called Religious Socialist movement, which was the attempt to bridge the ideological and practical gap between the churches and labor in postwar Germany. I never shall forget the conference . . . where I was to deliver the main address. . . . In order to make myself understood to those unfamiliar with or opposed to religious terminology, I had tried with great care to avoid any of the traditional religious words like God, sin, salvation, Christ, etc. . . . After I had finished, Martin Buber got up and challenged my paper, not with regard to its contents but its language. He stated with great seriousness that certain words are not replaceable, that there are *"Urwörter"* (primary words) which no other, especially no philosophical terms can ever supersede. Later liturgical attempts . . . confirmed for me the truth of Buber's assertion. And his whole interpretation of the "word" as more than the bearer of a logically defined meaning has become an integral element of my theological and philosophical thought, and a weapon against the attempts of modern semantics to reduce the words to a quasi-mathematical sign.[39]

The second incident is an evening spent by Buber in Tillich's house, as recalled by Tillich: "Another occasion which has impressed itself deeply on my memory was a night Martin Buber spent in my house. It was not the 'dialogue' (a favored term of his) we engaged in, but the radiation of a mind 'full of God' that I remember. It was a condensed, almost substantial presence of the divine, as I have seldom experienced it—at least to such a degree —among Christians."[40] Buber's influence upon Tillich is thus clearly acknowledged. The fact remains, as also indicated by Voss elsewhere in his essay, that they could and did challenge each other where religious and philosophic concepts did not converge. And it must be argued that Buber's influence would not have been as strong without that disagreement—again, an aspect of the larger issue of Christianity confronting Judaism.

Both Voss and the Paucks' biography of Tillich list the many occasions when Tillich took his stand alongside the Jewish community, both in Germany and in the United States. Attention is rightly given to the organization he helped to set up and which he led from 1936 to 1951, the Self-Help for Emigrés from Central Europe. Voss, in particular, lists many other articles by Tillich dealing with aspects of Jewish life and thought. At a colloquy in 1959 Tillich described changes in his thought about Zionism:

[I now had] the insight that the masses of the Jewish people cannot be identified with the historical destiny to be the people of *time*. The average Jew is not an embodiment of justice himself; and he partly provokes, by not being an embodiment of justice, the injustice of the nations against him. He, the average, the ordinary Jew, is in need of *space;* and this means an independent historical existence—and this changed my attitude towards Zionism. In realizing this, I saw that my attempt to play Providence by forcing—ideally, at least—every Jew into a prophetic situation was injustice of a metaphysical character. And so I became a member of the [American Christian] Palestine Committee.

Today [Israel] is a political reality with a definite space, with a very manifest structure of power, with the injustices of enforcing the law inside the country and the historical existence outside the country—partly, injustices against which the Jews always stood in foreign countries. Therefore, an identification of Israel as a nation with the nature and destiny of the people of *time* is wrong. There is only the hope that in Israel there will be Jews among the Israelis as there are Jews among the other nations, Jews meaning those who represent the prophetic principles of justice and of hope for the historical and transhistorical unity of the Kingdom of God. For all this the Jew was and remains as long as there is history. This is my belief, agent and symbol, whether inside or outside national Israel.[41]

At this point, we come back to the 1953 lecture in Berlin, where Tillich recognized that Jews have the right to make space for themselves in the world through the state of Israel, and where he reluctantly conceded that one cannot demand of the average Jew to be the righteous remnant, to proclaim time over space. But what is significant is that Tillich still looked for the special Jew—the Martin Buber and the Leo Baeck of his private encounters—who would represent the prophetic principle and who would be a witness for the coming Kingdom of God. In its way, the 1959 statement is a more negative judgment of the Jewish community, combining resignation with the recognition of the Jewish right to be imperfect. Buber had criticized Tillich in the past for clinging to "concepts" within philosophical and theological discourse.[42] Here, Tillich surrendered a concept of the Jewish people to the reality of experience. But he did so with sadness; and I would suggest that he still hoped for his concept (of the Jews as the people of time) to reenter the world as an existential reality. Meanwhile, there were still biblical dimensions within the life of the Jewish people to which he responded; there was the reality of the "suffering servant" that was present in his Jewish friends; and there was the inner knowledge that Christianity could not come to terms with its own identity without meeting the challenge of the Jew as a reality and as a concept.

On October 7, 1965, in a letter to his friends, Tillich wrote:

Die Endlichkeit die nur Hoffnung gegen Hoffnung zulässt, hat mich erpackt. Vielleicht ist es besser so für mich und gibt mir Stunden, in denen die Erfahrung dessen was Hoffnung berechtigt, stärker macht. [43]

Overtaken by finitude, the lines of Tillich's life move toward infinity. And our translation of this text would be: "May the Lord give strength, may the Lord give peace."

NOTES

1. Dietrich Bonhoeffer, *Letters and Papers from Prison*, 3d ed., rev. and enl., ed. Eberhard Bethge (New York: Macmillan, 1967), 180, entry for June 8, 1944.
2. Max Horkheimer, "Erinnerungen an Paul Tillich im Gespräch mit Max Horkheimer, T.W. Adorno, E. Heimann, Ernst Bloch, W-D Marsch," in *Werk und Wirken Paul Tillichs, Ein Gedenkbuch* (Stuttgart: Evangelische Verlagsanstalt, 1967), 15–24.
3. Tillich's lectures were originally published as *Die Judenfrage, ein Christliches und ein deutsches Problem* (Berlin: Gebrüder Weiss Verlag, Für die Deutsche Hochschule für Politik in Berlin, 1953). The lectures are included, under the same

title, in Paul Tillich, *Gesammelte Werke,* vol. 3 (Stuttgart: Evangelisches Verlagswerk, 1965), 128–70.

4. Ibid., 25.

5. Ibid., 25–26. The original text in Shakespeare reads:
   Horatio: O day and night, but this is wondrous strange!
   Hamlet: And therefore as a stranger give it welcome.
   There are more things in heaven and earth, Horatio,
   Than are dreamt of in your philosophy. (Act 1, scene 5)

6. Ibid., 27.

7. Ibid., 28–29.

8. Ibid., 33.

9. Ibid., 34–35.

10. Ibid., 40, 41.

11. Ibid., 46.

12. Ibid., 47–48. The final sentence quoted is the final sentence of the lecture.

13. Paul Tillich, "Letter to Thomas Mann," in *The Intellectual Legacy of Paul Tillich,* ed. James Lyon (Detroit: Wayne State University Press, 1969), 104.

14. Paul Tillich, *Biblical Religion and the Search for Ultimate Reality* (Chicago: University of Chicago Press, 1955), 3.

15. Paul Tillich, *Christianity and the Encounter of the World Religions* (New York: Columbia University Press, 1963), 29.

16. Ibid., 30.

17. Ibid., 31–32.

18. Ibid., 39.

19. Cf. epigraph to this chapter, from Bernard Martin, *The Existentialist Theology of Paul Tillich* (New York: Bookman Associates, 1963).

20. *Werk und Wirken Paul Tillichs, ein Gedenkbuch,* Beiträgen von Theodor W. Adorno (Stuttgart: Evangelisches Verlagswerk, 1967), 40.

21. Martin, *The Existentialist Theology of Paul Tillich,* 179.

22. "A Final Conversation With Paul Tillich," in *Out of the Whirlwind,* ed. Albert H. Friedlander (New York; Doubleday, 1968), 515–521.

23. Ibid., 52–53.

24. Paul Tillich, *The Religious Situation,* trans. H. Richard Niebuhr (New York: Meridian Books, 1956), 189, 190.

25. Ibid., 190–91.

26. Paul Tillich, *Love, Power, and Justice* (New York: Oxford University Press, 1954), 124–25.

27. Paul Tillich, "Born in the Grave," in idem, *The Shaking of the Foundations* (New York: Charles Scribner's Sons, 1948), 165, 166.

28. Ibid., 167.

29. Ibid., 50–51.

30. Dorothee Sölle, *Die Hinreise* (Stuttgart: Kreuz Verlag, 1976), 157 (my translation).

31. Paul Tillich, *The Shaking of the Foundations,* 41, 50.

32. Sölle, *Die Hinreise,* trans. *European Judaism,* no. 1 (1977): 22.

33. Tillich, *The Shaking of the Foundations,* 32–33.

34. The lines of life all differ, move apart,
    As pathways go, and where the mountains end.
    What we are here, God can still supplement
    With harmonies, peace and eternal reward.

My translation, from Johann Christian Friedrich Hölderlin, *Sämtliche Werke,* vol. 2, Grosse Stuttgarter Ausgabe (Stuttgart: W. Kohlammer Verlag, 1951), 268.

35. Paul Tillich, "Martin Buber. Eine Würdigung anlässlich seines Todes," in *Gesammelte Werke,* 12 (1971), 320–23.

36. Carl Hermann Voss, "Paul Tillich—Interfaith Pioneer," *Midstream: A Monthly Jewish Review* 25, no. 4 (April 1979): 70–74. This is a review of Wilhelm and Marion Pauck, *Paul Tillich: His Life and Thought* (New York: Harper & Row, 1976), vol. 1, *Life.*

37. Paul Tillich, "Martin Buber and Christian Thought: His Threefold Contribution to Protestantism," *Commentary* 5 (June 1948): 515–21.

38. Voss, "Paul Tillich—Interfaith Pioneer," 71.

39. Paul Tillich, "Martin Buber and Christian Thought," 515.

40. Ibid.

41. Paul Tillich, "My Changing Thoughts on Zionism," unpublished statement at Christian-Jewish Colloquy "Israel's Rebirth in the Middle East," Chicago, 21 January 1959, as quoted by C. H. Voss, "Paul Tillich—Interfaith Pioneer," 72. A German translation has been published in *GW* 13 (1972), 403–8.

42. Voss, "Paul Tillich—Interfaith Pioneer," p. 71. Voss refers to a discussion between Tillich and Buber in a meeting at Brandeis University during the year 1957–58.

43. "The finitude that permits only hope against hope has seized me. Perhaps it is better so for me and gives me hours in which the experience of that which vindicates hope strengthens me." (My translation.) The quoted words are added in Tillich's handwriting to a copy, addressed to Ernst Bloch, of a circular letter to some of his German friends. They are recorded in *Werk und Wirken Paul Tillichs: Ein Gedenkbuch,* 45.

11. Tillich, Kraemer, and the Encounter of Religions

JOSEPH M. KITAGAWA

In 1960 two prominent Western Christian scholars visited Japan —Paul Tillich in the spring, and Hendrik Kraemer in the autumn. Their visits aroused unusual interests among Japanese scholars and religious leaders—certainly among Christians as might be expected, but also among Buddhists and Shintoists as well. Although Tillich and Kraemer had never visited the Far East before, some of their published works had been widely read in Japan. Understandably, both the visitors and their Japanese hosts appreciated the opportunity to learn from each other through their personal encounter.[1]

What fascinated the Japanese scholars were certain similarities and sharp contrasts that they found in the two visitors. Tillich (1886–1965) and Kraemer (1888–1965) were contemporaries. Both were products of European culture, and both had experienced the devastation of World War I with the subsequent erosion of the foundation of the religious, cultural, social, and political fabric of Europe. Moreover, as committed Christians both were concerned with the encounter among various religions, more particularly between Christian and Eastern religious traditions.

On the other hand, their differences were striking. Tillich had always lived, according to his own account, on the "boundaries," between philosophy and theology, between religious and social and political issues, between religion and culture, and between his native Germany and America. Also, while he kept in close touch with people in various circles, his base of operation was always the academy. Even his connection with the Christian church was primarily through his theological reflections. In reference to Buddhism, he was particularly intrigued by the mental and spiritual training of Zen, which aims at "enlightenment." In sharp contrast to Tillich, Kraemer, who had been trained in Oriental languages and the history of religions, was an advocate of "biblical realism." He had served as an adviser to the Dutch Bible Society in Java, as professor of the history of religions at Leiden, and as Director of the Ecumenical Institute of the World Council of Churches in Switzerland. Also, while earlier he had been interested in Islamic mysticism in Java, he became deeply interested in the "salvation" experience of the Pure Land School of Buddhism.

It is not surprising, therefore, that despite Tillich's and Kraemer's professed keen interest in a meaningful "dialogue" between Christian and Eastern religious traditions, their perspectives had very little in common. More important, perhaps, for our present discussion is the fact that their respective approaches to Eastern religions may be regarded as two important options that are still viable today for the enterprise called a "theological history of religions," or a theological approach to comparative religions.

ENCOUNTERS AMONG RELIGIONS

Such designations as the theological history of religions and a theological approach to comparative religions are new, but their underlying concerns are very old. It is significant that this age-old question regarding the meaning of the encounter among religions has become a serious intellectual and existential problem in our time, especially among Christians.

As far as we can ascertain, various religious thinkers and philosophers throughout history have attempted to resolve the mystery regarding the division of humanity into various religious, ethnic, linguistic, and cultural groups. For example, Zoroastrianism affirmed the eventual resolution of the chaos and division of humankind in Ahura Mazda's eschatological war against the forces of evil and urged men and women to join this war in order to establish on earth the righteous and peaceful Kingdom of God. Ancient Hinduism taught the appearance of a just and virtuous world monarch, the Cakravartin, whose coming would be marked by the end of strife and division of the world. And, like the Cakravartin, the Buddha also was believed to turn his wheel—the Buddhist *dharma*—to unify the whole universe. Equally significant was the ancient Chinese vision of the grand commonwealth. "From the age of Confucius," says Fung Yu-lan, "the Chinese people in general and their political thinkers in particular began to think about political matters in terms of the [whole] world."[2]

In the West, the Greeks envisaged the unification of peoples in the "Oikoumene" by means of Hellenistic civilization and Greek language. While Alexander's dream to establish a universal empire was doomed to failure, Oriental-Hellenistic culture, consolidated further by Rome, remained for centuries the broad framework for cultural development in the Mediterranean world. Meanwhile, the once-tribal religion of the Hebrew community in the Middle East developed an ethical universalism under the influence of the prophetic movement, whereby the God of Israel came to be conceived of as the divine ruler of all humankind.[3] While Christianity and Islam developed within the orbit of Oriental-Hellenistic culture, both inherited their beliefs of the unity of humanity from the Hebrew example. Accordingly, the early Christian community considered itself the new Israel; Pentecost signified the reversal of the Tower of Babel in that the scattered and divided human race was now reunited, potentially at least, as the one true humanity. Similarly, Islam, which accepted the human division to be the inscrutable divine decree, nevertheless affirmed that all those who surrender to Allah are to be included in the universal congregation (*Ummah*) of Allah.[4]

In Asia neither the Hindus with their cosmic orientation nor the Chinese with their universal outlook propagated their beliefs outside their respective spheres of influence. However, the Buddhist King Asoka in the third century B.C. initiated an energetic missionary expansion beyond his empire, whereby the Buddhist community came to be understood as potentially a worldwide community, embracing peoples and nations outside India, uniting all humanity by means of Buddhist *dharma*.

It is interesting to note that Christianity, which also emerged as a missionary religion, had to come to terms with the traditions of pre- and non-Christian religions and philosophies in the West— just as Buddhism had to do earlier *vis à vis* other traditions in the East. In this task, some of the early Christian apologists affirmed the truths of other religions and philosophies as the *praeparatio evangelica*—a natural revelation by the *Logos spermatikos*—which were to be fulfilled by Jesus Christ, the *Logos-incarnate*. The appropriation of the Logos doctrine and the fulfillment theory enabled apologists to relate *Heilsgeschichte* directly to the general history of religions of humankind. Meanwhile, the Christian community gradually developed canons, orders, and creeds to consolidate the faith and practice of the community.

The emergence of Islam in the seventh century A.D. successfully confined the core of Christianity to Europe until the sixteenth century. Confronted by Islam's claim to be the fulfillment of all previous revelations, Christian dogmatists responded by portraying Islam as the "fulfillment" of the coming of the false prophet prophesied in the Johannine apocalypse. Although European culture benefited greatly from the Muslims, the attitude of Christendom toward Islam became fiercely antagonistic, as exemplified by the bloody Crusades. Moreover, subsequent religious developments in Europe—the Reformation, the counter-Reformation, and the rise of Pietism—added more and more fuel to Christians' prejudice against Islam as well as other non-Christian religions and cultures.[5] A remarkable exception in Christendom was Nicholas of Cusa, a Cardinal and a "renaissance man," who affirmed the existence of diversity of religions as a part of the divine plan, while acknowledging the Christian revelation as the fullest expression of divine truth and love. His irenic view of non-Christian religions, however, was not shared by the official church.[6]

The phenomenal colonial expansion of Iberian Catholic powers during the sixteenth and seventeenth centuries was marked by blatant economic exploitation mixed with fanatic motivation for religious conquest. These were residues of the Iberian Christians' campaign against Muslims. Meanwhile, in Europe the foundation of the Corpus Christianum was undermined by the Renaissance, which now equated the development of civilization with *Heilsgeschichte,* thus making in effect "civilization" a pseudoreligion of secularized salvation.[7] Many Europeans came to regard themselves as a new chosen people in the sense of being the inventors and transmitters of true civilization, which was to be propagated for the edification of the "backward" and "unenlightened" people in the non-Western world. This motivation was implicit in the second wave of Western colonial expansion in the eighteenth and nineteenth centuries.

It should be noted that the Pietists rejected this secularized view of the human being and of civilization. Thus, the initial ethos of Christian foreign missions, inaugurated by the continental Pietists and British evangelicals to "save the poor heathens from damnation," ran counter to the secular spirit of colonial policies. During the nineteenth century, however, Christian missions in Asia and Africa unwittingly cooperated with European colonialism, whereby Christianity was propagated as one—albeit an important one—of the constituents of Western civilization. While missionaries contributed much to education and philanthropy in the non-Western world, they viewed non-Christian religions, for the most part, as unenlightened paganism.

Ironically, while Christian missionaries were trying to save souls from pagan religions, English Deists and philosophers of the Enlightenment discovered the religious and ethical values of non-Western religions. For example, Voltaire praised China as the bearer of the true religion of Nature: "Worship God and praise justice—this is the sole religion of the Chinese literati. . . . O Thomas Aquinas, Scotus, Bonaventura, Francis, Dominic, Luther, Calvin, Canons of Westminster, have you anything better?"[8] The rejection of the Christian claim to be the sole bearer of the highest and absolute religious truth by the European intellectuals led to a new understanding of *Heilsgeschichte,* articulated by German idealism, that the whole history of humankind was the evolutionary history of self-realization of natural religion. "Here the idea of the absoluteness of Christianity was retained; however, it did not stand over against the remaining religions in the sense of negation but in the sense of crowning of a historical, developmental process."[9]

Significantly, the enormous body of data concerning the languages, customs, and religions of non-Western peoples made available to Europeans during the nineteenth century through the accounts of travelers, colonial officials, and Christian missionaries were devoured by the scholars of languages, ethnology, arts, philosophy, and religions. E. B. Tyler, James G. Frazer, E. Burnouf, F. Max Müller, Andrew Lang, E. Durkheim, and James Legge, to name only a few, pioneered the scholarly studies of primitive and

Eastern religions and philosophies. Following the establishment of the first chair of the history of religions in Geneva in 1873, similar chairs were instituted in other European universities. And the first full-scale Congress of the History of Religions was held in 1900 in Paris.

It is to be noted, as G. van der Leeuw suggested, that the scholarly study of religions came under the impact of three phases of romanticism: First, romantic philosophy, which regarded diverse religious manifestations as symbols of a primordial natural religion; Second, romantic philology, which, while rejecting unfettered speculation, still viewed religion as "the expression of a universal mode of human thinking"; and third, romantic positivism, which sought "to comprehend the objective appearances of religion in the light of subjective processes."[10] Understandably, because of their philosophical assumptions—whether rationalistic or romantic—pioneers of *Religionswissenschaft* dealt with religio-scientific data "philosophically." Even today the distinction between the history of religions and the philosophy of religion is not clearly understood in some quarters.

This is not the occasion to delineate the complex development in our century of the history of religions *(Religionswissenschaft)* as a nonspeculative religio-scientific discipline that deals with religious phenomena. It is pertinent, however, to point out that both the method and the data of the history of religions have come to be appropriated by other disciplines for their respective purposes, especially by Christian missionary thinkers and theologians who are concerned with the relationship of Christianity and non-Christian religions.

MISSIONSWISSENSCHAFT AND THE ENCOUNTER OF RELIGIONS

Before the emergence of modern *Missionswissenschaft,* medieval Christendom felt no need for scholarly studies of missions or non-Christian religions. The Roman Catholic dogma, *extra ecclesiam nulla salus,* explicated in the 1442 Council of Florence, was followed almost verbatim by Luther's statement that those who are outside Christianity, "be they heathens, Turks, Jews or false Christians," will remain in "eternal wrath and damnation."[11] Calvin, who felt that "the kingdom of God is neither to be advanced nor maintained by the industry of man,"[12] was not interested in missions or in non-Christian religions. It is commonly agreed that the father of *Missionswissenschaft* was Gustav Warneck (1834–1910) of Halle. Since his time many scholars, especially the members of the *Deutsche Gesellschaft für Missionswissenschaft,* have made valuable contributions to the study of non-Christian religions as a part of the agenda for their discipline.

The first international program of the scholarly study of missions was undertaken for the 1910 World Missionary Conference at Edinburgh. At the 1928 Jerusalem Conference of the International Missionary Council, which marked a second landmark of missiology, no other than Hendrik Kraemer insisted that while the missionary ought to proclaim the Gospel, "he must have an intense longing to discover the spiritual values of other religions." The council in the end concluded that "we rightly study other religions in order to approach men wisely, yet at the last we speak as men to men, inviting them to share with us the pardon and the life that we have found in Christ."[13] Thus, in effect the conference accepted the data and methods of the history of religions in their study of non-Christian religions for the service of *Missionswissenschaft.* The conference also expressed a native optimism about the future of Christian missions based on the "fulfillment" theory.

In 1931 the so-called "Laymen's Inquiry," comprised of laity from seven American Protestant denominations, evaluated missionary work in India, Burma, China, and Japan. Although this unofficial inquiry was not undertaken by scholars of missions, the prominence of the group headed by a Harvard philosopher, William Ernest Hocking, gave a special aura to its findings, entitled *Re-thinking Missions.* Among other important observations and recommendations, the findings called for a reappraisal of the relationship between Christianity and Eastern religions, since both were threatened by the spread of secularism, and also because of changes that were taking place in non-Christian religions. Thus, *Re-Thinking Missions* recommended a "creative relationship" that asked missionaries first to gain a knowledge and understanding of other religions, and "then to recognize and associate itself with whatever kindred elements there are in them." Moreover, the missionary aim was defined as follows: "to seek with people of other lands a true knowledge and love of God, expressing in life and word what we have learned through Jesus Christ, and endeavoring to give effect to his spirit in the life of the world."[14]

Not unexpectedly, a strong rebuttal against *Re-Thinking Missions* came from Hendrik Kraemer, who wrote *The Christian Message in a Non-Christian World* for the 1938 World Missionary Conference held at Tambaram, India. The main thesis of the book appeared in a later article, "Continuity or Discontinuity," in which he stated: "the Christian revelation as the record of God's self-disclosing revelation in Jesus Christ is absolutely *sui generis.*" As such, Kraemer saw only discontinuity between the world of spiritual realities defined by "biblical realism" and the whole range of other religious experiences and human endeavors. He insisted that the sole standard of reference for religion was revelation in Christ, and not a general idea about the essence of religion.[15] Accordingly, he felt that *Re-Thinking Missions* confused apostolic obligations with the noble human desire to respect other religions, which amounted to "the subversion of Christianity into a noble this-worldly idealism." Kraemer was convinced that the relation between Christianity and other religions was one of the gravest problems that "the Christian Church all over the world and the missionary cause have to face at the present time." As a trained historian of religions Kraemer acknowledged the legitimacy of the scientific study of religions. However, as a scholar of *Missionswissenschaft,* he resorted finally to a theological "dialectic" approach that was based on the affirmation that the revelation in Christ was the only way to acquire a true insight into the meaning of all human existence.[16]

Unfortunately, many of the serious and important issues raised at the Tambaram conference regarding the relation between Christian and other religions were not followed up during World War II; and when some of the same concerns were raised again after the war, the situation had changed radically.

EASTERN RELIGIONS SINCE WORLD WAR II

Historians tell us that the decline of Asia during the past four centuries was caused initially by an internal cultural erosion, which in turn encouraged commercial, political, and cultural encroachment by the West. Thus, Asian peoples' historic confidence in the autonomy and superiority of their cultures was rudely shattered by the technologically superior Western civilization, which was presented as a pseudoreligion of secularized salvation. In the course of time there developed a core of Asian intelligentsia with westernized education who endeavored to reform the stagnant Asian cultures and societies of their time. Some of them accepted the secular values of modern Western civilization, while others embraced Christianity or Marxism, although in their minds they were passionately Asians.

With this historical background in mind, we can appreciate the fact that the end of World War II signified to Asians not only the end of Western colonial imperialism but more basically a momentous redefinition of their destiny, their sense of dignity, value, and freedom. Confronted by such an enormous burden, Asians have been trying to come to terms with such issues as modernity and tradition, secularity and spirituality, liberation and freedom. We must understand recent religious developments in Asia in this broader context.

Already before the war, the "Laymen's Inquiry" team observed that contemporary Hinduism, Islam, and Buddhism were not those of a hundred years ago.[17] Hendrik Kraemer, too, noted that there was "along with the general national revitalization, a movement towards a heightening of religious group consciousness, consolidation and concerted opposition to Christian missions."[18]

After the war many religious leaders cooperated with political leaders in rebuilding a spiritual fabric for a new Asia with the firm conviction that their cultural tradition had resources that were no less remarkable than those of the West. Also noteworthy was the fact that, like their Christian counterparts, theoreticians of Eastern religions advocated their own versions of "fulfillment" theories by appropriating the data and methods of the history of religions.

Sarvepalli Radhakrishnan, for example, felt that studies in comparative religion reveal not only the bewildering variety of religious beliefs and practices but also show common features, such as ideas about incarnation, miracles, and festivals among different religions. To him, Christianity is the continuation of the perennial religion of the human race. Seen from his Hindu theological perspective, Gautama the Buddha as well as Jesus the Christ were

"God-men," or the manifestations of the Spirit through human media. As such, they are the precursors of the truly human: "The nature of man receives its fulfillment in them. They are our elder brothers."[19]

Similarly, D. T. Suzuki tried to show how Jewish and Christian insights could be "fulfilled" in Zen. He wrote:

When God saw the light which came out of his command, he said, "It is good." This appreciation on the part of God is the first awakening of consciousness in the world; in fact the beginning of the world itself. The mere separation of light and darkness does not demonstrate the beginning. The world starts only when there is a mind which appreciates, viz., a mind critically conscious of itself. This is also the eating of "the first fruit of the tree. . . ." The eating means "knowing good and evil," appraising the light and darkness, and in this appraisal, in this knowledge, there is the secret of living by Zen.[20]

During the immediate postwar era, leaders of Eastern religions expressed a jubilant optimism that their faiths were the way of the future not only in Asia but also in the materialistic West. For example, U Nu during his tenure as prime minister attempted to establish in Burma an earthly Nirvana, a Buddhist socialist state, with a firm confidence that it would permit "a maximum observance of the Dhamma to the point of perfection, making possible man's sublimation into future Buddhahood."[21] Similar endeavors elsewhere sought to actualize historic religious ideals in concrete programs. Pakistan, for example, was created in order to enable Muslims "to order their lives in the individual and collective spheres in accord with the teachings and requirements of Islam. . . ."[22] India, too, tried to synthesize its time-honored sacramental view of life and the ideal of socialist commonwealth by establishing a modern "secular" state in which religious freedom and the equality of opportunity were to be assured. Notwithstanding the apparent failures of these schemes, the fact that such attempts were seriously made was a matter of great significance.

By far the most serious challenge to postwar religions—including Roman Catholicism in the Philippines and other indigenous Christian groups elsewhere called the "younger churches"—came from communism. The emergence of Communist states in China,

North Korea, Vietnam, and more recently in Kampuchea, Laos, and Afghanistan confirms Hans Morgenthau's notion that Asian communism—unlike European communism, which was initiated by Soviet power—developed out of social revolution.[23] This does not mean that communism occasioned the social revolution in Asia. "What the communists claim to do is to explain the revolution and to have the right of leading it to a successful end." Equally important is the pseudoreligious appeal of communism in Asia where "the impact of the West has destroyed old religions and family and village loyalties, and robbed life of its spiritual comfort and purpose. People [now] ask a new code, a new certainty, a new religion, and some of them find it in communism."[24] In the course of time various modes of relationship, from hostility to submission, developed between religions and communism. In this respect, the common weakness of Eastern religions thus far seems to have been their failure to articulate to today's Asians the vision of their religious ends—for which the establishment of a social utopia is a precondition—in relation to viable concrete social or political theories.[25]

It is a great irony that today Eastern religions, which are threatened by antireligious humanism and communism in Asia, are gaining converts in the West. For the most part, constituents of Eastern religions in the West belong to three types—ethnic-cultural, intellectual, and cultic. The fact that Asian residents or their descendants hold their ancestral religious traditions is nothing new. What is new today is the phenomenal rise in the second and third groups.

Intellectual interest in Eastern religions is illustrated by a recent survey that lists 1,653 professors who teach Asian religious traditions in colleges and universities in Canada and the United States.[26] A wide variety of cultic groups—not only the established ones like Vedanta and Zen, but a whole series of new groups, for example, Hare Krishna, Transcendental Meditation, Nichiren Shōshū, and the Unification Church (known as the Moonies)—now are present in the West. Whether or not the presence of Eastern religions implies the spiritual colonization of the West by the East, it adds complexity to the encounter of religions in our time.

THEOLOGICAL HISTORY OF RELIGIONS AND THE INTERRELIGIOUS DIALOGUE

The last three decades have brought new modes of interreligious or interfaith relations, most notably the "dialogue" between Christian and non-Christian religious leaders and scholars. This dialogue has arisen primarily from the new mood of Eastern religions, coupled with new social and political realities in the non-Western world, and equally significant changes in religious outlook as well as in social, economic, and political spheres in the West. What is new on the Christian side is the fact that the encounter among religions, as a serious scholarly as well as existential problem, has captured the imagination not only of enlightened church leaders and scholars of missions but also of leading theologians.

Not surprisingly, the original impulse for the dialogue came from the indigenous Christian ("younger") churches in the non-Western world. Controlled for decades by churches in the West, these younger churches were an insignificant minority within global Christendom and were ineffective spectators of the social and political events in their own lands. The leaders of the younger churches were embarrassed by the denominational divisions of the church, and had a different approach from that of the Western church in the development of a meaningful relationship to the non-Christian religions to which the majority of their fellow citizens belonged. Hence their push for "ecumenical movement" and "dialogue."[27] The 1938 World Missionary Conference at Tambaram made a profound impression on the younger churches concerning the need for the scholarly study of non-Christian religions. The younger churches were also greatly affected by Asian political events, especially the national independence of former European colonies, and by the Chinese Christian churches' declaration of self-help after the establishment of the People's Republic of China. Thus, instead of returning to the prewar pattern of heavy dependence on the financial and theological resources of the Western churches, they redefined their relationship with the older churches in the West in terms of "mutual dependence" or "partnership in obedience."

One concrete outcome of the partnership of the younger and older churches was the establishment of the World Council of Churches' committee for a research program entitled "The Word of God and The Living Faiths of Men." A document of this committee, released in 1958, states that "each individual religion is *sui generis* and complete in itself. . . . This denies the concept that Christianity is the fulfillment of other religions," based on the ground that all religions, including Christianity as a religion, are "distorted responses" on the part of men to the works of God.[28] The committee envisaged the development of a continuing dialogue with other living faiths and ideologies, including Marxism, in order to listen to what they had to say "about their understanding, their vision, their hope of salvation."[29]

The notion of "dialogue" was not accepted universally by Western churches. There were many differences in motivation, procedure, and objective, even among scholars of missions who had accepted it. For example, one group of scholars, represented by those who contributed to the "Christian Presence Series,"[30] accepted coexistence with other faiths as an existential reality and dialogue as an expression of their deepest loyalty to the Christian Gospel's real content.[31] Thus, feeling that God had been in Asia and elsewhere before missionaries arrived, Max A. C. Warren suggested that "we must try to sit where [the adherents of other faiths] sit, to enter sympathetically into the pains and griefs and joys of their history and see how those pains and griefs and joys have determined the premises of their argument. We have, in a word, to be 'present' with them."[32]

On the other hand, Hendrik Kraemer and others considered the coexistence of religions as the foreshadowing of a future meeting of religions as well as of an "interpenetration and *Auseinandersetzung* of cultural attitudes and orientations contained in [Eastern and Western] civilizations." Kraemer felt strongly, as he told Buddhist scholars in Japan, that "the great responsibility of all thinking people . . . who belong to the great religions is that such a dialogue take place in a really worthy form." As a scholar of missions and the history of religions, Kraemer shared J. H. Gunning's critique of the narrow horizon of an orthodox theology that passed its value judgments on other religions without knowing them. But he also shared Gunning's conviction that "only theology, if rightly understood, is able to produce that attitude of freedom of the spirit and of impartial understanding."[33] Therefore he was persuaded that Christian participants in the coming dialogue needed the training in what might be called a "theological" science of religion or history of religion.

The concern for "dialogue," however, has not been confined to missionary circles or to the younger churches. Vatican II's "Declaration on the Relation of the Church to Non-Christian Religions"[34] also gave cautious encouragement to such a dialogue. In addition, a number of interfaith conferences have been held in recent decades in Europe and North America under different auspices. Moreover, the notion of "dialogue" as a principle for the academic study of religions has been promoted by the Union for the Study of the Great Religions in Great Britain, and has been implemented in North America by such programs as McGill University's Institute of Islamic Studies. McGill's policy is that half of the teachers and half of the students be Muslims. According to its founder, Wilfred Cantwell Smith, "it is the business of comparative religion to construct statements about religion that are intelligible within at least two traditions simultaneously." Smith hopes that "comparative religion may become the disciplined self-consciousness of man's variegated and developing religious life."[35]

Equally significant is the fact that the encounter and "dialogue" of religions have concerned many Christian theologians in our time. A prominent example was Paul Tillich who, as a systematic theologian concerned with the encounter of religions, attempted to develop a theoretical formula for the theological history of religions. Convinced that the Bible, church history, and the history of religions and cultures were legitimate sources of systematic theology, Tillich asked: "How are these contents made available for use in a way parallel to the method by which the biblical theologian makes the biblical materials available and the historian of Christian thought makes the doctrinal materials available?"[36]

Tillich acknowledged the following presuppositions in his theological history of religions: first, "revelatory experiences are universally human"; second, "revelation is received by man in terms of his finite human situation"; third, not only are there particular revelatory experiences throughout human history, but also "there is a revelatory process in which the limits of adaptation and the failures of distortion are subjected to [the mystical, the prophetic, and the secular forms of] criticism"; fourth, there may be "a central event in the history of religions" that "makes possible a concrete theology that has universalistic significance"; and fifth, "the history of religions . . . does not exist alongside the history of culture. The sacred does not lie beside the secular, but it is its depth."[37] It is worth noting that as early as 1919 Tillich wrote on a "theology of culture,"[38] in a theological attempt "to discover the ultimate concern in the ground of a philosophy, a political system, an artistic style, a set of ethical or social principles."[39] The theological history of culture or theology of culture, in his view, provided an important framework for the theological history of religions.

According to Tillich, the orientation for the theological history of religions is that of the history of salvation. The crucial task is to inquire whether there are great symbolic movements and moments (kairoi) in the general history of religions, here including prereligious and religious traditions. It is interesting to note in this connection that his earlier formulation of the theological history of religions pointed more directly to the Christian solution. In his own words: "A theological history of religion should be carried through in the light of the missionary principle that the New Being in Jesus as the Christ is the answer to the question asked implicitly and explicitly by the religions of mankind."[40] However, as he gave more thought to Eastern religions, Tillich acknowledged that "to them the Christian answer is not an answer, because they have not asked the question to which Christianity is supposed to give the answer."[41] Thus, he began to stress the importance of a "dialogue" with other religions, especially those in Asia, rather than a missionary encounter or an indirect cultural contact with them, provided such a dialogue presupposed that "both partners acknowledge the value of the other's religious conviction," "each of them is able to represent his own religious basis with conviction," there is "a common ground which makes both dialogue and conflicts possible," and there is "openness of both sides to criticisms directed against their own religious basis."[42]

In many ways Tillich's visit to Japan in 1960 was an eye-opening experience for him. For example, he was most curious about the nature of Shinto and asked many questions, but candidly admitted that his "categories simply are not sufficient to grasp the situation" of Shinto. He also found difficulties in establishing common grounds for discourse with Buddhists. For instance, his question as to how Buddhist leaders deal with popular piety, especially in countering the dangers of mechanization, superstition, and demonization, was summarily dismissed by a leading Zen scholar, Shinichi Hisamatsu, on the ground that even the most primitive piety "could be the way of awakening the Buddha spirit in every human being." He had, however, a more fruitful exchange of ideas with Buddhist scholars. Tillich felt that the task of Christianity in its encounter with Japan was to show that people had to make existential decisions by giving "their ultimate concern to the really Ultimate." He expressed the conviction that the Kingdom of God "is fighting in the tremendous spiritual experiences of the Buddhists" and adherents of other religions, "but the *criterion* is lacking." And while he affirmed that for him "Jesus as the Christ" was the criterion for the Kingdom, he did not pursue the question of the adequacy of the symbol of the Ultimate—"why Christ (not Jesus) and not Buddha?"[43]

Discussing "A Christian-Buddhist Conversation" (written after he returned from Japan), Tillich used a dynamic typology of telos formula in characterizing the typical structures of Christianity and Buddhism: "In Christianity the telos [is] of every*one* and everything united in the Kingdom of God; in Buddhism the telos [is] of every*thing* and everyone fulfilled in the Nirvana." It was his contention that "the decisive point in a dialogue between two religions is not the historically determined, contingent *embodiment* of the typological elements, but these elements themselves." Significantly, his earlier notion of the theological history of religions— to subject Christianity and other religions to "the criterion of final revelation"—gave way to his new approach based not on antitheses but on polarities, and "not conversion, but dialogue." According to his hopes for the dialogue, each religion would find in its depth "a point at which the religion itself loses its importance, and that to which it points breaks through its particularity, elevating it to spiritual freedom and with it to a vision of the spiritual presence in other expressions of the ultimate meaning of man's existence." In his very last lecture, given a few days before his death, Tillich used the expression "the religion of the concrete spirit" to refer to such an idealized feature of religion, an ideal that cannot be identified with any particular religion—not even Christianity—and yet can be found in the depths of every concrete religion.[44]

It is clear that Tillich was willing to encounter other religions as well as determined to remain an authentic Christian. Ironically, his earlier formulation of a theological history of religions based on his well-known theories of a "theological center," the "principle of correlation," "critical phenomenology," and the "latent church," was too formal to deal with concrete historical religious data and was too Christological to deal adequately with the motives and meanings of non-Christian religious expressions. To be sure, it was a useful tool against the scientific and philosophical criticisms of Christianity, but it was not entirely able to clarify the issues involved in the dialogue situation. Although he abandoned some of his formal categories in his conversations with non-Christian thinkers, he had definite ideas about the universality of religion lying in the depths of concrete religions. Thus, his approach to a dialogue was to compare, on his own terms, the typical structures of a unique form of historic religions with the typical structures appearing in Christianity as a historic religion. Therefore, when a Buddhist asked a prior question, such as why he chose as basic religious categories "being rather than nonbeing, life rather than death,"[45] it was difficult to continue the dialogue.

Also, as Mircea Eliade pointed out, Tillich was concerned not with *Historie* but with *Geschichte,* the existential meaning of history. In dealing with various religions, he was interested primarily in "their historical concreteness and immediacy, not in their modifications or changes or in the results of the flowing of time."[46] Nevertheless, Tillich's openness to engage in serious conversations with adherents of other religions opened new possibilities for Christianity to judge "itself in the light of its encounter with the world religions." This, of course, is a prerequisite for a meaningful dialogue.

NOTES ON "PUBLIC MONOLOGUE" AND "DIALOGUE"

Since the publication of the first volume of Tillich's *Systematic Theology* (1951), a number of Protestant and Catholic theologians and their counterparts in Jewish and non-Western religions have addressed the issue of the encounter of religions. Since all religions define the nature of reality, including ultimate reality, from their own "theological/religious center," any encounter of religions involves each participant's "public monologue" regarding this issue. Of course, each participant must realize the presence of others who also are engaged in similar public monologues. Thus, the encounter of religions compels each religious tradition not only to acknowledge the existence of others but also to try to make sense—here again from the perspective of each "theological/religious center"—of the sum total of a reality that includes the existence of other religions. Accordingly, each religious tradition must develop its own way of absorbing the data of alien religions into its own image of total reality. Such absorptions might be exemplified by historic Christian apologia of the Logos doctrine, the fulfillment theory, true versus false religions, *Heilsgeschichte* versus the history of empirical religions, and the Christian revelation versus historic religions. They are similarly represented by more recent proposals, such as Tillich's "latent church," Karl Rahner's "anonymous Christians," and Hans Küng's "ordinary and extraordinary [Christian] ways of salvation." All these proposals have helped to articulate the Christian "public monologue," which takes into account the relation of other religions to the Christian faith.

Ironically, the phenomenal expansion of Western colonial powers and civilization in the modern period has misled many Western Christians: Some feel that their "public monologue" was the most decisive factor involved in the encounter of religions. Fortunately, in recent decades an increasing awareness has developed that other religious traditions, too, have been engaged in similar efforts to absorb the existence of alien religions into their image of reality. Thus, in their efforts to develop a theological history of religions, Christians must recognize their non-Christian counterparts in people like Radhakrishnan and Suzuki. Only a mutual recognition will transform a series of "public monologues" into a "dialogue." In this connection, Eliade astutely observes that, in their encounter with Easterners, Westerners have tended to depend on the more westernized representatives of Eastern peoples and religions: "The Western world has not yet, or not generally, met with authentic representatives of the 'real' non-Western traditions."[47]

Each religious tradition in a dialogue must alternately talk and then listen, reflect and then observe, and articulate self-affirmations and then self-criticisms. Thus far, the encounter of religions has meant, for the most part, theoretical discussions of doctrines and ethics. But each religious tradition is not simply a stereotyped system of doctrines, cults, and ecclesiastical institutions; rather, each is a dynamic and ever-growing organism that defines total reality and provides its adherents with the meaning of life as well as guidance for their actions. Similarly, in recent encounters of religions, each religious tradition often has been presented as a unified system without due recognition of the diverse strands represented within it. Unfortunately, because of their overindulgent sense of identification with and tolerance of others, participants of many well-meaning interfaith conferences underestimated the difficulties in understanding other faiths presented by what Tillich called "offenses."[48]

It is sobering to realize that a dialogue among religions is not the solution to religious problems. Besides, as Yoshinori Takeuchi astutely remarks, "Where there is an enhanced possibility of mutual appreciation, there is also the increased risk of misunderstanding."[49] Even so, interreligious dialogues are some of the best ways to enhance religious persons' self-understanding as well as to encourage a mutual understanding among religious traditions in a time when humanity is divided not only along ethnic, cultural, and political lines but also along religious lines as well.

NOTES

1. See Robert W. Wood, "Tillich Encounters Japan," and L. Newton Thurber, "Hendrik Kraemer and the Christian Encounter with Japanese Buddhism," *Japanese Religions* 2 (May 1961): 48–71, 76–90.
2. Fung Yu-lan, *A Short History of Chinese Philosophy*, ed. Derk Bodde (New York: Macmillan, 1950), 181.
3. See R. G. Collingwood, *The Idea of History* (Oxford: Clarendon Press, 1946), 17.
4. See "Umma or Ummah," *Shorter Encyclopaedia of Islam* (Leiden: E. J. Brill, 1953), 603–4.
5. See J. M. Kitagawa, ed., *Understanding Modern China* (Chicago: Quadrangle Books, 1969), 24–26.
6. Ernst Benz, "The Theological Meaning of the History of Religions," *The Journal of Religion* 41, no. 1 (January 1961): 7–8.

7. William S. Haas, *The Destiny of Mind—East and West* (London: Faber and Faber, 1956), 298–305.

8. Quoted in Arthur E. Christy, ed., *The Asian Legacy and American Life* (New York: The John Day Co., 1942), 22.

9. Benz, "The Theological Meaning of the History of Religions," 10.

10. G. van der Leeuw, *Religion in Essence and Manifestations*, trans. J. E. Turner (London: George Allen and Unwin, 1938), 691–94.

11. See *Large Catechism.*

12. Charles H. Robinson, *History of Christian Missions* (New York: Charles Scribner's Sons, 1915), 42–43.

13. See the proceedings of the Jerusalem Conference of the I.M.C., vol. 1, *The Christian Life and Message in Relation to Non-Christian Systems of Thought and Life* (New York and London: I.M.C., 1928), 284, 410–12.

14. William Ernest Hocking, *Re-Thinking Missions: A Laymen's Inquiry After One Hundred Years* (New York: Harper & Brothers, 1932), 33, 59. Parenthetically, Hocking further delineated his own philosophical reflections on the future of relations between religions in his *Living Religions and a World Faith* (New York: Macmillan, 1940); and *The Coming World Civilization* (New York: Harper & Brothers, 1956). His famous theory was the "Way of Reconception."

15. Hendrik Kraemer, *The Christian Message in a Non-Christian World* (London: The Edinburgh House, 1938); idem, "Continuity or Discontinuity," *The Authority of the Faith*, vol. 1 (New York and London: I.M.C., 1939), 1, 2, 21.

16. Kraemer, *The Christian Message*, 45, 48, 102, 146.

17. Hocking, *Re-Thinking Missions*, 32.

18. Kraemer, *The Christian Message*, 46.

19. Sarvepalli Radhakrishnan, *Recovery of Faith* (New York: Harper & Brothers, 1955), 13, 179.

20. D. T. Suzuki, *Living by Zen* (New York: Rider, 1950), 13.

21. E. Sarkisyanz, *Buddhist Backgrounds of the Burmese Revolution* (The Hague: Martinus Nijhoff, 1965), 225.

22. Stated in the "Objective Resolution" (1949).

23. Hans J. Morgenthau, *In Defense of the National Interest* (New York: Knopf, 1951), 201–2.

24. P. D. Devanandan and M. M. Thomas, eds., *Communism and the Social Revolution in India* (Calcutta: Y.M.C.A. Publishing House, 1953), 7; W. MacMahon Ball, *Nationalism and Communism in East Asia* (Melbourne: Melbourne University Press, 1952), 198.

25. See Ernst Benz, *Buddhism or Communism: Which Holds the Future of Asia?*, trans. Richard and Clara Winston (Garden City, N.Y.: Doubleday, 1965), 217–94.

26. See *Professors in the United States and Canada Who Teach the Religious Traditions of Asia,* (Hamilton, N.Y.: Colgate University, Fund for the Study of Great Religions, 1980).

27. See J. M. Kitagawa, "Divided We Stand," *Religion in Life* 27, no. 3 (Summer 1958): 335–51.

28. Cited in Masatoshi Doi, *Search for Meaning Through Interfaith Dialogue* (Tokyo: Kyo Bun Kwan, 1976), 92.

29. S. J. Samartha, ed., *Living Faiths and Ultimate Goals: A Continuing Dialogue* (Geneva: World Council of Churches, 1974), xiv.

30. The "Christian Presence Series," under the general editorship of Max A. C. Warren included, Kenneth Cragg, *Sandals at the Mosque;* George Appleton, *On the Eightfold Path;* Raymond Hammer, *Japan's Religious Ferment;* and William Stewart, *India's Religious Frontier.*

31. See for example, Max A. C. Warren, "General Introduction," in William Stew-

art, *India's Religious Frontier: Christian Presence Amid Modern Hinduism* (Philadelphia: Fortress Press, 1964), 13.

32. Ibid., 15.

33. Hendrik Kraemer, *World Cultures and World Religions: The Coming Dialogue* (Philadelphia: Westminster Press, 1960), 14; Thurber, "Hendrik Kraemer and the Christian Encounter," 82; Kraemer, *Religion and the Christian Faith* (Philadelphia: Westminster Press, 1956), 53.

34. Cited in John Hick and Brian Hepplethwaite, eds., *Christianity and Other Religions: Selected Readings* (Glasgow: Collins-Fount Paperbacks, 1980), 81–82.

35. W. C. Smith, "Comparative Religion: Whither—and Why?" in *The History of Religions: Essays in Methodology,* ed. M. Eliade and J. M. Kitagawa (Chicago: University of Chicago Press, 1959), 52, 55.

36. Paul Tillich, *Systematic Theology,* vol. 1 (Chicago: University of Chicago Press, 1951), 39.

37. Paul Tillich, "The Significance of the History of Religions for the Systematic Theologian," in *Essays in Divinity,* gen. ed. J. C. Brauer, vol. 1, *The History of Religions: Essays on the Problem of Understanding,* ed. J. M. Kitagawa, (Chicago: University of Chicago Press, 1967), 242–43.

38. See Tillich's "Ueber die Idee einer Theologie der Kultur," in *Religions philosophie der Kultur* (Berlin: Reuther und Reichard, 1919).

39. Tillich, *Systematic Theology* 1:39.

40. Ibid.

41. Paul Tillich, *Theology of Culture,* ed. R. C. Kimball (New York: Oxford University Press, 1959), 204–5.

42. Paul Tillich, *Christianity and the Encounter of the World Religions* (New York: Columbia University Press, 1963), 62.

43. See Wood, "Tillich Encounters Japan," 60, 57, 71, 66, 63.

44. Tillich, "A Christian-Buddhist Conversation," in idem, *Christianity and the Encounter of World Religions,* 64, 65; idem, *Systematic Theology* 1:221; idem, *Christianity and the Encounter of World Religions,* 95, 97; idem, "The Significance of the History of Religions," 249, 255.

45. See Langdon Gilkey, "The Mystery of Being and Nonbeing: An Experimental Project," *Journal of Religion* 58, no. 1 (January 1978): 2.

46. Mircea Eliade, "Paul Tillich and the History of Religions," in Paul Tillich, *The Future of Religions,* ed. Jerald C. Brauer (New York: Harper & Row, 1966), 33.

47. Mircea Eliade, *Myths, Dreams, and Mysteries,* trans. Philip Mairet (New York: Harper & Brothers, 1960), 8–9.

48. While in Japan, Tillich tried to differentiate "justified" and "unjustified" offenses of the Christian Gospel. "I would, for instance, say it is unjustified to claim that one must accept the doctrine of the Trinity or the doctrine that Jesus was the Son of God and to throw them as stones at the heads of people, for both are completely misunderstood even by theologians. Now that is not the right offense. But the right offense is to accept the demand of ultimate seriousness of the Ultimate, as it is seen in the picture of Jesus in the Gospels. . . ." See Wood, "Tillich Encounters Japan," 69.

49. Quoted by Max A. C. Warren in his "General Introduction" to George Appleton, *On the Eightfold Path* (New York: Oxford University Press, 1961), 12.

12. Tillich and the New Religious Movements

JACK BOOZER

The news about the mass suicide of over nine hundred persons at the People's Temple at Jonestown, Guyana, on November 18 and 19, 1978, startled the world to such unbelief that only the subsequent photographs and details of the horror were able to bring convincing realism to the reports. How could that event of voluntary mass death have happened to a group that began, as Howard Moody suggests, by appealing to "the urban poor, the disenfranchised, the uprooted and dispossessed people seeking solid earth into which to sink roots, searching for unwavering truth in a world of total relativism, looking for some vision of some world kinder, more cooperative, more caring than the one they knew, and for a way of living that would express commitment to a cause larger than their own lives?"[1]

Thus questions as to the nature and function of religion became more insistent. Was the People's Temple a religious sect, a religious movement? Is there any relation between Jonestown and traditional religion? Is there a relation between Jonestown and the many new religious movements that have grown rapidly in the last twenty years?[2] Are there controls implicit in religious sects that temper or inhibit demonry? Is it possible for religion to continue to offer meaning and power to human life without at the same time manipulating or destroying the very life it promises to preserve and bless?

These are not new questions, but they become urgent in our day because of the ambiguity, disorder, disunity, and emptiness of contemporary culture for many people and their turn to new religious movements to find some "hold" or meaning in life. For many the stability of the future has been problematic, and for some a future of any kind has become questionable. The poignant remark of a fourteen-year-old girl indicates the precariousness of a constantly receding "present" for increasing numbers of people. When asked why she had got pregnant, she replied: "I didn't see anything else in my future."

FROM *KAIROS* TO THE "VOID"

In many striking ways the situation that Paul Tillich faced in Europe in the years before World War I was similar to the one in American culture in the last two or three decades. Sidney Mead has described that mood for America in an epilogue to essays on *The Nation with the Soul of a Church:*

I have written these pieces with the chilling realization that we live today under the shadow of man's power to destroy all life on this planet. In a happier time of more primitive technology, James Russell Lowell could say that when God gave man a matchbox he knew that the framework of the world was fireproof. . . . I agree with Arthur Goldberg that probably man now has less than a 50 percent chance of survival.

The appalling thing is that so many persons, including leaders in high places, seem to lack the imaginations to perceive the possibility of the end of man. But to our youth this possibility is an ever present reality; and perhaps this is the most important element in the gap between them and so many of the older generation who seem to conduct the business of living at the same old stand, in the same old way, and with the obsolete faith of James Russell Lowell.[3]

Although Tillich was able to maintain a somewhat optimistic expectation until he completed the text of *The Socialist Decision* on March 9, 1932,[4] on the eve of the Hitler darkness, that optimism was partly informed by the collapse of what he regarded as hopelessly rigid, conservative, and recalcitrant structures of life and order in the church, the state, and the culture.[5] Discussing his life in Berlin, 1919 to 1924, Tillich wrote:

The social structure was in a state of dissolution, the human relations with respect to authority, education, family, sex, friendship, and pleasure were in a creative chaos. Revolutionary art came into the foreground, supported by the Republic, attacked by the majority of the people. Psychoanalytic ideas spread and produced a consciousness of realities which had been carefully repressed in previous generations. The participation in these movements created manifold problems, ecstasies, and despairs, practically as well as theoretically.[6]

With several friends in the cause of Religious Socialism, a group called the Kairos Circle, Tillich sustained a hope for the future that entailed a radical transformation of the religious as well as of the economic and political situation. But that hope was held alongside the conviction that Western civilization as it has been known was near its end.[7] Indeed, one of the insights of the Kairos Circle was that theirs was "an outstanding moment in the temporal process," a *Kairos* of meaning-laden time, "a moment in which the eternal breaks into the temporal, shaking and transforming it and creating a crisis in the depth of human existence."[8] This moment contained a double move and a double assault by the eternal: a double move to destroy the hardened and self-righteous orders of manipulation and exploitation or, as Tillich puts it, "all sacramental demonries [and] their feudal . . . and ecclesiastical residues,"[9] on the one hand and, on the other hand, to create new forms of cultural life in which rights, justice, personality, and community prevail; a double assault "on the otherworldliness and individualism of ecclesiastical piety and on the this-worldly complacency and utopianism of the socialist movement."[10]

In his foundational essay of 1923 on the "Basic Principles of Religious Socialism" and in the book *The Socialist Decision* of 1932, Tillich, in the best tradition of the Hebrew prophets, claims an inextricable connection between holiness and justice, love and power, the right and the just, religion and culture, realization and expectation. A characteristic aspect of this combining of religion and ethics in a socialist form is the claim that "the religious principle is not confined to a specifically religious sphere,"[11] nor is the ethical principle confined to a specifically ethical sphere. All forms of provincialism as well as all forms of demonic manipulation were rejected in a vision of a holistic, spirited, rich, creative, and humane culture made possible by the power of the state to assure justice and the enlivening dimensions of religion and grace without the bigotry and self-centeredness of a "religious" sphere.

Combining the No to demonries, the Yes to emerging new possibilities of justice, and both of these with the recognition of the finiteness of every position, even that of Religious Socialism,

Tillich emphasized what he took to be the substance of Jewish and Christian ethics within the Kingdom of God:

In the struggle *against* a demonized society and *for* a meaningful society, religious socialism discerns a necessary expression for the expectation of the kingdom of God. But it repudiates the identification of socialism with the kingdom of God just as it rejects religious indifference towards constructive tasks within this world. It regards the unity of the socialist dialectic, a unity of expectation and demand of that which is to come, as a conceptual unity and at the same time as a concrete and contemporary transformation of the Christian eschatological tension.[12]

As might have been expected, Tillich's strong insistence on the religious dimension of socialism offended the socialists, and his insistence with Christoph Blumhardt that the secular struggle for social justice was an aspect of the Kingdom of God offended the traditional religions. Indeed, the superintendent of the Protestant Consistory of Brandenburg formally requested Tillich in 1919 to explain how he as an ordained clergyman could deliver a lecture at a meeting of the Independent Social-Democratic party of Germany.[13] Life "on the boundary," holding polar elements together, with the criticism and attacks that came from both sides, became a mark of Tillich's religious, social, and intellectual vocation for all his days.

The most agonizing aspect of this life "on the boundary" in the Kairos Circle was the break with his fellow student and friend, Emanuel Hirsch, over the religious meaning of Hitler and the National Socialist movement. Hirsch sided with ethnicity, Volkism, Fatherland, Blood and Iron, and Hitler. Tillich sided with humanity, autonomy, the Kingdom beyond the state, justice, love, and community. (See later in the present volume Tillich's published "Open Letter to Emanuel Hirsch," 1934.) It is not surprising, then, that *The Socialist Decision* was suppressed and copies destroyed, nor that Tillich's associates were stimulated by it to courage and resistance against Nazi power. Tillich's name was included in the first list of intellectuals to be purged on April 13, 1933, and he was dismissed from his chair in philosophy at the University of Frankfurt. He was among the first non-Jews to be dismissed, a fact he remembered with pride all his life.[14]

Professor John Stumme reports an interview with Adolf Lowe in

1972 in which Lowe reported that the Nazi Minister of Education called Tillich to his office in 1933 and offered him a chair in theology at the University of Berlin if Tillich would revoke his position expressed in *The Socialist Decision*. Of course Tillich refused, and the die was then cast. Of all his books, Tillich seemed to be most pleased with this one, about which a colleague observed that it was his "most prophetic book" as well as his "most Jewish book."[15] The rejection of the new messiah, Adolf Hitler, turned on the conviction informed by the prophets and by Jesus that the holy that is not at the same time righteousness and justice must be rejected.[16] As between Hitler and Religious Socialism, Tillich's position was clear: "The salvation of European society from a return to barbarism lies in the hands of socialism."[17]

Germany's decision for Hitler in 1933 rather than for Religious Socialism symbolizes those forces that caused Tillich gradually to make a radical shift from the ecstatic expectation of the post–World War I years to a mood after World War II of impending darkness, a mood of tragedy, a "mood of the end," of inner emptiness, "a vacuum out of which creation is possible," a void that may be a "sacred void" calling one to "wait" within the profundity of the divine No until the traces of the divine Yes are more clearly revealed.[18] Tillich has contrasted the general mood of "cynical realism" after 1945 to that of "utopian hope" after 1918, claiming the validity of the critical and creative aspects of the Protestant principle in justifying "the hope, though destroying its utopian form" and justifying "the realism, though destroying its cynical form."[19]

The purpose of this discussion of Tillich and the crisis in Germany after World War I has been to describe that condition and to appropriate Tillich's insights both for facing a somewhat similar situation in the United States in recent years and for assessing the significance of the new religions in that situation. Many of Tillich's insights illuminate the issue; among these are Logos, *Kairos*, idolatry, the Protestant principle, religion and quasi religion. But the demonic, which Tillich regarded as an important contribution to the interpretation of history, and the New Being are the most viable of Tillich's categories for the interpretation and assessment of the new religious movements. Before applying those categories, let us look at what is happening in the "new religions."

THE NEW RELIGIOUS MOVEMENTS

Theodore Roszak's book, *The Making of a Counterculture*, published in 1969, focused attention on a widespread discontent of the youth of America over the prospect of continued movement toward a technological utopia. Although he acknowledged that his interpretation was not accurate for all youth, especially for the more conservative and the more liberal as well as the militant black young, Roszak made positive claims for the counterculture as having "that healthy instinct which refuses both at the personal and political level to practice such a cold-blooded rape of our human sensibilities" as that entailed in mainstream's "ingenious rationalization" not only of the fact but of "the total *ethos* of the bomb."[20]

In that essay, Roszak pointed to and invited consideration of the two primary questions about the new religious movements: Why are Americans turning to the new movements, and what do these new movements offer?

In 1970 Jacob Needleman published *The New Religions* as a "portrait" of the "spiritual explosion" in which hundreds of thousands of Americans were turning "toward the religions of the East and toward the mystical core of all religion."[21] His partial list of those religions included Zen Buddhism, Meher Baba, Subud, Krishnamurti, Transcendental Meditation, Yoga, Sufism, Tibetan Buddhism, Vedanta, and Humanistic Mysticism. A more complete list would include the Hare Krishnas, the Unification Church, Process, the Children of God, Scientology, the People's Temple, the Living Word Fellowship, and revivals of American Indian religion. Some would also claim that many groups of evangelicals, charismatics, and mystics within Judaism and Christianity must be included as new religious movements within the "spiritual explosion."[22]

That a National Conference on the Study of New Religious Movements in America convened in Berkeley, California, in June 1977 under the primary sponsorship of the Graduate Theological Union is further evidence of the significance of these movements.[23] Indeed, that conference actually inaugurated a Program for the Study of New Religious Movements in America at the Graduate Theological Union.

The appeal of the new religious movements is related to the

cultural situation in post–World War II America. In general, the American people have been increasingly unable to answer their fundamental human questions through the traditional religious and secular forms of American culture. The culture honors proximate questions by providing proximate answers. But even the culture is becoming less dependable and proximate answers less satisfying. In this situation, as Langdon Gilkey observes, "ultimate questions grow out of the loss of proximate answers." Both Gilkey and Frederick Bird have emphasized the loss of the self in modern culture, either through a confused identity, a loss of "realness" and creativity at the center of self, or through the compromise of the self by restricting the meaning of the self to social roles which are themselves empty.[24]

Gilkey also speaks of the "external" orientation of American culture with its emphasis on skills of manipulation, organization, control, consumption, rearranging and reforming people and things, without adequate attention to the "inward life of the Spirit." "The self has become an elusive shadow, a hungry and lonely ghost, unrecognized and hidden, in a merely external process."[25] Further, American culture, while pampering the body, perpetuates the Hellenistic notion that the body is the house of the spirit, that the self *has* a body.

As one would expect, Gilkey sees the significance of the appeal of the new religions to be related in part to these two deprivations of American culture. He contends that, among many factors, an important one is that many persons "who in modern society find themselves unsure they exist or are effective, receive a new sense of the reality, value, and possibilities of the self," especially in the cults of meditation and self-awareness. "The discovery of the self is the initial gift of Oriental religions of meditation in our midst."[26]

The incisive ideas of William Irwin Thompson support Gilkey's observations while, at the same time, placing them within the broad context of a total cultural trend. In Thompson's vision, the civilization of modern culture has been built by the ego through competitiveness, consumption, externalization, mastery, separation, isolation and specialization. That assertion of the ego posits the worth of a person not in terms of what one receives, feels, conserves, gives, and preserves, but on the thin basis of what one achieves and owns. "And so, if you are what you own, the more you own, the more you are." The final tragedy of such a culture is that it consumes and destroys the human self, for the ego bent on consumption is insensitive to community, and an ego sustained by possessions is powerless (except for the pathetic gestures of remodeling the house, cosmetic surgery, and steel vaults) in the face of illness, old age, and death. "Where the whole way of life is devoted to consumption, it is people who become consumed."[27]

Thompson sees even the universities and the churches as complicit in the processes of consumption and death, with scarcely a word of criticism, re-creation, or revisioning of human life and culture.

The old university is now surrounded and contained as an artifact within the new postindustrial culture, just as once the Church was surrounded and contained as a content within the structure of industrial society. Harvard and MIT shift from being the critical wing of society to become a consulting agency for the government of the new corporate state. In the new university like MIT, the difference between education and business is blurred. Government, corporation, and university become one interlocking, bureaucratic corporate system.[28]

It is perhaps unnecessary to add that, in this view, the churches have become the "morale booster" for the universities, the corporations, and the state, and for all people in them who, for whatever reason, need reassurance from time to time that this is what God really intended for the creation.

Thompson's hopes for the future are not as specific and concrete as those of most of the new religious movements, but his proposals include many of the values of the new religions within a grand appeal for "resacralization." He sees dead ideas now supporting a dying industrial civilization and advocates new ideas that "hold the life of a whole culture for the earth." He expresses an alternative to civilization (in his special definition as the achievement of the ego) and savagery in several ways—as a move from competition and aggression to cooperation and symbiosis, as a revisioning of history, as a reunion of the ego with the self, as a transformation of the archetype of industrialization, as a shift from "civilization" to "planetization," as a shift from the center controlling the periphery to a situation in which "the center is everywhere and the circumference nowhere."[29]

The new ideas that he invites combine all of these. "What these new ideas call for is a revisioning or a remythologizing of nature, self, and society. In this remythologizing, charisma shifts from technology to contemplative science, from industry to ecology, from factories to communities." Here one is not what one owns, but one's being is what one is. Granting the trauma of removing our "selves" from status in the "civilization" that our ambitious egos have built, there is still the possibility of taking another road whose overall nature is "resacralization." That road leads toward "a spiritual awakening on the level of the great universal religions that have guided the cultural evolution of humanity." That awakening will include a "change of heart and mind, a new wedding of nature and culture, and a new kind of human community that can express the resacralization of earth."[30]

However one answers the question of whether specific new religions encourage resacralization of nature, human life, and culture, it seems clear that anyone who has reservations about the total investment of the self in the processes of agency and consumption over against communion and receiving/giving[31] is a candidate for *any* religious movement that honors *any* aspect of a more deep, moral, comprehensive, and spiritual intimation about nature, the self, history, culture, and even life after death.

In his essay for the National Conference on the Study of New Religious Movements in America, Theodore Roszak was sanguine as to the ominous destructive potential in some of the new religious movements. But he chose to focus on the "secular consensus" in American culture, which has come so close to a closure against the "religious" that it has, in effect, pushed anyone with religious sensitivity toward the new religious movements. While acknowledging that we live in a time of "religious awakening," he describes our situation in language strikingly similar to that of Thompson: "Science, technics, and social evolution—all radically divorced from religious tradition—sway the history of our time, and they do so globally, aggressively, militantly. They are fast taking over all the cultural ground, building a planetary synthesis that will soon bring our entire species within the urban-industrial dominance. We are very close to *Endgame.*"[32]

Roszak regards culture as a "splintered mirror coruscating that original splendor (visionary moment) into a million variations, all bearing some trace of the divine light, some remote spark or glimmer." From that it follows both that resacralization is possible, because a sacred "residue" remains in every fragment, and that secularization is actual when the "part is taken for the whole, the lesser reality substituted for the greater." Secularization, then, is an "idolatry" of a fragment, whether in the removal of ecstasy from ethics in secular humanism or in the exclusive fixation upon belief and doctrine in secular religiosity. Because of that kind of idolatry, Roszak is positive toward the current religious awakening, taken as a whole, in that it has brought "a sense of how much bigger and grandly various religion can be than the narrow fixation upon Belief and Doctrine that has for so long preoccupied the major churches of the West."[33]

The major flaws of the secular consensus in Roszak's judgment have to do with ethics. The first is the separation of ethics from ecstasy, thereby diminishing ecstasy, and portraying human enlightenment and fulfillment as fundamentally rational/moral and godless. The error underneath that position is to identify church and state as partners in tyranny and to regard only those outside the religious establishment as "the party for humanity," forgetting or denying the substantive claims for righteousness and human dignity within the religious vision of the prophets and of Jesus.

The second flaw Roszak sees in the secular consensus is a kind of "trivialization" of morality, as Abraham Heschel would put it. The ethical that rules out the religious has no way of exorcising or dealing with sin, except by more vigorous moral effort. Hence, there is an inordinate emphasis on approved conduct, winning merit badges, exemplary virtue in those things that keep the culture going. Intimations of guilt or sin, real or imagined, are repressed, and access to a higher level of morality (which Tillich called the "transmoral conscience"), through which release from bondage to the cultural consensus could be won, is closed off. As a result, Roszak sees "buried in the core of Western conscience . . . a festering accumulation of 'sin' that is simply unworthy of serious adult concern. It has nothing to do with justice, compassion, or good fellowship."[34]

It is because of the near closure of the secular consensus against the religious that Roszak can speak of a spiritual void as "the prime political fact of our time." Precisely at that point Roszak sees a

valuable lesson that can be learned from the renaissance of religion. "We can *use* what it tells us of human need and aspiration
to question the assumptions of the secular consensus. We can use
its conception of human potentiality to challenge the adequacy of
our science, our technics, our politics."[35]

Roszak leaves us to conjecture about many aspects of the new
religious movements, including whether or not they really promise
anything fundamentally different from isolation, achievement, exclusiveness, and trivial morality of the secular or of the religious
establishment. But he is quite emphatic in welcoming the religious
explosion overall, primarily because of its challenge to the secular
consensus, for that consensus does not go "deep enough to touch
what is fundamental in human nature, and so it cannot understand
our discontent or bring us fulfillment." That, for Roszak, is because people are not fundamentally "power and profit-seeking
creatures. . . . Power and possession are without significance for
the whole and healthy person. They become goals only by default
and to the degree that higher purpose withdraws from our lives."
The gurus in all the new religious movements are significant, then,
because they remind us of a project greater than that entailed in
the secular consensus and because they "awaken the god who
sleeps at the roots of our being."[36]

In a somewhat similar way Robert Wuthnow discusses "anomie"
and the relation of world order and disorder to religious movements.[37] Wuthnow applies two themes from Peter Berger,[38] "anomie" and "plausibility structures," to the varieties of religious
experimentation in recent years. In his view, the multiplicity of
religious movements in America is directly related to two facts:
that the only "plausibility structure" comprehensive enough to
perform a general "nomic" function is *world order,* and that since
World War II there have been fundamental uncertainties and
shifts in that world order. Wuthnow mentions a few examples of
this wavering: the cold war, the rise of China to world power,
uncertain relations with the Third World, the human rights movement, and the Vietnam War. The effect of the loss of any overarching plausibility structure has been to dissolve any general or universal moral authority or source of personal stability.

In that situation, the fundamental drive for order, stability, a
nomos, has taken a less general and universal form, but that drive
is so strong that it will not be denied. As power will not tolerate

a vacuum, persons will not tolerate anomie. "Americans have been forced to reevaluate the moral basis of their institutions. . . . The effect upon religion has been that the plausibility of the whole Western tradition, with its emphasis on modernity and rationality, can no longer be taken for granted quite as easily as it once was."[39] To be sure, this does not mean that the moral intimation and intention are lost, but only that the moral sense must place itself within a different plausibility structure. If the dominant orientation of American foreign policy has been an *amoral realpolitik* rather than the moral principles of religious vision and of the churches, persons must find a moral plausibility structure smaller and different from the nation.

That being the case, Wuthnow writes: "In the *lacunae* of ultimate confidence, many have turned inward to reconstruct their own personal experiences of the sacred, often by borrowing heavily from the tribal, magical, and mystical religions previously relegated to the fringes of Western tradition."[40]

On that analysis, Wuthnow proposes an explanation of why there is a kind of explosion of religious experimentation and of new and different religious movements. Without entering upon the difficult task of assessing them, he nevertheless urges patience toward them. Tightly constructed world orders have been achieved in the past "only at a tremendous cost in human freedom and social resources." Over against that kind of order "a loose confederation of local, national, and regional interests that can respond with flexibility to changing global conditions"[41] is probably a more viable alternative. Wuthnow welcomes the new religious movements partly because they add to the religious "pluralism, diversity and toleration" that could contribute to the "strength and adaptability" of that kind of loose confederation.

Steven Tipton wrote a dissertation at Harvard University in 1977 that has now been published as *Getting Saved From the Sixties: Moral Meaning in Conversion and Cultural Change*. Research for that study involved Tipton in extensive amounts of time with three particular groups: the Living Word Fellowship (a millenarian Pentecostal sect), the Pacific Zen Center (a Zen Buddhist meditation center), and Erhard Seminars Training *(est)*, a human potential training organization. Tipton describes these groups as conservative Christian, neo-Oriental, and psychologistic. Here we must slight his richly textured detail in order to concentrate on why persons in these groups rejected the three major options of the counterculture, Biblical religion, and utilitarian individualism, and what persons actually found in these groups.

Tipton claims that a profound change resulted from the conflicts of the 1960s, "the delegitimation of utilitarian culture, and with it the stripping away of moral authority from major American social institutions: government, law, business, religion, marriage and the family."[42] This conflict left scars on both the counterculture and utilitarian culture; that of disappointed expectations and subsequent withdrawal into private life on the counterculture, that of an inability to deal with substantive discontents on the utilitarian culture.

The attractiveness of alternative religious movements is vivid against that background.

Disoriented by drugs, embittered by politics, disillusioned by the apparent worthlessness of work and the transiency of love, they have found a way back through these movements, a way to get along with conventional American society and the demands of their own maturing lives. For some youths the social and ideological stability of these movements has meant psychological and even physical survival. For many more, membership in alternative religious movements has meant moral survival and a sense of meaning and purpose recovered through recombining expressive ideals with moralities of authority, rules, and utility. On one hand, these movements have thereby adapted and reconciled their youthful adherents to the traditional order. On the other, they have meant moral survival precisely by sustaining countercultural themes, albeit in altered forms.[43]

Although there are striking differences among the three groups, Tipton found that all three alternative religions enable their members to overcome the conventional opposition between instrumental conformity to modernized social conditions and expressive reaction to them. They mediate and recombine existing meanings to form alternative associations "better adapted to survival . . . than was the counterculture, supporting the attitudes of their members in specific ways: 1. Ecstatic experience vs. Technical Reason; 2. Holism vs. Analytic Discrimination; 3. Acceptance vs. Problem-Solving; and 4. Intuitive Certainty vs. Pluralistic Relativism." The primary conclusion Tipton reaches from this study is that the alternative religious movements are "experiments in the transformation of moral meaning."[44]

This necessarily abbreviated consideration of the new religious movements points inescapably to three general conclusions: that American culture has increasingly moved toward insensitivity to the transcendent and to the most deeply human; that the traditional religions have accommodated far too extensively the moral/social/political consensus; and that increasing numbers of persons have a strong intimation that there is something more profound than the secular consensus and competition for possessions. The outcome is a desperate search for physical, moral, religious, and intellectual integrity, which many are finding in the new religious movements. Whether that felt, willed, and thought integrity is genuine integrity, whether it leads to peace, justice, and love is another question. We will face that question now as we return to Paul Tillich for the value of his insights in relation to these new religious movements.

THE PRESENT VIABILITY OF TILLICH'S THOUGHT

The Conference on the Study of New Religious Movements in America met difficulties facing the question whether one religion is more true than another. Yet without some criterion, any claim to religious legitimacy by any group, even the People's Temple, can hardly be challenged. And without some norm, there is no way to prevent deterioration of religion into a threat to the human community. On these issues, few persons in this century have spoken with insight comparable to that of Paul Tillich. Because he has spoken clearly and profoundly, we may look to him on the way to our own answer to this question.

Tillich would understand and encourage the new religious movements insofar as they protest and stand against a destructive and demonic culture, "industrial society" as Tillich designates it. That society belittles the human by containing persons within the processes of production and consumption, making them into objects and things. The result for many persons in such a society is emptiness, meaninglessness, dehumanization and estrangement.[45] That the new religious movements themselves not only see the alienation but also lay claim to a holiness over against the culture places them within Tillich's category of the "courage to be," the courage to affirm the being of the self in spite of the threat

of nonbeing,[46] and within the category of "religion" as unconditional concern or seriousness about the meaning of life.[47]

But Tillich would also regard some of the religious movements
as pathological, idolatrous, and demonic. They are pathological
insofar as they are neurotic, having "settled down to a fixed,
though limited and unrealistic, self-affirmation."[48] They are idolatrous insofar as they elevate finite reality (such as leader, doctrine,
or organization) to the realm of the ultimate or unconditional.[49]
They are demonic to the extent that they use form-creating and
form-destroying power in the givenness of reality to obscure and
destroy the essence or meaning of people and things.[50]

Tillich's understanding of the demonic and of the New Being is
particularly illuminating for an understanding of the new religious
movements. That is partly because the effort of believers to "resa-
cralize" or to "make moral sense of their lives" tends to be so
intense as to set up an opposition that locates evil and destructiveness *outside* the religious altogether, with the result that both the
evil of the outsider and the goodness of the insider are exaggerated. In its most extreme form that exaggeration becomes a
hard dualism between the religious community and the profane
world or between this age, which is ruled by demonic "principalities and powers," and the new age of the Kingdom of God, which
is to come. If it is the former, the "new believers" must fortify
themselves against the polluting powers of the secular/profane
culture to the extent that they can neither accept anything from
that culture nor enter into open and mutual relation with persons
in that culture. They see themselves as having to be "in the world"
but determined not to be "of it" or contaminated "by it." If it is
the latter, the "new believers" assume the total domination of this
age by evil powers and discipline themselves through hope, faith,
and denial to await the coming of the Kingdom of God and the
overthrow of the rulers of wickedness in the present evil age.

Tillich would regard both these stances as "demonic" because
they cause a fundamental disruption or split in the self, in the
community, in the spatial order, and in the temporal order.
With the split there is a denial of risk and of the dynamics of history, as well as wholeness, because the possibility is claimed to
move from form-creation to form-creation, from value to value,
from goodness to goodness, without ever being threatened by

form-destruction, disvalue, or evil. For Tillich, such a view is static and flawed, because it misrepresents the nature of history and of human growth.

Over against these interpretations, Tillich emphasizes the mixture of good and evil, the form-creative and the form-destructive, in all persons, institutions, and events in history. The most all-embracing definition of what Tillich calls the "dialectics of the demonic" is "the unity of form-creating and form-destroying strength." The demonic describes "a power in personal and social life that is creative and destructive at the same time."[51] At this level Tillich is describing history and everything that "exists" in time. There is an inescapable ambiguity of good and evil, creation and destruction, in every movement in history. No creative act is possible without breaking and destroying the fixed form of things, and no completely destructive act is possible without borrowing or trading on form-creating energy. Often Tillich speaks of this as "existence" over against "essence." To exist, for him, is to be partially separated from that to which one, in essence, belongs, with the added poignancy that there is never certainty about an act toward essence or toward form or value creation. In philosophical terms one might say that everything that exists is a mixture of being and nonbeing. Tillich uses those terms often, but in order to stress the spiritual-personal-historical tension over against a possible static interpretation, he speaks of all acts of personal-historical existence as drawing on a fundament of power in which creative and destructive energies are inextricably intermixed.

This means that every action, every self, every institution in history inevitably participates in this dialectic, even if it uses power to resist change and to remain the same. Every move of self-affirmation (or toward the good or toward a just social order) draws energy and power from a level that is never simply form-creative or simply form-destructive. Within this dialectic of history persons must act and decide in order "to be" ("to be human"), and they are responsible for their action in spite of the fact that their actions draw on power and bring results that are partly destructive and partly creative. To recognize this demonic level of meaning does not imply that existence itself is evil. Existence is limited, ambiguous, fallen from essence. That may lead some to interpret the "myth of the Fall" to mean that existence as such is evil. Tillich would rather interpret the Fall as a concept that limits and defines all existence as ambiguous, as never completely good or completely evil; but for him, *this separation from essence is fundamentally good.*

Beyond this level of the universal quality of existence, the demonic designates the way in which individuals, communities, and institutions use power. Three possibilities present themselves: the divine, the demonic, and the satanic. Tillich dismisses the satanic, which he defines as a "devouring of every form" or as an "absolutely independent eruption of the abyss." As complete formlessness the satanic cannot come into existence because nothing can exist without form. "To come into being means to come to form. To lose form means to lose existence."[52] The divine indicates every manifestation of power in which the essence of things is preserved and destructiveness is controlled by the creation, liberation and fulfillment of form and by openness toward higher form. The divine gives form-creation a future and a transcendence. The demonic indicates every manifestation of power in which essence is defied and destroyed, personality is split, meaning is denied, and form is broken simply for the sake of breaking. The demonic denies a future to the fulfillment of the form appropriate to a thing (essence) and to the aspiration toward higher form. Since the demonic is form-destructive, it is destined to destroy what it creates, even the program of destructiveness, and destined finally to destroy itself.

The demonic often entails the elevation of something finite—a law, creed, person, race, community, institution, nation—to the status of the infinite, the absolute. "We see the horror resulting from the demonic elevation of something finite to absolute validity. I call it demonic because individuals and nations become possessed and are driven to destroy everything which stands in their way. And since this is done on a finite basis, they are themselves ultimately led to self-destruction."[53]

Because the ambiguous fundament of power comes to expression as predominantly creative (divine) or as predominantly destructive (demonic), there is a responsibility to "name" and oppose the demonic. "The battle against the demonries of a time becomes an unavoidable, religious-political duty."[54] The vivid symbol of history as the warfare between the "forces of light and those of darkness" takes the form of a struggle between the demonic structures of compulsive force and divine structures of enabling and persuasive power, of grace. "We are all involved in the conflict between these two structures. Sometimes we are ridden, as Luther described it, by the divine compulsion, sometimes by the demonic. However, the divine structure of grace is not possession or compulsion, because it is at the same time liberating; it liberates what we essentially are."[55]

It is important for Tillich, however, that in the struggle against the demonic, one not be led to regard the demonic as completely evil or one's own position as completely good. Nothing is "simply" demonic or divine. "The contrast of both principles is effective in every person and every phenomenon. An institution or community that should seek to withdraw from this judgment, would by this very act succumb to the pharisaic demonry."[56]

Further, the demonic can be limited, removed from dominance, even "conquered," but it is never completely banished. "The demonic power is banned but not eradicated, and it will return. In less mythological language, one could say that the demonic can positively be conquered in a special place and in a special time but not totally and universally."[57] It is only in eternity that the demonic is definitively overcome. Even so, every manifestation of the holy in history names the demonic for what it is, destructive and disintegrative, and limits the power of the demonic to destroy.

Hence, all true religion, on Tillich's terms, is engaged in the cosmic battle against the "principalities and powers" that would split and destroy the human person and the whole of creation, but engaged in that struggle with an awareness of the imperfection of one's own position. Because of the divine, the person of faith is called to name, oppose, and limit the demonic in order to show the demonic for what it is and for the sake of the fulfillment of all things in a higher form. This entails vigor but not stridency, a struggle for the good but without self-righteousness.

Tillich often spoke of love as the reunion of the separated, the reunion or reconciliation of the estranged.[58] Every act of love contains a denial of that which denies love, yet that act of denial is not for the sake of the denial (for the breaking or the cutting off), but for the purpose of the higher reunion that only love can bring about. The vision of Tillich, then, is grandly positive, constructive, healing, unifying and fulfilling, however fraught every concrete aspect within that vision is with the possibility of tragedy and demonic arrogance. But wherever, under the conditions of existence, the demonic is "conquered," denied its victory, there is New Being. Tillich understands the New Being as manifest most fully in Jesus as the Christ, but that conviction entails a rejoicing in every victory, however fragmentary, of the New Being, of the vital center and unity of persons, of the creation of the new, and of the drawing of all things toward their transcendent ground and aim.[59]

SOME CONCLUSIONS IN SUMMARY

What, in sum, do these aspects of Tillich's thought suggest specifically about the new religious movements?

First, Tillich would confirm the healing and wholeness, the effort to make moral, physical, emotional, and intellectual sense out of human lives. But he would question the health and integrity of any person or group that did not manifest that health in love toward nature and people in this world. For him separation to save oneself from the pollution and destruction of culture is suspect (except for hospitalization) unless the saving and healing powers are expressed to challenge and change the culture. For Tillich, resacralization can never apply to only a part of reality.

Second, Tillich would be sympathetic to the appeal of the new religious movements for many people, but he would urge caution about them until they showed seriousness in taking responsibility and risks in naming and opposing the demonic in present history. It is easy to offer something altogether new and pure as over against individuals and groups who have been compromised through involvement with the dominant culture. Tillich would be very suspicious of other worldly, eschatological groups that deny nonbeing and evil in such a way that they also deny being and the good.

Third, Tillich would challenge the claims for absolute certainty in most of these groups, whether that certainty attaches to a leader, a book, a doctrine, an ethic, a social program, or an organization. Human integrity entails the risk of courage, meaning, and love, and any group that removes that risk by claims to certainty in these forms obscures the mystery of history, of the holy, and of the human.

Fourth, though the situation would vary greatly with different groups, Tillich would welcome dialogue with them and invite speaking and listening at all levels. He would expect each to reconsider its position upon listening to the other, and he would insist upon internal criticism within each religion. He would confirm the sacral "treasure" in each, while insisting on the earthenness of all vessels, but he would avoid efforts for a common religion or for a collection of the truths of all religions.

Fifth, these insights together suggest that Tillich would claim that religion may be true on individual, social, moral, intellectual, communal, political, and spiritual levels. But he would insist that the more true and the more genuine religion would include them all: love (agape), power, and justice; hope for the fulfillment of the essence of all things and people in the Kingdom of God; sharing in the suffering of the sick, the weak, the abused, and the estranged.

A crucial question remains: Is it possible to have religion without the possibility of demonic destructiveness? To this question, Tillich would answer no. That is the answer, both because it is impossible to exist without the possibility of demonry and because every function of the human spirit is tempted by its own form of arrogance. That does not mean for Tillich that religion is thereby neutralized. On the contrary, Tillich identifies true religion as liberating, creative, community building, healing, and comprehensively unifying, but without arrogant self-centeredness. Any religion that functions against these qualities, whether in the bizarre instance of Jonestown or in the more mild forms of paternalism, manipulation, or sensationalism, deserves to be named, exposed, and challenged as demonic distortion. Nothing that destroys for its own sake, out of fear or hate or arrogance or idolatrous devotion, can possibly be to the service and glory of God.

NOTES

1. Howard Moody, "Jonestown and Ourselves," *Christianity and Crisis* 38, no. 21 (15 January 1979): 327.
2. A Gallup survey recently concluded that there are 6 million Americans involved in Transcendental Meditation, 5 million in yoga, 3 million in the charismatic movement, 3 million in mysticism, and 2 million in Eastern religion. George Gallup, Jr., "Afterword: A Coming Religious Revival?" in *Religion in America: 1950 to the Present*, ed. Jackson W. Carroll, Douglas W. Johnson, and Martin E. Marty (San Francisco: Harper & Row, 1979), 111–15.

3. Sidney E. Mead, *The Nation with the Soul of a Church* (New York: Harper & Row, 1975), 127–28.
4. Cf. the excellent introduction by John R. Stumme to Franklin Sherman's translation of Tillich's *Socialist Decision* (New York: Harper & Row, 1977), ix–xxvi.
5. Cf. Paul Tillich, *The Religious Situation,* trans. H. Richard Niebuhr (New York: Henry Holt and Co., 1932). Originally published as *Die Religiöse Lage der Gegenwart* (Berlin: Ullstein, 1926).
6. Paul Tillich, "Autobiographical Reflections of Paul Tillich," in *The Theology of Paul Tillich,* rev. ed., ed. Charles W. Kegley (New York: Pilgrim Press, 1982), 13–14.
7. Cf. the introductory essay by James Luther Adams to *Political Expectation* (New York: Harper & Row, 1971), vi–xx.
8. See Tillich's 1942 essay, "Kairos," in *The Protestant Era,* trans. James Luther Adams (Chicago: University of Chicago Press, 1948), 45.
9. Paul Tillich, "Basic Principles of Religious Socialism," in *Political Expectation,* 73. Cf. also 68, 69, 81, 82, 84.
10. Edward Heimann, "Tillich's Doctrine of Religious Socialism," in *The Theology of Paul Tillich,* 313.
11. Paul Tillich, "Religious Socialism," in *Political Expectation,* 41.
12. Ibid., 50.
13. Cf. James Luther Adams, "Encounter with the Demonic: From the Psyche to the Society," *Metanoia* 3, no. 3 (September 1971): 2–4, and Adams's translation of Tillich's reply to the superintendent in the same issue of *Metanoia,* 9, 10–12, and 16.
14. Cf. John R. Stumme's introduction to *The Socialist Decision,* ix–xxvi, and the illuminating work of Wilhelm and Marion Pauck, *Paul Tillich: His Life and Thought* (New York: Harper & Row, 1976), vol. 1, *Life,* 123–138, 151.
15. Stumme, introduction to *The Socialist Decision,* xxiv, xxv.
16. Tillich, "Basic Principles of Religious Socialism," 59.
17. Tillich, *The Socialist Decision,* 161.
18. Tillich, *The Protestant Era,* 60.
19. Ibid., xxix.
20. Theodore Roszak, *The Making of the Counterculture* (Garden City, N.Y.: Doubleday, 1969), 47.
21. Jacob Needleman, *The New Religions* (Garden City, N.Y.: Doubleday, 1970), xi.
22. Cf. Sidney Ahlstrom's essay, "From Sinai to the Golden Gate: The Liberation of Religion in the Occident," in *Understanding the New Religions,* ed. Jacob Needleman and George Baker (New York: Seabury Press, 1978), 3–22, especially 21.
23. To my knowledge two publications have appeared from the National Conference on the Study of New Religious Movements in America: In addition to *Understanding the New Religions,* there was a publication of *Working Papers* by the Rockefeller Foundation, which included much of the actual discussion among the participants.
24. Langdon Gilkey, "Toward a Religious Criterion of Religion," in *Understanding the New Religions,* 131–37, especially 133; Frederick Bird, "Charisma and Ritual in New Religious Movements," in *Understanding the New Religions,* 173–89.
25. Gilkey, "Toward a Religious Criterion," 134.
26. Ibid., 134.
27. William Irwin Thompson, *Darkness and Scattered Light* (Garden City, N.Y.: Doubleday, 1978), 67, 79.

28. Ibid., 21.
29. Ibid., 74.
30. Ibid., 43, 76, 101.
31. See David Bakan in his *Disease, Pain, and Sacrifice* (Chicago: University of Chicago Press, 1968) and in his *Duality of Human Existence* (Chicago: Rand McNally, 1966).
32. Theodore Roszak, "Ethics, Ecstacy, and the Study of New Religions," in *Understanding the New Religions*, 49. The entire essay covers pp. 49–62.
33. Ibid., 51, 52.
34. Ibid., 57.
35. Ibid., 61, 54.
36. Ibid., 60, 61, 62.
37. Robert Wuthnow, "Religious Movements and the Transition in World Order," in *Understanding the New Religions*, 63–79.
38. Cf. Peter Berger, *Facing Up to Modernity* (New York: Basic Books, 1977).
39. Robert Wuthnow, "Religious Movements and the Transition in World Order," 76.
40. Ibid.
41. Ibid., p. 78.
42. Steven Tipton, *Getting Saved From the Sixties* (Berkeley-Los Angeles: University of California Press, 1982), 29.
43. Ibid., 30.
44. Ibid., 21, 30.
45. Paul Tillich, "Aspects of a Religious Analysis of Culture," in idem, *Theology of Culture*, ed. Robert C. Kimball (New York: Oxford University Press, 1959), 40–51.
46. Paul Tillich, *The Courage to Be* (New Haven: Yale University Press, 1952), 66.
47. D. Mackenzie Brown, *Ultimate Concern: Tillich in Dialogue* (New York: Harper & Row, 1965), 20, 27.
48. Tillich, *The Courage to Be*, 68.
49. D. Mackenzie Brown, *Ultimate Concern*, 25.
50. Paul Tillich, *The Interpretation of History*, trans. N. A. Rasetzki and Elsa L. Talmey (New York: Charles Scribner's Sons, 1936), 77–93.
51. Ibid., 81, 58.
52. Ibid., 84.
53. Paul Tillich, *Perspectives on Nineteenth and Twentieth Century Protestant Theology*, ed. Carl E. Braaten (New York: Harper & Row, 1967), 50.
54. Tillich, *The Interpretation of History*, 116.
55. Paul Tillich, *A History of Christian Thought*, ed. Carl E. Braaten (New York: Harper & Row, 1968), 246.
56. Tillich, *The Interpretation of History*, 116.
57. Paul Tillich, *Systematic Theology*, vol 2 (Chicago: University of Chicago Press, 1957), 163.
58. Cf. Tillich, *Love, Power, and Justice* (New York: Oxford University Press, 1954), especially 24–34, 107–125; and idem, *Systematic Theology* 3 (1963), 134ff.
59. Tillich, *Systematic Theology* 3:134.

13. The Impact of Tillich's Interpretation of Religion

JOHN E. SMITH

Paul Tillich's religious and theological ideas have been welcomed with enthusiasm as both enlightening and liberating, they have been attacked by theologians as too speculative and unbiblical, and they have been criticized by philosophers as confused. Despite negative reactions, or perhaps because of them, it is fair to say that Tillich's ideas have not been ignored. On the contrary, they have served as the occasion for spirited responses on the American scene with the main emphasis falling on his basic conception of religion. Some have found his description of religion as the dimension of depth in all reality and of faith as ultimate concern both novel and fruitful, especially by comparison with traditional conceptions rooted in the beliefs of Western theism. Some philosophers and theologians as well, anxious to interpret religion within more familiar boundaries, have attacked Tillich's basic description as too undiscriminating. They have regarded as too facile the implication that everyone is "religious," since Tillich held that having an ultimate concern is no sporadic phenomenon, but belongs to the enduring structure of human existence. It has thus become somewhat commonplace among critics to say that Tillich was "converting" people by definition!

Any attempt to estimate the influence of Tillich's philosophy of religion in this country must make clear at the outset that what is meant by the philosophy of religion is not to be identified exclusively with his *Religionsphilosophie* of 1925. The impact of Tillich's interpretation of religion must be understood in terms of his numerous English writings concerning such topics as the dimension of depth in existence; faith as ultimate concern; the nature of religious symbols; the problem of reason, revelation, and truth;

and especially his idea of the relation between religion and culture. This is not to say that the ideas developed in what we may call Tillich's "official" philosophy of religion bear no relation to his later views; it is rather that the earlier work was largely unknown in this country and hence could not have been a major focus of response. The German work of 1925 was not generally available until it was translated in 1969 by James Luther Adams and published together with two other essays under the title, *What Is Religion?*[1] By that time, Tillich's writings in English had long been in the center of discussion.

Instead of seeking to discover what might be called genetic lines of influence stemming directly from Tillich's interpretation of religion—a study that could well turn out to be both forced and elusive—it will be more illuminating to consider certain points of contact or, better, crossroads of relevance between his ideas and some central concerns and problems manifest in American life. It is not that examples of direct influence cannot be found, for they do indeed exist. The book of the eminent geneticist Theodosius Dobzhansky, *The Biology of Ultimate Concern,*[2] was clearly inspired at several crucial points (and perhaps even in its main conception) by Tillich's description of religion and his view of man as both belonging to and yet transcending the world of nature. The force of Tillich's ideas on the development of depth psychology is well known. Nor should we overlook the responses of some philosophers. Charles Hartshorne, for example, whose neoclassical metaphysics is shot through with Leibniz, Whitehead, and modern logic that may seem alien to Tillich's ecstatic ontology, expressed appreciation for Tillich's work; and even when he criticized Tillich, he confessed some uneasiness about being on the other side.

The attacks upon Tillich by philosophers unsympathetic to his, or indeed any other, ontology are not without their import. They suggest some awareness of an element of truth in one of Tillich's main contentions about the relation between religion and philosophy. Without the goad provided by the religious and speculative questions, Tillich insisted, philosophy runs the risk of formalizing itself and of encapsulating itself within the issues of logic, language, and epistemology. That, of course, is precisely what has happened in so much of contemporary Anglo-American philosophy that has lost contact with both metaphysics and religion. It is, moreover, to be expected that anyone pointing out this danger would not be likely to receive a cordial welcome, especially if he were a descendent of German metaphysics. Consequently, in directing attention to what I have called crossroads of relevance in Tillich's thought instead of looking for genetic lines of influence, I do not mean to imply that the latter is either lacking or unimportant.

Before proceeding further I would like to set aside the quite futile dispute concerning how the philosophy of religion and theology are to be defined and related to each other. Some decades ago at the height of the neoorthodox revival with its antiphilosophical bias, a major issue was made of the proper distinction to be drawn between the two. Nor was the matter free from ideological implications. Some claimed that no philosophy of religion is possible or, if it is, that it would have to exclude Christianity, since the latter is not a "religion" as one among others, but is rather *sui generis* as "revelation." Others were prepared to acknowledge the legitimacy of the philosophy of religion, but took it to mean, in some cases, a kind of natural theology or, more dubiously, an "unorthodox" theology, unorthodox because of the use of either philosophical categories or nontraditional religious language. Largely by comparison with the antiphilosophical stance of Barth's "kerygmatic" theology, Tillich's thought was taken by some to be more philosophical than theological and when it was seen as theology it was often described as "apologetic," or engaging the culture in dialectic rather than proclaiming the Gospel.[3]

Ideology aside, there is a tolerably clear distinction to be drawn between the philosophy of religion and theology; there can be no question that Tillich engaged in both. A philosophical account of the religious dimension in human life and of the historical religions, including their relations to science, morality, art and, indeed, the entire spectrum of culture, constitutes a philosophy of religion. Examples of such accounts abound: James's *Varieties of Religious Experience;* Otto's *Idea of the Holy;* Hume's *Dialogues;* Kant's *Religion Within the Limits of Reason Alone;* and Hegel's lectures, *The Philosophy of Religion;* to name but a few.[4]

Theology, on the other hand, is in Tillich's view the systematic development of the concepts and symbols through which the concrete object of an ultimate concern is expressed, and which at the same time represent the faith and doctrine of an identifiable religious tradition embodied in a continuing community. Augustine, Aquinas, Luther, and Calvin were obviously theologians in this sense. Although there is some unavoidable overlap in the two enterprises, they are clearly not the same. Tillich's analysis of religion as the dimension of depth; his interpretation of faith in terms of ultimate concern; and his discussion of religious symbols, the relation between religion and culture, the connections between religion and depth psychology, and the relations between the world religions, plus related themes—all belong to his philosophy of religion. The dialectical *Systematic Theology,* aimed at a reinterpretation of Christianity by the correlation of the doctrine of God and the concept of Being, stands as Tillich's theology proper.[5]

THE DIMENSION OF DEPTH AND ULTIMATE CONCERN

With the understanding that our main concern will be with Tillich's philosophy of religion, we can proceed with a consideration of what I have called crossroads of relevance between his thought and some features of the religious and cultural situation in America. The first and most important of these crossroads is Tillich's conception of religion as the dimension of depth in human life and culture and the closely related understanding of faith as ultimate concern. It is highly significant that these concepts provoked the most spirited responses in the illuminating and freewheeling discussions Tillich held with students and faculty at the University of California, Santa Barbara, in 1963, published under the title, *Ultimate Concern: Tillich in Dialogue.*[6] There, in his distinction between a narrow conception of religion as belief in superhuman powers, and a broad conception involving an unconditional concern for the meaning of one's being, he struck a responsive chord, one that has been vibrating in America at a more or less audible level since the time of Emerson.

The more secularized a culture becomes and the more a preoccupation with things and possessions reduces the time for reflection and concern about who and why we are, the more religion becomes narrowed and transformed into a special department of life largely out of touch with the rest of what we think and do. The inhabitants of the secular city, many of whom have already decided that religion has been superseded, are further alienated by the narrow shape religion has been forced to assume. Religion as the dimension of depth and faith as ultimate concern, however, spark an interest and become a crossroad of relevance precisely because they evoke from the American psyche a deeply rooted sense that no religion is authentic if it is confined to a special compartment of life presided over by ecclesiastical authority. The possibility proposed by Tillich that religion need not be identified with its narrow and alienating form has served as a liberating force so that many have been led to reconsider whether it is true that religion is dead or outmoded. In addition, Tillich's arresting claim that both Jesus and Buddha were "antireligious," in that they challenged existing religious institutions, helped to consolidate the priority of his broad conception of religion over the conventional one that, as he said, is to be found as the dominant meaning of religion in any dictionary. For, on Tillich's view, it was in the name of the primordial religious relationship that Jesus and Buddha dared to criticize the religion of their time.

The California dialogues and many other discussions make abundantly plain that Tillich had great difficulty making clear and defending his concept of ultimate concern. However, that concept has one feature that assured its relevance; namely, the power of the idea to provoke self-reflection about one's priorities and thus to focus the problems of idolatry. Tillich was able to point out the extent to which American life is shot through with cases of individuals actually devoting themselves with an unconditional seriousness to finite causes—success in business and professions, the gaining of wealth and power, devotion to patriotism and the preservation of American dominance in world affairs. And he was also able to show why these finite and conditioned objects of commitment cannot, so to speak, bear the weight of an ultimate concern. Such objects, precisely because they are partial, transient, and subject to distortion and decay, are unable to provide an answer to the ultimate question of the meaning of life. Thus the concept of ultimate concern serves as a touchstone for exposing the many forms of idolatry that determine our life insofar as we seek to gain self-fulfillment and purpose through devotion to finite concerns.

Idolatry, moreover, is not, in Tillich's view, the only form of distortion besetting the possession of an ultimate concern. There is as well the demonic, which Tillich perceptively understood as the negative form of the sacred because it has within itself something of the power—unholy power, we may say—that attaches to the religious order. Tillich might have been clearer in distinguishing among misplaced ultimate concerns; all are to be sure idolatrous, but it is not clear that all are necessarily demonic. Some false ultimates may merely deceive us in the promise they hold out and, tragic though this is, the failure falls short of the destructiveness and horror manifest in the truly demonic. Tillich was particularly persuasive in the application of this distortion of ultimate concern to nazism and other forms of fascism. In many writings he led people to understand the stark reality of a misplaced ultimate concern. Speaking of the Nazis who, in his own words, "made people believe in Hitler as the voice of God for the Germans," Tillich declared their cause "demonic" because it was the embodiment of an evil power not to be accounted for merely by ignorance or faulty judgment.[7] Nor was he unaware of the penetration of the demonic into religion itself; consequently, he could describe the church of the Inquisition as a "demonization of Christianity" and the exploitation of superstition among the common people of all religions as further instances of the demonic distortion. Tillich's full appreciation of the "dangerous" character of the holy lent a weight of credibility to his message for, as he was fully aware, the destructive force of distortion is nowhere more powerful than it is when the ultimate is at stake.

Tillich's analyses of the human situation inspired conviction because of the extent to which he looked to actual experience in shaping his thought. Despite his insistence on the need for systematic and consistent thinking, he did not sacrifice to a theory the basic facts about life in the world—what people actually assume, believe in, and do, regardless of what they may say or claim to believe. Many of those who came to know his thought found themselves surprised and at the same time attracted by this experiential feature. They were surprised because his penchant for ontology led them to expect that his pronouncements would be "abstract" and "speculative" beyond the reach of anyone without special training. They were attracted because of the concreteness with which Tillich analyzed ordinary experience—anxiety, doubt, guilt,

forgiveness, faith and love—and set it in relation to the ultimate
dimension.

FAITH AND ITS DISTORTIONS

Another closely related crossroad of relevance in Tillich's philosophy of religion is found in his attempt to reinterpret the concept
of faith so as to give to it fresh significance in religion and at the
same time throw light on the relations between faith and knowledge, a topic frequently considered in connection with tensions
between religion and science. There is no escaping the fact that in
the biblical tradition, faith appears as having a decidedly ambiguous character, and it is by no means easy to overcome that ambiguity and synthesize the polar elements in it. On the one side, faith
means trust in its object, or what Tillich calls the total surrender
of the person in a centered act. On the other side, there is the
element of meaningful content to be apprehended by the knowing
mind, or, in Tillich's words, "in every act of faith there is cognitive
affirmation."[8] It is tempting indeed to set these two elements
against each other so that the former becomes all commitment and
engagement by comparison with what is then called "mere belief,"
and the latter becomes assent to or belief in correct doctrines, and
the trust, or surrender pole, recedes into the background as something merely emotional and quite unintelligent.

These distortions are to be avoided because it should be obvious
that neither pole can be taken without the other. One does not
trust or surrender to an ultimate about which one knows or understands nothing more than its name, nor does the affirmation of
doctrine by itself provide the transforming power of trust. As
Jonathan Edwards put it, having faith is not the same as having a
"mere notional understanding" of the things of religion. Tillich
tried to deal with the problem, which he states slightly differently
as the tension between one's cognitive function and one's emotion
and will taken together, by his claim that the meaning of faith is
distorted if it is entirely subsumed under any one of the three
functions of human being. Consequently, in his discussion of
"what faith is not," Tillich criticized the intellectualistic, the voluntaristic, and emotionalistic distortions of faith in order to establish
his conception of faith as "the embracing and centered act of the
personality."[9]

Appealing, as he so often did, to the notion of the "ecstatic," Tillich could claim that faith transcends the rational, the unconscious, the voluntary, and the emotional structures of the person while including all of them within itself at the same time. Whether this "transcending" solution, like many others in Tillich's thought, succeeds in illuminating the relations obtained between the elements transcended may be left as an open philosophical question. More important is the contribution he made to the understanding of faith in a scientific and technological culture. His analysis of the three distortions of faith represents an important crossroad of relevance since each of these distortions has exerted powerful influence especially on popular thinking, and he was fully aware of the extent to which they arose as abortive attempts to mediate between religion and science.

Tillich was convinced, and not without historical evidence, that the conflicts between faith and both ordinary and scientific knowledge stem from the notion that faith is a type of knowledge based on scanty evidence and supported or enforced by religious authority.[10] Instead, Tillich maintained that faith neither affirms nor denies the knowledge of the world and of ourselves gained by scientific inquiry because that is not a matter of faith but rather, as he sometimes put it, of belief. Although he was not unaware that an ultimate concern may lie behind an individual's devotion to a supposedly scientific method, he refused to confuse the dimensions. "The dimension of faith," he wrote, "is not the dimension of science, history or psychology."[11] The chief reason for this claim is that faith, being of an existential character involving the whole of human existence, *does not constitute a theoretical problem* of the sort we encounter in empirical inquiry, where knowledge is never complete or certain but is always dependent on evidence with a greater or lesser degree of probability. One highly significant consequence of the basic distinction drawn here is that Tillich could criticize those who, in the name of religion, either assert what stands in contradiction to what we know about reality on critical grounds or, even worse, claim that Scripture contains alternative explanations of natural processes, including the origin of the universe, which are to stand side by side with those of science.

It is clear that Tillich's rejection of the fundamentalist attitude toward science served as a liberating force in his own time, and it is even more sorely needed in our time with its resurgence of a superstitious belief in the "science" contained in the Bible. The impressive seriousness of Tillich's approach, moreover, made it possible for him to speak to an important segment of the intellectual community, namely those scientists who reject scientism because they are fully aware of both the proper tasks of science and its limitations, but who also know that there is no way of reconciling religious fundamentalism and modern science. Dobzhansky illustrates the point nicely; he quotes with approval and, one suspects, not a little relief, the following comment of Tillich's: "The first step toward nonreligion of the Western world was made by religion itself. This was when it defended its great symbols, which were its means of interpreting the world and life, not as symbols, but as literal stories. When it did this it had already lost the battle."[12]

While it is not possible here to consider both the advantages and problems posed by Tillich's conception of religious symbols, one decisive point can be made. In order to consolidate the distinction between the dimension of *theoretical knowledge* and that of *religion*, Tillich called attention to the different types of representation or language appropriate to each. The former dimension must find expression in concepts, whether it be in the fields of natural science, history, or philosophy, while religion in expressing ultimate concern must avail itself of symbols that, as Tillich insisted with many arguments, are entirely misunderstood if they are thought of as "mere" symbols. He successfully explained the unique role of religious symbols in their expression of faith, their disclosure of the various levels of reality and of human personality, and their historical destiny resulting from the fact that they have a life of their own and cannot be produced at will.

The theory of participating symbols was meant to resolve the same problem of determining an appropriate language for theology as the classical doctrine of analogy in Catholic thought. The chief obstacle Tillich had to encounter, however, consists in the simple fact that the term *symbol* has, especially in ordinary usage, an ineradicable connotation of something "subjective" or removed from reality, whereas no such unfortunate meaning attaches to the term *analogy*. On the contrary, doctrines of analogy have invariably been set forth as having an objectively logical or even "scientific" status. Despite this difficulty, Tillich's theory appealed to many scientists and philosophers as well as to some theologians as a way of preserving intelligence in religion and of overcoming the futile disputes that arise when it is supposed that sacred Scriptures are manuals of science rather than the record, expressed in symbol and myth, of the human encounter with the holy.[13]

Tillich's critique of the voluntaristic interpretation of faith forms yet another crossroad of relevance for American life. Energy, enterprise, and faith in the power of the human will have long been hallmarks of both thought and practice in a country whose future has always seemed more important than its past. William James's voluntarism is the perfect example of what Santayana unenthusiastically called "the strenuous life." It bespeaks the deep conviction that nothing is, in principle at any rate, beyond human capacity to create and control. Tillich saw the force of this distortion and sought to counteract it by stressing *being grasped* by a presence transcending human will as opposed to *grasping* or overcoming. Ultimate concern embraces all the capacities of the person, including the will, but it does not come into being by an act of will. The element of acceptance or surrender is essential. Royce had the same idea in mind when he declared that the supreme cause of loyalty "found me" and evoked his devotion. We encounter the limit of will at the edge of faith; in Tillich's own words, "No command to believe and no will to believe can create faith."[14] The point can be seen in ordinary experience; we often speak of a "commanding" personality, someone who evokes or calls forth a respect that is rooted in the individual's total being. The "commanding" aspect coincides with being grasped by a power we encounter in the person and it would be quite ludicrous to suggest that such respect could be evoked were the person to issue the command "Respect me!"

In his critique of the idea that the difficulties we encounter in treating religion in terms of intellect and will can be avoided if we regard religion as a matter of emotion, Tillich was engaging views strongly held by the advocates for religion as well as by their opponents. Tillich vigorously objected to the identification of religion with subjective emotions devoid of content, first, because it is supposed to provide religion with a "safe" abode from which it cannot be dislodged by science and, second, because, so situated, religion becomes innocuous and loses all possibility of influencing the culture in which it exists. In the first case there is the illusion that religion is out of danger because science cannot touch it, and in the second case there is the hope that religion has ceased to be dangerous because its prophetic voice has been silenced. The problem, moreover, was intensified by the prevalence among philosophers of a positivist outlook based on the belief that apart from matters of fact and logic, utterances purporting to express the concerns of ethics, aesthetics, metaphysics, and religion are one and all "emotive" in nature. Tillich confronted this situation directly by insisting that religion as ultimate concern claims the whole person and not just the emotions, and by calling attention to the deep concern manifested by the attempts of some philosophers and social scientists to relegate religion to an emotional corner. Moreover, as Tillich rightly saw, the stamping of certain questions as meaningless or as mere expressions of emotion does not of itself cause human beings to cease raising these questions. What the emotionalistic distortion, unfortunately, does accomplish is the impossibility of approaching the religious question in a rational way. Therein lies the real danger in the emotionalistic misconception of religion; superstition and fanaticism take command and every vestige of rationality vanishes. One can easily imagine how Tillich would respond were he alive today to witness the current revival of fundamentalism.

THE PROBLEM OF TRUTH IN RELIGION: THREE THEMES

Yet another of the crossroads of relevance to be found in Tillich's thought is his courageous, if not always successful, grappling with the cluster of thorny problems having to do with the meaning of revelation, the relation between faith and reason, and the truth of faith. Reinhold Niebuhr and those generally sympathetic to Barth criticized Tillich for orienting his thinking too exclusively to "intellectuals" and of neglecting the situation of the ordinary religious believer. Whether this criticism is justified or not, no one can deny that a major problem confronting all people of faith in the past half century at least has been how to maintain the meaningfulness of religious insight in a predominantly technological culture where facts take precedence over reasons, theoretical explanations over interpretations, and the motive to control over every form of grace. Three ideas served Tillich especially well in his efforts to show how religion can retain its intelligibility under such difficult circumstances.

CREATION, REDEMPTION, LOGOS

The first of these Tillich frequently expressed in theological language with the formula that God as Redeemer does not stand in contradiction to God as Creator. Citing the New Testament belief that all things were made through the Logos—that is, rational pattern, law, and intelligible structure—Tillich insisted that the sustaining and transforming power of God in humanity and world is manifested in accordance with the order that is the divine Logos. A most important consequence of this doctrine is that faith neither contradicts nor negates reason and secular knowledge; on the contrary, since the content of faith must be related to persons who are rooted in nature while also transcending it in their potential infinity, it is necessary to sustain an open process of interpretation aimed at determining the relevance to faith of the development of new knowledge concerning both people and nature. Tillich saw clearly that religious insight is not directed to people only insofar as they are "religious," but engages their entire being, including whatever we discover about them through empirical inquiry.

Living religion must address itself to the relevance of empirical knowledge to the meaning of the perennial content of faith. To take an example close to Tillich's concern: How is the biblical understanding of selfhood affected by the development of depth psychology? That is, to be sure, not an easy question to answer, but some answer, however complex and ambiguous, must be forthcoming if religion is to maintain a creative relation to the culture in which it exists. The situation calls for interpretation; it is not, as Tillich often pointed out, that faith itself is or can be based on scientific knowledge, but rather that the relation between faith and new discoveries about the world and humanity must be understood and not ignored. Accordingly, Tillich made an important contribution in seeking to overcome the belief that "secular" knowledge is inimical to faith. Such a belief has long been a corner-stone of the anti-intellectualism characteristic of conservative Protestantism, and it received classic expression in the rhetoric of William Jennings Bryan when he declared that it is far more impor-tant to seek out the Rock of Ages than the ages of rocks! It is highly significant that Dobzhansky should single out the following pas-sage from Tillich's *Systematic Theology* as making an admirable con-tribution to an understanding of the proper relation between reli-gion and science: "Of course, theology cannot rest on scientific theory. But it must relate its understanding of man to an under-standing of universal nature, for man is a part of nature and state-ments about nature underlie every statement about him."[15]

THE CONCEPT OF REASON

A second idea of central importance for Tillich's engagement with the problem of truth in religion was his attempt to recover the classical conception of reason that was obscured to a great extent in modern philosophy by the successes of scientific or technical reason. Historically speaking, Tillich was right in maintaining that in a tradition extending from Plato to Hegel there was a belief in reason as the foundation of all meaning and the source of princi-ples and norms pointing to goods and goals. Since the triumph of science in the seventeenth century and the triumph of the empiri-cal philosophies in the next century, reason had come to be iden-tified as formal logic, experimental method, and practical calcula-tion. It is obviously mistaken to deny the importance of this form of reason; it is, however, also an error to overlook the more inclu-sive conception of reason, especially since it has a crucial bearing on the problem of truth in religion.[16]

The distinction in question entails two important consequences for Tillich's thought. One is his perception that the religious di-mension and the type of meaning it involves cannot be adequately assessed with respect to truth or falsity, validity or invalidity, by reason understood in the technical and scientific sense. The sort of meaning expressed in faith is more akin to that embodied in the synoptic conception of reason, and if we are forced to understand reason only in the narrower sense, faith and reason become sepa-rated from each other, resulting either in the familiar conflicts between religion and science or in a situation where the two have nothing to do with each other. The second consequence following from the invocation of the classical conception of reason is that it provides a safeguard against the destruction of reason at the hands of an authoritarian religion whether based on Scriptures or on an ecclesiastical institution. For as Tillich rightly argued, reason as the source of meaning and of norms coincides with the humanity of man and represents his uniqueness in relation to all other creatures. Since, as Tillich maintained, reason is the basis of language, of freedom and creativity, and also makes possible the centered act of faith, the two cannot be opposed to each other without destructive consequences, including the loss of faith itself. The idea of an interpenetration of reason, synoptically conceived, and faith is superior to any position in which reason and faith are sharply distinguished from each other and then connected by a third power that is heteronomous to both.

If, as some have charged, Tillich was overly concerned with the intelligibility of religion, the importance of his motive is nevertheless clear. He was fully aware of the extent to which the erosion of religion in modern culture has been a result of the belief, expressed long ago by Auguste Comte, that the sciences have superseded religion. According to Comte, religion is not an enduring dimension of human existence, it is but the first and ineffective effort of human beings to consolidate their position in a precarious world. Religion, in short, is supposed to have been guided at the outset by the same aim as that of science—to master circumstances and control human destiny—except that it failed and therefore had to give way, first to philosophy and ultimately to science. Anyone who understands the concern that religion expresses, whether in Tillich's sense or not, knows that the Comtean thesis is false. Authentic religion can never be understood as a *means* to be used for human ends—the essential message of prophetic criticism. But even more important, the rejection of the religious concern in the interest of a theory does not lead to its disappearance, but rather to its being filled by quasi religions and cults that often assume the demonic forces about which Tillich so vividly wrote.

REVELATION AND ECSTATIC REASON

The last of the three ideas through which Tillich sought to reinterpret religion in an increasingly secularized culture was his paradoxical conception of revelation and its reception at the boundary of what he called "ecstatic" reason. Tillich vigorously opposed the belief that revelation is the communication of spiritual truths supposedly dictated by the divine Spirit to individuals who wrote down these deliverances, which were then collected in the form of a sacred book.[17] Such a conception seemed to him to distort both the meaning of revelation and the circumstances of its reception. This topic is too large to be treated in anything approaching adequate fashion here, nevertheless some central points can be underlined.

For Tillich, revelation essentially means the experience of being grasped by an ultimate concern and the consequent founding of a community expressing this concern in symbols embracing both thought and action. Although revelation is said to have a transforming and shaking effect upon the total situation in which it takes place, it is not, according to Tillich, the miraculous appearance of a "foreign body" that we are unable to receive because it is totally discontinuous with our experience and thought. Revelation is, to be sure, vouchsafed to persons in their estranged state and under finite, historical conditions, but it can be received meaningfully precisely because it is the fulfillment of reason driven beyond itself. Here Tillich appropriates an idea basic to Kant's philosophy, namely, that both persons and human reason are finite, but, in being able to raise the question of the unconditioned, persons become aware of their potential infinity and at the same time realize the inability of reason to answer from its own resources the ultimate questions to which it is necessarily driven.

Revelation is the fulfillment of reason become "ecstatic" or forced beyond its finitude by the experience of ultimate concern. Reason does not fulfill itself and answer its own questions; for that, revelation is required, but as Tillich made clear in his "method of correlation" for theology, the answers provided by revelation are addressed to a being who recognizes them as intelligibly related to what reason asks for but cannot provide. Many questions can be, and have been, raised about Tillich's general solution to this ancient and difficult problem, but his theory has one undeniable merit—it relates the Christian message to the concerns and perplexities of ongoing human life; Tillich, moreover, presents revelation not as a nonhistorical communication from some spiritual outer space, but as the experience and record showing humans how to fulfill the quest to overcome estrangement from their essential being. Reinhold Niebuhr has said that there is nothing more futile than offering a messiah to someone who is not seeking one. In this vein, it is equally futile to offer revelation as the answer to questions no one asks. But, as Tillich has so clearly shown, the questions and concerns to which revelation speaks are indeed those belonging to the fabric of human existence. The relevance of revelation, however, will be lost on anyone who identifies it totally with a sacred book believed to contain true propositions about everything under the sun.

RELIGION AND CULTURE

The issues considered thus far are all consequences of an underlying theory that encompasses Tillich's entire philosophy of religion —the theory of the relation between religion and culture. His conception of that relationship, expressed throughout many writings with minor variations, is stated in the following sentence: "Culture is a form of expression of religion, and religion is the substance *(Inhalt)* of culture."[18] A brief consideration of this thesis will serve to provide a unifying perspective from which to view all of Tillich's efforts to relate the religious concern to the spectrum of human cultural activities.

To begin with, Tillich was acutely aware, largely because of his Protestant heritage, of both the emergence and the powerful influence exerted on modern life by *autonomous* cultures no longer bound by ecclesiastical structures. It was his contention that it is imperative for philosophers of religion and theologians to come to terms with this new situation. The two have, to be quite precise, two different roles to play in confronting the problem. The determination of the generic relations between religion and culture is the task of the philosopher of religion, while it falls to the theologian speaking for the church to decide between several possible attitudes to be adopted toward what Tillich called a "theology of culture." This decision of the theologian is dependent on an understanding of the dynamics of religion and culture, but it is not entirely determined by that understanding.

Tillich envisaged three distinct possibilities for the theologian;

two have already been actualized, but difficulties inherent in both led him to look for a third and more adequate option. The first consists in lumping together all the aspects of culture under the rubric of the "world" and setting over against this complex the "church" as the bearer of religion. The chief consequence of this attitude is that the religious cultural functions performed under the aegis of the church inevitably take on the ultimacy that attaches to the religious principle the church represents. Thus, writes Tillich, "there are absolute science, art forms, morality, etc.—i.e., those realized in the church."[19] On this basis, he concluded, there cannot be a theology of culture, but only, one might say, a "theologized" culture. The second attitude, described by Tillich as "the old Protestant attitude," entails the separation of the church and culture, but with the retention of the supernatural revelation as absolute knowledge. This position Tillich regarded as inconsistent because, as a consequence of the Enlightenment, the absolute knowledge was deprived of support, since it no longer had the authority of the church behind it. Less paradoxically expressed, one may say that revelation was left with nothing but the authority of the church and this proved to be an insufficient foundation after the Enlightenment had done its work.

In the wake of these problems, Tillich conceived of a third alternative, which he described as a task for future Protestant thought; one can interpret Tillich's entire thought as an attempt to carry out this task. The new alternative has two aspects. First, it requires the drawing of a strict distinction between the religious principle and the manifest religious culture so that the character of ultimacy attaches *only* to the religious principle and not to any element of the religious culture. Second, the religious principle must be conceived concretely—that is, in terms of the meaning of the religious symbols for all aspects of life—and continuously maintained so that religion will not find itself subject to the fads and fashions of cultural development. Since a relationship of this sort is not something that can be "brought about" or established through human effort, Tillich repeatedly described it as a religion of paradox that breaks through cultural forms without having a "form" of its own. The religion of paradox is thus a creative possibility, forever realized only more or less, standing in the tension between extremes, each of which fails to do justice to the legitimate claims of religion and culture.

The position he was arguing for stands out most clearly when it is expressed through the contrasts Tillich drew between *heteronomy, autonomy,* and *theonomy.* For heteronomy, the holy and the supernatural become one, and religion stands opposed to culture which, in turn, becomes the "secular." Tillich's objection to this position rests on his dialectical conception of the holy as that power and presence which, to be what it is, must negate every form in which it merely "exists" as something standing alongside other things. The holy, in short, does not constitute a sphere.

He was equally critical of the position of autonomy, which he construed as a form of idealism aimed at transcending immediate existence in the direction of an ideal. In doing so, however, idealism loses sight not only of the fact that every finite reality has its ground in the unconditioned, but also of the negating force of the unconditioned with respect to the ideal itself. Tillich's conclusion is that heteronomy turns the holy into something finite because it stands over against culture, while autonomy causes the holy to be lost in an all-embracing ideal wherein real forms are sacrificed to ideal forms.

As against both attitudes, Tillich maintains the position of theonomy where the holy is present in all forms while at the same time breaking through every one of them paradoxically as the power of *grace* that has no "form" of its own. Here the holy is neither a separate sphere, on the one hand, nor an ideal demand, an "ought," on the other, but a transforming power and presence mediated through symbolic forms without ever becoming identical with any of them. It is for this reason, as Tillich frequently claimed, that religion as the living substance or soul of culture cannot find a "home" outside itself nor be assimilated to any single cultural form such as art, science, morality, or philosophy.

Tillich's philosophy of religion must continue to command our attention at the present time. For while Hegel could declare triumphantly that in religion all the enigmas of the world are resolved, the truth is that for many people today religion itself has become the greatest enigma of all. In view of this fact, what was said of Kant's thought is perhaps even more true of Tillich's philosophy of religion—you can think with him or against him, but not without him.

NOTES

1. Paul Tillich, *What Is Religion?*, trans. James Luther Adams (New York: Harper & Row, 1969).
2. Theodosius Dobzhansky, *The Biology of Ultimate Concern* (New York: New American Library, 1967).
3. See Reinhold Niebuhr, "Biblical Thought and Ontological Speculation in Tillich's Theology," and George F. Thomas, "The Method and Structure of Tillich's Theology," in *The Theology of Paul Tillich*, ed. Charles W. Kegley and Robert W. Bretall (New York: Macmillan, 1952). Nothing called forth greater indignation from Tillich than the use of the term *apologetic*, as if it meant "apologizing" for faith in the wake of insufficient courage to proclaim it; as Tillich knew well enough, *apologetic* in the tradition meant answering questions and responding to arguments advanced by critics.
4. See especially the monumental study of James Collins, *The Emergence of Philosophy of Religion* (New Haven: Yale University Press, 1967). This book is especially significant because it elucidates the issues raised by those modern accounts of religion set forth by philosophers whose standpoints were no longer determined basically by the theological traditions. Collins calls this situation "religion within the scope of philosophy."
5. It has always seemed to me that Tillich invited confusion by the title he chose for one of his most original and widely discussed papers, "The Two Types of Philosophy of Religion." See Tillich, *Theology of Culture*, ed. Robert C. Kimball (New York: Oxford University Press, 1959), chap. 2. The main distinction drawn is actually between the two types of *theology* represented respectively by Augustine and Anselm on the one hand, and by Aquinas on the other. I suspect that he chose that title because he wanted to distinguish the two different types of *spirituality* involved. In the ontological approach man is said to be related to God in the "overcoming of estrangement," while in the cosmological approach the relation is that of "meeting a stranger." We must not in any case overlook Tillich's own statement; in the *Religionsphilosophie* of 1925, he described theology and the philosophy of religion as "two elements constituting a single, normative cultural science of religion." *What Is Religion?*, 33.
6. D. Mackenzie Brown, ed., *Ultimate Concern: Tillich in Dialogue* (New York: Harper & Row, 1965).
7. Ibid., p. 21.
8. Paul Tillich, *Dynamics of Faith* (New York: Harper & Brothers, 1957), 7.
9. Ibid., 6.
10. This conviction manifests itself forcefully in his paper on the "Two Types" where he points out that Aquinas, in placing faith in the genus of knowledge where it must fall as the mean between ἐπιστήμη or knowledge (certainty) and δόξα or opinion, gave impetus to the idea that faith "falls short of that knowledge which is science" and hence is insufficient of itself to command assent; ecclesiastical authority must then fill the gap and does so through a determination of will.
11. Tillich, *Dynamics of Faith*, 33.
12. Dobzhansky, *The Biology of Ultimate Concern*, 34.

13. See ibid., 96–97, for a fine critique of those who attempt to locate God in the as yet unexplained features of the world—"the God of the gaps"—and of those who set up "Deluge Geology," supposedly derived from the Bible, as a rival to contemporary scientific theory. All this is especially pertinent in the face of the current revival of the fundamentalists' interpretations of the Creation stories.

14. Tillich, *Dynamics of Faith*, 38. Here Tillich is not entirely fair to James because part of what is meant by his "will to believe" is the person's *acceptance* of a possibility.

15. Dobzhansky, *The Biology of Ultimate Concern*, 109–10.

16. See Tillich, *Dynamics of Faith*, 75ff. The two modes of thought involved have received a number of parallel formulations by philosophers, although shifts in terminology have caused some confusion. The medieval thinkers distinguished between *intellectus* and *ratio*, the former being the higher synoptic and unifying power, and the latter serving as the means of analysis and classification. Leaving aside the reversal in terminology affected by Kant, his Reason stands as the synoptic faculty, and understanding is the power of analysis. Hegel distinguished between Reason and the finite understanding along the same lines.

17. Tillich's criticism of this view of revelation runs consistently throughout his writings: *What Is Religion?*, 105–9; *Dynamics of Faith*, 77ff; *Systematic Theology*, vol. 1 (Chicago: University of Chicago Press, 1951), 71–105; "Die Idee der Offenbarung," in *Zeitschrift für Theologie und Kirche* 8 (1927): 403–12.

18. Tillich, *What Is Religion?*, 73.

19. Ibid., 177. A striking example of this development is to be seen in the sphere of Catholic moral theology. According to Aquinas, the one absolute principle above all others is, "Follow the good and shun the evil." However, in the application of this principle to conditioned, historical situations involving, for example, marriage, procreation, education, etc., secondary principles of a contingent nature were developed and in the course of time these principles came to be invested with the same ultimacy attached to the one absolute principle.

14. Tillich and Contemporary Theology

DAVID TRACY

The impact of Paul Tillich's work in contemporary theology is the influence not of a school but of a pervasive presence. It is impossible to speak of Tillichians in the same way one can speak of Barthians, Bultmannians, Rahnerians, Whiteheadians, or Lonerganians. Perhaps the fact that there is no Tillichian school determines the major reason for Tillich's remarkable staying power as a live influence in contemporary theology. There are, to be sure, theologians whose work bears profound and explicit resonances of a Tillichian influence: above all, James Luther Adams, Langdon Gilkey, Nathan Scott, and Robert Scharlemann. Yet even these theologians, however great their debt to Tillich's work, clearly form no school. Although their work often shows the most explicit indebtedness to Tillich in contemporary theology, still each of these theologians remains highly individual, creative, and finally unclassifiable as strictly Tillichian.

Perhaps Tillich's success (not failure!) in not producing a "school" can now be recognized, as it deserves to be, as one of his most enduring legacies. In a discipline too often marred by the false security of "schools," the Tillichian influence has endured as a continuing set of concerns, a general method of approach, and a welcome inability to become too easily classifiable. Indeed that influence pervades contemporary theology as the "man in a macintosh" pervades James Joyce's *Ulysses:* He always seems to show up, but no one seems quite able to name or locate him with exactness. Yet there he is, again and again, invading the confines of every school, aiding every revisionary program, forcing his concerns (which turn out, at the end, to be our own in the contemporary situation)—upon all willing to risk the unending need for continual theological revision.

The most obvious impact of Tillich's program upon contemporary theology remains, of course, his famous method of correlation.[1] Since that method and the strife of interpretation that still rages around it are treated extensively in other chapters in this book, I shall here confine my own comments to a few brief observations. First, Tillich's choice of the word *correlation* over alternative possibilities was both logically and methodologically a brilliant stroke. To insist that the theologian "correlate" the interpretations of *both* "situation" and "message" into an ever-revisable contemporary theological position puts exactly the right methodological demand upon every theologian. For however tempted by one's other religious convictions and theological commitments an individual theologian may be, the broad category "correlation" implies that no one may simply assume an "identity," a "radical similarity," "a series of analogies," or a radical "nonidentity" or "confrontation" between the meanings in the situation and the message. *Every* theologian should *start* his or her inquiry with the assumption only of *some* correlation between the fundamental questions and concerns of each "pole" of theological inquiry. In sum, any particular instance of "correlation" may prove to be any single possibility on the fuller logical spectrum from radical identity through similarity to radical nonidentity.

The Tillichian insistence on a method of *correlation* reminds us that a particular case is always to be decided only on the basis of the particular subject matter under inquiry. We may believe that a radical nonidentity between message and situation prevails. Yet we cannot make that assumption prior to the hard effort at determining the actual correlation. Even Barthians correlate—if usually through a *Nein* to the situation. Even left-wing Hegelians among political and liberation theologians correlate—if often through an exposure of a confrontational, radical nonidentity of reason or the biblical message to the societal distortions in the present situation. Even those "liberal" theologians of culture who lack Tillich's own fine postliberal dialectical sense for the presence of negations correlate—if usually through a too-sanguine assumption of the identity or radical teleological similarity between the "highest values" of Christianity and the reigning liberal culture. All theologians, in fact, employ some method of correlation. Since Tillich's work, all are better able to recognize that this matter of fact implies a matter of methodological principle: the need to formulate explicitly and employ critically a theological method of correlation.

Since the work of Hans-Georg Gadamer on interpretation, moreover, it has become still clearer that insofar as every authentic interpretation of any classic (including the religious classics of the theological tradition) involves application to the contemporary situation, every theological interpretation logically involves an implicit correlation of message and situation. In Gadamer's correct insistence, every authentic interpretation will be a *new* interpretation.[2] There is, as a matter of fact, no alternative to a correlating interpretation save routinized repetition (in the manner of some naively anticorrelation models of "orthodox" fundamentalist and dogmatist theologies). In the present concern with hermeneutical theory, the enduring value of Tillich's insistence upon a method of correlation can be indicated by a few brief contrasts. Prior to the actual development of the technical resources of the postromantic hermeneutical theories of Gadamer and Ricoeur,[3] Tillich's method of correlation already spoke to the need for every theological interpretation to include a moment of *application* to the situation and thereby prove to be a *new* interpretation. Moreover, Tillich formulated his method of correlation (and thereby, I suggest, his method of theological interpretation) in such manner that he avoided three crucial difficulties otherwise prevalent in theological methods.

First, Tillich did not formulate his developed position (in *Systematic Theology*) in the then-prevalent terms of romantic hermeneutical tradition from Schleiermacher through Dilthey: empathy, divinization, and reconstruction of the "mind of the author" or the social-cultural life-setting of the work. Second, Tillich did not allow what Gadamer has correctly labeled "methodologism" to take over in formulating his theological method of correlation. Tillich's method is always an aid for interpretation (of an interpreted message and situation and their interpreted correlation), never a mechanical replacement of interpretation by method. The "truth" of any particular theological interpretation of any particular symbol, fundamental question in the situation, or hermeneutical correlation between the two (identity, similarity, analogy, nonidentity) is in principle always determined by the subject matter itself (the fundamental questions and responses in the symbols of both situation and message). Here is a method that renders explicit a matter-of-fact need for interpretation rendered as a need for some kind of application as correlation. Here is a method, as Gadamer might add, that does not sacrifice "truth" for "method."[4] Rather the method of correlation formulates a general method as a general guide for interpretative theological inquiry into particular questions and symbols demanding interpretation and application as correlation.

On more inner theological grounds, moreover, Tillich's method of correlation deserves the explicit, and more often implicit, victory it has gained in contemporary theology. Once again, a brief series of contrasts may serve to warrant this judgment. First, the method of correlation yields a postorthodox "dogmatic" theology. Indeed the very insistence upon "correlation," as I suggested above, highlights the fact that every theology, as interpretation, involves application to the situation (hence "correlation"). The ahistorical and ahermeneutical claims of traditionalist theologies are exposed in a stroke. When successful on their own terms, fundamentalist, dogmatist, and traditionalist theologies are mere repetitions of earlier theological (usually creedal) formulations. Thereby they are not hermeneutical reflections on the tradition at all. When successful (against their own ahistorical and ahermeneutical claims), these theologies become no longer simple repetitions of earlier theologies but new interpretations of them. Thereby they become subject to the same rules of interpretation of both "message" and "situation" (alternatively of the contemporary "application" of the tradition to the contemporary situation). The recent neoconservative resurgence in both culture and church suggests that Tillich's method here could once again prove liberating to all those frustrated by the ahistorical and ahermeneutical claims of the neoconservative crusaders. For the fact remains that insofar as theologians move past mere repetition into the risk of an interpretation, they are attempting to apply the tradition to the situation; attempting, in sum, to correlate the fundamental religious questions and responses of both situation and message. Tillich's method of correlation, on these grounds, may be recognized for what it is: one good way of rendering explicit the implicit matter-of-fact hermeneutical character of all theology.

Moreover, Tillich's actual use of his method of correlation throughout his *Systematic Theology* suggests that, on innertheological terms, he was fundamentally successful in formulating a theological position beyond the earlier confines of either liberalism or neoorthodoxy.[5] Once again, the key may be found in Tillich's choice of the word *correlation:* a concept, to repeat, that allows for the full spectrum of logical possibilities from identity to similarity and analogy to radical nonidentity. The "liberal" theologian is ordinarily concerned with "identities" between message and situation or, at the least, with radical similarities. The confrontations, the nonidentities, also present tend to be obscured either notoriously, as in much of the Ritschlian tradition or, less obviously but no less fatally, as in many too-benign "theologies of culture." The neoorthodox theologies (which, as Wilhelm Pauck has observed, are in fact *not* orthodox theologies but self-critical liberal theologies) tend to emphasize the stark nonidentities between the full message and our present distorted personal, political, social, or historical situation. The latter spectrum can range from an emphasis upon the distortions in the self, exposed by the confrontation with the "kerygmatic word,"[6] to the distortions in society, history, and culture, exposed by the liberating message of Christian eschatology.[7]

What is striking about Tillich's formulation of the method of correlation and, above all, about his wide-ranging and striking uses of that method is that one cannot predict before the actual investigation of a particular subject matter what kind of correlation will be demanded by the subject matter itself. Sometimes, as in Tillich's interpretation of some modern works of art, the correlation discloses profound analogies. Even there, however, Tillich ordinarily chose works to analyze (like Picasso's *Guernica* or works by his beloved German expressionists) that show the presence of the negative in and sometimes *as* the very analogy. His sensibility was almost always for art expressive in style of contemporary estrangement. The works of "finitude" (a Raphael, a Renoir) he tended to note but rarely to study. At other times, a genuine (for Tillich, a dialectical) *confrontation* was the major form of "correlation." It might be a confrontation of contemporary estrangement through the New Being disclosed in the New Testament "picture" of Jesus the Christ,[8] or it might be a confrontation of the Christian tradition itself as too unmindful of the profound negativities in its own classic portraits of humankind's actual state, disclosed in the symbols of the fall and the cross, by the portrait of the self-deception revealed by contemporary psychoanalysis and the distortions of the self exposed by existentialist thought (the "good luck" of Christian theology),[9] or the distortions in society revealed by contemporary socialist "utopian" demands.[10]

These examples (which could be easily multiplied) may serve to warrant my earlier methodologically formulated conviction: Tillich's method of correlation, in his actual pluralistic usage as distinct from some of his formulations (see below), allows for the full spectrum of logical possibilities from identity through similarity-analogy to radical confrontation. The method really guides but never determines the results of a particular study. A particular logical possibility becomes an actuality only after the study itself. The particular subject matter—and it alone—determines the final results. For correlation, logically, can allow for any one of the following possibilities: identity, similarity, analogy, confrontation. And the method of correlation, substantively, as Tillich actually employed it, can sometimes produce a remarkably liberal insistence upon identity or radical similarity. The same method at other times, produces a clearly neoorthodox insistence on radical confrontation.

The method's fidelity to the actual demands of inquiry and interpretation (in other words, its fidelity to the demands of the particular subject matter under investigation) is its pluralistic strength. Tillich's own pluralistic use of the method as well as the distinct usages of later theologians demonstrate the enduring vitality of an approach that need not become a school, a method that need not yield to methodologism, a hermeneutical position that exposes the naiveté of orthodox theologies, a postliberal and post-neoorthodox position that allows the enduring hermeneutical achievements of both liberal and neoorthodox theologies to live a hermeneutically transforming existence even now. The range of logical possibilities allowed by the method of correlation is wide indeed. Yet the particular possibility relevant to a particular question becomes an actuality only after the investigation itself.

A final critical word on Tillich's method of correlation demands attention, however, before we shift our focus to less methodological and more substantive theological concerns. Since I have argued the point at length elsewhere,[11] here I shall state my criticism more briefly and perhaps more pointedly. Any Tillich scholar will already have noted that in some of my earlier formulations of the method of correlation I changed Tillich's own more usual formulation. The issue here is this: Is the final moment of correlation to be a correlation of the "questions" from the situation and the "answers" from the message (Tillich's usual formulation)?[12] Or is a better formulation of the intent of the method the one suggested above: namely, a correlation of the questions and answers of the situation and the questions and answers of the tradition?

Tillich's own more usual use of the method, I believe, is more faithful to the reformulation suggested above than to his own usual formulation. The fact is that Tillich does allow the answers (not only the questions) of psychoanalysis, socialist theory, existentialism, and his own "self-transcending" naturalism to provide answers, not only questions, in his theology. The fact is that Tillich's own brilliantly dialectical use of his method (as Robert Scharlemann has decisively shown it to be)[13] demonstrates that his non-dialectical formulation of "questions" from the situation and "answers" from the message is not adequate to his own dialectical use. The fact is that Tillich's explicit refusal to allow "experience" to be a "source" for theology, while "culture" is allowed that position,[14] is confusing and perhaps confused. In sum, the method of correlation is better formulated not as he usually formulated it, but as he actually employed it: an interpretative correlation of the questions and answers of the message with the questions and answers of the situation.

This interpretation of Tillich's method is, I believe, not only more faithful to his own use of the method but also more in keeping with the hermeneutical character of much contemporary theology. What Tillich has given us all is a general guiding theological method that expresses in explicit terms the hermeneutical character of all contemporary theology. Each theologian, after all, must interpret the fundamental religious questions of the classics of the Christian tradition. In thus interpreting the tradition itself, each theologian also attempts to apply those questions and those responses to the contemporary situation. Thus does the tradition live as *traditio,* not as mere *tradita.* Thus does theology's own fidelity to its critically reflective task live in ever-revised forms. Thus does *applicatio* demand an interpretation of the questions and responses of the situation and thereby, in that very application, some appropriate form of correlation (identity, similarity, analogy, confrontation) between the fundamental questions and answers of the tradition and the situation.

In this manner, the influence of Tillich's method of correlation seems widespread in contemporary theology. In a recent symposium, for example, both Edward Schillebeeckx and Hans Küng (surely not Tillichians) have attempted to formulate a new consensus for contemporary "Catholic and ecumenical" theology.[15] Their formulations are remarkably resonant to the earlier formulations of Tillich: the task of the theologian is the attempt to provide "mutually critical correlations" between the tradition and contemporary experience: The words are the words of Edward Schillebeeckx, but the voice, like the voice of many theologians in our period, is the voice of Paul Tillich. By not founding a school, Tillich entered all schools. By formulating a method faithful to the theologian's task, a method genuinely guiding theology but never determining its results, Tillich aided every theologian. By insisting that the fundamental questions with which theology must deal are always the fundamental questions of the meaning and truth of our existence as human beings in the presence of the mystery of existence itself, Tillich listened to and still speaks to every questioning human being. His presence persists in contemporary thought because Tillich asked those fundamental questions that make a worthwhile existence authentically human. He asked those questions with the seriousness and the rigor they demand.

TILLICH'S QUESTIONS AND CONTEMPORARY THEOLOGY

Theology, as everyone knows, is too important to be left to the theologians. Theology presumes to ask certain fundamental questions incumbent upon every thinking being; for theology presumes to ask certain fundamental questions of the meaning and truth of human existence in relationship to itself, to others, to society, politics, history, nature, and the encompassing whole. Many theologians can content themselves with other questions. But Tillich recognized these fundamental questions and these alone as those religious theological questions that grasp and are grasped by an "ultimate concern." He found himself most at home with those artists, philosophers, political, and cultural critics who risked asking those perennial questions in a time of broken and distorted fragments in the self, society, culture, and history. He found himself most at home with the neoorthodox theologians' bracing rediscovery of the jarring, defamiliarizing, shattering power of the "kerygmatic" word in an age when what E. M. Forster named "poor, chatty, little Christianity" was in danger of becoming a nervous, well-meaning garrulous sentimentalist. Yet Tillich was not at home with many of the "answers" his fellow rediscoverers of the power of the Word actually gave. He saw—and surely here he was correct—that the Word in our day forced upon our consciousness as many questions as answers, indeed often questions as the answers.

The answers forged for other situations—the *"imago dei"* for the patristic period; a cry for architectonic order in Aquinas and Kant; a sense of forgiveness in Luther; a sense of the overpowering, overflowing power of nature in Schelling—became, in Tillich's hands, a rediscovery of the fundamental questions lurking in those classic responses—finitude; estrangement; technical and ontological reason; the mystical, questioning sense of the whole. He could not in honesty write a *Church Dogmatics.* But he could and did write a *Systematic Theology:* a theology structured by the method of correlation, ordered by the drive to the concrete from the necessary abstractions of essence through "existence" to the concrete actuality of "life"; a theology empowered by the fundamental questions embedded in all the classic symbols of Christianity and lightened by the obscure clarity of the new responses rendered available by those classic symbols to our own situation. As a series of answers, Tillich's systematics seems more what Whitehead called an assemblage than a system. *Systematic Theology* of Tillich is more comparable to the unsteady *Sentences* of Peter Lombard than to the architectonic whole of Aquinas' *Summae,* more faithful to the existential richness and partial order of the works of Tillich's true mentors, Luther, Kierkegaard, and Schelling, than of the ordered and ordering patterns of Calvin, Schleiermacher, or Hegel.

If one reads only Tillich's *Systematic Theology,* one may miss the liberating and defamiliarizing disorder lurking in those ordering volumes. The ontological language—at once analogical, symbolic, and dialectical—yields no single final second-order language for theology. Tillich's other works—his brilliant essays on art, socialist politics, psychoanalysis, nature, and sacrament; *Kairos* and the demonic; his sermons and occasional pieces—all reveal better than *Systematic Theology* the power of his insight and his authentic questioning of existence by means of Christian symbols. There is no reason to disparage Tillich's real achievement in *Systematic Theology.* Yet there is need to rediscover that the major legacy of his entire work there and elsewhere is his stunning ability to ask those fundamental questions again, to face the possibility of a *Kairos,* the actuality of the demonic, the necessity of attempting some order while facing the urgency and reality of the chaos in the self, society, history, and nature.

The fundamental questions that the contemporary situation forces upon the consciousness of every human being—above all, for Tillich, the question of possible nonbeing, of possible meaninglessness and absurdity in existence—[16] frees the defamiliarizing, questioning, liberating classic responses of the Christian symbols to become retrievable responses once again. In some cases, for Tillich, those classic responses intensify the questions themselves. In all cases, those responses become genuine responses to authentic questions of human beings attempting to live a worthwhile life in an age of distortion and fragmentation. In all cases, those questions force the question of an honest, believable faith and an honest, irretrievable doubt in that very faith upon the conscience of the contemporary Christian. Above all, Tillich's theology may teach any thinking person to ask those fundamental questions again and to see the classic symbols of Christianity for what they are: classic, retrievable responses to just such questions.

In our own post-Tillich situation, his favored questions are not necessarily ours. For many contemporary theologians, for example, the fundamental question of massive global suffering and oppression outweighs the Enlightenment questions of "reason and revelation" in a historically conscious age or the existentialist questions of alienation, absurdity, meaninglessness and alienation of the solitary human being in a mechanized age of fragments. There is little doubt that in *Systematic Theology* (or at least in the first two volumes), it is that existentialist question of authentic existence that predominates. Like so many of the other classics of that early period of postmodernity—Camus's *Stranger;* Eliot's *Waste Land;* Yeats's "widening gyre"; Sartres's *No Exit;* Giacometti's emaciated, evocative sculptures; Hemingway's nonmessy code; Ortega's revolt of the masses; and Tillich's own German expressionists—Tillich's work (especially his essays on modern art and psychoanalysis and the first two volumes of *Systematic Theology*) stands as a major candidate for a classic theological expression of existentialist postmodernity.

Even as the major attention of many contemporary theologians shifts from the alienation and sense of absurdity of the solitary, alienated individual trapped in a technological world to the sense of the interconnectedness of all in a situation of massive global suffering, oppression, and alienation, it would be foolish to dismiss Tillich and other classics of an earlier existentialism as merely "personalist" much less as purely "individualist." Rather we honor these existentialist classics best as we honor all classic expressions of the human spirit: by attempting to reformulate their questions—their fundamental perennial questions—in our different situation. Tillich honored many questions, both relativizing them and retrieving them: the questions of finitude and mortality from the patristic period; the question of the need for forgiveness in Luther; the questions of enlightenment reason and revelation in Kant and liberal and modernist theologians; the question of the depths of ontological reason in Hegel and Schelling. Theologians of the present also can honor Tillich's existentialist questions of alienation, absurdity, and meaninglessness, even as we relativize and retrieve them, in our postexistentialist situation.

For our own situation has become postexistentialist not because we have adequately answered those existentialist questions, much less because any thinker has now finally become an "authentic individual" in Kierkegaard's or Nietzsche's or Tillich's demanding sense. Rather the only real postexistentialist move forward has been the recognition that one cannot and should not become an individualist, an alienated, solitary self isolated from all the rest—isolated, above all, from the oppressed who were honored by the prophets and by Jesus, those who were oppressed, too often ignored or scorned by official Christendom, and just as often scorned by the scorners of Christendom. Contemporary political and liberation theologians can see their new political and historical formulation of the fundamental questions of an authentic existence as just that—a reformulation of the fundamental question incumbent upon every human being and surely demanded of anyone who has ever listened to the word for the oppressed in the great prophets and in Jesus. Political and liberation theologians continue, even as they revise the theological conversation of Tillich and his existentialist contemporaries, just as Tillich continued his predecessors' conversations in his justly revisionary formulations.

Although Tillich is best known for his "existentialist" theology, it is remarkable how diverse his posings of the fundamental questions in fact were. Although his better-known American period (and, therefore, his *Systematic Theology*) and his concern with the distortion in the individual self disclosed by existentialism and psychoanalysis) does disclose a relatively apolitical, personalist, existentialist thrust, his earlier German work (and the principal reason for his forced exile from Germany) expressed a political theology with a socialist thrust long before the recent demands for one. The recent resurgence of interest in these aspects of Tillich's work, it seems to me, is an altogether positive phenomenon. Not that Tillich's own inevitably dated solutions can be ours. Rather his early work in political theology shows how every political theology that is a genuine theology must ask its political questions as fundamental theological questions.

Political and liberation theologies, as theologies, are not a retreat from those questions that theology as theology asks. Rather, these theologies are nothing other than better, as more relatively adequate, formulations of the kind of fundamental, existential questions theology must always ask. From the point of view of their new concrete, liberating, political, and historical praxis, liberation theologians are freed from the misunderstanding of praxis as the mere application of theory in the manner common in much classical and enlightenment discussion of theory and praxis.[17] Liberated from the existentialist temptation to a rigid and often elitist notion of what will count as authentic individuality, liberated from enlightment dreams of a purely autonomous reason dialectically becoming the trap of a contemporary merely technical reason, liberated from the law of diminishing returns enforced by an all-consuming concern with one's own secretly cherished alienation, the political and liberation theologians ask their fundamental questions. They ask those questions (as did the early Tillich) in the context of a questioning retrieval of the concrete, political, and historical resources of the classic biblical symbols of prophecy, eschatology, and apocalyptic[18] and the resources of once-forgotten "sectarian" movements in every age.

In the contemporary theological situation, therefore, some of the earlier "political" aspects of Tillich's work (along with some aspects of volume 3 of *Systematic Theology*) demand further retrieval: not, to be sure, as a proposed solution to our present questions but as a retrievable example of how those questions can be posed theologically. Indeed, what most strikes a reader of Tillich is how single-mindedly theological his questioning remained, yet how diverse, and finally how radically pluralistic, his actual questions were.

CONCLUSION: TILLICH AND RADICAL PLURALISM

In our own postexistentialist situation, a distinctive note is the failure of any one situational fundamental question to command attention of all. Whether one interprets this situation in the European fashion as an irresolvable conflict of interpretations, or in the Anglo-American mode as a radical pluralism of questions, responses, and traditions is a relatively minor point. What a contemporary analyst needs to note, above all, is that no one fundamental question (not even the fundamental question of meaninglessness of Tillich and his existentialist contemporaries) now dominates. Rather we seem caught in a situation where all the questions, often all at once, force themselves upon the attention of every theologian.

For some theologians this seems to occasion the inability to ask any fundamental question at all. The question of meaningfulness becomes itself meaningless as thinkers retreat to more manageable questions: manageable in terms of what Tillich aptly named "technical reason" and its revolt against all ontological or religious concerns. For other thinkers, this radically pluralistic situation occasions an unnerving sense of the uncanny, which releases a myriad of fundamental questions.[19] For these theologians, Tillich remains a dependable guide. It is, in fact, striking how pluralistic Tillich's own work is in both its questions and its answers. Despite the dominance of the fundamental question of meaninglessness in an estranged world and its brilliant evocation of a possible response of a New Being in Tillich's most famous works, there is present throughout his work a constantly shifting analysis of the fundamental questions present in contemporary culture and in the symbols of classic biblical and traditional theologies.

His formulation of the question of "reason and revelation"[20] for example, shares both enlightenment concerns for reason and liberal theological concerns for historical consciousness. Yet his formulation also shares the concerns of the "Frankfurt School" with the "dialectic of Enlightenment" reason, as one notes the devastation forthcoming from a merely "technical reason."[21] Like Adorno and Horkheimer, Tillich is concerned with forging concepts that, by incorporating the negative, are not reducible to mere categories. Like them, he insists upon the need for a negative dialectical moment—for him, theologically as the Protestant Principle; for them in a "posttheological" fashion, as the ancient Jewish refusal to name God or to provide an image for a future paradise. Unlike them, Tillich's retrieval of the possibility of a "theonomous" reason in the classic symbols of revelation and in the classic traditions of ontology, frees his dialectical language from either the impossible self-confidence of Hegel or the despairing critique of the solely negative dialectic of Adorno and Horkheimer.

This move, in its turn, freed Tillich to incorporate the question and concerns that other "dialectical theologians" found foreign to their single-minded concentration on the defamiliarizing negative dialectic of the "kerygmatic" Word. For Tillich, the dialectic of the Word really did free one from the world and, by that negative freedom, freed one for the world. This freedom is a theological freedom for reason, in its fully ontological, not merely ontic sense;[22] for participatory symbols, not only dialectically negating signs;[23] for nature and its nonverbal manifesting powers, not only history illumined by the dialectical word;[24] for Catholic substance and Protestant principle[25] and thereby to a classic Lutheran retrieval of word *and* sacrament and a remarkable theological resonance by means of his own symbolic-dialectical language to the traditional Bonaventurean and occasionally the Thomist use of analogical language in theology.[26] Indeed in his final extraordinary lecture, "The Significance of the History of Religions for the Systematic Theologian," Tillich expanded his concerns yet further to suggest the need for a radical rethinking of his own and other Christian systematic theologies in the context of the world religions.[27]

A theological position that can incorporate such pluralistic concerns without easy compromise and that can dialectically relate these questions into an ever-revised ontological theological language, while never allowing the easy exit of eclecticism, commands respect. For what is notable in Tillich's work is that the "and" in his famous polarities (reason and revelation, situation and message, Being and God, word and sacrament, nature and history, Catholic substance and Protestant principle, Christianity and the other religions, the existential and the political, the utopian and the eschatological, faith and doubt) is never an easily juxtaposed "and." The latter easy "and," so beloved by professional moderates in theology, was well exposed in its timid and tedious eclecticism by the full force of the negative dialectics wielded by Tillich and the other theologians of the Word. Tillich knew that a theologian can never simply assent to that easy "and." Rather each theologian must earn the right to affirm it.

With the intrinsically dialectical character of Tillich's own use of his method of correlation, with his retrieval of the dialectical and the participating power in the classic symbols, with his honest refusal to move forward into a new concern (psychoanalysis, "the Catholic substance," the "other religions") until the genuine otherness of that "other" actuality was dialectically related through a tensive "and" to his own grounded religious core (the Protestant principle),[28] Tillich earned the right to his theological "ands." How many contemporary theologians can claim as much?

In a post-Tillich theological situation, too many calls to pluralism are really disguised eclecticisms, too many denunciations of the pluralistic actuality of our situation are new exclusivist "onlies." In such a situation the pluralistic reality and the theological integrity of Tillich's mode of thinking strikes home anew. The welcome renaissance of interest in Tillich's work, I suspect, is not principally occasioned by a belief in his particular answers to our later and often different questions. Rather that renaissance is occasioned by the belief that the mode of inquiry that Tillich brought to bear upon his situation is what most needs retrieval today. That kind of theological inquiry, as I have tried to suggest in these reflections, is characterized above all by a fidelity to the kinds of questions the theologian must ask in every situation, by a decent sense that every answer is at best relatively adequate, that every question and response needs constant revision as the questions and the classic resources come more and more clearly into view, that a radical pluralism of both questions and responses is our actuality while an earned, a dialectical analogical "and" should be our ideal.[29]

Tillich achieved something more important than giving correct answers. He taught his contemporaries anew, as he can teach us, how to ask a religious theological question today. He did something more enduring than found a school; he set an example of how nonultimate all our responses to the ultimate concerns in our fundamental questions must be. Tillich teaches the most important lesson any contemporary theologian needs each day to relearn: what it means in the contemporary situation really to believe and to think and to do both in the gifted clearing of that participating, defamiliarizing "and."

NOTES

1. See especially Paul Tillich, *Systematic Theology*, vol. 1 (Chicago: University of Chicago Press, 1951), 59–66.
2. See Hans-Georg Gadamer, *Truth and Method* (New York: Seabury Press, 1975).
3. Ibid. Cf. Paul Ricoeur, *Interpretation Theory* (Fort Worth: Texas Christian University Press, 1976). For the development from "romantic" hermeneutics to Gadamer, see Richard Palmer, *Hermeneutics: Schleiermacher, Dilthey, Heidegger, Gadamer* (Evanston, Ill.: Northwestern University Press, 1969).
4. The charge is often made by Gadamer against "methodologisms." Indeed, the title of Gadamer's famous work could just as well read *Truth or Method.*
5. See especially the prefaces to Tillich's *Systematic Theology*, vols. 1 (1951) and 2 (1957).
6. See, for example, Rudolf Bultmann and Tillich, vol. 2, *Systematic Theology.*
7. See, for example, the early writings of Tillich, vol. 3, *Systematic Theology;* and

contemporary political theologians ranging from James Luther Adams through Jürgen Moltmann, Johann Baptist Metz, Dorothee Sölle, and the liberation theologians of the Third World or oppressed groups in the so-called first world.

8. Tillich, *Systematic Theology* 2:118–38. Despite its well-known difficulties (*analogia imaginis,* etc.), Tillich's Christology by its basic stand for the "picture" of Jesus in the New Testament, instead of the more familiar, historically reconstructed "historical Jesus," deserves restudy among contemporary hermeneutical and literary critical theologians. For a discussion of these issues in contemporary Christology, see David Tracy, *The Analogical Imagination: Christian Theology and the Culture of Pluralism* (New York: Seabury Press, 1980), chaps. 6, 7.

9. See Tillich, *Systematic Theology* 2:27–28.

10. Paul Tillich, *The Socialist Decision* (Washington, D.C.: University Press, 1977).

11. See David Tracy, *Blessed Rage for Order: The New Pluralism in Theology* (New York: Seabury Press, 1975).

12. Inter alia, see Tillich, *Systematic Theology* 1:62–64.

13. See Robert Scharlemann, *Reflection and Doubt in the Thought of Paul Tillich* (New Haven: Yale University Press, 1969); see also James Luther Adams, *Paul Tillich's Philosophy of Culture, Science, and Religion* (New York: Harper & Row, 1965), and Marion and Wilhelm Pauck, *Paul Tillich: His Life and Thought* (New York: Harper & Row, 1976), vol. 1, *Life.*

14. Tillich, *Systematic Theology* 1:34–46.

15. See Küng and Schillebeeckx in *Consensus in Theology?,* ed. Leonard Swidler (Philadelphia: Westminster Press, 1980). My own criticism of Küng's preference for a model of confrontation over correlation may also be found in that volume,

16. See Tillich, *Systematic Theology* 1:188–99; see also idem, *The Courage to Be* (New Haven: Yale University Press, 1952), passim.

17. For a good study here, see Matthew Lamb, "Theory and Praxis in Contemporary Theology," in *Proceedings of the Catholic Theological Society of America* (Yonkers; CTSA, 1976), 149–78.

18. Tillich's actual interpretation of the eschatological symbols in *Systematic Theology,* vol. 3 (1963), differs notably, of course, from the contemporary political and liberation theologians' retrieval of the political import of biblical eschatology. Still, Tillich's interpretation of eschatology, for all its inadequacies by present exegetical and theological standards, did not allow eschatology to become purely vertical (Barth) or purely personalist-existentialist (Bultmann). Tillich's earlier interests in utopian symbols, in fact, shows some resonance to the influential work of Ernst Bloch on the political theologians.

19. I have tried to analyze this radical pluralism of fundamental questions within a horizon of the "uncanny" in chapter 8 of *The Analogical Imagination.*

20. *Systematic Theology* 1:71–105.

21. See Theodor Adorno and Max Horkheimer, *Dialectic of the Enlightenment* (New York: Seabury Press, 1971). It might also be noted that Tillich had direct connections with the Frankfurt thinkers, including his somewhat mysterious role as director of Adorno's thesis on Kierkegaard.

22. One of Tillich's major contributions to the theology of his period was his keeping alive ontological concern in the ontic revolt against all ontology of the existentialist theologians.

23. For some formulations of this justly famous Tillichian distinction, see *Systematic Theology* 1:235–41, and 3:111–29.

24. Paul Tillich, "Nature and Sacrament," in idem, *The Protestant Era*, trans. James Luther Adams (Chicago: University of Chicago Press, 1948).

25. Tillich, *Systematic Theology* 3:245. See Thomas O'Meara, chap. 16 of this book.

26. For some good studies here, see *Paul Tillich and Catholic Thought*, ed. Thomas O'Meara and Celestin Weisser (Dubuque, Iowa: Priority Press, 1964).

27. See Paul Tillich, *The Future of Religions*, ed. Jerald Brauer (Chicago: University of Chicago Press, 1966), 80–84.

28. See the insightful essay of James Luther Adams, "Paul Tillich on Luther," in *Interpreters of Luther: Essays in Honor of Wilhelm Pauck*, ed. Jaroslav Pelikan (Philadelphia: Fortress Press, 1968), 304–34.

29. I have tried to study the relationships of these two classic theological languages in Tillich and other theologians in *The Analogical Imagination*, chapter 9. A major reason for Tillich's influence among theologians is the remarkable way in which his second-order analogical-symbolic language always includes a negative dialectical moment and his dialectical language always implies (for example, through his emphasis on "participation" and his insistence on the need for a *"reunion* of the separated") an analogical-symbolic result.

15. Tillich and the Art of Theology

JOHN POWELL CLAYTON

No one who visits the Musée Rodin in Paris can fail to be struck by that sculptor's capacity to find ever-new uses for fragments previously cast for a different purpose. Rodin's early experiment with this technique can be seen in the statue known as *The Walking Man,* in which new legs were added to an already existing torso.[1] In later years, Rodin would often make multiple castings of individual body parts to be assembled at will in every imaginable combination or he would take several finished terra-cotta works of similar size, chop off their arms and legs and heads, mix up the pieces, and then glue them back together again with hot wax. Rodin's studio must have been a macabre scene, its shelves and drawers filled with dismembered limbs, torsos, and heads, all awaiting the resurrection of new creation. As *creator ex membris disjectis,* Rodin was not in every case equally successful. Some assemblages seem awkward, even arbitrary.[2] Even so, novel and often unexpected combinations of separately cast parts frequently give Rodin's sculpture an expressive power and vitality that can be overwhelming in intensity.

Rodin's combinatory technique can be seen especially in his monumental portal known as *The Gates of Hell.* Begun in 1880, it was to have been his masterpiece, a work intended to rival Ghiberti's *Gates of Paradise.* Some of Rodin's most famous individual pieces, including *The Thinker,* began life as studies for this never-quite-completed monument on which he labored for nearly forty years until his death in 1917. During much of that time, Rodin would remove and remold individual figures from the *Gates* and experiment with them in different positions and combinations. A torso might be borrowed from a body in one part of the panels, be given new limbs, and then be used for a quite different purpose in an entirely different context. Two figures might be juxtaposed that had existed and, indeed, that continued to exist elsewhere on the panels. The tension, which had been there from the beginning, between the sculptural and the architectural requirements of the artist only increased with the passing years. As Rodin returned again and again to the individual components, the unity of vision with which he had begun the project was gradually lost, so that it is most unlikely that he would ever have completed his "master-piece." And yet some of his finest individual pieces were initially associated with work on that faulty monument.

The Gates of Hell contains within it many masterpieces[3] but is itself no masterpiece. It is a most unsatisfactory fragment. It is not at all like the partial figures for which Rodin is so admired, the fragments in which—as Rilke rightly adjudged—"nothing necessary is lacking."[4] *The Gates of Hell*, by contrast, is a fragment that —while having the form of a whole—is nonetheless devoid of unifying vision or message. Admire as one may the "many master-pieces" that it contains, one stands before Rodin's intended masterpiece profoundly disappointed.

Tillich's intended masterpiece, the three-volume *Systematic Theology,* can evoke a similar response. Tillich, like Rodin, spent some forty years of his professional life shaping and reshaping the work that was intended to be the highest expression of his craft as theologian.[5] In those years, concepts that had been formed for a particular purpose in a specific context were removed and made to serve quite a different purpose. This is especially true of such key terms as *Kairos* and *theonomy.* In Tillich's early writings, the *Kairos* is *now* and *theonomy* is an empirical possibility in the *present;* in his later writings, *Kairos* is increasingly identified with some past time, most notably with the appearance of Jesus as the Christ, and *theonomy* is transformed into an eschatological hope of which there are in time only anticipations.[6] The weld marks are still visible in *Systematic Theology,* in which an unsatisfactory mixture of motifs is subsumed under the terms *Kairos* and *theonomy,* each of which seems by the end of the third volume to have lost its force and focus.

The way Tillich would remold his basic concepts to do new and varied jobs can be illustrated clearly by calling attention to certain similarities and dissimilarities between the original 1922 version of the article "Kairos" and the English-language version of it, which appeared only in 1948.[7] Whole sections of that article were thoroughly reworked in order to accommodate changes in the subsequent direction of Tillich's thought over the intervening twenty-five years. This had two main consequences, the second being by far the more important of the two.

First, the symmetrical structure of the argument in two major sections of the article was weakened.[8] The various lines of argument in "Kairos" were intended collectively to support the claim that Tillich's philosophy of *Kairos* both unites and supersedes every relativist and every absolutist view of history. These two main competing views of history and the interconnections between them are developed with a dialectical symmetry that would be delightful possibly to Hegel himself.

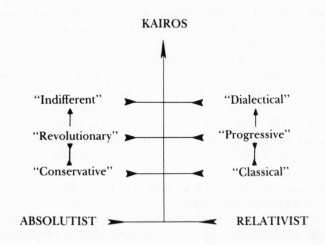

This visual representation of the structure of Tillich's argument exhibits clearly its symmetry. The opposition between what Tillich calls the "conservative-ecclesiastical" absolutism of Augustine and the "revolutionary-utopian" absolutism of the sectarians is overcome dialectically in the "indifferent" absolutism of the theologians of crisis, such as Barth and Gogarten. Moreover, absolutist philosophies of history are said to generate as well their dialectical opposites, namely, relativist philosophies of history.

Within relativism, a similar dialectic occurs: the opposition between the "classical relativism" of Herder and the "progressive relativism" of Lessing is said to be overcome in the "dialectical relativism" of Marx and others. For this Hegel-like argument to be complete, it then remains for Tillich only to show that the opposition between "indifferent absolutism" and "dialectical relativism" is overcome in his own *Kairos* philosophy. But the *dialectical* symmetry of the argument further requires that "conservative-ecclesiastical absolutism" stand directly parallel to "classical relativism," that "revolutionary-utopian absolutism" stand directly parallel to "progressive relativism," that "indifferent absolutism" stand directly parallel to "dialectical relativism." And it is precisely *this* symmetry that was disturbed in the 1948 version of "Kairos" when Tillich—who had perhaps in the meantime forgot why he had ordered things as he had—carelessly inverted the order in which he placed the "conservative" and the "revolutionary" varieties of absolutist philosophies of history. It might be objected, and not unreasonably, that these finer points of dialectical mediation need not worry us overmuch. For those of us still living in the cave, so to speak, this matter affects at most our aesthetic sensibility as to the elegance of the argument's structure.

Secondly and more importantly, the term *Kairos* is itself radically redefined in the 1948 version of Tillich's famous piece. For the first time in print, Tillich distinguishes three meanings of the word *Kairos:* [9]

Kairos in its *unique* and universal sense is, for Christian faith, the appearing of Jesus as the Christ. Kairos in its *general* and special sense for the philosopher of history is every turning point in history in which the eternal judges and transforms the temporal. Kairos in its *special* sense, as decisive for our present situation, is the coming of a new theonomy on the soil of a secularized and emptied autonomous culture. [10]

These distinctions are wholly unknown in Tillich's earlier writings, including the 1922 version of the article that is the putative basis for the 1948 translation. [11]

Giving *Kairos* a new range of meanings has the consequence that even those passages of the article that are left unaltered in the new translation gain a different significance. For instance, compare the opening paragraph of the fifth section in the two versions:

Wir sind der Überzeugung, daß gegenwärtig ein Kairos, ein epochaler Geschichtsmoment sichtbar ist. Diese Überzeugung zu begründen ist hier nicht der Platz, es mag auf die immer wachsende kulturkritische Literatur hingewiesen werden, vor allem aber auf Bewegungen, in denen das Krisenbewußtsein lebendige Gestalt genommen hat, *wie die Jugendbewegung und der Sozialismus.* Beweise zwingender Art sind das alles nicht; es kann sie nicht geben. Denn das Bewußtsein des Kairos ist abhängig von einem inneren Erfaßtsein durch das Schicksal der Zeit. Es kann da sein in dumpfer Sehnsucht der Massen, es kann sich klären und formen in einzelnen Kreisen bewußter Geistigkeit; es kann Kraft gewinnen im prophetischen Wort; aber es kann nicht demonstriert und aufgezwungen werden; es ist Tat und Freiheit, wie es zugleich Gnade und Schicksal ist.[12]

We are convinced that today a Kairos, an epochal moment of history, is visible. This is not the place to give reasons for this conviction, although we should refer to the ever growing literature that is critical of our culture and to movements in which the consciousness of the crisis has taken a living form. These may not be proofs that are objectively convincing; proofs of that sort cannot exist. Indeed, the consciousness of the kairos is dependent on one's being inwardly grasped by the fate and destiny of the time. It can be found in the passionate longing of the masses; it can become clarified and take form in small circles of conscious intellectual and spiritual concern; it can gain power in the prophetic word; but it cannot be demonstrated and forced; it is deed and freedom, as it is also fate and grace.[13]

With the exception of the six italicized words in the German text, which are omitted from the English text, the 1948 version is entirely faithful to the 1922 original. Even so, the *sense* of the passage in the two versions is measurably different. In 1922, *today* was regarded as *Kairos* in the sense of being a moment in which new meaning was already breaking through from within the structures of human existence; in 1948, however, *today* was regarded as *Kairos* in the sense of being a time of emptiness in which one can only wait in hope for new meaning, at some unidentified future moment, to break into human existence from without. The phrase *the passionate longing of the masses* rings differently in the two versions, as does the reference to "being grasped by the fate and destiny" of the present time. So, the very same words in the two versions gain their particular significance in each case from their specific context. And that context is prescribed in part by the changing meaning of *Kairos* in the two versions.

We learn from this single example, and the example could be multiplied severalfold, how Tillich characteristically refashioned his own texts to suit present needs. He was, so to speak, simply joining new limbs to old torsos.

What was common of key texts outside *Systematic Theology* is not in the least unknown within that work. Two brief examples will suffice. First, the well-known "two formal criteria of every theology" propounded by Tillich in the first volume of *Systematic Theology* have their genesis in his 1927–28 lectures at Dresden on "The Structure of Religious Knowledge." Only the most minor alterations were made in adapting the "criteria" to their new, more straightforwardly theological context:

Die Gestalt der religiösen Erkenntnis	*Systematic Theology*
§26. Religious knowledge is knowledge which concerns us unconditionally. No statement contains religious knowledge which does not deal with an object insofar as it concerns us unconditionally.	The object of theology is what concerns us ultimately. Only those propositions are theological which deal with their object insofar as it can become a matter of ultimate concern for us.
§27. That concerns us unconditionally which determines our being. No statement contains religious knowledge which does not deal with an object insofar as it determines our being.	Our ultimate concern is that which determines our being or nonbeing. Only those statements are theological which deal with their object insofar as it can become a matter of being or nonbeing for us.[14]

Needless to say, these two sets of "criteria" do not have precisely the same sense in the two contexts, separated as they are by more than two decades of theological reflection. Secondly, the familiar slogan from Tillich's early writings, "Culture is the form of religion and religion is the substance of culture," has quite a different meaning within *Systematic Theology* from that which it enjoyed in Tillich's writings during the Weimar Republic.[15] Here, as elsewhere, the way Tillich casts and recasts the individual pieces that make up his composite texts reminds one of the technique exploited so well in Rodin's works. One might be willing by now to grant the similarity and yet not be convinced that the similarity is very illuminating of the theologian's craft or of "the art of theology." For it could well be the case that such a technique might be suited to the work of the sculptor and yet not be at all suitable for the theologian. Indeed, the effects of such a technique could be entirely unwelcome within the theologian's guild. I want now to suggest not only that Tillich's use of this technique is theologically justifiable, but that it also constitutes his most enduring legacy to the future of theology.

Tillich's notorious tendency to reform constantly even his most basic concepts certainly causes difficulties for anyone who would comprehend his thought. It is also one ground for the frequent charge of inconsistency. That this constant restlessness of his occasioned tension and inconsistency within his thought cannot be denied. Tillich himself was more aware of the presence of inconsistency in his thought than his more uncritical admirers have been; but he was apparently less worried by such inconsistency than his less sympathetic critics. For Tillich, the ἔρως of thinking theologically compelled him continuously to reshape concepts to meet new needs, to look for connections between concepts that had previously seemed unrelated, to apply concepts to contexts that had been previously untried. Tillich was not in every case equally successful. At its best, however, Tillich's thought achieves a certain timeliness and vitality, as is witnessed by the remarkable effectiveness of his addresses, essays, and shorter books. Yet this tendency of his always to rethink and remold basic concepts also meant that he would in all likelihood never bring his system to a satisfactory end. Not even the sort of "open-textured" system that he projected.[16]

For all the stress in his writings on the importance of systems, Tillich was no more suited to construct a theological system within the traditional mold than Rodin was suited to execute a monumental portal in the manner of Ghiberti. I must make myself clear. I do not mean by this possibly outrageous statement that either Tillich or Rodin was defective in the skills of his craft. I want to emphasize, rather, that the medium was in each case too constrictive. Movement and ἔρως do not yield easily to such discipline. It is perhaps not accidental that the preparatory "studies" by each man tend to be more successful than their intended masterpieces.

Tillich and Rodin's evocative powers were more suited to the essay, to the fragment, to the partial figure in which "nothing necessary is lacking."

Rodin first feared and was then resigned to leaving his great work unfinished. After all, he once rationalized, even the greatest cathedrals of Europe are themselves unfinished![17] Tillich, too, often expressed the fear that his own magnum opus would remain an unfinished fragment, to be completed perhaps by some of his students. The anxiety of uncompleted work led him at times to the brink of despair: "The system crumbles. What shall I do? Shall I collect fragments? Declare that the attempt failed?"[18] Tillich was in his later years under great pressure from his friends and students, from his publisher and, most of all, from himself to finish the work that had occupied more than half his life. The final volume appeared in 1963, as we know, only two years before his death. No one was satisfied with it. Especially not Tillich. He published it resigned to "the incompleteness of the completed." His already keen sense of the unsatisfactory state of the final volume must have been intensified by the sometimes savage reviews that it received.[19] Tillich was so dissatisfied with the results that he talked seriously of rewriting the text of volume 2. Had he proceeded in earnest with that plan, it is not clear whether he would have been content simply to revise the existing text, for at the same time he was coming increasingly to feel that the whole of the work —from first volume to last—should be recast to take more account than it did of the history of religions.[20] Death halted any serious progress in that direction.

THE OBSOLESCENCE OF ALL THEOLOGICAL SYSTEMS

Systematic Theology is no masterpiece, even if it should be judged by some to contain within itself "many masterpieces."

What does that settle? Is there nothing more to be said regarding Tillich's possible significance for the future of theology? Perhaps the reckoning is not fully complete. Indeed, I want to propose that Tillich's significance for theology is no more settled by reference to the disappointing state of his *Systematic Theology* than is Rodin's significance for his craft settled by reference to the disappointing state of *The Gates of Hell.* Both men are significant, and for much the same reason: They were both masters of their craft. This is to be seen principally in the *manner* of their activity as artist, as theologian. I think that I would probably want to stand by this judgment, even if *The Gates of Hell* had been satisfactorily completed and *Systematic Theology* more adequately executed. I shall explain what I mean in reference to Tillich.

The monumental systems in the history of Christian theology have their import primarily for the situation in which they were produced. Study them we must, learn from them we should—just as Rodin studied and learned from the classical expressions of his craft. But imitate them in detail we cannot. Their time is not our time; their questions are not precisely our questions—even if we were to hold that their faith is in some sense our faith. So even if *Systematic Theology* were the best of all possible systematic theologies, it would still be a mistake to attempt to defend Tillich's significance for the continuing work of the theologian by reference to the success in detail of his theological system. As Tillich himself was aware, no theological system can speak convincingly to all people in all times.

New organizing principles appear, neglected elements acquire central significance, the method may become more refined or completely different, with the result that a new conception of the structure of the whole emerges. This is the fate of every system. But this is also the rhythm in which the history of Christian thought has moved through the centuries. The systems were points of crystallization toward which the discussion of particular problems moved and from which new discussions and fresh problems arose.[21]

Every theological system is at best "a station at which preliminary truth is crystallized on the endless road toward truth." This means that every theological system can and must be superseded, that "every concrete system is transitory and that none can be final."[22]

Each theological system, even the finest, has an inherent obsolescence factor: As the time for which the system is a "crystallization" recedes into the past, the contemporary significance of that system diminishes. This is an insight shared by such theologians as Schleiermacher, Troeltsch, and Tillich, for each of whom the object of theology was conceived as a mediation between historical Christianity and contemporary culture.[23] In Tillich's words, *"the task of theology is mediation,* mediation between the eternal criterion of truth as it is manifest in the picture of Jesus as the Christ and the changing experiences of individuals and groups, their varying questions and their categories of perceiving reality."[24] Elsewhere he speaks of theology's "moving back and forth between two poles," namely the Christian message and the cultural context, "the eternal truth of [Christianity's] foundation and the temporal situation in which the eternal truth must be received."[25] Both poles are said to be necessary to the theological task, and neither on its own is sufficient, such that the theologian is regarded as having done his job properly if and only if "message and situation are related in such a way that neither of them is obliterated."[26] This "revelatory correlation" of message and situation alters as the cultural situation changes, with the result that the theologian must begin afresh in every new situation.

Tillich's work as a whole records a serious and sustained attempt through the years to respond theologically to the uncertainties and questions implied in the cultural situation of the first half of the present century. By responding so single-mindedly to the questions of a single generation, Tillich achieved a certain timeliness for his work. He also thereby insured that as the time for which he was writing becomes past history, the contemporary significance of his particular "correlations" will diminish accordingly. Such obsolescence is the fate of every theological system, even the most nearly perfect. Given his own characterization of the transitory worth of "every concrete system," Tillich could hardly dissent from the judgment that his significance for the future work of theology cannot be determined by reference to the details of his own system. For this judgment is clearly in line with his own declared intention to construct a historically conscious theology, a theology that is κατὰ καιρόν.

Tillich made no claim to speak "for all times." He spoke, instead, out of his own time and to his own time. This holds not only for Tillich's *Systematic Theology,* but also for the individual phases of his activity as theologian. The determination to do theology κατὰ καιρόν entailed for him the recognition that "not everything is possible at every time; not everything is appropriate [*wahr*] to every time; not everything is required in every moment."[27] Speaking "according to the *Kairos*" meant something different in 1922 than in 1948. The demands of the present were in each case understood differently. Nor should one underestimate the impact of the intervening years upon Tillich. If nothing else, the Third Reich, and with it the shattering of his political hopes for Germany, stands between the two versions of the article "Kairos." Within each context, Tillich rethought not only the details of the present moment, but also what would count as a *Kairos*. The *concept* of *Kairos*, as well as the *content* of any specific *Kairos*, remained subject to revision throughout his writings. But this is consistent with the intention to do theology contextually.

Tillich's intention to do theology *in* "the situation" accounts in large measure both for his success and his failure. It helps account for his tendency constantly to remove and to remold individual concepts and to experiment with them in different combinations and in different contexts. It also accounts for many of the glaring inconsistencies in his thought, and for his own tendency not to take them too seriously. Finally, it accounts for his significance and his limitation for the theology of the future. From Tillich one can learn to do theology κατὰ καιρόν. Other things one must learn elsewhere.

NOTES

1. On the significance of this particular piece of sculpture, see two important articles by Albert E. Elsen: "Rodin's *The Walking Man*," *The Massachusetts Review* 7 (1966): 289–320; and "Rodin's *The Walking Man* as Seen by Henry Moore," *Studio International* 174 (July 1967): 26–31.

2. Cf., for example, some compositions in the *Iris* and *Crouching Woman* series of c. 1890–92.

3. Bourdelle, cited in Bernard Champigneulle, *Rodin* (London: Thames and Hudson, Ltd., 1967), 145.

4. "Completeness is conveyed in all the armless statues of Rodin: nothing necessary is lacking. One stands before them as before something whole." Rainer Maria Rilke, *Rodin*, trans. Jessie Lemont and Hans Trausil (London: Haskell House Publishers, Inc. 1946), 24.

5. I am taking Tillich at his word that work on *Systematic Theology* had begun by at least 1924. Cf. *Systematic Theology*, vol. 3 (Chicago: University of Chicago Press, 1963), 7.

6. The matter is actually more complicated than this suggests. For one useful account of the development of many key terms, including *Kairos* and *theonomy*, see Eberhard Amelung, *Die Gestalt der Liebe: Paul Tillichs Theologie der Kultur* (Gütersloh: Gütersloher Verlagshaus Gerd Mohn, 1972).

7. The article "Kairos" originally appeared in *Die Tat: Monatsschrift für die Zukunft deutscher Kultur* 14 (1922): 330–50. The issue in which it appeared was devoted

entirely to the theme "Religious Socialism" and had Carl Mennicke as its editor. The 1948 version of the article was reworked by Tillich before being translated by James Luther Adams for the collection of essays *The Protestant Era* (Chicago: University of Chicago Press, 1948), a volume that did much to make Tillich's thought accessible to the English-speaking public. The version of the article that appeared in *The Protestant Era* was also used for the German translation of "Kairos" that is printed in Tillich's vol. 6, *Gesammelte Werke* (Stuttgart: Evangelisches Verlagswerk, 1963).

8. Compare pp. 332–40 of the version of "Kairos" published in *Die Tat* with pp. 35–42 of the version printed in *The Protestant Era*.

9. The distinction is adumbrated, however, in Tillich's 1927–28 lectures at Dresden, "Die Gestalt der religiösen Erkenntnis." The course outline and main propositions from those lectures have now been published in the appendix of J. P. Clayton, *The Concept of Correlation: Paul Tillich and the Possibility of a Mediating Theology* (Berlin and New York: De Gruyter, 1980), 269–308.

10. Tillich, *The Protestant Era*, 46–47.

11. Cf. Tillich, "Kairos," *Die Tat*, 346–47.

12. *Ibid.*, 347.

13. Tillich, *The Protestant Era*, 48.

14. Compare Tillich, *Systematic Theology* 1 (1951), 11–15, with "Die Gestalt der religiösen Erkenntnis," in Clayton, *The Concept of Correlation*, 280.

15. On this point, see Clayton, *The Concept of Correlation*, 191–249.

16. Tillich, *Systematic Theology* 2 (1957), 3.

17. Cited in Champigneulle, *Rodin*.

18. Quoted in Rollo May, *Paulus: A Personal Portrait* (New York: Harper & Row, 1973), 71. See also Wilhelm and Marion Pauck, *Paul Tillich: His Life and Thought* (New York: Harper & Row, 1976), vol. 1, *Life*, 244–45.

19. An especially savage review by Paul van Buren appeared in the *Christian Century* 81 (5 February 1964):177–79. For a selection of more kindly, but nonetheless critical, reviews, see those by J. H. Randall, G. H. Tavard, and Kenneth Hamilton reprinted in the *Journal of Religion* 46 (1966):218–28.

20. See Paul Tillich, *The Future of Religions*, ed. Jerald C. Brauer (New York: Harper & Row, 1966), 80–94; cf. 31–32.

21. Tillich, *Systematic Theology* 3 (1963), 4.

22. Ibid., v, 4.

23. See Clayton, *The Concept of Correlation*, 7–10, 34–83.

24. Tillich, *The Protestant Era*, xiii.

25. Tillich, *Systematic Theology* 1:3; see also 3:185ff.

26. Ibid., 1:8.

27. Tillich, *Gesammelte Werke* 6:10.

16. Tillich and the Catholic Substance

THOMAS FRANKLIN O'MEARA

THREE STAGES OF DIALOGUE

THE CATHOLIC SUBSTANCE

The wise but self-indulgent countenance of the great baroque pope *Urban VIII Barberini* or the radiant expression of *Teresa of Avila* in ecstasy—these sculptures by the quintessential Roman Catholic artist Bernini are not quite what Paul Tillich meant by the "Catholic substance." Tillich intended something more abstract, more dynamic, and more profound by that pole of the Christian dialectic that he named "Catholic" and "substantial." Towards the end of his *Systematic Theology* he wrote:

> The Protestant principle is an expression of the conquest of religion by the Spiritual Presence and consequently an expression of the victory over the ambiguities of religion, its profanization, and its demonization. . . . The Protestant principle . . . is not restricted to the churches of the Reformation or to any other church; it transcends every particular church, being an expression of the Spiritual Community. . . . It alone is not enough; it needs the "Catholic substance," the concrete embodiment of the Spiritual Presence; but is the criterion of the demonization (and profanization) of such embodiment.[1]

The following pages offer some theoretical and personal remarks on Tillich and on his relationship to two aspects of catholicity in Christianity: his theory of the Catholic substance and the dialogue between him and Roman Catholicism in this century. One of the more surprising aspects of Tillich's long career was the warm conversation with Roman Catholics that began twenty-five years ago. The framework for this exchange, coming at the end of Tillich's life and at the beginning of Vatican II, was Tillich's own theology of "Catholic substance."

For the first sixty years of his life, Tillich was not lacking in fear and criticism of Rome.

From earliest times I was opposed to the most potent system of religious heteronomy, Roman Catholicism, with a protest which was at once both Protestant and autonomous. This protest was not directed and does not direct itself in spite of theological contrasts to the dogmatic values or the liturgical forms of the Catholic system, but is concerned with its heteronomous character, with the assertion of a dogmatic authority.[2]

So, it was not the icon or the sacrament but the canon and *motu proprio* that had come to stand for Rome and Catholicism. To Tillich, *Rome* meant excessive, constricting, ahistorical authority, while *Catholic* meant religious presence, kairotic power, cultural diversity. When Tillich was a university student, Roman Catholicism would have been described by his German Protestant teachers much as Herder had described it in 1780: "A ruins from which one does not expect new life." New life, however, did come, and Tillich was part of the rebirth.

Around 1940 the young theologian wrote an essay that enunciated his dialectic of reality and critique, substance and principle. He went beyond the competing claims drawn up in wars of words between the Christian churches. Catholicism, he wrote, needs a prophetic criticism, for its very essence contains a tendency to confuse the finite with the absolute and so to turn sacrament into idol. Protestantism, on the other hand, cannot live by an intangible faith and word alone but needs concrete forms. This dual experience of the absolute and the holy as reality and as address gives rise perennially to two types of religion: the sacramental and ontic, the prophetic and eschatological. Both are present in the Gospel. What Catholicism should offer is not the legal but the sacramental side of Christianity. At its best, Catholicism's ontic concreteness owns a holiness whereby the church sanctifies as well as calls the community by leading it to New Being. In the Catholic substance Tillich searched for and prized the symbolic and ontological, a clarity both mystical and metaphysical.[3]

A DIALOGUE

Nazism changed the political and psychic atmosphere and very briefly pushed Tillich toward Roman Catholicism even as it intensified his fear of limitless authority. Emigration to America brought him contact with a new landscape of Protestant church life. Dominated by Rome, however, Catholicism continued to pursue from 1850 to 1950 a program of authority and organization (Pius XII was more powerful than any pope in the thirteenth or sixteenth centuries), and so the Catholic substance—unrealized in any particular church—seemed to be something abstract, an ideal element for every church, including Protestant bodies.

With the advent of ecumenism in the United States in the 1950s, a dialogue between Tillich and American Catholic theologians began. Why was American Roman Catholicism, conservative and unimaginative in theology, attracted to this Protestant systematician? Not because he offered new expressions of dogma, such as Christ, Trinity, or church. Indeed, around 1960, as they looked at the dogmatic content of Tillich's incomplete system, Roman Catholics would have initially viewed his thought as largely naturalistic in religious stance and thin in content. Because he had chosen the direction of Bultmann over Barth, Tillich's Christology, one could argue, had become a demythologized transference into existentially articulated myths. Roman Catholic theologians were drawn, rather, to Tillich's theological method, to his transcendental anthropology, and to his theology of God. As this conversation began, the first volume of *Systematic Theology* had just appeared as well as essays on theology and culture. In them were three attractions: a deployment of Greek, medieval, and modern metaphysics; a new method called "correlation"; and a theology of the full history of Christian thought (and not one that began in 1520).

Tillich was not the first Protestant partner for Catholic ecumenists and theologians. That distinction had gone to Barth even though, thundering forth out of tiny Switzerland, he delighted in lusty denunciations of Rome. Barth seemed to Catholics to be free of a previous century of German Protestant liberalism. There was no wholesale denial of Christian beliefs, and traditional dogmas were reinforced in the *Church Dogmatics*. Barth, like Trent, was a theologian of the letter of revelation and not a theoretician of an evolving, collective consciousness. Books and articles poured forth from European Dominicans and Jesuits, from Jerome Hamer and Hans Urs von Balthasar; Hans Küng's doctoral dissertation claimed an astonishing agreement on justification between Barth and the Council of Trent. Paradoxically, Barth pointed out that he and Rome differed not over biblical content but over philosophy. The doctrine of analogy, he wrote, grounding both the papacy and Mariology, was the issue.[4] The depth of this philosophical crevasse between Barthian and Catholic minds was not at first perceived, and only later would its difficulty be understood.

It probably surprised Barth as much as Tillich when a group of theologians led by Gustave Weigel turned to Tillich with sympathy rather than denunciation. Before we look at the nature of the affinity that Catholics discovered they had with the Protestant systematician, let us review briefly, and bring up to date, the history of what Tillich generously called "a dialogue done in listening love."

LISTENING

In his pioneer essays written after 1956, Gustave Weigel singled out Tillich's use of Augustine, his openness to Aquinas, his rare appreciation of the legitimate usage of Plato and Aristotle in theology. "Wherein lies the importance of Tillich? In the fact that he made an all-embracing system of Protestant thought and doctrine. . . . What is more, this synthesis takes into consideration the Catholic elements which are latent in Protestant belief, though often unrecognized.[5]

George Tavard argued that Tillich's use of symbol and New Being suggested to Roman Catholics a new expression of sacraments and Christian life in faith, existence, and love. He concluded:

His intention is to establish an existential correlation between the human condition today and the Christian message. His thought stresses, understresses or overstresses the aspects of Christianity that need to be stressed, understressed, or overstressed to make such a correlation meaningful. The resulting "system," as he calls it, cannot be integrated as such and without changes into an established type of Christianity; it is not Catholic or Orthodox; nor is it, for that matter, Protestant, as Luther and Calvin were Protestant. Yet, whatever label we give it, and how much we may wish to rewrite his thought for the sake of orthodoxy, we should heed Paul Tillich's eagerness to interpret Christianity for the man of today.[6]

Appearing in 1964, *Paul Tillich in Catholic Thought* brought together in one volume a dozen representatives of what we might call the first generation of this dialogue. The success of this book was due not only to the *Kairos* but also to Tillich's "Appreciation," written in the winter months of 1964. The promise from Pope John XXIII of a new style, along with a visit to Japan, seemed to be an opportunity to enter new horizons, worlds which the spirit at the end of life could visit but for which there remains no time for dwelling. Tillich concluded his careful evaluation of these still somewhat unrefined, ecumenical essays with a soaring paragraph:

I want to repeat that I did this replay with the same joy about a fruitful dialogue with which I read the articles. One thing I learned in doing so is the necessity that we learn more about each other's thought, the classical as well as the contemporary. Much misunderstanding on both sides could be prevented by such better information. But fundamental differences cannot be removed and must be acknowledged. Only the divine Spirit and historical providence can overcome the splits amongst those representing the Spiritual Community which transcends every particular church and every particular religious group. A dialogue done in "listening love," can be a tool of providence and a channel of the divine Spirit.[7]

Books and articles were written in the last half of the 1960s that represent a second generation of Roman Catholic interest. Their scope was broader, their tone more sympathetic; they could build upon the metaphysical interests of Weigel and McLean.[8] Their authors were younger, less bound to the things and words of scholastic or Tridentine texts, and more caught up in the excitement of Vatican II. Kenan Osborne's *New Being* and Carl Armbruster's first, fine overview, *The Vision of Paul Tillich*, both focused upon the Christian anthropology of Tillich and not upon his theodicy (so interesting to the first generation) nor upon his Christology (so problematical in its existentialism).

By 1970 interest in Tillich had diminished. The transitory theologies of the death of God and of secularity—both of which Tillich had forecast in the spirit of Nietzsche and Heidegger—as well as the upheavals of postconciliar Roman Catholicism, led students and believers away from the high glaciers of system. By the mid-1970s, however, one could detect a third wave of interest. Under the direction of Hans Küng, Ronald Modras examined Tillich's ecclesiology; J. C. Petit in Montreal and R. Bulman in New York studied Tillich's analysis of religion, particularly in the early writings; John Dourley presented an analysis of Tillich and the Franciscan, medieval tradition as represented in Bonaventura.[9] Under the direction of L. Chapey at Lyons, a French Tillich society was formed and its proceedings have been published.[10]

In Germany, interest in Tillich had not declined. It was there that his complete works began to be published, although monographs on him and Catholicism appeared late. Two books came from the direction of Heinrich Fries, a force for German Catholic interest in Tillich and himself a representative of the Catholic Tübingen tradition. A. Siegfried's *Das neue Sein* looked at the mixture of ontology and grace in New Being, while E. Rolinck's *Geschichte und Reich Gottes* drew the dialogue into the third volume of *Systematic Theology* with an examination of Kingdom and history from the viewpoint of contemporary German theology. Two other books compared Tillich with Karl Rahner: K. Bümlein's *Mündige und schuldige Welt* and G. Schepers's *Schöpfung und allgemeine Sündigkeit;* although this comparison was in limited areas such as freedom and secular responsibility.

The history of this theological dialogue is not over. Our summary of its three stages suggests an analysis of why Roman Catholics have been consistently attracted to Tillich.

GROUNDS OF AFFINITY

THE RELIGIOUS CHARACTER OF CULTURE

The affinity between Roman Catholicism and Paul Tillich's thought is explained by their similarity in three areas: metaphysics, culture, and mysticism. These three words even describe the process, the chronological progress, in the exchange.

Like the Roman Catholics of neoscholastic sympathies, Tillich spoke of the late twelfth and thirteenth centuries as a time of theonomy (the interplay of infinite in finite), which he preferred over heteronomy or autonomy. When we look at sculpture from Chartres, we discern some inner life in the stone head or hand. There is a balance in the features of individuality and humanity; somehow the lines of the brow unlock a luminosity within the stone. The outline of the earlier, forceful heads of Greek athletes or Roman Caesars seem to etch limits and secularity. A sad expression plays across the face—neither hope nor heaven has been fully entertained by this man. And by the late fourteenth century, a certain undistinguished individuality stands out in statues. But at Chartres, among the two thousand carved figures, philosophers and art historians, experts and tourists have caught something of stone containing fire, of the struggle to express not only grace but graced human beings, the human being as more than symbol or posed portrait. This is what Tillich meant by theonomy, and theonomy's orchestration of philosophy and culture, above all else, destined this Protestant theologian to play a role in contemporary Roman Catholic theology.

Why has Tillich's thought had a lasting attraction for the Catholic mind? The answer lies not only with his employment of philosophy, for instance with a quasi identification of *analogia entis* with symbol. At a deeper level, we see that Tillich's theonomy is similar to the "sacramental" or "mediative" essence of Roman Catholicism. The Catholic spirit or thought form (the "Catholic substance") is, in fact, guilty of Barth's charge: it does intermingle the human and the divine, it admits degrees of participation, of ministerial cooperation, by the finite in the infinite's gracious presence. Tillich's dialectic—found in correlation, theonomy, revelation, and culture—appears as a comrade in the exposition of how the divine Logos is present in nature, mind, and revelation. Although Roman Catholicism, since the end of the baroque era, has frequently suppressed acculturation and diversity, it endures *au fond* as a cultural religious phenomenon: not a mental or verbal articulation of belief, but a tangle of tangible presences of grace. Let us turn now to the similarity between the Tillichian enterprise and the inner dynamic of Western Catholicism as exemplified by three areas: metaphysics, culture, and mysticism.

Metaphysics

A century ago Pope Leo XIII recalled the medieval thought forms of scholasticism to serve as the official structure of philosophy and theology in the Roman Catholic church. From the fourteenth century on, Catholicism had decided at several key moments to retain that particular version of Aristotelian and Platonic thought which had found its beginnings with Abelard and its climax with Aquinas. Both the explanation of a largely Semitic sacred Scripture and the life of Roman or Celtic church should best be expressed in this metaphysics. The first volume of Tillich's *Systematic Theology* presented a rich mastery of the history of Western ontology. That a Protestant theologian should map and employ ontology prior to Kant, that a German student of Heidegger should appreciate the conviction of Western Catholicism that ultimately metaphysics and not exegesis determines one's theology—this was a novelty within American Protestantism, where popular slogans had kept the Cinderella of philosophy out of view, preferring preaching and exegesis. Here was a Protestant thinker who, without always agreeing with him, took Aquinas seriously, and who understood that colors from Plato and Aristotle painted the logo for the history of Western Christian thought. Tillich explained how Protestantism with Böhme and Kant, Hegel and Troeltsch, had not lived exclusively in a pageant of biblical personages and words, but the churches of the Reformation, too, had been formed by a *Kairos* and its world. Tillich's comprehension of the structure of ontology in theology first drew Catholics to him, and to a comparison of him with Aquinas. Next, in Tillich's juxtaposition of thinkers—for instance, Kant with Scotus—Roman Catholics learned a lesson they desperately needed, namely that every metaphysics is a product of a historical time and that theology could not escape postmedieval, post-Kantian thought.

After World War II, pioneers like de Lubac and Rahner, Chenu and Congar, were mulling over the problem of theological method, brooding over the challenge of history and situation to scholasticism. Tillich's theological method of correlation helped not them but a younger generation of theologians to find a new direction; for when we look at the literature on theological method in the first half of this century, we notice its weakness in identifying the very nature of theology either with research into the thirteenth century or with Aristotelian logic where a syllogism whose major premise was a passage from Scripture produced a new, logical conclusion.

There must be more to theology than research and logic. Tillich's method of correlation, admitted in principle, consciously or unconsciously, by every great theologian, related revelation to a defined culture and situation. But to accept a new method for theology, two old problems had to be solved: history and subjectivity. We have already seen that Tillich joined with Catholic scholars in turning the lights of historical birth and death upon metaphysics. As a modern thinker whose mentor had been Schelling and whose colleague had been Adorno, Tillich gave allegiance to the primacy of the subject. In his world of the 1920s, where change and despair raged through Europe, both focus and anchor came from the creative self. Roman Catholicism was only beginning to ask the question whether it might be possible (without capitulating to agnosticism and relativism) to accept the stance of the modern world, which is that of the apprehending and creating subject rather than that of arranged objects. A first fulfillment of this shift in Roman Catholic theology from object to subject would come from Karl Rahner and others of the school of transcendental Thomism. What is intriguing about Tillich is that with him we have an explorer of faith and revelation whose commitment to the subjective and existential side of faith did not eliminate the objective dimension but endured in the correlation of Scripture and ontology, of revelation and culture.

Culture

Paul Tillich was a theologian of culture in several ways. His theological method correlated revelation with dimensions of culture. His self-description was that of someone standing on the boundary where both self and culture are revelatory, and his theology entered into and drew from politics, psychology, and art. Tillich was a spokesman for culture and its devotees, a first theological advocate for psychotherapy, an apologist for nonrepresentational art.

Tillich's use of *Kairos* to circumscribe a cultural period in history explains how the theologian and the artist share an analogy of style. Beneath ethics, art, law, politics, and ontology are the forms of a cultural epoch. Style is "a key to understanding the way in which a particular group or period encounters reality."[11] A cultural era is the context and the catalyst not only of poetry and economics but also of theology. Whatever we might think of revelation and its inspired evangelists and bishops, its human expression in liturgy or spirituality does not descend from heaven but expresses, incarnates, a cultural epoch. Every Christian tradition is a collage from past cultural periods as well as an attempt to interpret the realignment of newly occurring forms in faith and church. Tillich's dictum that culture is the form and religion the substance helped believers comprehend abstract or Byzantine art, and it helped theologians understand both the power and the limits of theology.

Each epoch is holy in its own way, and each culture offers to faith-reflection new forms of thought. Out of personal, national, and historical styles, a *Zeitgeist* determines the style of a period. Vision has a history. Theology consists, then, not simply in the creation of new ideas (a situation that ends up with systematic theology being indistinguishable from religious journalism) but in the discernment of "a point in the structure of man as man in which the finite and infinite meet or are within each other."[12]

Whatever we may think of Mexican Guadaloupe's pilgrims on their knees; the Latin language and baroque manners of the papacy; the Carthusian's solitude where books on icons or, today, on Zen are absorbed into the mystical flame, Roman Catholicism is a heavily cultural entity. Its drive toward incarnation and universality is nourished by the visual and structural, by art and liturgy. Tillich wisely saw that a universal, incarnational, essential dynamic (the "Catholic substance") was also the cause of Rome's woes and infidelities such as superstition, obstinacy, and antiquarianism. Like Tillich, however, Catholicism unfolds its campground tents and battens its faith within cultures. It is always searching for (or trying to reproduce) a theonomous time.

What Tillich called "theonomous," Catholic theologians like E. Schillebeeckx called "sacramental": not in the sense of a liturgical sacrament but as an event, a tangible object, a person in whom the holy and gracious have been present.[13] The sacramental is the union of the human and the divine; and Roman Catholicism is a vast cathedral or museum, workshop or gypsy caravan, of sacramentality. Varied mediations of the divine, Platonic degrees of light in darkness mix with violence and exploitation. The theonomous seeker will tolerate some failure for moments of a *Kairos* when feeling and intuition perceive the intersection of the human and the divine. Tillich wrote:

If any one, being impressed by the mosaics of Ravenna or the ceiling paintings of the Sistine Chapel, or by the portraits of the older Rembrandt, should be asked whether his experience was religious or cultural, he would find the answer difficult. Perhaps it would be correct to say that his experience was cultural as to form, and religious as to substance. . . . The highest stage of culture is attained where human existence, in complete and autonomous form, is comprehended in its finitude and in its quest after the Infinite.[14]

"In its finitude and in its quest after the Infinite"—here is the theonomous, the sacramental.

For Barth, however, this analogy between the human and the divine grounding of sacramentality in life/culture was the root of all that was awry, heretical, even evil in Western Catholicism. Although they might agree on creedal content, Catholicism and Barthianism had eventually to drift apart, and they did.

Mysticism

The word *mysticism* assumed in some Protestantism (in contrast with Roman Catholicism and Eastern Orthodoxy) a pejorative meaning. The mystic seemed culpable of an almost divine works-righteousness or of an evangelical freedom charismatically out of control. In other Christian churches, although the mystic's life suffered at times from being the domain of the monk or the private ascetic, mysticism was viewed as a grace-given intensification of prayer. It was a normal, if infrequent, flourishing of the gifts of the Spirit where intuition replaced pictorial prayer. Miracles and prophecies were rare and marginal; the authentic mystic wished to avoid them.

Today Tillich appears differently from the way he did in the 1940s and 1950s: no longer an existentialist in the vein of Jaspers or Sartre, but a nineteenth-century romantic-idealist systematician. We grasp that it was no coincidence that Tillich's first inspiration, Schelling, was also the romantic-idealist mentor for Roman Catholic intellectual life in Germany from 1798 to 1848. Although metaphysics, as with Aristotle, can stand at the end of a meticulous process of syllogistic thought, it can also be, as with Schelling, a theology of the unfolding of what has been intuited in the esoteric life of the Absolute. Tillich liked to cite the saying of Oetinger, a Swabian eschatological Pietist: "Corporality is the end of the ways of God."[15]

Mysticism is no more or less than the access to the holy in culture. Metaphysics and religion are both places for what Heidegger calls the task of our godforsaken age, "the piety of thinking."

In these ideas and thinkers we have the source for the friendly communion within our triad of metaphysics, culture, and mysticism. Tillich wrote that he stood within the mystical tradition. He favored the Augustinian-Franciscan tradition of immediacy for God's presence to human spirit. Tillich pointed out that his Lutheran background, as well as his appropriation of Rudolf Otto and his sympathy with the expressionism of artists such as Marc and Rilke, led him to reevaluate all mysticism and to accept a legitimate mystical side to the life of faith.[16]

In Tillich's thought one has an aesthetic system of theological reflection that was grounded in Western ontology and history but that was also drawn from insight searching the universe (culture, consciousness, nature, history, religion) for theonomy. Roman Catholics were not offended when Tillich said that he preferred the mysticism of Augustine and Bonaventura to the rationality of Aristotle and Aquinas. Western Catholicism has been conscious of a dialectic in its theology: between ontological system and intuitive experience. There is a tradition of pride that early theologians such as Origen and Augustine were both scholars and mystics. If Roman Catholicism glimpses the objects of faith incarnate in culture, often this glimpse comes through intuition.

There is a similarity between the theonomous and the mystical, for what is mysticism but the intuition of spirit into the world of material symbols and people grasped as theaters or liturgies of a transcendent and transcendental presence? Liturgy is the field of celebrating the mystical, while Christian life is the source of contemplation. Even in ethics and social action, one can see a confrontation with evil, injustice, and suffering that is mystical, that is, an experience that brings conversion to a deeper hope and effort for the Kingdom of God at work in the daily life of an individual or a community. Where art is the paradigm of religion, the mystical will be the stance of the life of the believer. The mystical dimension can be repressed but never long hidden, and in favorable times the mystical returns. When Tillich expressed his preference for Böhme and Augustine, when he said his Lutheran background led him to the mystical, he was interpreting the Lutheran tradition. Lutheranism strikes Roman Catholics as mystical, not a mysticism but a spirituality, for Luther's own theology was born of experience, insight, paradox, exaggeration.

This mystical dynamic behind Tillich's thought helps to explain why the dialogue between Roman Catholicism and this Protestant theologian will continue. In it Böhme speaks to Eckhart. Metaphysics was the original attraction for Catholic scholars, but the Tillich of a search for an immediate experience of the presence of Spirit has replaced philosophical congeniality. Speaking of Rilke's poetry, Tillich wrote: "Its profound psychoanalytic realism, the mystical fullness, the form charged with metaphysical import, all that made this poetry the expression of what in the concepts of my philosophy of religion I could seize only abstractly."[17] If metaphysics is the inner form of a culture, mystical insight gives the thinker and the believer access to the meaning of a *Kairos:* to the incarnational presence of the holy in the finite. So, the three areas of mutual interest are not isolated syndromes but the same interplay of consciousness and reality viewed differently.

AN INTERPRETATION UNDER THE GUIDANCE OF THE SPIRIT

Although books and articles still appear and dissertations are still composed, there has been a lessening of Roman Catholic interest in Tillich.[18] One reason for this is that Roman Catholics found a theologian similar to Tillich, someone who, beginning with the horizon of subjectivity and employing existential language, was intent upon dogmatic interpretation: this is Karl Rahner. Rahner had little by little evolved a coherent system based upon modern German philosophy and applicable to all areas of theology. Rahner achieved a subjectual approach to revelation and grace but, above all, this was done without the previously required dilution of traditional belief. Rahner has been able to shift the horizon of Christian and Roman Catholic theology from object to subject and to maintain the facticity of what revelation proclaims in a history of salvation. An interest in distinguishing, comparing, these two systematicians is only at its beginning.

SPIRITUAL PRESENCE IN HISTORICAL HUMANITY

Tillich was a pioneer in interpreting the potential holiness of modern painting to believers and agnostics. Cézanne, van Gogh, Klee battled with form and dreamed of colors to show the cosmic dread and ontic power in nature and human consciousness. Rather than being shocked by an absence of human figure or message, Tillich rejoiced over the emergence of expressionism in the first decades of this century. "The abyss of Being," he wrote," was to be evoked in lines, colors and plastic forms."[19]

Tillich and the Roman Catholic mind agree upon the search for the gestalt of grace in a salvation history that is more than a history of words and hermeneutics. Therefore, Tillich's theological method, if not his conclusions, will remain of interest to, even serve as a guide for, the Catholic mind.

To conclude, let us return to Tillich's dialectic, to the Protestant principle and the Catholic substance. Some of the world that Tillich found modern is declining: existentialism, demythologizing, European hegemony in the humanities, the dictates of the Enlightenment, Anglo-Saxon Protestantism. Nevertheless, the dialectic that we have been exploring has not been rendered obsolete. Like Schelling, Tillich wanted to overcome the duality that Christian orthodoxy and the Enlightenment posited. So he spoke in nondualistic, pantheist, mystical phrases.

For over two centuries the world of culture and intellect had taken sides either for or against the values of the Enlightenment, for or against faith in a presence that was more than nature and reason. American culture still exists partially within a framework of the *Aufklärung,* for scientific rationalism and political naturalism control government, university, public policy. The theological dialectic that the Enlightenment's continuing influence suggested was rational/supernatural or science/myth. Religion in its varied forms was to be reinterpreted and criticized in terms of naturalist, scientific presuppositions, and every form or group that resisted was to be set aside. Neither post-Kantian philosophy nor Christianity was contained or univocal enough to be absorbed by this enterprise. Academic theology prior to the 1960s presumed that the pattern from Enlightenment through liberalism to secularity (as the German theologians had forecast) would occur. This did not happen, and a gap opened between the form of academic theology and American church and religious life. Almost two decades later, the religious scene in the United States is in even greater disarray. Fundamentalist and charismatic churches grow, innumerable religious movements (mystical in one form or another) appear, Roman Catholicism appears to be simultaneously dynamic and suicidal. On the other hand, mainstream Protestant churches lose members, and the impact of university theology in public life is minimal.

Tillich never accepted secularity as the normal outcome of modern, Protestant Christianity, although he took the secular dimension seriously. He proposed to look for a theonomy of spiritual presence in every era and structure of history.

If one turns to Protestantism, the other form of the profanization of the ultimately sublime appears—secularization. It appears under the heading of the Protestant principle, which makes of the priest a layman, of the sacrament words, of the holy the secular. Protestantism . . . does not escape the tendency to dissolve the holy into the secular and to pave the way for a total secularization of Christian culture, whether it is by moralism, intellectualism, or nationalism.

The question then arises as to why a secular world broke away from this union in modern Western civilization. Was not and is not the power of the New Being in Christ strong enough to subject the creations of modern autonomous culture to the Logos, who became personal presence in the center of history? This quest, of course, should be a decisive motive in all contemporary theology, as it is in the present system.[20]

Tillich did not choose the combat of natural versus supernatural; like his German romantic-idealist teachers, he formulated a dialectic that would include two poles, each organically serving the other for growth.[21]

The Catholic substance is not the same as a particular tradition of Christianity; it is deeper and richer; it changes, yet it is the source of faithful Christianity's past, present, and future. At every moment, this substance can be buried or manipulated; and so a critical principle, equally grounded in the Spirit, comes not to repress but to bring forth. In Tillich's theology, the presence of God, apart from its linguistic expression, is neither myth nor divine cause, but a presence infinite and real. Despite his Protestant phrasing, there is no religion or revelation that is only words and faith. The Protestant principle is not the critique outside the substance, paring down grace or honing new terminologies, but a flame within the spiritual presence. In this dialectic, where even transcendental analysis and secularity must be criticized in light of both poles, a *Kairos* directs the expression of revelation. Theonomous encounters with the divine give hope in the midst of history's suffering.

As Tillich himself recognized, the 1960s were a new *Kairos.* For Tridentine Roman Catholicism, Vatican II was and remains a liberating and shattering experience. Catholic dialogue with Tillich has had several generations. What remains with us from this conversation is not the first interest but a slowly developing consensus about revelation, culture, theology, and theonomous presence. In the narrow and mediocre neoscholasticism of the century after 1848, the Catholic mind forgot its roots in Bernini and Urban VIII, in the Parisian architects and Louis IX. Perhaps Tillich's writings drew from the Catholic unconscious its own essential commitment to all aspects of culture, to epochal theonomy in social action as well as in art.

Now we are struck by how much the enterprise of Tillich resembles those of Rahner, Teilhard de Chardin, and South American theologians. All are exploring, first and foremost, the dialectic of God's reign and evil's tenaciousness in human history. Their interpretations of Spirit, presence, theonomy, sacrament, and grace are not the same. Nevertheless, there is a communion in the approach and the task, in the straining to see in the last years of this century the movement of galaxies of grace and culture around and through each other.

NOTES

1. Paul Tillich, *Systematic Theology,* vol. 3 (Chicago: University of Chicago Press, 1963), 245.
2. Paul Tillich, *The Interpretation of History* (New York: Charles Scribner's Sons, 1936), 24–25. In volume 3 of *Systematic Theology,* Tillich frequently criticized the heteronomy of Rome, even when Roman theology might serve his own theological view (p. 149). In this book, concluded in 1962, Tillich wondered if Pope John XXIII could bring the Council to the astonishing point of theological critique and creativity (p. 168).
3. Paul Tillich, "The Permanent Significance of the Catholic Church for Protestantism," *Protestant Digest* 3 (1941):23ff.
4. Karl Barth, *Church Dogmatics,* Part 1, book 2 (Edinburgh: T. and T. Clark, 1956), 143.
5. Gustave Weigel, "The Theological Significance of Paul Tillich," in *Paul Tillich and Catholic Thought,* ed. Thomas A. O'Meara and Clestin D. Weisser (Dubuque, Iowa: Priory Press, 1964), 4.
6. George Tavard, "Christ as the Answer to Existential Anguish," in ibid., 236.
7. Paul Tillich, "Appreciation," in ibid., 311.
8. Continuing the earlier dialogue with Aquinas are D. Keefe, *Thomism and the*

Ontological Theology of Paul Tillich: A Comparison of Systems (Leiden: Brill, 1971); T. Hall, *Paul Tillich's Appraisal of Saint Thomas's Teaching on the Act of Faith* (Rome: Angelicum, 1968); A. Milmore, *Paul Tillich's Idea of Sacrament* (Rome: Pontifica Studiorum Universitas A. S. Thoma Aq., 1976); J. P. O'Brien, *The Doctrine of Revelation in the Theology of Paul Tillich* (Rome: Angelicum, 1971).

9. There is a large number of dissertations on Tillich and Roman Catholic interests, for example, psychology, culture, worship.

10. *Etudes théologique et religieuses* 53 (1978); this includes a full bibliography of writings in French on and by Tillich.

11. Tillich, *Systematic Theology* 3:61.

12. Paul Tillich, *Perspectives on Nineteenth and Twentieth Century Protestant Theology*, ed. Carl E. Braaten (New York: Harper & Row, 1967), 231.

13. One could claim that the heart of Catholic theonomy is Aquinas's theology of grace in which "grace does not take away nature but brings it to fulfillment." (*Summa theologiae*, vol. 1, question 1). Tillich wrote: "The Spiritual Presence does not destroy the structure of the centered self which bears the dimension of spirit. Ecstasy does not negate structure." *Systematic Theology*, 3:114.

14. Tillich, *The Interpretation of History*, 49–50. At the end of his life, Tillich railed against "the enormous amount of superstitious devotion in some sections of the Catholic world, both Greek and Roman, in both national and social groups." *Systematic Theology* 3:379.

15. Tillich, *Systematic Theology* 3:201.

16. Paul Tillich, *My Search for Absolutes* (New York: Simon and Schuster, 1967), 25ff.

"The question which arises from the extended discussions about faith and mysticism in Protestant theology is that of the compatibility and, even more, the interdependence of the two. They are compatible only if the one is an element of the other; two attitudes toward the ultimate could not exist beside each other if the one were not given with the other. This is the case in spite of all antimystical tendencies in Protestantism; there is no faith (but only belief) without the Spirit's grasping the personal center of him who is in the state of faith, and this is a mystical experience, an experience of the presence of the infinite in the finite." (Tillich, *Systematic Theology* 3:242.)

J. R. Horne fails to make a case that Tillich rejected the mystical itself rather than the abuses of some mysticisms, in "Tillich's Rejection of Absolute Mysticism," *Journal of Religion* 58 (1978): 130ff. Perhaps new light on Tillich and spirituality will be thrown by a first Indian study on him: S. Paindadath, S.J., *Dynamics of Prayer* (Bangalore: Asian Trading Corporation, 1980) presents the entire Tillichian system from new perspectives of spirituality.

17. Tillich, *The Interpretation of History*, 17.

18. There have been a few dissertations comparing Rahner and Tillich in English; on the edge of this comparison is John Roberts, "Tillich's 'Two Types' and the Transcendental Method," *Journal of Religion* 55 (1975): 199ff.

19. Paul Tillich, *The Religious Situation*, trans. H. Richard Niebuhr (New York: Henry Holt and Co., 1932), 55.

20. Tillich, *Systematic Theology* 3:380.

21. Cf. M. Westphal, "Hegel, Tillich, and the Secular," *Journal of Religion* 52 (1972): 223ff.

17. The New Being and Christology

LANGDON GILKEY

THE CENTRALITY FOR TILLICH OF THE NEW BEING

There can be little question that the New Being represents the central category or symbol for Tillich's theology. Let us, therefore, begin our discussion with a brief look at the significance of the New Being for Tillich's thought as a whole: for his understanding of Christology, Christianity, religion, God, finitude, church, and culture. As disciplined reflection on the self-interpretation of the Christian community (1:15, 28),[1] theology for Tillich sets into intelligible, and thus contemporary philosophical (ontological) discourse, the message that is constitutive of that community. In the case of the Christian community, that message is the message of the appearance in history of the New Being, the "new state of things," the "new reality," in Jesus who is therefore the Christ (2:97). The New Being is thus, first of all, the fundamental principle explanatory of Tillich's Christology and so represents the determinative "Christian" aspect of his system.

That is to say, when one asks, "What does the Christ represent, do, or bring?" or alternatively, "How does he save, if at all?", Tillich's answer is that in him the New Being makes its appearance in historical existence. Jesus is said to be the Christ because he brings in the New Being, in "time and space" (2:98–99). For Tillich the central problem of life as modern persons experience it is the self-destruction and despair of estranged existence. Correspondingly, for him the central reality to which all religions dimly and often misguidedly witness, and the center of the Christian good news, is the appearance of a healing reality, the reality of reconciliation and reunion, that "in which the self-estrangement of our existence is overcome" (2:49). All religions presuppose the presence of this redemptive reality (2:80–86; 3:138–41, 147); Christianity is based on witness to its *explicit* and *definitive* appearance in a personal life, in Jesus who is therefore affirmed to be the Christ, the bearer of this new reality. Thus for Tillich the New Being as it is manifested in Jesus represents the decisive criterion for all *religions* (especially 1:137)—"that revelation is final if it has the power of negating itself without losing itself" (1:133; cf. also 2:150ff.); and it represents, amid the variety of Christian documents, theories, and themes, the "norm" for *present* Christian self-understanding, for a modern, relevant interpretation of Scripture and tradition alike with regard to their most fundamental message (1:47–52). Since the New Being is the creative principle for religions generally and for the Christian religion among the religions, the decisive manifestation of the New Being in Jesus—the description of which is the task of Christology—provides the basis for the most fundamental interpretation of religions and of Christianity.

Second, this message of the appearance of the New Being works its way, so to speak, "backwards" in the system as a whole to give definitive shape to Tillich's most fundamental conceptualizing of God, of the nature and purposes of Being Itself. Being Itself is known in experiencing the victory of being over nonbeing through the presence of courage; this "conquest," creative of culture and religions alike, in turn is the work of the creative, reuniting work of God as Spirit; finally, the divine Spirit is *itself* known as such (as *divine*) in the universal appearance of the New Being, the creative principle in all religions. Thus as the universal principle of religion, the New Being provides the entrance into the knowledge of Spirit, and through Spirit of God, of Being Itself; it is, as Tillich insists, in *religion* that reason finds its own ground.

It is characteristic of Tillich's thought that the positive is always experienced "over against" the negative, being "over against" some form of the "shock of nonbeing." (Note that while Tillich always holds that "the negative lives from the distortion of the positive" [2:86], still for him, as for Kierkegaard, the positive is *experienced* and *known* only through the experiencing of the negative [for example, 1:110].) The negative depends ontologically on the positive, the positive epistemologically on the negative. Thus the constitutive principle of actuality (Being Itself) is experienced in and through a redemptive principle of actuality, that which manifests itself in overcoming separation, alienation, and the threat of the conquest by nonbeing.

Being for Tillich is always existentially encountered; that is, it is known and so defined within the context of the experienced conquest or victory of being over the nonbeing inherent in *finitude;* in turn, the New Being is existentially known when the divine power and meaning is experienced as conquering the *estrangement* characteristic of existence. Now as finitude and estrangement are in our experience inextricably mixed, so is the experience of their conquest—that is, the experience of the ontological courage resulting from Being Itself and the experience of the salvific, unifying *healing* resulting from New Being. For both experiences presuppose and manifest the reuniting activity of God, the ground of being and meaning.

The experience of the ground of being presupposes, first, the shock of nonbeing and, second, the "religious" experience of reunion with the ground through the universal reuniting work of God. That reuniting and so redemptive principle within the divine is, of course, God as Spirit: "the most embracing, direct, and unrestricted symbol for the divine life" (1:249), and so "the ultimate unity of both power and meaning" (1:250). It is, therefore, through the work of the Spirit as the constitutive principle of the divine life that the uniting and reuniting of finitude with God in all aspects take place: in the actualizing of creatures, in the appearance of courage throughout finite existence, and in culminating fashion in the New Being.

To repeat, the category of the Spirit is the symbol for the divine forces of redemption and healing (1:251); correspondingly, the category of the New Being represents the *way* in which the creative and redemptive work of God is experienced in human history, that is, in religion generally, and especially in the Christian community. In this sense the long, detailed description of the Spiritual presence in the third volume of *Systematic Theology* represents the effects in continuing history of the New Being, as Tillich's Christology in the second volume represents the definitive manifestation of the redemptive Spirit of God in history. And even the content of the first volume on finitude and Being Itself is, as Tillich says, *known* through "revelation" and not autonomous reason; in other words, through the appearance of the New Being as the reuniting, reconciling work of the Spirit.

As the understanding of God moves *from* the knowledge of God as Spirit (via some form of the New Being) *to* the knowledge of God as Being Itself (*from* religious experience *to* philosophical theology), so the true understanding of *finitude* as real and good is made possible by the appearance of the New Being, by the experience of essential humanity under the conditions of existence. Tillich is convinced that the power of estrangement is such that in *estranged* finitude, the nonbeing inherent in all finitude in the end always conquers, smothers, dissolves the "being" also inherent in finitude. This is his continual and omnipresent polemic against secular humanism: Without the divine ground, finitude in every one of its aspects is unable to *be*, or better to maintain its being, over against nonbeing (1:192–201; 2:66–75).

Thus the universal presence of the courage to be reflects or manifests the universal reconciling work of God as the transcendent ground of that courage. Without that reuniting work, therefore, finitude would not experience itself as "real" or as "good"; the possibility of a creative finitude, in fact the possibility even of a *theory* of creative finitude, is thus dependent on the New Being. Without that, finitude would be experienced—as it is in the depths of despair—as unreal and vacant of possibility, as "illusion," and as "evil." Correspondingly, for Tillich, pantheism, as reflecting the experience *alone* of the divine ground, an experience without the courage of self-affirmation and so of finitude as "maya," represents a relatively imperfect apprehension of the New Being. In contrast, in the *full* appearance of the New Being, estranged existence is united with essence, essential humanity with our alienated condition. Here the destructive effects of nonbeing and the marks of estrangement are overcome. Finitude as *essential* and yet *actual* manifests itself; thus is it possible to speak of a real and a good finitude (and so of *creatio ex nihilo*). Systematically, the anthropological and cosmological implications of the symbol of creation, as is the knowledge of God as Being Itself, are dependent on the experience of the New Being in Jesus as the Christ.

Incidentally, it is here that, despite his well-known identification of the Creation and the Fall, Tillich presents a *fundamental* defense against the accusation of pantheism: Finitude, seen through the experience of the New Being, represents neither an essentially fallen humanity nor an unreal "maya"—nor is its reality identical with that of the divine ground; on the contrary, it is "finite freedom," real, good, and potentially creative and self-creative if also absolutely dependent.

The concept of the New Being, defined through its definitive appearance in Jesus as the Christ, likewise represents the central symbolic source for Tillich's view of religious symbols, for his ecclesiology, and for his interpretation of culture. The fundamental character of the New Being in Jesus (of essential humanity under the conditions of finite existence) is that here a finite actuality "negates itself without losing itself." That is, on the one hand, it points beyond itself by its criticism and ultimately by its sacrifice of itself ("by surrendering its finitude"), and yet on the other hand, in so doing, that finite actuality "becomes completely transparent to the mystery he reveals" (1:133, 147). In this, Jesus represents, first, the perfect medium or symbol of the unconditional, of the divine, of God, and so the paradigm for all other religious symbols as that finite actuality through which the infinite is fully *communicated* to others; second, the conquest at once of unbelief, of "hubris," and of self-destructive concupiscence and as a consequence, the religious-ethical model for all other individual finite entities (each of *us* is also called to become just such a "symbol"); and, third, the source of the picture of a *creative* community as well as of a creative individual and so for the definition of creative hope in historical life.

Spelled out in this fashion, the New Being in Jesus is the ground in Tillich's system for his well-known, and ecumenically helpful, ecclesiology: The church is "a true church" when it embodies both the Protestant principle (the principle of self-criticism and so of "pointing beyond itself" to the divine source of its grace and power) and the Catholic substance (principle of the presence, through the media of dependent revelation, of divine power, divine truth, and divine grace). As in the paradigm of the Incarnation itself, these two principles are polar, mutually dependent: Without Catholic substance (the presence of the divine in the church's symbols of Word, sacraments, and "saints"), the Protestant principle is empty, unredeemed, and unredeeming—and the church becomes vulnerable to other, alien "spirits"; without Protestant principle, the Catholic substance is demonic, a medium that claims ultimacy for itself and becomes heteronomous and destructive to cultural life.

The church is the church, therefore it "continues the incarnation" (to use an old phrase). That is, it first points beyond itself to its message of judgment on itself and its world and of grace to that world—the message about the appearance of the New Being in Jesus—and *through* that message to God as Spirit, as power united to meaning; and, second, it communicates *through* this self-negation and this affirmation of grace the divine creative power to the world, to culture in all its phases. The church thus points beyond itself to God as ground and to the Kingdom as end; essentially, if latently, it represents on the pattern of its Lord the communal "symbol" communicating the divine life to culture, the potential center for a "religious substance" of culture that could be creative and not demonic; that is, a theonomous culture.

As these last remarks indicate, for Tillich, ecclesiology interpreted through the category of the New Being shades quickly into a theological understanding of culture. As he notes, church and cultural world are separated only in estrangement (for him, the doctrine of the Two Kingdoms is an *error* resulting from the Fall, not a *truth* illuminating the Fall's consequences); eschatologically, they both are fulfilled in becoming one in the Kingdom. More specifically, as the category of a real and good finitude (a finitude united to the divine ground and yet creative rather than destructive in and through its own finite powers) resulted from the experience of the New Being, so the concept of a "theonomous culture" has its origin there as well.

A developed autonomous culture is a culture cut off from participating in its ground; like the church without Catholic substance, it is empty and subject to other, alien, destroying spirits. As autonomous, such a culture has ceased to be a "symbol" of the divine ground, of unconditional meaning, and thus will it die. A heteronomous culture is one where the necessary unconditional base of the culture, its "religious substance," has *itself* become absolute and beyond criticism (a *cultural* Catholic substance without Protestant principle); in other words, in such a culture, the cultural community has refused to "negate its finitude," to sacrifice itself, to point beyond itself—and so it too will die, ultimately of internal or external conflict.

As finite beings cannot escape estrangement and be without the divine ground, so cultures, teetering between demonic hubris and destructive emptiness—and history with them—vacillate between autonomy and heteronomy, longing for "theonomy." Theonomy, therefore, represents a culture at once autonomously creative and yet dependent upon, and so affirmative of, its unconditional ground, its religious substance: "autonomous reason united with its own depth" (1:89). Here, as Tillich notes (1:147–48), a culture in touch with and expressive of the divine ground possesses "a spiritual substance to all forms of its rational creativity" (1:147). But equally, a theonomous culture, through "the self-sacrifice of the finite medium, keeps heteronomous reason from establishing itself against rational autonomy" (1:148). Thus as the church qua Catholic substance and Protestant principle represents the latent center for the new theonomy (1:148), so a *culture* expressive of its religious substance and yet prophetically self-critical of its own absolutes, represents the cultural environment for theonomy and for a creative church. Both together culminate in the Kingdom, the symbol of historical fulfillment, of a "complete theonomy" (1:54).

THEOLOGICAL IMPLICATIONS OF TILLICH'S POSITION

The purpose of this section has been to indicate the centrality of the concept of the New Being for the entire scope of Tillich's theology. We have sought to show not only that his view of estrangement and of Christology is derived from this category, but also that the particular shape of his conceptions of Being Itself and so of God, of finitude and so of human being, of religions generally, and finally of ecclesiology, of culture, and of history and its hopes, are formed by this category as it is defined in and through his Christology. Several important implications follow if this presentation is correct.

First, Tillich's is a *Christomorphic* theology.[2] While by no means does awareness or cognizance of God stem for Tillich from Christian revelation alone (revelation and the presence of the New

Being are *universal*), nevertheless for his theology the revelation of God in Christ gives to every significant theological symbol its basic shape and definition. To be sure, the whole, from beginning to end, is set within philosophical/ontological categories; nevertheless, knowledge of God, and so *all* theological symbolism—as Tillich repeatedly insists—comes through revelation, and so, for the Christian community and theologian, through the decisive revelatory appearance of the New Being in Jesus who is the Christ. (Many have wrongly concluded that *because* his is a philosophical theology, *therefore* revelation is deemphasized, if not negated.)

Second, as the answer to estrangement—estrangement in turn being expressed in the language of "halfway myth"—the New Being is itself to be spoken of in "mythical" rather than in strictly ontological terms, though its categories (as with estrangement) are ontological. Although Christology, says Tillich, must be "deliteralized," it cannot be "demythologized" (2:29, 152). For the appearance of the New Being cannot, any more than the Fall can, be deduced from the universal structures of being as these are experienced in ordinary existence. Thus is the appearance of the New Being "paradoxical" (against all opinions); thus is it a subject of reception, of faith, and of believing witness; thus does Tillich speak "mythologically" of "event," of "bringing," of "appearance," of the "coming of the new reality"—as well as of the traditional mythological symbols of the Messiah, Son of Man, Mediator, Logos.

There is much more mythical, as well as ontological, symbolic language in Tillich than is usually recognized. In fact, one might argue that the fundamental theological symbols (Fall and New Being, estrangement and grace, and "event" of actual revelation) are linguistically "halfway myths" or "mythological symbols" that are in turn interpreted *symbolically* by means of the epistemologically secondary categories of ontology, of being, of finitude, and of the polarities. After all, for Tillich, all fundamental ontology is begun and completed via some form of religious ecstasy, when reason comes in touch negatively and then positively with its own ground.

Third, it has for some time been recognized that Tillich's theological system represents a "dynamic" ontology, an ontology in which process and becoming are the central aspects of being, and so in which historical passage, rather than timeless forms or static being, constitutes the most fundamental notion. This point can be argued in a number of ways: dynamic life, and not rest, is the basic symbol for God; the Spirit is in turn more fundamental than is Logos, and so on.

If correct, our interpretation makes much the same point. As "mythical," the categories of estrangement and of New Being are *historical* as well as ontological; neither one is an aspect of the timeless (Logos) structure of things; rather they "happen," although universally, and thus include a temporal element as well as form or structure, human and divine, the one being an "irrational" Fall, the other an "event" "against all historical opinions." It is *from* these fundamental events that Tillich derives ontological knowledge and the timeless structures of being. As he repeatedly insists, and as we have argued, *valid* or *fulfilled* ontology or philosophy is derived from religious apprehension, cultural or theological (though ontology is necessary to deliteralize the latter). Logos, therefore, has a *Kairos* dependent on revelation. The knowledge of the structures of finitude, of existence, of authentic humanity and community, of history and of God, have their origin in some aspect of universal revelation and achieve their most valid form in an ontological theology based thereon.

Tillich's earlier political works were centered on history and the relation of religion to history, and his earliest interpretation of Christianity viewed Jesus as "the center of history." Although much of his thought seems to carry us beyond the finite to its timeless and infinite ground, the corpus of his theology taken together points to an understanding of truth and of being alike as *historical*, to a consequent interpretation of being as dynamic and in process (life), and to a view of a completed philosophical ontology as existentially and religiously grounded (philosophical analysis plus religious answers) through participation in revelatory events as well as in the rigors of philosophical analysis of structures.

Theological reason is philosophical and religious at once; it is *reason in touch with its own ground*, "theonomous" reason or "ontological" reason. Thus it is an ontological reason that combines reflection and participation, analysis and ecstasy. And our present point is that this religious element relates itself to religious events and uses the language of myth to interpret what is there uncovered. Theological or ontological reason (reason in touch with its own ground), uncovers the universal structures of finite actuality *because* it also witnesses to events revelatory of the ground and meaning of those structures. It is at once *historical* (as Christian, Christomorphic) and *ontological* (as cultural, philosophical).

THREE ISSUES IN TILLICH'S CHRISTOLOGY

It is now time explicitly to discuss Tillich's Christology. I shall deal only with three somewhat puzzling and controversial issues: first, his reinterpretation of the Incarnation; second, the question of the historical Jesus; and third, the relation, for Tillich, between the particularity of the Christological event and the claim—necessary for any Christian theology and especially for any philosophical theology (1:137)—to universal relevance or significance; that is, the question of universality, a question that concerns at once the relation of theology to philosophy and of Christian witness to other religions.

REINTERPRETATION OF THE INCARNATION

As he is well aware, Tillich offers a radical reinterpretation of the Incarnation. That this interpretation is *not* a humanistic one is beyond question. Human powers are for him helpless, caught in estrangement, condemned to self-destruction and despair. It is through the divine "activity" alone, the appearance of the New Being, that rescue appears, that an answer—existential or religious in life, theoretical in philosophy or theology—to the question of existence (estrangement) appears; and, as we have pointed out, that insight into the essential nature of finitude itself becomes possible.

For Tillich, therefore, the appearance of the New Being, the new reality of salvation, the Incarnation in that sense, is not at all to be interpreted as an achievement of human powers or of history, or even as representing merely a new presentation or uncovering of human possibilities. Rather, the central message is that *God* has "acted" for human salvation, has established a new reality in which we may now participate, and that on the basis alone of that divine act, new possibilities for us and for our powers are opened up.

Thus Tillich's reinterpretation of the Incarnation represents a reinterpretation of *how* God saves, not a denial *that* it is God who saves. In that sense the "myth" of the divine "descent" and the philosophical category of the divine nature, which for Tillich to be sure must be deliteralized, are by no means rejected, denied, or even removed from his theology. Rather they are reinterpreted or represented by the central assertions, first, of the divine event on which and through which the New Being appears ("God is the subject, not the object, of mediation and salvation" [2:93]) and, second, by the presence of the divine Spirit as constitutive of the New Being definitively present in Jesus as the Christ (3:144ff.).

Tillich begins his reinterpretation by a criticism of the classical theology of incarnation. In that traditional theology, incarnation has been understood, or misunderstood, as the juxtaposition in Jesus the Christ of two contrary, even contradictory, opposites: eternity and the temporal, the changeless and the changing, the immortal and the mortal, God and a man. Tillich regards this interpretation, if taken literally, as "pagan": The conception of God becoming man is an inheritance from pagan mythology; the conception of a divine nature uniting with a human nature is an inheritance from pagan philosophy. Both presuppose polytheism, the assumption of the finitude of God, for only a finite entity can become or have "a nature" to which it belongs. Thus both are nonsensical if God is, as in Christian thought, the source and ground of finitude; God cannot will to become a man without ceasing to be God (for Barth, of course, this is precisely the wonder of the divine freedom).

The "paradox" of Christology is, therefore, not the paradox of God becoming a man, or of the divine and the human united in one. Rather it is the paradox of the unexpected, of the seemingly impossible, granted human, estrangement, of the radically new in the alienated history of human existence. It is, as noted, a *historical* paradox contrary to historical experience and to our own existential situation, not an *ontological* or a *metaphysical* paradox contrary to the logic of philosophical reasoning.

This unexpected, paradoxical reality, which is radically new, is that essential humanity, what we really are, the structure of authentic humanity, and so what we ought to be ("human possibility"), has in Jesus appeared in actuality, in historical life, and so (most important of all) under the conditions of finitude and of the estrangement of finitude. This is the New Being, the new creature: essential humanity not, as hitherto, merely as an unreachable, impossible possibility, but as actuality, as a historical person, "under the conditions of existence." Here, therefore, the powers of existence—of bondage, of the structures of destruction, of the old age—are broken. Essential humanity, and therefore humanity in unbroken relation to God, has appeared as actuality, and therefore for us as actual, though fragmentary, possibility. "The paradox of the Christian message is that in *one* personal life essential manhood has appeared under the conditions of existence without being conquered by them" (2:94).

Tillich interprets the most important Christological symbols of the New Testament—Son of man, Son of God, Messiah, and Logos —in the light of this reconception. For him, each points to the appearance of the new and yet essential humanity, or humanity in intrinsic relation to God, a humanity therefore that ushers in the new age of salvation.

As we have noted, this unique, transformative, and decisive event, the appearance in fullness of the New Being, is for Tillich the work alone of God: it is a divine event whose subject is God as Spirit (3:144ff.). This unprecedented unity with God that establishes the New Being is for him, therefore, not the work of a man called Jesus; no human, however good, could for Tillich break the power of existence and establish this new reality, *essential* humanity *within* existence. For this reason, despite the fact that seemingly the "divine" nature (God) of orthodox Christology has been replaced by "essential humanity" in Tillich's formula (a "Monophysite" Christology in which Jesus the Christ is essential humanity within existence, not a divine nature united to a human nature), this view is neither humanistic nor adoptionist. Here the category of divine nature is replaced by the category of the reconciling and reuniting, redemptive activity of God that establishes the New Being through the presence of the divine spirit, uniting in one person essential humanity with the conditions of existence. Jesus, of course, as finite freedom, must accept this, his unique destiny, and through his own act of self-constitution embody and reembody the New Being in his person, his lifestyle, his teachings, his deeds, his passion, and his death. Nevertheless, the whole event of his appearance, life, death, and resurrection is the work primarily of God as Spirit.

The similarity in structure, though not in language or category, to Schleiermacher's Christology, is apparent: Perfect God-consciousness is here replaced by New Being and "unbroken unity with God." Nevertheless, in both cases there is no supernatural, transhuman nature present in Jesus; instead it is through the work and presence of the divine Spirit that the perfection of the human appears in history.

As the historical person who brings in the new reality—essential humanity within existence—Jesus is for Tillich wholly human. Since there is no supernatural nature, there is here no qualification of his humanity: He is simply and solely a human being ("Jesus") but one in this unique role, embodying throughout his being this new redemptive reality. One notes the modern emphasis on the humanity of Jesus, and the Protestant emphasis (perhaps the one consistent note in all Protestantism) that redemption (even in the case of Jesus) represents the *fulfillment,* and not the *transcendence,* of the human. Tillich underlines both of these points through his critique of the usual designation *Jesus Christ.* This usual "name," he says, sounds like a proper name, one with a human given name and a divine family or surname. Thus *Jesus Christ* expresses and implies not only a two-natures theology, it tends also to compromise the reality of the human—for inevitably the divine, as constituting the person, overshadows and smothers the human. Preferable for Tillich is the title "Jesus *who is* the Christ," that is, the human person who has this role or function, namely to bring in the new reality, the man therefore who is the Messiah or, "Jesus *as* the Christ."

THE ISSUE OF THE HISTORICAL JESUS

As the implications of our remarks to date indicate, the *actuality* of the historical person "Jesus" is crucial to Tillich. To deny that actuality, to deny that essential humanity entered existence, submitted to its conditions (for example, finitude and the categories of finitude: space, time, substance, and causality—the polarities; and all the anxiety, suffering, doubt, and weakness implied in them), is to deny Tillich's whole point, the crux of the Gospel message. If this paradox is not real, if no essential humanity actually entered existence, then nothing ultimately significant or new has happened, the New Being remains merely a hope, religion merely a quest—and there *is* no message, no faith, and no hope (2:98). The validity of the message (that the New Being has appeared in history) therefore implies, on the one hand, a divine event in which essential humanity entered historical existence in an actual person in space and time (in Tillich's terms, the "miracle" side of an originating revelatory event). And it implies, on the other hand, the reception of that event; that is, understanding of it, acknowledgment of it, witness to it, and commitment in relation to it by the nascent community of disciples (the "ecstasy" side of an event of revelation).

It is important to emphasize the crucial importance for Tillich's Christology of *both* of these sides of the revelatory event: the objective event, the actual personal life denoted by the name Jesus; as well as the responding witness. The reason is that Tillich has frequently been interpreted as regarding that actual life as irrelevant to faith, as not only unknowable by us but even more as unimportant in comparison with the picture of the New Being in the Gospel records, a picture clearly created by the responding witness. This misinterpretation has probably mainly been caused by Tillich's rather novel view of the roles of historical inquiry and faith in relation to this actual, personal existence.

The correct question initially to ask, if we are to understand Tillich on the issue of the role in Christology of historical inquiry, is not "Is there for Tillich a historical Jesus?"—for he asserts unequivocally there was an actual, historical person, Jesus, who was said to be the Christ. The real question is "How do or can *we*, in the twentieth century, *relate* to this person or to this 'fact' who was said to be the Christ? How can we know of him, or be in any way certain of him, of the actual character of his life, teachings, destiny, and so on—if, as we agree, his actuality is essential to faith?" Premodern (pre-Enlightenment) Christians would have answered these questions by appeal to the infallible authority of the New Testament accounts, or of the church, or both. In contrast, most post-Enlightenment Christians would probably say, "We can be sure of him only through historical inquiry, that same inquiry by which *any* historical fact is known if it is to be known at all." It is this last reply that Tillich finds inadequate and proceeds to refute.

Tillich first distinguishes two different meanings, or referents, to the phrase *the historical Jesus*. The first referent is the actual, living person or individual life ("Jesus") who was received as the Christ, the person who was the referent of the witness of the Disciples or Apostles, the historical figure "behind" the records of the New Testament; as noted, *this* referent Tillich affirms unequivocally. The second referent is the figure or picture reconstructed *by* historical inquiry out of and on the basis of the data present in the scant sources available to us today, "what we can know about him through scientific inquiry." Usually these two referents are fused into one: "What we can be sure of about Jesus is what historical inquiry can tell us about him." Tillich, on the contrary, wishes radically to distinguish the living person *behind* the texts from the historian's reconstruction *out of* the text. For him the first is crucial for the validity of the Christian message; the second, however, is of only preliminary, scholarly interest, and in no way is it essential to the message or to faith.

Let us begin with the second referent, the historical Jesus reconstructed by historical inquiry. Why is the historical person Jesus in this sense only of preliminary, scholarly concern? Because, says Tillich, no certainty or stability is ever possible here. Our records represent the believing witness of his followers and so they portray Jesus *as* the Christ; as is appropriate, they give us their *reception* of this event, not the event itself independent of their reception and witness. Thus the reconstruction of the event *independent* of the believing witness is a hypothetical reconstruction, one necessarily created anew by each historian on the basis of his or her own theory with regard to the data. Thus, like all historical reconstructions from the data, it is and can be only "more or less probable"; it will be, as are all hypotheses, subject to critique because of new data, new perspectives, new theories. The shape, size, and certainty of this historical picture will continually shift, and every one adopted at this or that time is in principle disprovable.

Historical reason, in other words, is "technical reason"; it can only achieve more or less probability; it is always in principle falsifiable—hence it can never be the vehicle of either certainty or of ultimate concern, of the personal, existential (participating) sort of knowing essential to religion. As Tillich frequently remarked, "I do not wish the telephone to ring and to hear from my New Testament colleagues: 'Paulus, our researchers have now finally removed the object of your ultimate concern; we cannot find your Jesus anywhere.' " For him, that phone call represented an obvious confusion of categories, a misunderstanding of different facets of reason, technical and ontological/participating reason, and of the relation of each of these to religion. It represented the mistaken claim of autonomous, technical reason to be able to legislate through its knowledge of "the facts and their relations" for every realm of life: for morals, art, politics, philosophy, and religion—in the end, a false and dangerous claim because it dissolves all rational bases for ultimate concern and thus prepares the way for a new heteronomy.

If we cannot know Jesus, or know of him, through historical inquiry, then how can we be assured of knowing Jesus through "faith"? Can our faith be an authority for certainty about the historical details of his life contained in the Gospels? Can we say, "I believe he is the Christ; therefore I know he lived, he said such-and-such and did so-and-so"? Or can we say, "In the New Testament the Word of God has been heard; therefore I know in the acknowledgment and obedience of faith that its historical account of Jesus' life and death is valid"?

For Tillich these bases of certainty represent the reverse confusion. Here ultimate concern or belief attempts to legislate as an authority in the realm of historical fact and in the place of historical inquiry; religious knowing makes the claim to impart scientific information. Such a confusion represents heteronomy, the restrictive control or determination of autonomous reason about the facts and their relations by the claims of religious knowledge; a claim that, when successful, is infinitely dangerous and when unsuccessful, makes religion seem a game for blind fools. Religious knowledge of the *ground* of fact cannot be derived from, nor legislate for, scientific reason about facts and their interrelations. The essence of Tillich's answer, therefore, is the attempt to steer between these two opposite, but interrelated, confusions.

Faith, says Tillich, can be guaranteed or supported neither by historical knowledge nor by heteronomous belief. It can be guaranteed alone by *itself*, by its own experience or awareness of its object and its source or ground; the new reality or New Being. The basis for *my* faith has been the appearance of that New Being in my experience; the presence of faith is the direct result, the experiencing in consciousness, of the new reality in my existence—and therefore *in* existence. No historical uncertainty, no skepticism, can question this appearance of the New Being in existence —for it characterizes *my existence*. Thus to participate in this reality is already to know the appearance of the New Being, and it is to know that it entered and transformed *a* historical existence. Behind my participation in the New Being, therefore, stands as its necessary source and ground a definitive participation in and through another historical existence, when essential humanity entered the conditions of existence and was not conquered by them. No hope by enthusiastic persons caught in existence, no picture imagined by the Disciples or believed by them could exert this transformative power, the power of a new reality—of which I am in my own awareness certain. Thus through participation, I can know there is and was a historical reality, an actual life embodying the New Being.

Once again—as in the appearance of courage and the knowledge of God—Tillich, like Schleiermacher, argues from the experience of a New Being, and from the impossibility of human self-salvation, to a crucial theological conclusion, in this case the reality of a "historical" embodiment of that same New Being. *If* humans cannot extricate themselves from self-destruction, and *if* they experience such rescue, *then* the reality of the divine, the active presence of the divine, or in this case the appearance of divine redemption in and through a personal life, follows.

It is, moreover, not the case that we can, through our own experience of the New Being, be certain only *that* a historical embodiment has been actual. For this experience of the New Being has been mediated to us through the picture of Jesus in the New Testament and through the *whole* picture (the Johannine and Pauline, as well as synoptic, writings). The picture has functioned, therefore, as a *true* medium or symbol of the originating event, communicating the latter's power and meaning to us. There thus must be, reasons Tillich, a parallel, an analogy, between the picture as a true symbol and the historical reality that evoked it, that was its historical ground.

In this intriguing argument, one notes that Tillich (again like Schleiermacher) emphasizes the essential role of the community as the bearer of the picture and, even more, as the locus of the divine

Spirit communicating through the picture the reality of the New Being to each succeeding generation. It is also evident that Tillich has sought to rescue the *religious* validity and power of the whole New Testament, including the Johannine and Pauline writings; for it has been this total picture that has communicated the New Being. As Tillich perceptively remarks, only when the historical Jesus of scientific inquiry (the first referent) becomes crucial for faith, do the synoptic Gospels have more theological and spiritual importance than the rest—and this is to misunderstand them, for as Gospels, they too are witnesses to Jesus as the Christ.

The picture of Jesus as the Christ in the New Testament is thus the definitive picture of the New Being, the criterion or norm, as we have noted, of Christian self-understanding, of religions generally and, expanded out into ecclesiology and theonomy, of Tillich's conceptions of church, culture, and interrelations. It is a picture made up of two interwoven polarities. First, there is the polarity of essential humanity on the one hand and the conditions of existence on the other (the categories, the polarities, and the marks of estrangement). Jesus participates fully in the former (finitude), and despite that participation, conquers the latter (estrangement). Second, there is the polarity of unbroken unity with God ("God-manhood") on the one hand and self-surrender and self-sacrifice on the other.

For Tillich, this profound and moving picture and its interwoven themes can be summed up in the two symbols that dominate that picture; namely, the cross (total participation in existence and self-surrender) and the Resurrection (essential humanity and unbroken unity with God, the ground of power and meaning). Since Tillich's account of the further elements of this picture and the relation of those elements to the major events of Jesus' life as portrayed in that picture, is straightforward, we shall cease our description at this point and move to our final theme.

RELIGIOUS PARTICULARITY AND UNIVERSAL TRUTH

One of the most intriguing notions connected with Tillich's Christology is his resolution, or implied resolution, of the problem of universality. As the case of Lessing shows, this question represents for Christian theology an old and extremely troubling issue: How can a particular religion, especially one based on a particular historical event, claim to embody a universal truth and so to be of universal relevance? We should note that the question raised by the Christian claim to universal relevance "offends" two quite different alternative claimants to universality: on the one hand philosophy and on the other hand particular non-Christian religions. We shall, therefore, discuss Tillich's understanding of universality in relation both to philosophy and to other religions.

How is universal thinking and, as a consequence, a knowledge of universal truth, possible for us? The most obvious answer is of course "through science," which abstracts from the particularity not only of the inquiring *subject* but also of the various *objects* of any scientific inquiry. Thus appears the "universal language of science," a language apparently usable by members of any cultural or religious community. On the other hand, scientists from another culture, or religious community, must be "converted" to the general world view and epistemology presupposed by science before they can speak this universal language. By definition, this universal language of science deals with no issues of ultimate concern. It excludes the questions of ontology; of value or ends; of meaning, which science itself presupposes and with which any wider cultural life must perforce deal. If science seeks to deal with these questions, it can do so only if the scientist in fact takes on the role of philosopher or theologian.

We must, therefore, look beyond science to some other answer, and the answer obviously next in line is philosophy. Is it not the case that by abstracting from the particularity of the thinking subject (by its objectivity and "distance"), and by seeking for the universal structures of being (not for particular entities within being), philosophy has universal truth and relevance as its intentional object? It need not be stressed how committed Tillich himself is to this philosophical intentionality, how respectful he is of philosophy's claims to "know the universal structures of being," and how he views religious awareness or knowledge as *completed* only through the use of philosophical thinking. Nevertheless, for him the final path to universality (even by means of philosophy) is *religious* and not philosophical (and certainly not scientific). Because this claim—that through the religious the universal is apprehended—is seemingly so bizarre in the modern world, it is deeply interesting and deserves explication.

For Tillich, while all philosophical thought aims at universality, it remains in fact relative to its cultural base and thus itself incurably particular. Philosophy is the deepest and most universal expression of the culture's substance, its "religious substance"; that is, the particular and yet creative response of that culture to the manifestation of Being as reality, as truth, and as value. This represents the "mystical a priori" of all philosophy from which no philosophy can escape. Thus does "Logos" have a *Kairos,* a "fate";[3] it is subject to the deepest presuppositions of its time and place, of its cultural epoch; and it cannot by the powers of abstraction transcend that particular base.

Aristotle represents the spiritual substance of Hellenic culture; Hegel, the spiritual substance of modern European culture; Whitehead, the substance of recent scientific and democratic culture. Each surveys the universal structures of being from the perspective of a particular cultural point of view or epoch. If the cultural particularity is removed from such philosophical abstractions, the assumptions of Hellenism from Aristotle, of modern European culture from Hegel, of early twentieth-century science and liberal democracy from Whitehead, nothing is left.

Even the process of abstraction, therefore, retains the marks of finitude (the particularity of time and space) and, since philosophy is confident it *can* become universal knowledge, more often than not these marks are compounded with the marks of estrangement (the self-elevating claim to an unconditional knowledge). Philosophy in existence is in effect *doubly* particular, once as finite and then a second time as claiming not to be.[4] Thus for Tillich, whatever great value for cultural and religious life the philosophical enterprise may have, and despite its intentionality, philosophy is not the path to the universal any more than it can, unaided, achieve the knowledge that is its own fulfillment, namely, the knowledge of Being Itself.

For these reasons (note they represent *reasons* and not merely an arbitrary adherence to a religious tradition) Tillich offers a *religious* path or way to the universal, or better, *toward* the universal— which, for Tillich, as for Kierkegaard, is about as far as a finite creature can go. This "path" involves the *recognition* of the finitude and so the relativity of one's own truth (scientific, social, philosophical, or religious), the *negation* of the particularity, or the elements expressive of that particularity, and so the pointing *beyond* that particularity (beyond my truth or our truth) to the unconditional expressed in it. Since the attempt to transcend particularity through the abstractions of thought is regarded as futile (though useful for other purposes), the transcendence of particularity is here achieved existentially, personally, or subjectively, by the stance, the mode of existing and thinking of the thinker himself or herself.

Thus is this an *existential* resolution. It is a *religious* resolution since it points beyond the finite, beyond all rational elucidation or expression or categorization to the unconditional, to God, and because such a pointing, presupposing union with the divine ground, presumes religious ecstasy, the reception of revelation. For Tillich, the universal lies there, in the unconditional, in God; that is his religious affirmation. We in turn can become "symbols" or "media" of that universality only as we point beyond ourselves, beyond our thoughts, our systems, our doctrines, to *their* infinite and transcendent referent, to God. But the medium of unconditional truth, the system of thought, of doctrines, of scientific knowledge, cannot without demonic distortion or absurdity claim to be that to which it points.

As Tillich recognizes (1:135–37, 150–53), the model of the *true symbol* (and so of the New Being) that "negates itself without losing itself" (1:133), and in so doing points beyond itself and communicates the transcendent; that is to say the picture of Jesus as the Christ lies back of this novel and suggestive conception of the path to universality. The revelation in Jesus as the Christ is a universal (and so final) revelation, of universal significance (1:133–37; 2:150ff.); on its pattern, then, human being, thinking, and acting can approach universality.

For Tillich this view answers, or suggests answers, to the issue of universality vis à vis both philosophy and other religions. For philosophy its own culture, specifically the religious substance of that culture, is "the medium" through which being, truth, and good are manifested, and each philosophical viewpoint represents one specific form of that general medium. As noted, with regard to philosophy as such, the question of the *sacrifice* of the medium (which is the basic question of finality and universality, [1:133]), that is, the sacrifice of the elements of that culture's particularity, is an unresolvable one—except as philosophy become itself religious or theonomous. Only if philosophy participates in the religious, if its final revelation is located in the New Being, and so if it can point beyond itself, can it transcend its particularity in the universal, can it become "theonomous" philosophy embodying ontological reason. To achieve union with its own ground, in other words, means, as it does for all true media, its sacrifice of its own particularity and of its claims to possess universality. It means that it must point beyond its own systematic conclusions in order to be transparent to the universal, to the unconditional. As Tillich has insisted from the start, only in religious philosophy ("theology"— if the latter understands itself aright) can philosophy itself be fulfilled (1:150).

With regard to the question of universality vis à vis other religions, Tillich was also only suggestive; this was a subject he wished further to explore but for which he knew he had "no time." As noted, Tillich regarded the New Being in Jesus as the paradigm for the quest of culture and religion alike for universality. As Jesus "sacrificed" or "negated" all that was particular about himself— even "himself as Jesus" (1:136–37); his lifestyle, teachings, deeds —and pointed beyond even himself, so Christianity as a religion must sacrifice and negate its particularities as a religion—doctrines, laws, rights, polity—and point beyond itself to the New Being, to God as Spirit. Indeed, it must point beyond even those theological expressions of New Being and of God as Spirit (1:136–37).

Tillich has the greatest confidence (again on the model of Jesus as the Christ) that these concrete and particular media are not lost or dissolved in that sort of sacrifice; rather, that sacrifice is of the very *essence* of any final revelation (1:148). (One might remark that "the Church" has never agreed with this, though many Christians have.)

In any case, this sacrifice of all elements of particularity, while retaining "unbroken unity with the ground," represents the path, and the only path, to universality, to a transcendence of particular religious traditions that results neither in a secular universality that is culturally particular nor in a new religion made out of transcended elements of old religions. Only if each tradition negates itself in pointing beyond itself can the particularity of religion, and especially the estrangement embodied in that particularity, be, not dissolved or removed, but "overcome." In this, for Tillich, Christianity shows its finality, because its own center in Jesus who is the Christ represents precisely this process of self-negation and yet of unity with the transcendent ground.[5]

NOTES

1. Citations in this chapter refer almost entirely to Paul Tillich, *Systematic Theology* (Chicago: University of Chicago Press, vol. 1, 1951; vol. 2, 1957; vol. 3, 1963). Therefore references are included parenthetically within the text, with the first number referring to volume and the numbers following the colon referring to pages.

2. For the development of this helpful descriptive category, I am indebted to Richard R. Niebuhr's book *Schleiermacher on Christ and Religion* (New York: Charles Scribner's Sons, 1964), especially chap. 5, 210ff.

3. See Paul Tillich, *The Protestant Era*, trans. James Luther Adams (Chicago: University of Chicago Press, 1948), chap. 1; and idem, *The Interpretation of History*, trans. N. A. Rasetski and Elsa L. Talmey (New York: Charles Scribner's Sons, 1936), part 2.

4. See Tillich, *The Interpretation of History*, part 2.

5. The strange relation—both positive and negative—of this interpretation of Christianity among the religions to the analogous resolutions in Barth and Pannenberg might well be a subject for further study.

18. The Role of the Theologian in Contemporary Society

LANGDON GILKEY

This chapter is an exercise in imaginative extrapolation. Its purpose is to describe the role of the theologian in our contemporary situation as Tillich would (or might) have seen it. Since I have long found Tillich's view of this role both helpful and persuasive, this account will sail pretty close to my own view of that role—though unfortunately it took Tillich to embody and enact it! Still I shall seek to steer as close to Tillich's emphases and categories as I can, as *he* might have used them in *our* context.

THE CORRELATIVE FORM OF THEOLOGICAL REFLECTION

We must begin, as all Tillich's thought did, with the keystone of his system: God (the supreme object of religion) equals or is identical with Being Itself (the ground of all finitude and so of the whole range of common experience). From this center flow the principles that determine and structure the theologian's role. First of all, with this identity is entailed the interrelatedness of religion and of culture (of creative human being), for thus is "God" the depth of every aspect of cultural life. As a consequence religion enacts itself in and through the forms of culture, and culture is characterized by an essential religious dimension. Secondly, from this identity also stem the interrelatedness and interdependence of *theology* (as reflection on religion, on the *meaning* of being) and *philosophy* (reflection on the *structure* of being). From these two principles follows the correlative form of theological reflection: on the one hand a philosophical/theological analysis of the *structure* of finite existence (philosophy), including culture, in order to uncover its problematic, its "questions," so to say its *negative meanings* (theology); on the other hand, a theological/philosophical description of the received "answers" to these questions, that is, a reflection on the religious symbols expressive of that answer (theology) and a reflection structured by the categories of finitude (philosophy) analogically and mythically used.

The important point is that contrary to most simplistic and incorrect interpretations of Tillich (correlation means philosophical questions, theological answers), philosophical and theological elements lie on *both* sides (philosophical/theological questions and theological/philosophical answers). In turn, this understanding of correlation is crucial for the role of the theologian.[1] He or she does *not* saunter through a distraught cultural scene passing out theological answers at each corner; Tillich never saw his own role thus. More than most theologians he was aware that culture in all its aspects, including philosophy, was fairly bristling with "answers" as well as wracked with problems. His point was *not* that secular men and women can only ask questions. His point was rather that the answers that characterized culture, even a secular culture, whether in politics, law, art, morals, or philosophy, had as their deepest ground the *religious* dimension of the culture in question, its religious substance (in philosophy its "mystical a priori"), and that these answers were structured by the "mythos" of the culture and enacted in its common rites. As a consequence one of the important cultural roles of the theologian was to uncover, analyze, and criticize those answers.

In other words, there were *theological* elements on both sides of the correlation that is represented by *philosophy* (some important questions of philosophy are questions of *meaning,* and all ultimate answers of philosophy have a *religious* source and mythos), as there are *philosophical* elements on both sides of the correlation that is represented by *theology.* All profound and significant thought (embodied ontological reason) is a combination of philosophical and theological elements, of analysis of structure and uncovering of meaning, of reason and the depths of reason; separated out into philosophy (autonomy) and unphilosophical theology (heteronomy), both lose their power, their depth, and their significance, and fail utterly—for then culture is cut off from its own religious substance and religion from its possibilities of reflective power. Only in concert together can philosophy and theology either ask important questions or find healing answers, whether in cultural or religious matters, in "philosophy" or "theology."

There are, to be sure, differences between a secular community implicitly built around a religious substance and a religious community explicitly concentrating on its religious center, and so in reflection between a "theology of culture" and Christian systematic theology. But in neither is it a simple case of cultural and philosophical questions receiving Christian or theological answers; and in both theology of culture and in systematic theology, questions of structure and of meaning, and so philosophical elements, are intertwined.

The role of the theologian is, therefore, a dual role, a cultural as well as an ecclesiastical role; in this sense, too, he or she is "on the boundary." As philosophical analyst of the structure of finitude and theoretician of the religious dimension and of religious symbols, he or she is, if Tillich is right, as much relevant and at home in culture with its religious substance as in *ecclesia* with its religious center. In the end, in a *theonomous* culture and in a *true ecclesia* (in other words, in the Kingdom as the norm for both), theology of culture and systematic theology would in principle coalesce into one enterprise, all *Kairoi* or creative epochs of culture or of history now being centered about *the Kairos* to which the Christian community witnesses. Thus is the role of the theologian "public" as well as "churchly." By this Tillich would *not* mean that the theologian should seek to defend theology or theological conclusions by the criteria of culture (a sort of natural theology). Such self-defense on the part of theology would, I suspect, have represented for him a relevantly insignificant enterprise, a bit narcissistic in character; on a deeper level, it would (at least in our age) also have to submit ontological (philosophical/theological) reason and its conclusions to the barren and profanizing criteria of technical reason.

On the contrary, the public task of the theologian is the analysis of public life and of communal experience with regard to its religious issues and dimensions, not with regard to its economic, sociological, or psychological dimensions, though each of these has a religious basis and ground. As noted, while by no means representing all the important issues and dimensions there are, those that are religious are important; and they are "ultimate."

That is to say, these issues involve questions of our being and our nonbeing, the security and insecurity of our being, and our courage in the face of this contingency, the deepest threat to and the deepest supports of our common life; the public task of theology is thus desperately significant even if its voice is not heeded.

Every aspect of culture has its ground in the culture's religious substance. Art, science, morals, law, economic and political structures each reflect and depend upon a particular apprehension characteristic of *that* culture of the unconditioned. Consequently, the history as well as the forms of a ⌐ulture, its sequence of developments and events, takes its shape as much from the character and career of this religious dimension as from its sociological, economic, or political developments. Both the negativities of a culture's life, its "structures" of contradiction, of disintegration, and of destruction, *and* the positive possibilities of that culture's life are, therefore, functions of the culture's relation to its religious substance, of its continuing temporal relation to eternity; and they are to be understood *only* in relation to its religious substance.

For example, "The World Situation"[2] is a typical Tillichian analysis of the relevant recent public history of the West. Reason, the culture-creative power of men and women, can only understand itself in its creativity as well as in its forms of alienation, in relation to the *depths* of reason. And socialism, as an example of a cultural possibility, can only understand itself, its distortions, and its genuine possibilities as *religious* socialism. Theological analysis and critique is as essential for cultural and historical self-understanding as it is for religious self-understanding. To recall our starting point, if "God is Being Itself," then the career of *being* must be understood through "God" (culture in terms of its religious dimension) as well as "God" through the structure, the contradictions, and the possibilities of being (religion in terms of philosophy).

THE THEOLOGICAL INTERPRETATION OF CULTURE

Granted, then, the important public role of the theologian for Tillich, what in our day might a theologian, understanding his or her task in Tillich's terms, contribute to our common self-understanding? Tillich's own analyses penetrated with illuminating power into an amazing variety of areas of culture: art; economic, social, and political life; psychological existence, both individual and social; science and technology; law and morals as well as organized religion. Since, therefore, the Tillichian theologian in our day might well discourse with effect on any number of presently relevant themes, any selection is fairly arbitrary. I shall choose three such themes. With these themes Tillich himself was deeply concerned, and because each of them has if anything become more significant since his time, I have chosen to represent them here. In each case we see a problematic area of current cultural existence illuminated by the kind of philosophical/theological analysis that Tillich was wont to provide. In offering to the wider public these "theological" interpretations of culture, the theologian fulfills a significant part of his or her role in contemporary society.

The Unity of Fragmentary Realms of Existence

The problem of the *unity* of the diverse realms of personal and cultural existence was a question reflected frequently in Tillich's thought. The apprehension of this unity, he thought, was particularly weak in our time; as a consequence, on many levels a destructive sense of disunity prevails. The consequence of this in intellectual or reflective life is the disunity of the university; the noncommunication between disciplines; the lack of common categories bridging the physical, the psychological, and social sciences, and bridging all these sciences with humanistic studies; and the absence of a language relating all of these cognitive or theoretical disciplines with the practical, shaping, and, so, normative disciplines concerned with technical development, political action, legal practice and reformation, and the moral obligations of life.

This disunity on the linguistic, conceptual, and theoretical level, crippling enough to be sure, indicates a deeper disunity in our personal and social existence. How is the self that, as a body, sleeps, eats, exercises, makes love, shops at the market, and goes to the doctor related to the professional self who has a job, the political self who votes, the mortal self who sees a lawyer about a will, the anxious self late for an appointment with an analyst, the self in love or desolately rejected—the self who asks about the meaning of life? Is there any possibility of unity, of identity, of *one's own* self amid these diverse functions and activities of daily life; is it only the same body in all of them, and if so, how is *it* related to its own activities? The disunity of the universities is a theoretical reflection of the disunity of each self in culture, and of the professions and functions of the wider culture itself. It represents estrangement of body from spirit, of desiring from willing, of knowing from valuing and doing, of individuals from themselves and from each other. Its personal terror, as Tillich often referred to it, is that of "falling into a hundred pieces"; its social and political threat is the separation of expertise and purposes, of means and ends, of *techne* and norms, of rational knowledge and political decision. A part of Tillich's own amazing significance for American culture as a whole was his role in providing in all he said a deep sense of the unity of human being and of being generally, and of supplying a philosophical language for expressing that unity in categorial form.

This task is, of course, primarily philosophical. It is the precise task and aim of ontology (or "metaphysics" in Whitehead's sense of that word), to provide categories "in terms of which every aspect of our experience may be interpreted." For Tillich, however, the unity of finite being and so the unity of the reflective interpretation and so the expression of it, stems from the *depth* of reason in which subject and object, self and world, thought and external reality find their common ground and so the point of unity. Thus a *philosophical* explication of the unity of finite being is itself dependent on a *religious* apprehension of the depth of reason. Again, both philosophy and theology unite and complete themselves in the union of these two elements, namely, philosophical/theological thinking. The first public role of the theologian is the explication, nurturing, and preservation of the unity of personal existence, and in that the unity of cultural life.

RATIONALITY

The second area in which, for Tillich, theology would make a significant contribution is the issue of *rationality,* in our epoch the question of technical rationality. For Tillich "reason" did not represent, as it does for most of us, only one aspect of creative spiritual power, opposed to or at least differentiated from imagination, valuing, or the moral, the artistic, the emotive, or even self-giving and self-dedication. Rather, and again that powerful drive toward unity manifests itself, reason represents the total creative spiritual power or capacity of human being encompassing as a consequence not only cognitive and organizational capacities— science and technology—but every other realm or dimension of cultural life as well—morals, law, political and economic structures, art, even religion.

As it is found at work in us, reason, even in its most objective cognitive endeavors, evinces elements not usually recognized as aspects of the rational: a deep, even "ultimate" concern (for the truth); an emotional attachment to an end and to the community devoted to that end (as in science), dedication to the moral norms of that community and its aims, a degree of empathetic participation in its object, and so on. To separate these elements from "reason," to strip the rational down to bare cognitive and technical organization, is, therefore, to divest it of characteristics essential to its *own* functioning, to endanger its own creative exercise—and above all, to subject a now purely technical, rational expertise, unguided by its own norms and directionless without its own ends, to the lethal risk of itself being used for other, nonrational, even demonic, purposes. For reason, having been confined to the laboratory, the planning office, and the factory—technical reason—is now itself alienated from the larger issues, questions, and decisions of culture—political, moral, existential, and religious. These latter, therefore, bereft of rational norms, rational goals, and the capacity of rational assessment and decision, tend to the irrational and the absolute. Thus can a "pure" science and a merely instrumental technology become the potent instruments of economic or political purposes (of vast corporations, Fascist and Communist ideologies, even religious fanaticism) that are now *themselves* utterly irrational, absolutist, and oppressive. In this way, autonomous rationality pushed far enough finds itself metamorphosed into its dialectical opposite, a demonic religious heteronomy.

Such was Tillich's own view of the "fate" of rationality if an unimpeded autonomy was allowed to run its course: from a powerful and creative originating theonomy or ontological reason (that is probably rebellious against a previous heteronomy); through an autonomy centering more and more on technical reason; to a final oppressive and self-destructive heteronomy. To him, the development of modernity since the Enlightenment and down to his own experience of Germany of the 1920s, '30s, and '40s, more than justified empirically this speculative/historical schema (a kind of mirror-image of Hegel) of creative synthesis, unraveling thesis, and final destructive antithesis.

The even greater relevance of this schema to developments into our own present seems uncontestable. Philosophy has become even more nonontological since Tillich's day (he never really believed that positivism, language philosophy, and analytic philosophy could be serious); political science, social and psychological theory, tend more and more toward "science" and away from theory; technical and vocational, rather than liberal or humanistic, patterns of education rule more and more college and university curricula; politics is more and more directed by the requirements of public relations and the media—to mention just a few signs of the dominance of *instruments* and their needs over the humans who use them and *their* purposes. It is obvious that the understanding of the rational as the capacity or use of a tool or skill (expertise) has enlarged and grown dramatically away from such categories as insight, understanding, and wisdom—capacities both rational and also necessary for cultural health. Whereas, moreover, in Tillich's day fideism, nationalism, fascism, and an authoritarian communism represented to him almost apocalyptic signs of a coming heteronomy, of the end of an era, in our own day even clearer, if not more dramatic, signs have appeared of the lethal consequences of technical rationality and of the deepening split between the dwindling forces of rational autonomy and the advancing evidences of a new religious heteronomy.

The first, which we shall briefly mention, is the crisis in the relations of a scientific and technical culture to nature. Tillich had been well aware of the political and social dangers of a technical reason that made "objects" out of the human beings it sought to know, categorize, and manipulate; in knowing them thereby and using them as mere objects, technical reason, he said, not only does not know its object but destroys the very object it seeks to know. Recently it has become clear that a merely instrumental knowledge of nature, and so a merely manipulative use of her, also fails in the end to understand her and culminates by destroying her —and in destroying her, it destroys us. Nature is *misunderstood* as merely an object over against us, as are we, its knowers, if we

understand ourselves as merely objective knowers and manipula-
tors of her forces. What is lacking here is the *correlation* of objective
Logos (system) and subjective Logos (knowing and policies), the
participation of subject and object in one another, as well as their
difference and distance—in this case, the necessary participation
of human culture in, and its fostering of, the system of nature if
either one is to survive.

A Tillichian philosopher/theologian has much that is relevant to
say about the spiritual origins of the present ecological crisis and
a good number of categories to offer that may be helpful in the
rethinking of the relation of human being to nature. An ontological and a religious understanding of the unity of the natural and
the human world—and on what other grounds could that unity be
comprehended?—long scorned by the empirical sciences as representing the dying vestige of a primitive, animistic view of nature,
may well in our day provide the West's best opportunity for the
retrieval of that lost unity. Technical reason can know the human
only as an object, as an objective product of nature, and it can
know nature only as objective, and so separated, from the human
subject; thus does it lose both humanity and nature. With his
background in German romanticism and *Lebensphilosophie*, Tillich's
approach is now relevant in an area for which his generation had
little direct concern, since the problematic of that area had not yet
surfaced: the correlation of Logos in human being *and* in nature,
and the unity of human being with nature in the ground of being.

One further word on the subject of the technical, industrial, and
commercial culture. In the last decade, this worldwide culture has
revealed itself to us as a veritable predator of nature's resources,
not only of fuel, but of air, water, and soil, of fecundity itself.
Human being here manifests itself as infinitely greedy, as seeking
to use and to use up everything there is, in Tillich's colorful
phrase, to "take the whole world into itself" for its own well-being
—and ultimately for its own self-destruction. Certainly there are
elements of pride or hubris in this demonic process, pride of
knowledge and of expertise and, above all, of power, the economic
power evidenced by exploitation. However, there can be little
doubt that Tillich's category of "concupiscence," of infinite and so
inordinate desire, desire to grasp and use the whole world (a
category he lifted right out of Augustine) hit the nail squarely on

the head long before the ecological crisis made its appearance. As Tillich would put it, this demonic use and using up of nature bespeaks a deep alienation of human being from itself, from nature, and from its own infinite ground; consequently, it seeks that infinity of meaning, and so itself and its unity, through taking the infinite into itself, by possessing and using the finite *infinitely*. To a post-Freudian generation, "concupiscence," oriented as it had been exclusively to the bedroom, had long gone out of fashion as a primal form of sin. Tillich has, in reinterpreting it, given it a much wider meaning as the prime symptom of the estrangement of human being from the whole world of goods and so of nature —and as the key "sin" of our technical, commercial culture.

The second new "sign" of the progressive disintegration of an autonomous, rational culture into one split into technical and heteronomous elements is the appearance in the last decade of religious cults.[3] This would not have surprised Tillich. A technical culture does not eradicate the depth of reason or the need of the culture for it. On the contrary, ends, meaning, and hope remain as essentials for existence; myth and cult remain as the only verbal and behavioral forms in which these can be expressed; and the infinite and holy ground of all is continuously apprehended. So far Tillich. Fifteen years after his death, this has been amply confirmed. Religious cults have mushroomed among the middle classes and the intelligentsia, especially, one may note, around the great university centers. (The contemporary scene in a college pub where graduate students in chemistry and mathematics hold discourse on yoga, karma, astrology, and homeopathic medicine is a bizarre one!) For the individual, and so for "set-apart" religious communities, these religious cults, structured in theory by mythical language and in practice by transrational meditative rites, provide principles of personal moral discipline, of personal goals and ends in life, of meaning in wider history, and of religious union totally omitted from the secular, technical, and commercial culture and yet desperately needed by the inhabitants of that culture.

A Tillichian analysis can help immensely to illuminate the social and spiritual conditions that prepared the way for the "new" religious cults, in providing anthropological categories that may mediate the present split between an official autonomous, scientific, and technical culture and these new separated religious elements in it, and in providing theological categories that can express and thematize the positive healing powers without question present in many of these movements.

THE UNDERSTANDING OF IDEOLOGIES

The central theme, as we noted, of Tillich's theology of culture was the interpenetration of religion and culture, the presence of a religious dimension or substance in each aspect of cultural life. Thus, whenever religious elements are officially excluded from daily life in secular culture, ultimate concern manifests itself in new and "unreligious" forms; and myth, cult, and rite reappear in exotic, "set apart" religious communities. And ironically, according to the same principle, though its self-understanding is secular to the core, the National Science Foundation itself quite unsuspectingly takes on the role and the appearance of a "religious" establishment, with its marble temple placed appropriately near the seat of political and economic power, and its anachronistic, tuxedo-clad rites of initiation! On an even more significant level, however, the same principle of the religious substance illuminates the deepest and most formative traits of our contemporary political epoch, namely, the "ideological" character of our fundamental politics.

By ideology here I refer to the subtle transformation of political and economic theory into a "religious" symbolic structure, that is, into myth, when it begins to function as the uniting, shaping, and guiding *ethos* of a social community. This is what has happened to capitalistic and democratic social theory as they have been reshaped into, say the "American Way of Life"—that set of social, economic, and political symbols which shape fundamental American aims, norms, institutions, vocations, education, and many patterns of behavior and judgment. To the Marxist, this whole symbolic structure is, of course, a "capitalist ideology," that which *claims* to be science but which actually sanctifies and so justifies the capitalistic social structure, provides a moral cloak for imperial self-interest, and serves the sole interests of the ruling bourgeois classes. Interestingly, this is *also* what has happened to Marxism as it has moved from a critical social theory to becoming a constitutive ethos shaping, directing, sanctifying, and justifying the structural elements of Russia's economic and political life, its patterns of vocational and educational life, and its most fundamental policies. To the Western social scientist, certain that his theory is "objective science," this Marxist symbolic structure is by no means science but pure ideology, assented to on the grounds of authority and not of evidence; asserted because of faith, not rational assessment; and functioning as the cloak for the predatory aims of world communism and of party rule. Probably both are right about the other—though not in their flattering estimates of their own objectivity!

In any case, as many commentators have pointed out, the appearance and dominance of powerful ideologies, of national, racial, religious, as well as political and economic ideologies, marks our epoch. The systematic denial of ideological elements in the science of each bloc—because "we are empirical and pragmatic" if we are bourgeois, and because "we are proletarian" if we are Communist—indicates the pervasive importance of ideology. In turn, criticism of the ideological elements of modern theory, so that communication between communities can become possible again ("ideology critique"), has become a major enterprise for philosophers and social theorists alike.

Our point is that the dominant presence of ideologies in our epoch and this active current interest in them provide an opportunity for a significant public role for the Tillichian theologian/philosopher. For such an analyst has something unique and helpful to add to a philosophical/epistomological, economic, sociological, anthropological, political, or psychological interpretation of this phenomenon. And that is because, as Tillich reiterated, ideologies contain a religious dimension as well as economic, political, and social dimensions. In fact, one could say that in a secular epoch, ideologies express and thematize the mythic structure, the religious substance, of the culture—as in traditional societies organized religion provided that mythic structure.

It is, therefore, no accident that the fact of ideology (and the word itself)—a secular, symbolic structure unifying a community —appeared just after the French Revolution, when organized religion was officially removed from the center of public life. The religious dimensions of ideologies consist not only in the fact that they *function* as traditional religions once did, though that is surely significant. On the contrary, these religious elements on the

objective side consist in the intrinsic constitutive elements of ultimacy, universality, and meaningfulness that characterize each ideology. Each ideology appears for its adherents as *the* truth about
all of history and society, and in so doing, it answers the most
pressing problems of *meaning* in communal life and provides the
most fundamental norms and goals for that common life. On the
subjective side, individual persons relate to these ideologies
through commitment and assent ("faith"); they entail loyalty, obedience and, in the end, self-sacrifice, and in thought they generate
the polarity of orthodoxy and heresy or deviationism. "America,
love her or leave her" expresses an advanced ideological attitude
that implies all of the above, as do countless elements of present
Russian life. It is evident that in the same way that the developing
gulf between technical rationality and religious cults, and between
a technical culture and nature, called for a Tillichian interpretation, so the dominance of ideology in a culture seeking to base
itself solely on autonomous rationality *also* calls for a Tillichian
theological hermeneutic if the full dimensions of our ideological
age are to be uncovered and understood.

THE TASK OF SYSTEMATIC THEOLOGY

We have cited and analyzed several elements of our current cultural scene, which a Tillichian analysis, based on the philosophical
and theological presuppositions intrinsic to his thought, might
vastly illuminate. This illumination of his surrounding culture,
through creative theoretical interpretation of cultural developments, cultural problems, possibilities, and perils, constitutes *one*
of the major public roles of the theologian in the Tillichian tradition. It represents part, and a major part, of what he meant by a
theology of culture. This is, however, not the only public role of
the theologian. For the central theological task is the creative, and
so contemporary, self-interpretation of the message of the religious community itself, the setting of that message in the terms of
the present cultural "situation," namely, the task of systematic
theology.

This theological task also represents a public as well as an ecclesiastical role, and for two reasons. First, because systematic
theology represents the correlation of cultural and religious ele-

ments, of philosophy and theology, theology possesses a common ground with every theoretically alert member of that culture and so presents to us a public, rather than an esoteric, set of materials.

Second, the church is an institution with a mission *to* and therefore *in* history, and so within the cultural communities of history. Ideally (eschatologically) the church would bear, represent, express, and mediate the spiritual presence to the wider cultural community; it would express and manifest the theonomous center of the culture, its religious substance; it would be the religious center of the "Kingdom" as a theonomous culture would be its historical manifestation. In actuality, because of the alienation or estrangement *both* of the culture *and* of the church, no theonomy is ideally actual, nor is the spiritual presence anything but fragmentary, even in the church. The present church, therefore, is diffused with ambiguity as well as with grace, and it must await its own redemption before it can fulfill fully its own historical task. Nevertheless, its role is *in* the world, united with culture both in estrangement, in grace, and in promise. The New Being, to which it witnesses, is a gift to the *world,* to the world's *entire* life, and so to culture; the problems or contradictions that the New Being heals are the *world's* problems and contradictions; its promises are promises for the world. The present task of the church is, therefore, within culture, not apart from it. It is as much the task of nurturing, criticizing, and reshaping the religious substance of *culture* closer to the New Being it seeks to bear and to the Kingdom it proclaims as it is the task of nurturing and fostering the community of the *ecclesia.* (The many *Kairoi* of cultural history are submitted by the *ecclesia* to the criterion of the *Kairos* or center of history in the New Being; the Kingdom refers as a symbol to that point where history and New Being are united in an eschatological theonomy).

Thus the church retrieves, nurtures, and fosters the "Catholic substance" of *culture* as well as its own, and it enacts over against *culture,* as well as over against itself, the Protestant principle of criticism and judgment. As the one whose task is the theoretical self-interpretation of the *ecclesia,* itself a cultural-religious institution, itself "on the boundary," the theologian qua systematic theologian has, therefore, also a cultural role. In the following brief comments I shall try to describe five elements of that role in our present, that is, the ways the development of a contemporary and relevant *systematic theology* can—if heeded at all—contribute to the present wider contemporary cultural and social situation.

A THEOLOGY IN CONTEMPORARY TERMS

The most direct and central task of the theologian is the creation of a systematic theology, a unified, encompassing, and intelligible statement of the Christian message. As noted, as a correlation of situation and message, this statement is couched within the terms and categories of the cultural situation; it seeks to answer the culture's problems and contradictions; and it states its message through the categories of the culture's self-understanding. A systematic theology so constructed is, therefore, also a contemporary *cultural* document, a part (the Christian part, to be sure) of the culture's self-interpretation. It unites the religious and the intellectual (scientific, social scientific, psychological, historical, and philosophical) traditions of that culture, and in uniting them brings each "up to date" in terms of a novel, contemporary interpretation.

This *reinterpretation* of a given historical destiny in terms of new perspectives on new problems (of new possibilities) represents precisely Tillich's view of creative cultural and historical activity, of the way the new creatively enters into passage as a union of tradition and possibility. Thus systematic theology unites past and future "through the Eternal Now," into a new synthesis, as well as the other often disparate elements of a separated present cultural life referred to earlier. This temporal, as well as spatial, unifying task must take place in every area and discipline of culture; in systematic theology it occurs in that area closest to the religious substance of the culture, in fostering and criticism of that substance. A classic statement of the eternal message in contemporary and novel form represents the paradigm of historical creativity for Tillich, a model, if done well, of creative spirit.

INTERPRETING HUMAN FINITUDE

Systematic theology begins with the analysis of the *structures* of our finitude (philosophy), and its aim is to uncover the *meaning* for our being and our nonbeing of those structures (theology). By "meaning" here we refer to the crises and possibilities with which being finite and yet free (that is, being human) seem to present us; the deep, ineradicable modes of anxiety that accompany this finitude; and the possibilities of courage that are open to us and that alone can overcome ("conquer") that anxiety. The point *theologically* of this philosophical/theological analysis of our finitude is of course to show in the "answering" section what in our experience God is, and so that to which this central word in religious discourse refers, namely, the infinite power of being conquering the experienced nonbeing of our finitude, and therefore the source of the courage common to all creative human existence. However, it is evident that that theological point, central as it is, does not exhaust the value—for believers and unbelievers alike—of this philosophical/ theological analysis. To uncover and so illuminate the structural sources of our deepest and most pervasive anxieties, granted the latter are there, is of great value to all.

To be aware of the unconscious but always effective terrors, as well as the possibilities, of our temporality, our spatiality, our causedness, our contingency, and to face realistically in the context of the divine ground the overwhelming threat of death, presents to culture as a whole—which groans also under these anxieties—the only way with which these anxieties can be dealt. This form of theological analysis brings to consciousness the *religious* (existential) problems involved in our human being as such, and brings to awareness and so into real possibility an answer to them. Since these are problems fully as characteristic of ordinary persons in culture as of ordinary persons in church, this sort of analysis has a most creative cultural role to play. The particular forms that anxiety (about, for example, space) takes will shift with each cultural context; they are of *one* sort in a nomadic culture, of *another* sort in a high-rise apartment in Chicago. Thus must this analysis of the meaning (theology) of spatiality (philosophy) be continually renewed with an eye to each particular social situation—but the value of this theological/philosophical enterprise as a most creative form of religious reflection is constant.

It might also be added that this sort of ontological theological analysis, analysis of the structures of our finitude and of the religious problems involved in those structures, is particularly relevant to American religion. Stemming from the Calvinist and the evangelical traditions, most American Protestantism has been primarily concerned with the *moral* problems of being human, as if these were the only issues in which true Christianity should be interested. Insofar as death remained an important issue, it was understood within moral categories: A "bad" life resulted in eternal death after death, a "good" life in salvation from death. Thus vast regions of genuine and devastating spiritual problems were left unaddressed, problems as debilitating to Americans as to any other humans: growing older, loss of place, radical contingency or insecurity, utter dependence on undependable factors, and so on. To be sure, selfishness and inordinate desire add to these problems of our finitude; they do not, however, create them. In fact, as Tillich pointed out, it is more often than not in despairing *reaction* to these ineradicable sources of anxiety in our finitude that we go morally sour, that is, become overly selfish or inordinately concupiscent. Thus an ontological theological analysis of a Tillichian sort can open up many significant areas left unexplored by other types of American religious witness and theology.

THE POLITICAL ROLE

On the most important facet of the role of the Tillichian theologian in contemporary society I shall be brief, for this obvious facet is well-covered in this volume. This concerns the political role of the church and so of theology, a role that quite dominated Tillich's early career in Germany and that he continued to take very seriously to the end of his life.

The grounds for this political concern have already appeared and reappeared in this essay: the interweaving of religion and culture, an interweaving that penetrates to every aspect of both culture and theology. Thus on the side of culture, the health of culture depends on the character of its religious substance, on its capacity for self-affirmation and courage, and so the character of its fundamental aims and norms; further, its health is a function of the justice of its structures, a function of its capacity for self-criticism, self-judgment; and lastly, it depends on its courage and hope in the face of the future. All of these capacities represent "religious" issues intrinsic to creative cultural life; each of them appears in relation to the eternal ground of being and meaning, to the divine; each is compromised if politics seeks to remain autonomous and not theonomous. Thus are a religious and a theological dimension necessary for passage toward a healthy culture and so a creative politics.

On the theological side, the Gospel (and therefore theology) becomes esoteric and possibly heteronomous when it is unrelated to culture; it loses its touch with the structures of life and becomes empty and irrelevant. It loses its claim to justice and becomes fatuous or ideological. In centering on the individual, it loses both community and history, and so becomes meaningless to the individual who lives in both. In sum, the categories of history and the Kingdom drop out as relevant to the New Being and so as religious and theological concerns. Such an omission is untrue both to the original message and to the human situation. The drive toward justice and so toward the Kingdom is, therefore, as essential an aspect of any theological statement of the message as is any other aspect; thus is theology essentially political if it is to be theology at all.

Possibly more than any other issue of the essential aspect of theology, the political aspect changes as the cultural situation changes. This Tillich discovered when he moved to America; political problems and requirements now took in his eyes a different form than they had in Weimar Germany—and he wisely and humbly chose to be largely silent on these issues until late in his career. The factor of change is even more evident of the political situation, both domestic and international, since his time. Vast historical and social transformations have occurred from the '30s, '40s, and '50s, changes which require reformulations of sociotheological theory, some of them radical, at every point. The problems of justice in economic life, in social status and opportunity, and among the races and nations remain, of course; but in the following areas quite new issues have arisen.

The dominance of the West, both in political and in cultural power, has all but vanished. Socialism has joined capitalism-democracy in showing deep, actual, and so theoretical, ambiguity (especially in politics) and thus as also in need of essential rethinking and reformulation. The international rectitude of the liberal democracies has been challenged by their economic dominance of other cultural centers, especially Africa and South America; and the virtue of their domestic institutions by the black and feminist movements. The Third World has appeared as an originative,

348 / THE THOUGHT OF PAUL TILLICH

autonomous part of the common world with its own needs, values, and aims. Finally, a common ecological crisis has suddenly appeared (since 1970) that dominates every political and social question for the future. Each of these new appearances requires a formulation different from Tillich's religious socialism in the '20s, and even (one suspects) from the simplistic socialistic aims of recent liberationist theology. Yet with all this need for reformulation, the crucial role of the theologian in political matters remains, and for all the reasons Tillich so clearly stated. Other chapters in this book have developed this theme more fully than this chapter can.

THE PROMISE OF *KAIROS* IN A TIME OF TROUBLES

As the above makes clear, ours is an age not only of vast change for the West but of apparent decline, a "time of troubles," when few of our established institutions seem able to cope with a mounting sequence of crises. Tillich realized all this deeply; but the reality of the appearance in power of *other* cultural traditions to near dominance as well as the fissures in our own cultural house, was not a part of his world as it is of ours. Thus the sense of dismay at the present and of despair over the future is perhaps deeper now, and the grounds for hope in the future less certain—for now much less depends on *us* than in his day, when only the Western powers seemed to be able to make important decisions. Added to these historical changes is the ecological crisis, looming darkly and menacingly over every political and economic possibility for the future. In this historical situation, courage, hope, and confidence in relation to the future are very important, for the culture as a whole, as well as for the church.

An anxious nation, increasingly insecure, with little remaining confidence in its destiny and little hope for new possibilities in its future, becomes a danger to all at each new threat. Thus is the theological message of promise, of a *Kairos* to come—even if it is not what we expect or want—of vast significance. The theological analysis of the forms of our estrangement is constantly crucial, else we understand neither our problems nor ourselves. But in our contemporary situation, it is the promise of providence "in spite of" all the visible facts, of a new *Kairos* developing out of the contradictions of the present, that is most important.

THE RELIGIONS OF THE WORLD

The final contemporary cultural issue to be noted is one to which the theologian can make a significant contribution. The recent "oneness" of the world economically and politically has made the continual and deep interrelation and interaction of cultures more and more a reality, increasing even since Tillich's time. Added to this is the crucial aspect noted, the "shaking of the foundations" of Western culture itself and, as a consequence, the disappearance for Westerners and non-Westerners alike of any sense of Western superiority, and so of the superiority of Western religions. This latter point has opened the West to the influence of "alien" cultures and religions in a way undreamed of before, except among esoteric circles. Thus non-Western religions have appeared in *power* amongst us, that is, as traditions obviously possessing both truth and grace. No modern Western theologian can possibly deny this last point, nor fail to take account of it in his or her systematic theology.[4] Tillich felt deeply this new set of relations between religions in his last years and wished above all that he could live to deal with it. He knew well that the easy ways by which Christian theology had previously demoted its rivals were now irrelevant or impossible, and that a new understanding of "religions" and of their relation to Christian (and Western philosophical!) claims was necessary. This is one of the two or three major and inescapable theological problems of our present, one that has appeared in a quite new and radical form in our present generation.

Anyone familiar with Tillich's carefully articulated view of revelation and with his sense of the immanent presence of the divine power of being and meaning to every creature, every culture, and every religion will see at once the immense possibilities latent in his thought with regard to this problem. To him revelation was universal and universally effective. To him, being grasped by the divine power gave courage to each creative human existence, and an apprehension of some facet of the divine meaning founded every cultural gestalt. To him, each religion embodied answers as well as questions and so reflected, in however fragmentary a form, the New Being. All of this offers immense opportunity for understanding the truth and the grace present in other religions. Tillich's doctrine, moreover, of the true "medium" that sacrifices itself and its own particularity in pointing beyond itself can provide one way of understanding how a religion can relate creatively and humbly to other religions and yet preserve its own characteristic witness.

My main point, however, is the contribution of a theological analysis of this problem to culture as a whole. That our understanding on the deepest level of other cultures is now imperative for us in the West is obvious to all. It is equally obvious—at least in relation to them!—that each of these other cultures contains a "religious substance" that must be understood first of all: How can an Islamic land, India, China, or Japan, be understood at all without comprehension of its religious heritage?

Tillich helps to explicate this point elegantly, and he provides categories that mediate between that *religious substance,* to be comprehended by the methods appropriate to the study of religion (among them a *theological* understanding), and the *cultural substance* in question: its history, economic and political institutions, art, morals, and so on. Area studies departments concerned with the Middle East, India, China, and Japan have begun to recognize this point and to give important place to an analysis of their religious heritage alongside analysis of other elements of the culture. Insofar as the religion in question (or, as noted, a current ideology) is central to the shape of the entire culture, a *theological* analysis like Tillich's, uniting the religious center with its cultural expressions, is also necessary for intelligibility—lest all else be understood through the psychological or the economic aspects of that culture alone. Thus in a world of interacting and now of interlocking cultures, *our* world, a theological analysis of a Tillichian sort, but reworked to fit this very new situation, is necessary. As is evident, there is much for a Tillichian theologian to do in our age!

NOTES

1. See the discussion of this issue in chap. 14 of this volume by David Tracy.
2. Paul Tillich, "The World Situation," in *The Christian Answer,* ed. Henry P. Van Dusen (New York: Charles Scribner's Sons, 1945).
3. See the discussion of this issue in chap. 12 by Jack Boozer.
4. See the discussion of this issue in the last part of chap. 17 by Langdon Gilkey and the whole of chap. 11 by Joseph Kitagawa.

SUPPLEMENT

SUPPLEMENT

Open Letter to Emanuel Hirsch

New York, October 1, 1934
Union Theological Seminary*

Dear Emanuel:

I have never been made more aware of the tension-filled unity of our friendship and the real enmity between us than by reading your new book, *Die gegenwärtige geistige Lage im Spiegel philosophischer und theologischer Besinnung* (The present spiritual situation as reflected in philosophical and theological consciousness). I agree with Karl Barth's opinion of its significance, but, what is more, I believe that I can feel what is at stake in it for you. At the same time, I know that I must be frank and unsparing in my opposition to it. This severity has always been characteristic of our scientific *(wissenschaftliche)* conversations, but now, in this historical moment, when the whole of our spiritual existence is in doubt, it is more necessary than ever. Whereas the epistolary form is meant to maintain the informal character of our debates, its publication, which was made necessary by the publication of your book, signifies that what is needed is not a private conversation, but a clash of conflicting principles that for years have been associated with our names. I ask that you interpret this letter, which has been more difficult for me to write than any other, in this twofold sense.

I was very much surprised by your most recent book,[1] as were others (Compare the review by Pastor Aé in *Junge Kirche*[2] as well as various letters that I have received). The reason for our surprise is the fact that in order to interpret theologically the new direction of German history, you used every crucial concept of your adversaries, against whom you have struggled for fourteen years, and whom now you appear to have vanquished. I could rejoice in this

*English translation by Victor Nuovo and Robert Scharlemann. The translation is made from the text printed in Paul Tillich, *Gesammelte Werke*, suppl. vol. 6, pp. 142–176. The notes are those of the editors of that volume, Renate Albrecht and Rene Tautmann, but have been supplemented by them for English readers.

as proof of the spiritual power of the intellectual labor of our Religious Socialist movement, by which even its victorious enemies must live. But two things disturb my joy. First, you deliberately conceal your agreement with Religious Socialist categories; second, in using these categories, you deprive them of their deepest sense. For both these reasons, I write this letter. For personal reasons, I was glad to remain silent for a long time. The use and abuse in your book of the *Kairos* doctrine, which is associated with my name, compels me to speak out.[3]

What I should like to say, first of all, remains within the framework of this personal introduction. Of all that I have to say, this is the most difficult, but it must be said, and said clearly and publicly, for it concerns the crucial relation of scientific truthfulness to the needs of political conflict. At a time when political affairs have attained a significance surpassing all others—something that none of us ever anticipated—when, given the world situation, there is little prospect that in the foreseeable future these political affairs will lose their significance; when, not by accident, "the adversary" of the categories of historical thinking has appeared; in such a time as this, it seems to me necessary that one be clear, at least for his own good, about the relation of the affairs of science to the political ethos. Now I must confess that I—and not I only—have the feeling that, while writing your book, you were not clear about this relationship or, if you were, then in a direction that I deeply regret. I was grievously distressed by your book not on account of its actual content, which justifiably inspired in me the will to attack it in force, but on account of your attitude which, in contrast to our work, cannot be reconciled with intellectual veracity. I view it as a violation of our intellectual work when, in your account, there is not the least hint that the work that we have done has provided the methodological groundwork for the new attitude in philosophy and theology that you call for. You treat it with respect and at least do not suppress the presentiment that you are indebted to it in all sorts of ways. But, at the same time, you concoct for it the name *religious Marxism* which, given the propagandistic use of the word *Marxism* during the last ten years, must defame it for its readers while depriving it of any real content. Nevertheless, this is not what matters, but rather that your presentation would have looked differently if you had publicly acknowledged the work of those whose thoughts resound in every one of your sentences. Then you would not have been able to hide the fact that the feeling of change, the crisis of the bourgeois age and of the new departure and the hope for a spiritual, social, and political renewal of Germany and, thereby, of Europe, were as alive then as they now are because of the rise of our movement; that existential-historical thinking and its consequences for philosophy and theology were first experienced and discovered by those who joined themselves to the German workers' movement, because they believed that there necessarily lay the starting point of every actual change. You believe that the conservative, middle-class revolutionary powers offer a better approach, indeed, that they have brought fulfillment in principle. But can this difference in political-sociological judgment be a reason to deny commonality in that basic attitude and in all the concepts flowing from it? You criticized our application of these concepts, pointed out the causes of our lack of practical efficacy, and were able in this way to keep your distance from us, but there is nothing at all to be found in your book that can be said to interpret the present historical situation in the light of the past.

And this now is the question that motivates me and troubles me: Are you prevented by some unconscious power from recognizing the truth of your relationship to us? Does some half-conscious concern about the consequences prevent you from expressing it? Or (then your attitude would have fundamental significance) do you intend to subordinate truth to political values, not only in diplomacy and propaganda, but also in history and theology? If this were so, then at the very least we would have the right to demand that this transvaluation of values be treated openly in your book and founded on principle. Lutheran social ethics has indeed for a long time been reputed to be Machiavellian. You might have renewed this alleged or real tradition, and you could have transferred its application from the "prince" to the "philosopher." Then you would have created a clear situation. Now I stand before a wall, and the sorrow that I feel because I can no longer push through it to reach you has wrought from me these words.

But enough of this! I must consider what is at issue. Two closely related tasks lie before me. One is to show how you have taken up the basic concepts of Religious Socialist thought, especially the

Kairos doctrine, and, at the same time, by eliminating their prophetic-eschatological elements, have twisted or emptied them; and the other is to present an actual critique of your theological method through a discussion of your basic attitude as well as various particular solutions. One is not possible without the other. Nevertheless, the first task will predominate in the first part, the second task in the second part.

I

1. It is surprising to what extent you have adopted the concepts and thoughts of Religious Socialism in general and of the *Kairos* doctrine in particular and, methodologically, have based your interpretation of the present situation upon them. I intend to prove this charge as thoroughly as possible—so thoroughly that, perhaps, even you will be surprised. Hence, what is at issue is not whether one thought or another has been developed simultaneously and independently by you and by us, but that you have adopted the basic methodological attitude of our thinking. And even if you also had developed this attitude simultaneously and independently of us, the coincidence would have been all the more amazing and should have required of you a separate account.

About nine years ago, when I sent you my *Religiöse Lage der Gegenwart* (Religious situation of the present),[4] you asked somewhat ironically why I had assumed the role of an onlooker. Now that you have had your *Gegenwärtige geistige Lage* (Present spiritual situation) sent to me, I ask no such question. For I think I know and am forced to say that unless one takes a position that comprehends past, present, and future, it is not possible to fulfill the demand to "think in terms of the present." Even the title of your book is an indication that you have come much closer to the Religious Socialist approach to philosophy and theology than you had before.

This accusation, however, applies not only to the form of thought but to its content. You reproduce the same rhythm in which we perceived the development of Western civilization since 1919, and which has been the guiding star of our concrete interpretation of history: the noble attempt of autonomous reason, following the destruction of the religiously based unitary culture of the Middle Ages, to accomplish from its own resources the spiritual and political reconstruction of society; the catastrophe of the "world-shaping will"; *ratio* in the World War and its consequences; the present as a decisive period of crisis; the struggle for a new founding substance. Even the particular historical moments to which we have given prominence reappear in your work. The significance of the Reformation and the counter-Reformation for the rise of autonomous thought; the triad of science, technology, and economy as symbols of the age; the rational dominion over nature and the rational structure of society; the struggle for human rights; the rejection of idealism; the surpassing significance of Karl Marx and Friedrich Nietzsche for the nineteenth century—thus, in general and in particular, the Religious Socialist view of the course of history up to the present crisis.

The same coincidence appears among your basic concepts. I give only brief references.

To denote certain powers that are both creative and destructive, Religious Socialism uses the concept of the demonic in a precise religious and philosophical sense.[5] You adopt this central concept and interpret German events as the conquest of demonries that have massed together in an age of crisis (whence you, along with Dacqué, Leese,[6] and many others have been influenced by the judgment of Ernst Krieck who in *Volk im Werden* speaks of "falling for Tillich's fraudulent demonology" and utters the sigh, "Is there anything that German intellectuals don't fall for?").[7]

When introducing the concept of the boundary you feel that you have to justify appropriating it from an older doctrine. But if, in doing so, you assert that what formerly had been an infinitely extendable limit is for you a "sacred center," then not only are you altogether in disagreement with the doctrine of the boundary situation as it was developed by Jaspers and me,[8] but you have thoroughly twisted the fact. And you must have been aware of this when you wrote concerning the bourgeois attitude: "They see only one side, the Yes; they know him [God] only as ground, not as boundary; they remain in their bourgeois piety. The unconditional judgment that calls the world into question before God is to them a . . . scandalous thought." These sentences prove that your "sacred boundary" is a translation of the "abyss" in the formula "ground and abyss," and also that your "boundary" as "sacred center" that at the same time sustains and unconditionally judges, repeats exactly what we have wrested in serious conflict with bourgeois neo-Kantianism. This becomes completely clear by your sociological reference to bourgeois society, which is introduced here suddenly and only once and which you, in complete agreement with the Religious Socialist critique, characterize as a piety lacking the experience of the abyss and of the boundary situation.

Your agreement with the *Kairos* doctrine is decisive in principle and in its consequences. Why you avoid the Greek word cannot as a matter of fact be explained, since you have adopted Stapel's term *nomos*[9] and translated "boundary" as *Horos*. Instead of *Kairos* you speak of the "present hour" and of the "beginning" to which it points, of a "special responsibility, which it contains for theology and philosophy," of the "religious meaning of our historical moment," of the "confession of the Holy in the situation of the moment," of "openness to the demand of the historical hour," of the demand to acknowledge "what is imposed by the hour of the Lord of History," etc.

The fundamental agreement in philosophy and theology results from the reception of the *Kairos* idea. You are aiming at an existential philosophy of history, something that I tried to develop in my last German lecture as an "existential-historical method."[10] A sentence like "The existence [*Existenz*] of philosophical thinking is the measure of the historical existentiality of philosophy" is an almost word-for-word rendering of a basic thought of my "Realism of Faith" (Gläubiger Realismus).[11] And the sentence "Philosophy must avoid appropriating the claim of strict science to be ahistorical" is a rendering of the thought that the philosophical Logos must abandon its avoidance of the *Kairos*. "Self-illumination of modern German reality in the light of its existential depths" has been the endeavor of Religious Socialism from its first to its last utterance. None of our writings has, in principle, any other content than this. We have tried, just as you require, "in our last great question of decision, to let the present hour enter into us mightily, so that we might not fail to take up our task."

But do you also know what you are doing with this demand of existential-historical thinking? First, negatively, you break decisively with the Gogartenian form of the dialectic and only by self-deception can you maintain a close relationship with him. In his

book, *Ich glaube an den dreieinigen Gott,* [12] Gogarten attacks the philosophy of *Kairos* as the "plague of the philosophy of history." Will
he greet your version of the same with more grace on account of
your political connections? I doubt it! Instead of with him, you
have taken your stand with someone who, among all the dead and
the living, could not please you less, the young Marx. Whereas,
according to Kierkegaard, to whom you appeal, and Heidegger,
whom you reject, and Jaspers, whom you do not mention, an
understanding of existence *(Existenz)* is gained from the standpoint
of the existence of the individual, the young Marx has, against
Hegel and even more against Feuerbach, called for existential-
historical thinking in terms that appear similar and often interchangeable with Kierkegaardian ones. Religious Socialism, which
in this connection actually is religious Marxism, has responded to
this demand as its single task and has done its best to realize it. You
are dependent on this demand and on the young Marx, when you
call for existential-historical thinking. And you and we and Marx
and everyone who thinks existentially-historically are dependent
upon ancient Jewish prophecy, whose attitude of existential-historical thinking has penetrated philosophy. On this point, you
stand clearly in the tradition of (prophetic) Judaism and (religious)
Marxism.

The *Kairos* doctrine is rich in consequences for you as well as for
us, above all in apprehending the idea of truth. Your decisive
sentence states, "Reason is the law of life determined humanly and
historically, which unfolds and comprehends itself spiritually as
Logos, and science is nothing other than this reality-determined
Logos's cultivating and reckoning, in its own presence, the reality
that has determined it." Without here entering into a discussion
of your formulation, may I remind you that the problem that you
pose by means of it is the theme of every work that aims at the
philosophical grounding of the *Kairos* doctrine, that the solutions
have been influential well beyond our circle, and that we have
spoken since that time of a "dynamic truth" and have tried to
develop a "dynamic method"? Must I remind you of these things?
And, if not, why don't you remind those who need to be reminded
of the original sense of this doctrine, when, in the name of dynamic
truth, they sacrifice the "truth" to the "dynamic"?

All other consequences, which you rightly derive from the idea of truth, have been drawn in detailed expositions from Religious Socialism: for the risk character of knowing I refer to the discussions about knowledge as fate and risk in "Kairos and Logos."[13] For the demand that knowing, in order to avoid a free-floating willfulness, must take place from the community and for the community, Religious Socialism testifies through its existence [*Existenz*]. It looks within the nation [*Volk*] for the place of greatest historical power and, from community with this group, to bring to light the historical existence of the nation and its cultural circle.

Finally, we have derived from our idea of truth consequences for the pursuit of science and for the university no less radically than you have done. Our conflicts with the reactionaries among the faculties and in the senate have revolved entirely around this point. An article has caused all the representatives of the old humanism to rise up against us. In July, 1932, on the day before the political reaction deprived us of all possibility of realization, we stood up against the old humanism in favor of the experimental structure of a university, in which the new existential attitude would be the standard and the struggle against the corruption of the university, which we pointed out, would be taken up.[14]

Your construction of history is determined by the opposition between autonomous and theonomous ages, hence, by the basic presupposition of Religious Socialism. You characterize the late antiquity as "God-estrangement of the late culture," which knows God only as the unhistorical beyond of being, the bourgeois age as the self-determination of reason and freedom, pre-Christian paganism as an unbroken theonomy, namely, as a simple unity of the historical and sacred *Horos;* and you characterize both pagan theonomy and autonomy as demonic. On the other hand, you characterize true theonomy by saying, "The historical *Horos* is also the sacred *Horos,* and nevertheless, in return, the sacred *Horos,* endowed with the power of the eternal, is a boundary that consumes the historical as something transient." We spoke of theonomy as the "breakthrough of the bearing and consuming ground and abyss," invading the forms of historical life. You are aware even of heteronomy, when you speak of the "destruction of knowledge by an antinatural impulse," and you have tried to show that, therefore, there is something in the new theonomy that is not intended.

Your description of Protestant theology, of its development and its task, contains almost every decisive thought, on account of which the theology of Religious Socialism was branded heretical by the church theologians: the "evangelical turning against itself" and the insecurity that goes with it as the basic attitude of evangelical Protestant theology; the surprising agreement with the doctrine of the fundamental identity of theology with a theonomous philosophy (compare *Das System der Wissenschaften* [15] and *Die Religiöse Verwirklichung*); the power of such a philosophy or theology "to know the fundamental motive power of the common life (compare the brief programmatic essay "On the Idea of a Theology of Culture" and the development of its themes in the *Kairos* volumes);[16] the conquest of historicism by the interpretation of the history of Christ as the "center of history" (compare this formulation in the essay *"Christologie und Geschichte"*);[17] the significance of Feuerbach for theology (compare the expression "the constant suspicion of religion of itself as ideology"); the protest against the use of faith to "exalt historical facts" and the resultant freedom for radical historical criticism; the characterization of Barthian transcendence of history as indirectly supporting the demonry of the time (compare page 119 of your book, and the many places in our works); and finally, what also surprises me is your assertion that the idea of justification be applied also to thinking,[18] against which you have, until now, always protested.[19] And when you oppose a "reflective historical self-constitution of the Church [*geschichtsüberlegenes Eigenwesen der Kirche*]," you then are affirming our conception of Protestantism and secularism; when you want to keep theology from "tossing at men a traditional theological conceptual scheme, as though putting a sack over their heads," you thereby repeat a demand that all Religious Socialists never cease to make of the church, and then I absolutely do not know how you can side with Gogarten and not with us. I can explain this only as a consequence of the frightful confusion of all fronts in the present spiritual conflict. But you have had the spiritual means to contribute to the dispelling of this confusion. And that, through keeping silent about your actual relationship to the work of Religious Socialism, you have not done this, for this I blame you in behalf of the present spiritual situation.

I am amazed and disturbed when I survey the evidence, not so much because of the degree of your dependence on the intellectual labors of Religious Socialism—although this is much greater than I had expected—but because of the real agreement in basic principle and in almost every particular. And I ask you, how can you write, "It is by the power of the present hour in nation and state that we are all together drawn into the pure and original questioning," when all the pure, original questioning that you put forth has, for years past, been put forth and answered by those whom you call your keenest opponents, in such a way that you are able to make their answers the foundation of your own? The older generation still know of these things and shake their heads. But how can you justify it to the younger generations, who are entirely ignorant of all this, when you paint for them a picture of current developments that, from the outset, blocks their access to an understanding of actual development?

2. You may nevertheless respond that what is decisive is not something categorical but a concrete application of concepts and that a difference of application justifies your remaining silent about the extent of our common foundation. I cannot acknowledge this defense. Instead of freeing you from blame in the first instance, this excuse brings a second charge against you: To make them serve your own purpose, you partly empty, partly twist the categories that you use, and thereby you deprive the *Kairos* doctrine of the credit among your theological opponents that it has in broader theological circles. And this is why I react so forcefully and comprehensively to your dual relationship to the *Kairos* doctrine.

Perhaps you recall our distinction between the sacramental and prophetic attitudes. It is the distinction between the holy as consecration given in space and time, and the holy that, in the sense of Jesus' preaching of the Kingdom of God, "is at hand" and therefore is both promise and demand. This eschatological moment belongs inseparably to the *Kairos* doctrine, in early Christianity as in Religious Socialism. It unites us with Barth, insofar as we, with him, combat the tangible presence of the divine in a finite being or event; it separates us from Barth, because for him the eschatological has a supernatural character, whereas for us it is paradoxical. We put transcendence not in an undialectical opposition to history, rather, we believe that it can only be understood as genuine transcendence when it is understood as something that breaks into history again and again and shakes it and turns it. In this conception you and we are united. The theology of *Kairos* stands exactly in the middle between the theology of young national Lutheranism and dialectical theology. It regards the latter as a deviation into abstract transcendence, and the former as a deviation into the demonic sacramental. Coming forth against both is the prophetic early Christian paradox that the Kingdom of God enters *into* history and remains *above* history. It is clear that such an attitude neither was nor is suitable for the undialectical necessities of church political conflicts. But I cannot abandon the hope that in both situations there will be theologians and nontheologians who will find in the undistorted *Kairos* idea a way out of the cul-de-sac into which you as well as Barth must, in the long run, lead theology and the church. So long, indeed, as the battle rages, we shall stand with those who defend the eschatological standpoint against the assault of a demonic sacramentalism. If even a higher price must be paid for this, in terms of a narrow supernaturalism and an obdurate orthodoxy, it is better to pay it than to abandon the eschaton to an absolutely posited finite entity.

In the light of these remarks, I can summarize my critique of your book in this sentence: *You have perverted the prophetic, eschatologically conceived Kairos doctrine into a sacerdotal-sacramental consecration of a current event.* This can be shown at every point where you agree with the *Kairos* doctrine and the ideas of Religious Socialism that it entails.

In your book, you have put yourself on the ground of the Religious Socialist interpretation of the bourgeois age. But with this decisive difference: *We* understand the present as a struggle for what is coming, in which theonomy will face more defeat than victory and in which a realism of faith will keep us from perceiving the fulfillment in one romanticized event or another. Our whole presentation is oriented toward this rule. First you look to this rule, then you forsake it, first for the year 1918, then for the year 1933. In the first case, in the sense of an unbroken negativity, in the second case, in the sense of an unbroken positivity. You exalt absolute values, as they may be necessary in political propaganda, to theological validity. Since, however, this is impossible, since nothing finite can remain standing under the unconditional Yes or No, in your interpretation of the present, you actually thus deny the theological plane in favor of the propagandistic. The age of "confusion and corruption"; "abyss of the nation and of the end of history"; a "people and a state sick to death"; a "nation sick to death"; "a time of need and of conflict"; "frightful crisis of the age of history" that, perhaps, would devour everything; "recognition of the situation of the time of decomposition"; "the death crisis of our nation"; "secularism, unbelief and superstition"; "degenerate public order"; "flight from the crisis of history"—it is what Fichte called "the age of consummate sinfulness."

But there is no such age. And no age has the religious and theological right to designate another to be such. "Judge not, that you be not judged," applies also to ages and nations. A judgment such as you give is possible on the ground of the self-certainty that one lives in the age of perfect bliss; for only in such an age does one have the possibility of knowing perfect sinfulness. And just this feeling comes to expression in every one of your words, most clearly where you attribute to current events the quality of holiness. "The new will . . . has come upon us and swooped us up like a sacred storm." Our most recent history has "plunged [us] into the consecrating power of a dark fate." "Here is to be perceived the work of the Almighty Lord, whose instruments we essentially must be." "The sacred spring of the nation," "from this God works uprising and upheaval." The theological consecration of the present is expressed most sharply in the section entitled "The Present Hour of Theology." Here I would have to quote almost every sentence. For you, Protestant theology is possible only "if it is altogether open from within to the great and the new, which has broken through with the National Socialist movement. Its world view should be the sustaining, naturally historical basis of life for the German man of evangelical faith." And finally, with your italics: *the liberation of our nation, the uprising of a new age of history* [is] also the liberation and the uprising of evangelical Christianity." Therefore, you have approximated the year 1933 so closely to the year 33, that it has gained for you the meaning of an event in the history of salvation.

These absolute values, the negative as well as the positive, stand in clear contradiction to the *Kairos* idea and have never been used by the theology of Religious Socialism. We have never characterized the immediately preceding so-called Wilhelmine Epoch as the

age of consummate sinfulness, although politically and propagan-
distically we have had every occasion to do so, since we have made
it responsible for the lost war and for all its consequences up to
the present. But to draw from this a theological and therefore
absolute value judgment would make no sense to us. We have
never called an age sinful, but we have called powers demonic.
And what is more important, we have interpreted the demonic
dialectically:[20] It is never destructive but always also creative and
sustaining. If you had considered this dialectic, then you would
have taken the objection that you yourself raise more seriously
than you do: You ask whether the current events might not be a
concealed form of salvation of the capitalist system. You answer by
renouncing every analysis of the actual events with reference to the
paradoxical unity of originality and reflection in the present movement. This, however, is in no way an answer to the question.

Instead of this evasion, you should have asked further whether
in general a political movement in a particular country, however
powerfully it prevail, is able at the outset to abolish a social structure in which it is involved and by which it lives. Indeed, if one calls
persons, groups, and trends demonic, and moreover in the entirely undialectical sense of wicked, then it is easy, after abolishing
them, to prove triumphantly the victory over "the mass of demonry." But one only shows by this that he has understood nothing of the true depth and power of the demonic. And for this I do
indeed blame you and at the same time prove that through our
understanding of the demonic dialectic we have avoided consecrating even the most important and value-laden events. It was
Kairos for us, because the demonry of capitalism was disclosed,
because resistance to it arose out of the world catastrophe full of
promises and demands. Nothing more can or may be inferred from
the *Kairos* idea. We cannot and may not go beyond promise and
demand. This is the realism of faith that belongs to the theology
of *Kairos*. It is no accident that you have not been alone in using
this category of Religious Socialism. From your standpoint you are
justified, for you are impelled not by the realism of faith but by an
unbroken enthusiasm that deprives you of critical insight and critical utterance. As a Protestant theologian and a spokesman for the
present cultural situation we should expect this from you.

3. Allow me to offer now two examples from theology and

philosophy. When we first joined the socialist movement, it was at once clear to us that, at one decisive point, we must enter as uncompromising critics and revisionists. Intrinsic to every prophetic eschatological movement is the danger of utopianism. Utopianism, however, is the absolutizing of a finite possibility, even of a possibility that can be expected. We must resist this, but we may not and want not to break the burden of demand and the passion of expectation. In this necessity—I can recall the exact day —the *Kairos* idea was discovered. Many, perhaps, do not know that it was discovered in the struggle with the problem of utopianism. By means of this struggle we reached a position from which we had the possibility to appreciate the significance of the historical moment for the formation of the future, yet without becoming utopians, for at the end of every utopian enthusiasm stands disappointment and doubt. And I believe that it would have been your task, as a theologian in the current victorious movement, to adopt the same attitude that we held against utopian enthusiasm, against ideological enthusiasm, which is the danger of every victorious power. Here lies the true theological task. Your book shows me that you have neither seen it nor fulfilled it. The concepts of the theology of *Kairos* would have made it possible for you to do this. However, you have adopted only their form, and just there where they should have been applied to your particular situation, you twisted them. An unbroken sacramentalism of the given is the consequence. Instead of breaking theologically ideological enthusiasm and transforming it into a realism of faith, you strengthen it and therefore share the responsibility for the crisis of despair that must erupt with every single apparent or real failure. You admit that such failures lie within the realm of possibility. You have not become so intoxicated as not to see these possibilities, but you have not been sober enough to find the theological word that sobers those who are intoxicated without depriving them of courage and daring.

Here is another example to distinguish our theological attitudes: You speak of the "filth of economic materialism." About this I make two observations: First, in your choice of a metaphor, I perceive the complex suppression of a situation with which you have not inwardly come to terms; second, the plain ignorance of the fact that economic materialism is a method of inquiry that arose in the struggle against the metaphysical materialism of Feuerbach and in connection with a high-flying ethical idealism that was always prepared for martyrdom. Otherwise, this method has found its way into all of the historical sciences and is indispensable in any deeply penetrating investigation. Nevertheless, you are right to criticize insofar as there was, at the end of the previous century, a way of metaphysical materialism that flowed from the bourgeoisie into the worker movement, so that Religious Socialism faced an antireligious front. Again, it was our task to take a sharply critical stand against this situation without falling into the pharisaism of "church" theologians, which you denounce. From the necessity of this situation, the ideas of the "secularism of faith" and of the "latent church" were born. But for you, there is no struggle against metaphysical materialism or against enmity toward religion. The confession of positive Christianity belongs to your political program. But should you not as a theologian now have the task of bringing to light the fate of every political confession that binds it to religion and to subject this to the same sharp criticism that we applied to materialism? Indeed, you should have been able to find this doctrine in Luther, who waged war mightily enough against the self-made gods; but this can be treated as a matter of personal piety.

This is not so with Feuerbach, who applies the ideology doctrine to man in his natural constitution, or with the young Marx, who applies it to social classes, or with Freud, who applies it to the mass psyche. Here especially, the ancient demand of "know thyself" finds a methodological fulfillment of inevitable clarity. It should have been your theological duty to use these concepts to disclose the ideological misuse of religious confession by reactionaries and petit bourgeois in their antiproletarian class struggle. It is nevertheless the case that behind an ideological theism lies concealed a—now more filthy—practical materialism, whereas a heroic idealism can stand behind materialistic atheism. I can hardly conceive of a more important, concretely theological task in the present hour than to work this out. You, however, take every ideology, positive as well as negative, according to what it says instead of according to what it is. Here also there is a critically unbroken enthusiasm as opposed to the realism of faith, priestly consecration instead of prophetic disclosure.

4. You also make demands of the new philosophy that is associated with the theology of *Kairos*. Here also I must follow you and show you how you have twisted the original intentions of the new philosophy because of your basic sacramental attitude. I cite as a first example your critique of Heidegger. In fact, Heidegger must be criticized from the standpoint of existential philosophical thinking. He has concealed the concrete historical limitations of his concepts by his abstract use of the concept of historicity. However, he cannot be charged as an existential philosopher on account of his negativity, for this amounts to an attack on existential philosophy itself, to which you yourself, indeed, formally subscribe. Existential philosophy is what it is because, in contrast to idealism, it presupposes existence outside of the idea, and it makes this its theme. That which makes existence into existence is not the same as that which causes existence to stand in the idea, in some essence. The later Schelling recognized this, when, in connection with his doctrine of evil, he discovered the basic antithesis of both philosophies; so did Kierkegaad, when he found the basic human existential category in despair; so did Marx, when, in opposition to Feuerbach's doctrine of man, he took as his starting point the process of dehumanization in proletarian existence; so did Jaspers, when he made failure the last existential possibility of man; so did Heidegger, when he posited radical questioning before the abyss of nothingness. Thus did I try to develop existential historical categories from an analysis of the threatening aspect of our historical existence. This existential threatening is not cancelled when a historical group has gathered power to itself. Should it not, therefore, be the task of the existential philosopher in the present situation to elaborate, in general and in concrete applications, the existential threat of every historical actuality, even when it contains concealed promises? In your critique of Heidegger, as well as in your own philosophical attitude, you prove to be an enthusiastic idealist, not an existential philosopher. You consecrate instead of disclosing.

From this standpoint, I question your demand for a new Socrates. Historically, everything contradicts it: Socrates at the end of a determinate period of history, by his discovery of the concept, is the bearer of the rational and autonomous development that follows him; a dialectician in the strict sense of one who leads dialogues, not to clarify this matter or that, but to ground human and political existence in thought. In contrast is our situation: the end of a rational and autonomous development; in transition to a new determinate period; bound by the necessities of a late capitalistic organization of the masses, which makes free dialogue about foundations more and more impossible—as indeed it has also been explicitly excluded by you.

All that remains is what Kierkegaard, in contrast to the systematic thinker, perceived as the existential *(existentiell)* element in Socrates, a questioning about questioning itself. This, however, is neither the exclusive nor the predominant characteristic of the Socratic method. You take the Kierkegaardian symbol, not the actual Socrates. And this has deeper foundations: You conceal thereby that you side with Nietzsche and his struggle against Socrates. What you say about Nietzsche is such a mass of historical injustice that it can be explained by your determined will not to disturb the consecration of present events by recalling their ancestors. For you would have disturbed nothing more than the hardly to be overrated influence that Nietzsche had on the development of the feeling and thinking of the younger generation and that it continues to have on the formation of the new political dogma. And this influence is due precisely to his protest against the Socratic influence on every spiritual and political realm. It is as easy to show that the ideas that you defend are present in Nietzsche, seminally or developed, as it is to show that all of these ideas are explicitly aristocratic.

I write this not to regain for a violated historical truth what rightfully belongs to it; rather, I write this to show you once more how, for the sake of your enthusiastic consecrating attitude, you have denied the primary, namely, critical duty of the philosopher. Otherwise, you should have resisted the unbroken stream of vitalism, irrationalism, and voluntarism, as we have tried to counteract an empty rationalism, intellectualism, and mechanism. We have developed the significance of the vital, of eros, of the will, with such emphasis that we have been repeatedly blamed for fascism. I do not see that you have demanded of philosophy or even undertaken the corresponding converse task.

Therefore, I come to your doctrine of truth, of Logos and *nomos.* It might appear as though your doctrine were a—very spiritual—

development of our doctrine of dynamic truth. But this is not the case. You deprive the Logos of its critical power, which it must preserve in spite of its strong commitment to the *Kairos*. This happens in three steps. First, you bind the Logos to the *nomos* of a historical actuality; this may be its scientific self-consciousness. Second, you recognize only the *nomos* of a nation. Third, this *nomos* is interchangeable with and dependent upon the actions of the political shapers of the nation. The result is, necessarily, that the Logos is dependent upon that group within the nation that happens to be the bearer of power. The Logos is the scientifically shaped self-consciousness of whatever this group decides to make of the *nomos* of the nation. Practically, this means that you justify what is said in great chorus with Nietzsche, that truth is the expression of the group that bears power and of its being. This stands in indissoluble contradiction to the Socratic method, but also to the *Kairos* doctrine that has endeavored to go beyond the Socratic.

First, that which you call *nomos,* and which, as the law of form, is closely related to the Platonic idea, has been interpreted by us as the unity of unity and inexhaustibility. For the sake of the moment of unity, logical knowledge is possible; for the sake of inexhaustibility, this unity cannot be static. The relationship between both elements is different in every sphere of knowledge, but in no case is the possibility of critical control lacking. I cannot develop this any further here. Second, we have bound the Logos not to the law of form of any nation, but to the form of a historical constellation in which the nation can take a decisive place, but it has its form only within a comprehensive network of forms and can discover Logos only in this context. How important this insight is methodologically will be shown below in the treatment of some historical sociological questions. In this way, joining truth to power is eliminated insofar as every power finds its limits within the whole constellation. No particular historical form can bind the Logos to itself, just as no nation can bind God to itself. The first insight we owe to Plato, the second to Amos. In an "hour of history" in which the comprehensive critical seriousness of the idea of truth is threatened to be swept away in a flood of speech against the objectivity of knowledge, the philosopher and the theologian must bear witness to both. Third, for us, the joining of truth to a historical actuality has never meant that truth is nothing more than the expression or self-interpretation of this historical actuality. We have often treated the relation of "expression" and "validity," and we have come to the opinion that for one who knows there can be only *one* intention, namely, validity; but that precisely when his intention is directed for the most part and most strongly to validity, to the in itself, and to the objective, does the power of expression enter his thought. And, what is more, the less he intends it the more will he yet at the same time be filled with the inner power of its presence. But in every act of knowing, it is not this inner capability that is intended, but truth. You have not developed this distinction, and you could not, because you yourself have endeavored more for "expression" than for "validity," and therefore—this is the guiding dialectic of the idea of truth—you have failed to reach even the deepest expression of what has occurred.

Through these philosophical and theological examples and their critical treatment, I believe that I have shown sufficiently that you have twisted the meaning of the *Kairos* doctrine, in whose categories you think, until it has come to mean just the opposite of what it is supposed to mean. I have contended that the concepts themselves offer the possibility of such a use. You must have wrested from each one of them a decisive element, in order to force them into the service of your theological and philosophical will. I must defend myself against this and shall continue to do so, while I investigate particular problems.

II

1. Theologically, it is not clear at all in your case how you conceive, in strict concepts, the relation between contemporary history and new theology. Is current history a source of revelation alongside the biblical documents? That almost seems to be so with you. If it were so, then those who judge contemporary history differently from you would be excluded from one source of revelation, and would be so on the basis of a political judgment about political events. In the "German Evangelical" church they, like Jewish Christians, could only be members with fewer rights than others. And their theology would be lacking a source of religious knowledge that would be accessible to those with a different political judgment. I wonder whether such a conception can in any way be

justified by the *Kairos* concept. I do not see how; but I grant that we did not sufficiently pursue the problems that arise here and that therefore such mistaken interpretations were not clearly enough excluded. To the extent that current history and its record in your book force a clarification of these problems, I am grateful, despite all my criticism. The concept of revelation has two sides that must be clearly separated. In the first place, revelation is real only as "a correlation of revelation *(Offenbarungskorrelation)*." Revelation is not a concept of objectifying thinking. It is revelation only as an actual revelation for someone. But—and this is the other side— when it does take place, that is, when it is actualized correlatively, it is exclusive. There can be no other revelations beside it but only other situations from which one enters into the revelational corre- lation. Every new situation changes the correlation but does not change the revelation. If I wanted to express the matter without using the word "revelation," I would speak of the place from which our existence gets its meaning, a meaning that is unconditioned and exclusive, simultaneously sustaining and directing. Revelation is that to which I am conscious of being unconditionally subject as the final criterion of my thinking and acting.

The *Kairos*, the historical time, can thus never of itself be a revelation. It can only indicate the entering of a new correlation of revelation. It designates the moment in which the meaning of revelation discloses itself anew for knowledge and action, in which, for example, the final criterion of truth over against a temporal constellation is visible anew, as, say, the cross of Christ over against capitalistic or nationalistic demonry. If you call the Yes to such a new disclosure of revelation a "risk," I agree with you, presupposing, first, that you do not call the standing in a correla- tion of revelation itself a risk and, second, that you acknowledge the relativizing of what is risked in all its consequences. Revelation is the *prius,* not the object, of the risk. It is that which has already grasped me before I take any daring action. It would be neither exclusive nor unconditioned if it depended on my risk, or daring. "To risk something for Christ or for God" is a formula that has always sounded to me somewhat blasphemous.

In a *Kairos,* by contrast, taking a risk does have its place. From this it follows that the community of revelation is *not* dependent on the community of risk. In every historical time there is more than can be exhausted by one interpretation. Hence, one theological group may indeed claim to stand more deeply in the *Kairos* than another, but it does not exclude the other group from the revelatory correlation in which they stand together. Risk includes the consciousness that one may fail. It is neither unconditioned nor exclusive. So, for example, in our case: For you and for others, *Kairos* is the time that you designate "the German hour," whereas for us it was a time that could be called the "hour of socialism" and of which, in our view, German history is a part that cannot be understood in isolation from the whole. For Barth, who thereby pays tribute to the *Kairos* without intending to do so, it is the hour of the liberation of the church from the secular elements by which it had been penetrated during the bourgeois centuries—something that is possible only because secularism as a historical phenomenon has been weakened in itself.

All three interpretations of the *Kairos* are risks. Now, do you exclude from fully legitimate work in German Protestant theology the two that you do not affirm? Instead of struggling with them for the best and truest interpretation? Is German theology not a powerful spiritual tradition that has long since laid a manifold foundation even beyond the boundaries of Germany, and that can continue to work on numerous theological problems in the authority of this its tradition even when it is hardly affected by current history? The decisive point is—and I owe a clear insight into this from my contradiction to your book—that revelation and *Kairos,* the pure state of being grasped and the taking of a risk, the exclusivity of the criterion and the relativity of the concrete decision, lie on different planes. Having an intention toward the first is what makes a theologian a theologian, it provides the final criterion; standing in the second is what gives him a proximity to current events and a power to affect history. For the sake of the second, you have left the first out of view in your book; and you have done so just at a time when, because of the eruption of the powers of origin, it was more necessary than it had been for centuries to give powerful emphasis to the cross as a criterion.

2. As I did with your theological attitude, so too I must attack your scientific attitude. Do you seriously think it is scientifically responsible to write a book on the present spiritual situation without providing a sociological analysis of the groups and strata by

which particular spiritual tendencies are borne? I mentioned these things while discussing the theological meaning of investigating ideologies; now I come to it in connection with my scientific, historical critique. Many of your historical judgments can be understood at all only because you have consciously or unconsciously refused to consider the most manifest sociological insights. That, in turn, can be explained only because sociology is one of the sharpest weapons against an unbroken enthusiasm. Some examples: You boast of having stood against the "tide covering the breadth of public life." Has it never caught your attention that at the universities, in so-called higher society, in the middle class, and among the farmers nothing of such a tide could be noticed, though one could notice an exactly opposite tide? Now, if you have not noticed it, then *I* can tell you that we who stood alone hopelessly in these groups were made to feel at every step what the real tide was: the reaction of all levels of the bourgeoisie against participation by the workers in political activity! Had you seen that with a sociologically sharpened vision, you would not boast of having "hollowed out" the postwar state and of having stripped it of as much authority as possible. That occurred much more effectively through the bourgeoisie. Furthermore, if that really is the case, you should not have neglected to mention the world economic crisis and the accompanying acute threat to the middle class and the new social type created by it, the permanently unemployed.

In view of the worldwide scope of these phenomena and of the similar reactions in many countries, you ought to have used the picture of late autumn rather than that of spring, and you should not have restricted it just to Germany. How can a cultural circle that has already passed its classical period, that is, the period of its blossoming, suddenly begin again with spring? These insights would not have had to alter your positive judgment about present events. But they would have given it the scientific support that it now lacks. One cannot deduce facts from enthusiasm any more than from faith. If as a theological historian you wanted to show what is the spiritual situation of the present, you could have performed a great service, had you done nothing more than call attention to other sociological connections than those that we see, and had you pointed out the present sociological structure in Central Europe as the background of the present spiritual situation. Then you would have been able to make visible the vast and, in a philosophical historical sense, the threatening wealth of tensions within the present political unity; and therewith you would have given a genuine analysis that would have been concrete, existential, and historical.

Furthermore, such an effort, which from a scientific standpoint is unconditionally requisite, would have prevented you from taking passing shots at foreign countries so superciliously: your assertions that philosophy in other countries gave essentially "subhuman-naturalistic definitions of ultimate validity," that cultural imperialism is a "specifically Welsh" idea, that "authoritarian government [is] Welsh," that non-German Protestant Christianity could not of its own, without German power, maintain its evangelical character; to say nothing of your judgments about Russia, which, too, however perceptive they are, should at least be material and pertinent. That leads me to the question: Is this invitation to unchecked judgments about other peoples really a service to one's own? And if you are justly indignant about the "lie of the world conscience" and the "culpable silence of the churches at Versailles," you ought at least to have mentioned the indignation that the silence of the German churches on the day of the Jewish boycott, for example, evoked in the churches and nonchurches of the whole world! Just because you do approve, for philosophical and theological reasons, laws concerning races, it would have been an ethical duty of the time and a religious responsibility toward our nation if you had made so sharp a distinction between racial legislation and racial hatred as we did between the structural necessity of class warfare in capitalism and class hatred, a hatred against which we then also did battle. It is your unrefracted sacramentalism that, again, prevents you from seeing what otherwise you should have and could have seen.

3. To speak with you about the nation, the state, and the church demands more space than the limits of this letter allow. So I will restrict myself to what is indispensable in the framework of my whole critique of your book. In order to make it possible to absolutize the national *Kairos*, you restrict the *Horos*, the creative darkness, to the limitedness of human existence by people and blood. Using the language of my last book, *Die sozialistische Entscheidung* (The socialist decision),[21] you call it the "original"; and the

question, which I raised systematically there, of how reflection could create originality you answer with the assertion that there is a paradox and a mystery. It seems to me, now, that no passage in your book contains as much fiction as this one. The identity of the sacred *Horos* and the origin is not proved; neither is the identity of origin and people, nor the identity of people and blood-bond. Yet these three identifications are the scaffolding of your whole argument. Without them the decisive presupposition of the whole book would amount to nothing. "In the whole of our human historical life the limit is effective. Everywhere in it this limit reveals itself . . . its luminosity the light of thinking, its glow the blood of life,"[22] you say, in agreement with what we said about the abyss, the inexhaustibility, the meaning-giving depth of our existence over against a rationalistic philosophy of form. But why do you then restrict the *Horos,* which is to be a power in the whole of our historical life, to the origin? Is it not also effective in the created forms in which man creates something beyond the origin, is it not effective in the "where to" through which, in historical life, the "where from" is transcended? Is the "light of thinking" in Plato's or Lao-tse's thought only the origin that limits them? How could it then provide illumination through times and spaces that have nothing to do with their origin? Is this not to be understood only because the transcendent, meaning-giving center shows its power precisely in this that it breaks through the boundaries of origin? And is the same not true of living as it is of thinking?

The sacred boundary as "the blood of life" glows in Saint Francis and in Buddha not in virtue of their origin but in virtue of an explicit break with their origin. You do know, of course, that the sacred *Horos* can devour the natural and historical one, but you never give any indication that it can transcend it, that it can lead to a new actualization, historical, but no longer bound to an origin. This is exemplified partly by the exilic community and unrestrictedly by the first Christian community. Here the "where to" and not the "where from" is the basis of existence. Hence comes the necessity for you to distance yourself so strongly from the New Testament attitude and to call the most religious period of human history an "alienation from God on the part of a late culture." It was indeed a time of estrangement from origin. Autonomy and the crises of autonomy had preceded it. But a new theonomy had broken in, and the document of this irruption is the New Testament. If alienation from a piety of origin is as such an alienation from God, then there is no book more alienated from God than the New Testament.

Concretely, origin means, for you, the people. Unfortunately, you do not define that term clearly. But if one puts together the various elements that you name (natural, historical, blood-related, political), what emerges as a picture of the ideal type is the European nation-state as it was created by the French Revolution in opposition to the feudal and dynastic state. Now, there can be no doubt that the nation-state in this sense is the reality that most immediately has historical power. And I would concede that Religious Socialism, because of its interest in the social order of society, paid too little attention to the nation-state and the powers of origin that are concentrated in it (I myself did so only in my last book). I also concede that there can be moments in history in which the destiny of a people can signify not only for it itself but also for the world a *Kairos,* a historically outstanding time that is to be religiously interpreted, a promise and a demand.

If your book had said only this, I could have spared myself the subsequent critique. But it says very much more and very much else. It says, for example, that origin and nation are identical. But how can that be justified unless "nation" *(Volk)* becomes a name for every natural, historical group at all: that is, kinship, clan, blood group, racial group, topographical group, social status group, linguistic group, state group. All these groups can get together and exclude one another. In all of them there are powers of origin. But the *Volk* that has the marks you cite is neither the dynastic state nor the linguistic group nor the social stratum (for example, medieval knighthood, which, having a power of origin, represented a cross section of the countries of Christianity), nor the race, and so on. The "nation" that you speak of in a circumscribed sense is a unique phenomenon scarcely a hundred and fifty years old. If that is so, it is exceedingly dubious to posit it with metaphysical absoluteness as the power of origin in general and consequently as the only actualization of the sacred *Horos.*

Indeed, I must confess that, from this perspective, the enticing concept of a nation's *nomos* (law of form [*Gestaltgesetz*]) and the less enticing concept of a people's Logos (concept of the law of form [*begriffene Gestaltgesetz*]) has become dubious to me. For what does a law mean if it not only comprehends changing phenomena but rather, as you often put it, is itself undergoing constant change? If historical action changes the laws, the *nomoi,* of the nation in every moment, what does it then mean to act in accord with the structural law? If I change it through what I do, then it is no longer a law for my doing. And that is how, as a matter of fact, it is. At present a new form of the German nation is being created through the strongest exertion of will, but what is it supposed to mean concretely to say that a law of form, previously at hand, is being actualized, when you say at the same time that the coming law of form must first be created? Of what value is a concept for which there are no possibilities of concrete application? Such words might make sense in a solemn, ritual, and priestly language; they do not communicate fruitful scientific knowledge.

Now to the third identification, which leads wholly into the sphere of the mythical: the equation of nation and blood-bond. You give the greatest weight to this identification when you assert that through the idea of a blood-bond the call "This far but no farther" is made against the plunge of "Euramerican culture from cliff to cliff." The idea of a blood-bond thus has outright salvatory significance for one part of mankind. That would make it all the more important to work out clearly what is involved. Obviously, you do not mean the making of racial laws, which practically is directed only against the Jews and not against the other peoples of the Euramerican cultural circle. Thus, blood-bond must mean something more narrow. It may mean the specific blood constitution of the so-called Nordic man; but, on the one hand, that comprises non-German nations and, on the other hand, does not apply to large groups of the German nation. That leaves only the German nation itself and the demand to prevent any mixing of blood beyond its borders and, along the lines of the racial laws, to deprive of their rights those who already bear mixed blood of this kind. Such a thing would mean tearing to pieces the tradition of more than a thousand years that the Christian, occidental world represents one family of nations just because, from its historical beginnings on, it has been formed in common by Christianity. Do you, precisely as a theologian, want to advise the German leaders to take such a step, which they themselves obviously have not had

in view? Are you, precisely as a theologian, called to subordinate
the sacramental consanguinity of Christianity, which is given with
the Lord's Supper, to the natural historical consanguinity? Again
I ask, as I have already so often asked: As a theologian, and precisely if you wanted to emphasize so much the power of origin in
blood, would it have been your task to work out the boundary of
its power with the aid of the symbolism of the Lord's Supper?

What is original in your doctrine of the state is your concept of
the "hidden sovereign." I shall go into it because it also touches
on matters theological. You use the concept in order to give the
state a content that, as a total state, it needs and, at the same time,
in order to provide a basis for the right of revolution in contrast
to the older Lutheran doctrine. I shall begin with the second. Have
you never asked yourself the question that I have so often encountered, that has misled so many about the honesty of our church,
and that is so obvious: How is it possible that a church that for
centuries yielded to every feudal-dynastic government, even those
that most corrupted the people, and taught unconditional obedience to just these "bad governments" suddenly forgot that doctrine the moment when a state was created in which someone other
than the old classes represented the government? In the moment
when certain groups had lost their inherited privileges, Lutheranism, represented by the neonational Lutheran theology, developed a doctrine of "conditional obedience." Would this not have
been the place to ask about the ideological character of both doctrines? From this point of view, I must almost shudder when you
write: "It was necessary . . . to wrest from the existing state as much
of its formative authority as possible." Whose unconscious tool
were you when you did that and justified it theologically? And what
kind of consequences must it have if *that* becomes the theological
doctrine?

The "hidden sovereign" is a mystical reality, if it is a reality. No
one can derive from it a concrete decision. Everyone can assert,
and even give one's life for the assertion, that the manifest sovereign of a time is disobedient to the hidden one. Neither the old
Calvinist doctrine of the right to resist on the part of the subordinate authorities nor the socialistic doctrine of the class character
of the capitalist state gives so unlimited a right of revolution, a
right so free of all objective norms, as does this doctrine. Or is it

to be applied only once and never again? But does it then deserve the name of doctrine? Furthermore, what does the idea of a hidden sovereign mean for the activity of the state itself? It gives the state the task of protecting and developing the natural, historical nationality, a demand that in the nation-state is self-evident; but there is simply no way of seeing how the idea of a hidden sovereign brings something new besides that.

I suspect, therefore, that it has a third task to fulfill, the one most important for you: In place of the realm of God's grace on one side and of the sovereignty of the people on the other, it is to create for the rulers an obligation and a responsibility. In a state in which the will of one man is the only law, that is indeed of greatest significance. But again I ask: Is the hidden sovereign suited to that? The domain of God's grace provided a corrective against arbitrariness insofar as the Christian notion of God had definite explicit traits by which the conscience of the ruler could be oriented and by which the people could judge the actions of the ruler. And the sovereignty of the people was represented in a determinable form as the will of the majority. The hidden sovereign has no such definiteness. He gets it, according to your own view, through the current historical destiny, above all, through the action of the rulers, for whom he is, however, to be the sovereign.

But what is a sovereign that is created and changed by those who are subjected to him? Does not your wish to avoid the autocratic consequences of the destruction of democracy, which you yourself fear, drive you into a mysticism from which nothing concretely follows? Would it not have been more correct and more honest to have here precisely a realism that seeks for real antiautocratic correctives than an enthusiasm that declares the return to autocracy to be "improbable"? What kind of doctrine of man can bring you as a theologian to such an expectation? And what is the category of the probable doing in a fundamental doctrine of the state?

You yourself feel the weakness of this way out in your discussion of leadership. You know from church history that charismatic leadership is a gift of the historical time and is so, as you rightly say, both for the leaders and for the led. You also know that the charismatic must be transformed into the institutional according to understandable laws. But if that is so, then autocracy can be prevented in no other way than by shifting to correctives of an

aristocratic or democratic character. That, however, brings the
new doctrine of state to the point at which the Religious Socialist
doctrine of state long ago arrived, namely, the proposition that
democracy cannot be constitutive but only corrective in politics.
(Compare my essay "Der Staat als Erwartung und Forderung.")[23]
Can your hidden sovereign offer what the concrete correctives of
autocracy have offered in all higher development of mankind and
must also offer in the future? Is Hegel really so wrong when, in his
history of philosophy, he sets the Christian-Germanic notion of
freedom in opposition to the Asian and pre-Christian principal of
despotism? And is there not contained in the democratic ideal,
alongside the Stoic-Epicurean, the Christian-Germanic element—
the valuation of the individual person, in distinction from the
complete lack of individual significance in Asian thinking? Could
one, for example, justify from the Christian-Germanic tradition a
legally unlimited power, given to *one* individual, to dispose over
the life and death of *every* individual? Would it not have been your
task as a Christian and German philosopher of history to call
attention to this tradition historically and systematically instead of
releasing a declaration of hate, without any critical restriction,
against everything democratic? Even in your statements about
justice among equals and unequals, with which I can formally
agree, you have forgotten to show what *justice* means when there
is no equality. Would that not have been a theological word "of
the hour"?

With enthusiastic approval you portray the claim to totality
made by the state that you see as ideal. (The actual state is significantly more reticent, for example, in economics. Your description
is true only of Russia.) Your approval is especially interesting to
me because I am just now working on an essay[24] in which I try to
make intelligible the rise of the totalitarian state in Eastern and
Central Europe out of the late capitalistic situation of crisis
(spiritual, social, and economic) in countries that do not have an
older democratic formation, namely, out of the necessity of "rein-
tegrating" the increasingly disintegrated masses. Above all, it is
important to me that you think the basis for such a total formation
has to be provided by a *Weltanschauung.* For *"Weltanschauung"* I use
a word that is less intellectualistic but more in accord with current
usage: a "myth." But as soon as that is recognized (and here we

seem to have seen similar necessities from different standpoints), a series of difficult problems arises.

First, a political and dialectical problem: The total state must be sustained by personalities that make decisions on the basis of "creative responsibility." How can such personalities come about? Certainly not without what you yourself call a *Widerspannung*, a resistance, against the hardened forms. You yourself confess that you have gained strength by resistance against the political and spiritual powers of recent times. Democracy provided space, surely too much space, for such resistance. Nevertheless, it provided, according to you, space for the development of uniquely many leader personalities. But what would happen if every such space would be occupied with spirit and with power? What would happen if there were no possibility, either inwardly or outwardly, of getting out of the way? Can personalities in general, or leader personalities in particular, arise without there being space in which, through existential decisions, they grow into the authority to decide for others? Was not the history of Europe from the beginning so rich and creative because there always was enough room to get out of the way?

This question applies, further, to the spiritual. I miss painfully in a book about the present spiritual situation a section on the present situation of spirit. I grant that spirit has had to pay a price because its bearers have been teachers with the security of civil servants or coddled literati. For a century already the real bearers of spirit have for that reason stayed away from those two forms of existence, either voluntarily or involuntarily. In contrast to many liberals, I assert that insecurity, persecution, homelessness, prison, and the threat of death have never been able to harm the real spirit and now too will serve that spirit. But there is a limit. In order to be threatened and persecuted, spirit has first of all to be there; and in order to be there, it must have a space in which it can come to yea-saying through nay-saying. The first step of spirit is to say no to what is immediately given. Does it not contradict the totalitarian idea, as you portray it, to provide space for the development of an existential no? There have been states that have denied spirit this space and have destroyed spirit in itself. Has the seriousness of this question never disturbed you in your enthusiastic portrayal of the total state and in the demand of ruthless intervention, which is said to be better than persuasion? Is there not, between the two, the category of "convincing"—not through words but also through the positing of realities that have the power of symbols? Where are such considerations in someone who simultaneously makes appeal to Socrates?

4. It is above all the church that needs room to get out of the way. What would have become of primitive Christianity or of Protestantism if they had not had such room from the start, and if they had not been able to mature so that they could take up the decisive battles against the powers that wanted to deprive them again of their space? Now, you grant to the Catholic church such space without discussion. You ascribe to this church historical possibilities of life that are independent of the destiny of the German people, and you do not attack these vital possibilities, even though you do regret them. To the Protestant church you deny the possibility of such an independent life. The death crisis of the people was also the death crisis of the church. Now, we did agree that a total state with its claim on the whole man is possible only by the power of a *Weltanschauung* that takes hold of all aspects of the human, the power of a myth. You rightly say that one should not view national socialism simply as a movement to which only a "portion of human existence is entrusted." For only a religiously filled, and not a rationally produced, *Weltanschauung* has such power. But if what is involved is a myth, then the question, which you yourself pose, is very serious indeed: whether this myth "is the sustaining, natural historical vital ground and creative space for Germans of the evangelical faith and evangelical spirit," whether the new picture of the German and the old picture of the Christian agree.

I need not investigate whether they do. I must concern myself, as I have done in this whole letter, only with matters of method, with the theological principle. And in that regard, I ask: Who is to decide this? A serious decision is only one in which a no is possible. If the claim of the total state is justified, then Protestant theology must subject itself to the claim since, according to you, it lacks a historical existence of its own. If the state then says: "No, they do not agree," then the church would have to give itself up in favor of the new myth constituting the totality of the state. The danger that it will openly say no is not large. But what if it says no in a hidden, perhaps unconscious way, if the standard-bearing leaders erase certain features from the picture of the Christian man or paint them over because they do not agree with the new picture of the German man? Why have you not treated this possibility, which in many ways has already become actuality, as a problem of its own? But even the other possibility exists that church and theology might question the agreement of the two pictures. Do you grant to them the same alternative as to the Catholic church? And if you did so, what would become of the totalitarian claim of the state, since the churches too lay claim to the whole man?

At this place there lie the questions that, with totalitarian claims of the state breaking out all over, will be decisive for Protestantism and Christianity and that you in your book—yes, I must say it—enthusiastically bypass. Or do you intend to indicate a solution when you threaten Protestant theology, lacking unity and resisting your demands, in the following words: "If a despot has to come and to impose a doctrine on all of us, the principle of the Reformation would collapse in us"? Are you inclined to summon the despot if theology says no to the unity you presuppose? Are you prepared to sacrifice the Protestant principle for that? You speak here as Religious Socialism would have had to speak if it had been religious Bolshevism. It did not so speak. But if you did not intend to speak so either, then what does this threat mean, what is meant by your unbroken acknowledgement of the state's totalitarian claim on us beyond what the state actually does? What is meant by sacrificing a historical space of its own for German and even for world Protestantism?

In your other statements about the church I can ascertain one welcome agreement among Barth, you, and me. None of us regrets that the state has taken from the church many social and cultural works and that the church can now devote more consideration to its own work. But even in the Berneuchener circle we were already far beyond your positive formulations. Besides proclamation of the Word and meditation, we assigned to the church the task of actualizing symbolically and representatively within itself the Christian idea of love in social forms and of being for the state an impressive indicator of the limits of all compelled actions and an indicator of a reality of a higher order. But we could agree in this matter if you would concede room for such Christian representative activity in the total state. No agreement is possible, however, with the following propositions of yours: "Only leadership as the burning desire . . . to force into the coming forms and shapes of the people's state-life the preachers and the church helpers and workers and all the living religious members with all their goods and work and gifts can protect our church from becoming a dead church now. . . . " To this I can only say: In the first place, you confuse the tasks of state leadership and ecclesiastical leadership. The state will have an interest in actively incorporating into its life the church preachers and workers as it does all of its citizens. But not even the state can have much interest in a church whose leadership imitates the state—with means more imperfect than the state's own—instead of fulfilling its own task and "forcing" its proclaimers and helpers into the coming Kingdom of God. Whether the church is living or dead depends on the power with which it awaits the Kingdom of God and with which, in accord with the time, it seeks to actualize an anticipation of the Kingdom; it does not depend on anything else. The judgment concerning what the time is and how it appears is a risk. And it can be a sign of the highest vitality when different risks are undertaken in the same church and contend with each other. If you declare a church dead when it does not unanimously go along with your risk, you are claiming that it is more than a risk, you do not place yourself with your risk under the cross but elevate it to the rank of revelation alongside the cross.

5. In my *Grundlinien des religiösen Sozialismus* [25] I made a distinction between a *reservatum* and an *obligatum religiosum*. The *reservatum* corresponds to the attitude of the New Testament time which, as you rightly say, was one-sided and conditioned by its time to the extent that it could feel no *obligatum* for people, state, culture, society. The *obligatum* with the *reservatum* is your attitude. You do give to the individual a *reservatum*, the personal relation to God, but not to the church, whose independent historical place you contest. But with that you cancel it, you make it impotent over against the *Weltanschauungen* or myths that sustain the totalitarian state. And it is not fitting, although it is an ancient way out, to reinterpret this defenselessness, as you call it, as a power. Protestantism is defenseless enough as it is. If there were no *reservatum* to which it could withdraw from historical powers, it would be not

only defenseless but long since not even extant. Religious Socialism knew, when accepting the doctrine of the *reservatum religiosum,*
that the religious can never be dissolved into the socialist, that the
church is something quite apart from the *Kairos,* that is, from the
promise and demand that Religious Socialism saw in the broadly
visible irruption of the new social and spiritual arrangement of
society. You took over the *obligatum* but gave up the *reservatum—*
the charge that is basically the theme of my whole letter.

You cannot escape the charge as you try to do in your last letter
to me and repeatedly indicate in the book. You contest the need
to have a *reservatum* over against current history because your
personal relation to God can give you the courage to enter a
historical movement with an unrefracted yes. I quote the relevant
sentence of your book: "When we have the courage, on the basis
of the faith that obeys this truth [of the Gospel], to enter into
something human-historical with our yes, then the unfathomable
sublimity of the truth accompanies us and, in its way, reigns in this
human-historical thing." To the whole line of thought I can only
say that not only I but others as well were shocked and repelled
by it. That each of us must bear the risk of having decided for this
finite possibility and must answer for it before eternity and that,
in so doing, we are dependent on grace, as we are in all our doing,
are certain for a Christian. But to derive from that the right to say
an unrefracted religious and theological yes to this finitude cannot
only not be derived from it but stands in complete contradiction
to our human situation. We should and must enter into finite
things, into human-historical things. But when we enter them conscious "of the unfathomable sublimity of the truth," that is, as
Christians, as theologians, then it is forbidden to us more than to
others who are not filled with this consciousness to become victims
of an enthusiasm that says yes, when nothing other than a simultaneous yes and no ought ever to be said. It would be false if we
wanted to avoid deciding altogether on that account, even to avoid
deciding religiously and theologically in the sense of risk, in order
to spare our theology the judgment that is passed on everything
human-historical. Neither you nor we have tried to escape such
judgment. That holds us together. But you have said yes, whereas
we could say yes only in connection with many a no; not because
we considered our cause to be worse—it was, after all, our risk—

but because we believed that, from the point of view of the eternal, this is the only thing that can be said about something finite and to someone finite.

You once wrote to me that I should write a book that could be of use to Germany in its present situation. I dare to believe that this letter can help Germany more than your book and many similar ones of less value. For if the thoughts of this letter would penetrate deeply into the consciousness of many Germans, *if enthusiasts could be made into believing realists,* this would limit the enormous danger, which you have increased, that enthusiasm, whether on the small scale or the large, will abruptly change into disappointment. To protect the German people, oppressed as they are by their destiny, from that would be the greatest service that could be performed for the people today, and it would include all other philosophical and theological services.

With cordial greetings,

Paul

NOTES

1. Emanuel Hirsch, *Die gegenwärtige geistige Lage im Spiegel philosophischer und theologischer Besinnung: Akademische Vorlesungen zum Verständnis des deutschen Jahr 1933* (Göttingen: Vandenhoeck and Ruprecht, 1934).
2. See Karl Aé (pastor in Dresden) *"Die gegenwärtige geistige Lage: Anmerkungen zu dem Buch Emanuel Hirschs,"* in *Junge Kirche,* Jahrgang 2 (Göttingen: Verlag Junge Kirche, 1934): 507–9; see also Karl Aé, in *Theologische Blätter,* taken from the *Neuen Sachsischen Kirchenblatt,* no. 26 (25 November 1934).
3. See Paul Tillich, *Kairos: Ideen zur Geistlage der Gegenwart,* vol. 6, *Gesammelte Werke* (Stuttgart: Evangelisches Verlag, 1963), 29–41; "Kairos und Logos: Eine Untersuchung zur Metaphysik des Erkennens," in *Gesammelte Werke* 4 (1961), 43–76 (English trans., "Kairos and Logos," in *The Interpretation of History* [New York: Charles Scribner's Sons, 1936]). Hereafter, *Gesammelte Werke* is referred to as *GW.*
4. See Paul Tillich, *Die religiöse Lage der Gegenwart,* vol. 10 (1968), *GW,* 9–93 (English trans., *The Religious Situation* [New York; Henry Holt and Company, 1932]).
5. See Paul Tillich, "Das Dämonische, Ein Beitrag zur Sinndeutung der Geschichte," in *GW* 6:42–71 (English trans. "The Demonic," in *The Interpretation of History*).
6. Edgar Dacqué, palaeontologist. Kurt Leese, philosopher and theologian; see *GW,* supp. vol. 6 (1983), 299ff.
7. See Ernst Krieck, *Volk im Werden* (Oldenburg: O.G. Stalling, 1932).
8. See Paul Tillich, "Die protestantische Verkündigung und der Mensch der Gegenwart," in *GW* 7 (1962), 73–79 (English trans., "The Protestant Message

and the Man of Today," in *The Protestant Era* [Chicago: University of Chicago Press, 1948]).

9. See Wilhelm Stapel, *Der christliche Staatsmann, Eine Theologie des Nationalismus* (Hamburg: Hanseatische Verlagsanstalt, 1932).

10. See *GW* 14 (1975), 301f. See also, Paul Tillich, *Auf der Grenze*, vol. 12 (1971), *GW*, 33 (English trans., *On the Boundary* [New York: Charles Scribner's Sons, 1966], 51f.).

11. Paul Tillich, "Gläubiger Realismus 1 und 2," in *GW* 4:77–106 (English trans. of 1 only, "Realism and Faith," in *The Protestant Era*).

12. See Friedrich Gogarten, *Ich glaube an den dreieinigen Gott* (Jena: E. Diederichs, 1926).

13. See Paul Tillich, "Kairos und Logos," in *GW* 4, especially 53ff.

14. See Paul Tillich, "Fachhochschulen und Universität," in *GW* 13 (1972), 144–49.

15. See Paul Tillich, *Das System der Wissenschaften nach Gegenständen und Methoden, Ein Entwurf*, vol. 1 (1959), *GW*, 111–293 (English trans., *The System of the Sciences according to Objects and Methods* [Lewisburg: Bucknell University Press, 1981]).

16. See Paul Tillich, "Über die Idee einer Theologie der Kultur," in *GW* 9 (1967), 13–31 (English trans., "On the Idea of a Theology of Culture," in *What is Religion?* [New York: Harper & Row, 1969]).

17. The reference is clearly to Tillich's paper "Christologie und Geschichtsdeutung," in *GW* 6: 83–96 (English trans., "The Interpretation of History and the Idea of Christ," in *The Interpretation of History*).

18. See Paul Tillich, "Rechtfertigung und Zweifel," in *GW* 8 (1970): 85–100; and *Auf der Grenze*, vol. 12, *GW*, 33 (English trans., *On the Boundary*, 51). Doubtless, Tillich was also referring to his earlier (1917–18) correspondence with Hirsch; see *GW*, suppl. vol. 6, 98–136.

19. In addition to such pupils of Karl Holl as Emanuel Hirsch, Hans Ruckert, Heinrich Bornkamm, Hermann Wolfgang Beyer, and Erich Vogelsang, such proponents of young reform movement as Walter Künneth and Helmuth Schreiner attempted to interpret the year 1933 theologically. Also, Paul Althaus, Friedrich Gogarten, Adolf Schlatter, Ethelbert Stauffer, and Karl Heim tried to understand the Fascist seizure of power as a challenge to theology that could not be refused.

20. See "Das Dämonische," in *GW* 6: 42–47.

21. See Paul Tillich, *Die sozialistische Entscheidung*, vol. 2 (1962), *GW*, 219–365 (English trans., *The Socialist Decision* [New York: Harper & Row, 1977]).

22. Combined quotation from pages 33 and 36 of Emanuel Hirsch, *Die gegenwärtige geistige Lage.*

23. Paul Tillich, "Der Staat als Erwartung und Forderung," (English trans. "The State as Expectation and Demand," in *Political Expectation* [New York: 1971]).

24. Paul Tillich, "The Totalitarian State and the Claims of the Church," in *Social Research* 1, no. 4 (1934): 433; later published as "Der totale Staat und der Anspruch der Kirchen," in *GW* 10 (1968):121–45.

25. See Paul Tillich, "Grundlinien des religiösen Sozialismus: Ein systematischer Entwurf," in *GW* 2:91–119 (English trans., "Basic Principles of Religious Socialism," in *Political Expectation*).

Appendix: A Short Chronology of Tillich's Life

Paul Tillich's ideas and actions were intimately related to his personal history and the public history of his times. This brief chronology indicates the major periods of his life and several pivotal events that are important in the chapters of this book. It mentions only a few of Tillich's most important publications. The many other writings described in this book are dated in the notes to the chapters and can easily be related to the chronology below.

For a fuller chronology see Wilhelm and Marion Pauck, *Paul Tillich: His Life and Thought,* (New York: Harper & Row, 1976), vol. 1, *Life,* 287–90. That book is the standard source for biographical information.

20 August 1886	Birth, followed by boyhood in Starzeddel, Schönfliess, Berlin, with schooling in Königsberg.
1904–10	Education at Universities of Berlin, Tübingen, Halle. Ph.D., University of Berlin.
1911–14	Pastorates, Nauen and Berlin.
1912	Ordination to ministry, Evangelical Church of the Prussian Union
1914–18	Army chaplain in World War I.
1919–24	*Privatdozent,* University of Berlin. Origins of Kairos Circle and Religious Socialists.
1924–29	Faculty, theology and philosophy, Marburg, Dresden, Leipzig.
1926	Publication of *Die religiöse Lage der Gegenwart (The Religious Situation).*

1929–33	Professor of Philosophy, University of Frankfurt.
1932	Publication of *Die sozialistische Entscheidung* (*The Socialist Decision*), quickly suppressed by government.
1933	Hitler formally became German chancellor. Dismissal of Tillich from Frankfurt professorship by Nazi government. Appointment to faculty at Union Theological Seminary, New York.
1936	Publication of *The Interpretation of History*, Tillich's first English-language book.
1939–45	World War II.
1948	First return visit to Germany. Publication of *The Protestant Era*.
1951	Publication of *Systematic Theology*, vol. 1.
1952	Publication of *The Courage to Be*.
1955	Retirement from Union Theological Seminary. Appointment as university professor, Harvard.
1957	Publication of *Systematic Theology*, vol. 2.
1960	Visit to Japan, conversations with Buddhists.
1962	Retirement from Harvard. Appointment at University of Chicago.
1963	Publication of *Systematic Theology*, vol. 3.
22 October 1965	Death in Chicago.

Contributors

James Luther Adams is professor emeritus of Christian ethics, Harvard Divinity School. He is a past president of the American Theological Society, the Society of Christian Ethics, and the Society for the Scientific Study of Religion. He is a fellow of the American Academy of Arts and Sciences and has been a leader in many organizations related to the arts, civil liberties, politics, and of help to drug addicts and emotionally disturbed people. He translated and edited *The Protestant Era* and other books by Tillich. Among his own books are *Paul Tillich's Philosophy of Culture, Science and Religion, Taking Time Seriously,* and *On Being Human Religiously.*

Jack Boozer is Charles Howard Candler Professor of religion at Emory University and for many years chaired the Department of Religion. He has been president of the Southern Section of the American Academy of Religion. He is author, with William A. Beardslee, of *Faith to Act: An Essay on the Meaning of Christian Existence,* and editor of *Rudolf Otto: Aufsätze zur Ethik.* His research and writings include work on medical ethics, Christianity and Judaism, the military chaplaincy, and the thought of Paul Tillich.

John Powell Clayton teaches in the Department of Religious Studies at the University of Lancaster (England), where he is also principal of Cartmel College. He was a Humboldt Research Fellow at the University of Marburg and has been visiting professor at the University of Bayreuth, Rice University, and the University of Houston. He is author of *The Concept of Correlation,* a book on Tillich. He is editor of *Ernst Troeltsch and the Future of Theology* and, with S. W. Sykes, of *Christ, Faith and History.* He is associate editor of the *Neue Zeitschrift für Systematische Theologie und Religionsphilosophie.*

Albert H. Friedlander, born in Berlin, has been a rabbi in England since 1966, and before that was a rabbi in the United States. He is dean of Leo Baeck College in London (the seminary training progressive rabbis in Europe) and minister of Westminster Synagogue. His books include *Out of the Whirlwind,* an anthology of literature of the holocaust; and *Leo Baeck, Teacher of Theresienstadt* (also the enlarged German edition, *Leo Baeck: Leben und Lehre*). He is one of the founders of the Conference of Christians, Jews, and Muslims; a vice president of the World Union for Progressive Judaism; and chairman of the European Conference of Progressive Rabbis.

Langdon Gilkey, Shailer Matthews Professor of theology at the University of Chicago Divinity School, has lectured widely in the United States, Canada, Europe, and Japan. He is a past president of the American Academy of Religion. His many books include *Maker of Heaven and Earth; Shantung Compound; Naming the Whirlwind: The Renewal of God-Language; Religion and the Scientific Future; Reaping the Whirlwind: A Christian Interpretation of History; Message and Existence: An Introduction to Christian Theology; Society and the Sacred: Towards a Theology of Culture in Decline.*

Joseph M. Kitagawa, born in Japan, is professor of history of religions at the University of Chicago, where he was also dean of the Divinity School from 1970 to 1980. He has held many visiting professorships and lectureships in Germany, Australia, Japan, and the United States. He is founding coeditor of *History of Religions* and former president of the American Society for the Study of Religions. He is editor of many books on Asian religions and methods of studying religion; and he is author of *Religions of the East, Gibt es ein Verstehen fremder Religionen?,* and *Religion in Japanese History.*

Dennis P. McCann teaches in the Department of Religious Studies at De Paul University in Chicago, where he specializes in the area of religious social ethics. His essays on theology and ethics— dealing especially with themes in Tillich, Reinhold Niebuhr, Jacques Maritain, and Latin American theology—have appeared in a variety of scholarly journals. He is author of *Christian Realism and Liberation Theology* and coauthor of a forthcoming book on the discipline of practical theology.

Victor Nuovo is professor and Chairman of the Department of Religion at Middlebury College. He is the translator of *Mysticism and Guilt-Consciousness in Schelling's Philosophical Development,* and *The Construction of the History of Religion in Schelling's Positive Philosophy, Its Presuppositions and Principles,* two very early works of Paul Tillich.

He has recently visited Germany to participate in the preparation of a new biography of Paul Tillich to be published in Germany.

Thomas Franklin O'Meara is professor of theology at the University of Notre Dame. He has taught and lectured in several seminaries and universities in the United States and Africa. He has written extensively in the areas of ecumenism, ecclesiology, and nineteenth- and twentieth-century theology. He edited *Paul Tillich in Catholic Thought,* and his books include *Paul Tillich's Theology of God* and *Romantic Idealism and Roman Catholicism: Schelling and the Theologians.* He is a past president of the Catholic Theological Society of America.

Wilhelm Pauck (1901–81), after a youth in Germany, had a fifty-year teaching career in the United States. At the time of his death he was Charles A. Briggs Graduate Professor of church history emeritus of Union Theological Seminary, New York. After retirement from Union, he was distinguished professor of church history at Vanderbilt University Divinity School and then visiting professor at Stanford. He was author of many books on the Protestant Reformation and on later Christian thought. With his wife, Marion Pauck, he was coauthor of *Paul Tillich: His Life and Thought,* vol. 1.

William R. Rogers became president and professor of religion and psychology at Guilford College after ten years on the faculty at Harvard Divinity School and the Graduate School of Education. He has been a visiting professor at the University of Louvain. He is coeditor of the book *Nourishing the Humanistic in Medicine: Interactions with the Social Sciences.* He is author of *The Alienated Student* and of many articles on education, psychology, and theology. He is active in community, educational, and cultural organizations; and he has been consultant to many colleges, educational commissions, and religious organizations.

Robert P. Scharlemann is Commonwealth Professor of religious studies at the University of Virginia. He has lectured widely in American and European universities. He is a past president of the North American Paul Tillich Society and is editor of the *Journal of the American Academy of Religion.* His articles have appeared in many scholarly journals. His books include *Thomas Aquinas and John Gerhard, Reflection and Doubt in the Thought of Paul Tillich,* and *The Being of God: Theology and the Experience of Truth.*

Nathan A. Scott, Jr. is William R. Kenan, Jr. Professor of religious studies and a professor of English at the University of Virginia. He is a fellow of the American Academy of Arts and Sciences and president-elect of the American Academy of Religion. His many books include *The Broken Center: Studies in the Theological Horizon of Modern Literature; Craters of the Spirit: Studies in the Modern Novel; The Wild Prayer of Longing: Poetry and the Sacred; Mirrors of Man in Existentialism; The Poetics of Belief: Studies in Coleridge, Arnold, Pater, Santayana, Stevens, and Heidegger.* He has edited several books, including *The Tragic Vision and the Christian Faith* and *The Legacy of Reinhold Niebuhr.*

Roger L. Shinn is Reinhold Niebuhr Professor of social ethics at Union Theological Seminary, adjunct professor of religion at Columbia University, and occasionally visiting professor at the Jewish Theological Seminary of America. He is a past president of the American Theological Society and the Society of Christian Ethics. He has lectured widely in North America, Europe, Asia, and Africa. He has participated in studies of social issues for the National Council of Churches and the World Council of Churches. His many books include *The Existentialist Posture; Wars and Rumors of Wars;* and *Forced Options: Social Decisions for the 21st Century.*

John E. Smith is Clark Professor of philosophy at Yale University. He has been president of the American Philosophical Association, the American Theological Society, the Metaphysical Society of America, and the Hegel Society of America. His lectures and participation in philosophical conferences have taken him to many universities and intellectual centers of Europe, Asia, and North America. He is general editor of the Yale edition of *The Works of Jonathan Edwards.* Among his books are *Reason and God, The Spirit of American Philosophy, Experience and God, The Analogy of Experience,* and *Purpose and Thought.*

David Tracy is professor of theology at the University of Chicago, where he is coeditor of the *Journal of Religion.* He serves on the editorial boards of other publications, including the *Journal of Pastoral Psychology, Concilium* (Louvain), and *Theology Today.* He is a past president of the Catholic Theological Society of America. Author of scholarly articles in many journals, he has also written several books, including *The Achievement of Bernard Lonergan; Blessed Rage for Order: The New Pluralism in Theology;* and *The Analogical*

Imagination in Systematic Theology: Christian Theology and the Culture of Pluralism.

Ann Belford Ulanov is professor of psychiatry and religion at Union Theological Seminary in New York, a Jungian analyst in private practice, and a member of the board of directors of the C. G. Jung Training Center in New York. She is author of *The Feminine in Christian Theology and in Jungian Psychology* and *Receiving Woman: Studies in the Psychology and Theology of the Feminine.* With her husband, Barry Ulanov, she is coauthor of *Religion and the Unconscious; Primary Speech: A Psychology of Prayer;* and *Cinderella and Her Sisters: The Envied and the Envying.*

Walter A. Weisskopf is professor emeritus of economics at Roosevelt University, visiting professor of economics at Stanford University, and a trustee of Roosevelt University. He came to America from his native Austria in 1938. He is author of *The Psychology of Economics* and *Alienation and Economics.* He has contributed essays to many books and journals and has participated in extensive international conversations on issues relating values and ideology to the social sciences and public life. His work brings together insights from such varied disciplines as economics, philosophy, theology, psychology, and sociology.

Index